Debate and Dialogue

Alain Chartier in his Cultural Context

EMMA CAYLEY

CLARENDON PRESS · OXFORD

OXFORD
UNIVERSITY PRESS

Great Clarendon Street, Oxford OX2 6DP

Oxford University Press is a department of the University of Oxford.
It furthers the University's objective of excellence in research, scholarship,
and education by publishing worldwide in

Oxford New York

Auckland Cape Town Dar es Salaam Hong Kong Karachi
Kuala Lumpur Madrid Melbourne Mexico City Nairobi
New Delhi Shanghai Taipei Toronto

With offices in

Argentina Austria Brazil Chile Czech Republic France Greece
Guatemala Hungary Italy Japan Poland Portugal Singapore
South Korea Switzerland Thailand Turkey Ukraine Vietnam

Oxford is a registered trade mark of Oxford University Press
in the UK and in certain other countries

Published in the United States
by Oxford University Press Inc., New York

British Library Cataloguing in Publication Data
Data available

Library of Congress Cataloging in Publication Data
Data available

Typeset by Laserwords Private Limited, Chennai, India
Printed in Great Britain
on acid-free paper by
Biddles Ltd., King's Lynn, Norfolk

ISBN 978-0-19-929026-0

Preface

This book is the first full-length study of Chartier's complete Latin and French *oeuvre* in its cultural and material context and, as such, is long overdue. The dearth of critical material available on Chartier seems entirely unjustified given his reputation among contemporaries and successors as a master in his field; the 'pere de l'eloquence françoyse' as Pierre Fabri (1521) puts it. Recent criticism has all but passed over Chartier, perhaps in favour of medieval authors more easily claimed for modern theoretical movements. Chartier's French verse debates have often been dismissed as formulaic and frivolous. I present a revisionary take on these works in particular, based on their material context of transmission and intertextuality. The interdisciplinary nature of my study, which draws on models from sociology and game theory, will, I hope, appeal to scholars in diverse fields, and open up a wider future investigation into the works of this pivotal figure.

There are many individuals whose help and expertise has proved invaluable to this study. First and foremost, my thesis supervisor, Jane Taylor, whose constant support, advice, and encouragement, above and beyond the call of duty, has helped me to navigate the often fraught sea of academia, and without whom I would no doubt still be floundering like Chartier's shipwrecked sailor. I thank my thesis examiners Adrian Armstrong and Miranda Griffin for their penetrating criticisms, excellent suggestions, and good humour. I also thank Tony Hunt and Roger Pensom of Oxford University for their kindness and expert guidance. This study has been much improved thanks to the OUP's specialist readers, whose astute observations and suggestions I have attempted to address. Of the many medievalists who have personally offered me advice, insights, and have commented on my work, I would particularly like to thank Peter Ainsworth, Barbara Altmann, Adrian Armstrong, Katie Attwood, Kevin Brownlee, David Cowling, Rebecca Dixon, Francesca Galligan, David Hult, Michael Jones, Sarah Kay, the inimitable late Elspeth Kennedy, Jim Laidlaw, Peter S. Lewis, Linda Paterson, and Jean-Claude Mühlethaler. I thank Gretchen Angelo, Adrian Armstrong, Bill Calin, Ashby Kinch, Joan E. McRae, and Craig Taylor for allowing me to read their unpublished work and to refer to it in my book. I would also like to acknowledge the comments and suggestions I have received in response to the papers drawn from my research for this study, which were delivered at numerous national and international conferences and seminars. Parts of this book have previously appeared in different guises in print (listed in the Bibliography): '"Tu recites, je replique; et quant nous avons fait et fait, tout ne vault riens": Explorations of a *Debating Climate* in Early Humanist France' (Chapter 2); 'Collaborative Communities: The Manuscript Context of Alain Chartier's *Belle Dame sans mercy*' (Chapter 4, part II); 'Players and Spaces of Play in Late Medieval French Manuscript Collections' (Chapter 4, part II). I thank the editors for their kind permission to reuse some of this material here.

I have been privileged to work in various libraries and archives over the years and owe a particular debt to the Taylorian Institution, Oxford; the Bodleian Library; the Bibliothèque nationale de France; the Bibliothèque de l'Arsenal; the Institut de Recherche et d'Histoire des Textes; Cambridge University Library; and the British Library. I was fortunate in securing an affiliation to the École Normale Supérieure in Paris for a term, where I was able to pursue the codicological research that forms the backbone of my book; further trips were made possible through the generosity of the Queen's College, Oxford, during the tenure of my Laming Junior Research Fellowship there. I would have been unable to carry out my research without the financial support of Oxford University and St Anne's College who jointly awarded me the Paget Toynbee Olwyn Rhys scholarship to enable me to pursue my doctorate. I am also grateful to the Arts and Humanities Research Council, who financed me through my MSt and final year of doctoral research. Other thanks go to Kate and Adrian, and to my colleagues at Exeter who continue to support and encourage my research.

In memory of Nick Hanlon, our friend and colleague.

Finally, this is for my parents, Christine and Digby, who have always believed it was possible; my brothers, Thomas and George, who may read it some day; my beautiful sister, Catherine, who sets the standard; and for Michael, whose endless patience and love keep me afloat.

Contents

List of Plates

Bibliographical Note

Full bibliographical details or titles are given in the notes or text for the first reference, and thereafter in abbreviated form. All translations from Latin are my own unless otherwise stated.

Arsenal	Paris, Bibliothèque de l'Arsenal
BDSM	Alain Chartier, *La Belle Dame sans mercy*
BL	British Library
BM	Bibliothèque Municipale
BN	Biblioteca Nazionale
BnF	Bibliothèque nationale de France, Département des Manuscrits (division occidentale)
BR	Bibliothèque Royale
Breviaire	Alain Chartier, *Breviaire des nobles*
CNRS	Centre National de la Recherche Scientifique
CUP	Cambridge University Press
DDFA	Alain Chartier, *Debat des Deux Fortunés d'amours*
DHVV	Alain Chartier, *Debat du Herault, du Vassault, et du Villain*
Dialogus	Alain Chartier, *Dialogus familiaris amici et sodalis*
DRM	Alain Chartier, *Debat de reveille matin*
EETS	Early English Text Society
fr.	fonds français
lat.	fonds latin
Godefroy	Godefroy, *Dictionnaire de l'ancienne langue française*
GRLMA	*Grundriss der romanischen Literaturen des Mittelalters*
IRHT	Institut de Recherche et d'Histoire des Textes
KB	Koninklijke Bibliotheek
LQD	Alain Chartier, *Livre des Quatre Dames*
MSS	Manuscripts
NB	National Bibliothek
OUP	Oxford University Press
Rose	Guillaume de Lorris and Jean de Meun, *Le Roman de la Rose*
SATF	Société des Anciens Textes Français
Vat. Reg.	Rome, Bibliotheca Apostolica Vaticana, Regina

Introduction

Pensés doncques d'estre soubtil
En donnant responce affinee,
Car droit le premier jour d'avril
Journee est et heure assignee
Pour la cause estre examinee:
Lors par raisoinz judiciaires
Sera commencee ou finee
Entre vous et voz adversaires.[1]

In this extract, three 'ladies' of the court apparently challenge Alain Chartier to defend himself and his poem *La Belle Dame sans mercy* (1424) at a judicial hearing in the face of growing unrest at the 'court amoureuse'. Chartier's only recorded 'responce affinee' to the allegations supposedly made against him and his poem comes in written form: a debate between himself as *acteur* and the *Dieu d'Amours*, framed as a dream sequence: *L'Excusacion aux dames*. These pieces form the 'noyau' of what came to be termed the *Querelle de la Belle Dame sans mercy*, a fifteenth-century socio-literary engagement whose repercussions linger even today.[2] The virtual courtroom to which Chartier is summoned here is the textual space occupied by the *Querelle* itself, where author and creation are fused in a series of fictional trials, and judgements are perpetually deferred or reversed, moving between two fixed points in space and time: 'commencee ou finee'.[3] Chartier and his works are summoned to attend a virtual trial in this study too. In assessing Chartier's verse debates for the first time in the light of his whole *oeuvre*

---

[1] Taken from the verse redaction of a letter in prose: *Copie des lettres des dames en rithme envoyees a maistre Alain*, VI, vv. 41–8. See *Le Cycle de La Belle Dame sans Mercy. Une anthologie poétique du XVᵉ siècle (BNF MS FR. 1131)*, ed. David F. Hult and Joan E. McRae (Paris: Champion, 2003), p. 479.

[2] A nineteenth-century revival of interest in Chartier's poem was sparked by John Keats's version; see Keats, *Selected Poems*, ed. Barnard, rev. edn. (London: Penguin, 1999), pp. 160–2. Pre-Raphaelite painters (Sir Frank Dicksee, John William Waterhouse, etc.) subsequently adopted the subject and it is mainly through this Romantic filter that we know *La Belle Dame sans mercy* today. Twentieth-century responses to Chartier's/Keats's poem include Sting's ballad, 'La Belle Dame sans regrets' on his album *Mercury Falling* (Magnetic Publishing Ltd, 1996).

[3] See Armstrong, 'The Deferred Verdict: A Topos in Late-Medieval Poetic Debates?', *French Studies Bulletin* 64 (Autumn 1997), 12–14.

and in their material and socio-cultural context, I dismiss the case for the prosecution. The case for the defence presented here establishes the social and political significance of Chartier's poetic moves within a collaborative debating and game-playing community. In a strategic move which echoes that made with Chartier's *Belle Dame sans mercy*, this book aims to open up further debate and dialogue on this unfairly neglected poet, so restoring him to his rightful place at the heart of any discussion of a late medieval literary culture.

Over the course of the initial exchanges in the *Querelle de la Belle Dame sans mercy*, it emerges that what we are witnessing is not the recording of an actual dispute between named parties, as some critics have assumed, but an intellectual and literary exercise whose continuation is part of an elaborate competition or game between poets, and which is fostered by a flourishing climate of cultural and literary debate and exchange in late medieval France.[4] The literary production of the later Middle Ages in France is characterized by a participatory culture that is essentially competitive. Contemporary enthusiasm for literary competition is manifested both by the proliferation of debate poems which are written at this time, and by prolonged literary quarrels acted out in verse and prose. The primary driver of this vogue for debate is the convergence of two debating traditions in early humanist France. The first, literary and vernacular, is exemplified by debate poems such as Machaut's *Jugements* or Jean le Seneschal's *Cent Ballades*; the second, more intellectual, and often conducted via Latin epistles, is prevalent in learned, humanist circles at Paris and Avignon.[5] Both modes are essentially playful: the protagonists assume *debating positions*, and adopt complex personae.[6] In this study, I explore the operation and dynamics of the communities that these debate traditions suppose,

---

[4] See Piaget, ed., 'La Belle Dame sans merci et ses imitations', *Romania* 30 (1901), 27–8; and Alain Chartier, *The Poetical Works*, ed. James C. Laidlaw (Cambridge: CUP, 1974), pp. 7–8. My view is shared by Hult and McRae; see their discussion in *Le Cycle de La Belle Dame sans Mercy* (2003), xv–xix. I would go further than this to suggest that the letters were themselves written as part of the fiction by Chartier himself, or possibly another court poet.

[5] See Guillaume de Machaut, *Le Jugement du roy de Behaigne and Remede de Fortune*, ed. William W. Kibler and James I. Wimsatt (Athens/London: University of Georgia Press, 1988), and *Le Jugement du roy de Navarre*, ed. R. Barton Palmer (New York/London: Garland, 1988); see also Jean le Seneschal, *Les Cent Ballades*, ed. Gaston Raynaud (Paris: Firmin-Didot, 1905).

[6] All terms in italics (except already established critical terms) are paradigms that I have developed in the interests of this study and, after the first occurrence, they appear in normal font.

building on important recent work in this field by Jane Taylor and Adrian Armstrong. In her study of Villon's poetry, Taylor traces intertextuality across his *oeuvre* and assesses the implications for a discussion of late medieval poetic culture. Armstrong is primarily concerned with issues arising from competition and tension in late medieval poetry.[7] Both Taylor and Armstrong open up a fascinating and productive vein of research, which remains largely untapped. Taylor's study complements my own with its examination of the operation of late medieval poetic communities. However, Taylor's investigation is more strictly focused on the immediate literary background to debate and competition in this period, while the current discussion covers a broader spectrum of influences including the theological, intellectual, and historical antecedents of debate.[8] Taylor uncovers a network of complex intertextual references in Villon's work and so assigns him a central role within a dynamic culture of literary game-playing. I trace similar patterns in Chartier's Latin and French works, and show how a clear intertext identified within and across these works themselves informs the French verse. My study, though, is more closely linked than Taylor's to the material context and reception of these works. Armstrong's recent work on late medieval poetic collaboration also complements my own, though the scope and focus of our studies differ. While Armstrong also examines patterning in the *Querelle de la Belle Dame sans mercy*, his material extends further forward than mine, to embrace *rhétoriqueur* poetry and early print culture until *c*.1530. My period of investigation primarily covers the years 1400–*c*.1466. There are differences in the nature of the focus too. My focus is more properly sociological, while Armstrong concentrates on formal poetics and politico-social tensions. Finally, Armstrong considers production as well as reception, whereas my study shifts the weight to reception and its implications for a revision of current critical trends and canons which have tended to marginalize Chartier. My present contribution to this fertile research field aims to establish Chartier's centrality to a *debating climate* in early humanist France through an intertextual reading of his French works in the context of the Latin works, in their wider

---

[7] See Taylor, Jane, *The Poetry of François Villon: Text and Context* (Cambridge: CUP, 2001); and Armstrong, *The Virtuoso Circle: Competition, Collaboration and Complexity in Late Medieval French Poetry* (Arizona: Medieval and Renaissance Texts Studies, forthcoming in 2008/9).

[8] See Taylor, Jane (2001).

manuscript context, and in the context of other earlier or contemporary
debates and exchanges.

Alain Chartier (1385/95–1430)[9] was born in Bayeux, and after a
university education in Paris, became notary and secretary at the court
of Charles VI,[10] and at that of the Dauphin (later to become Charles
VII). Chartier's prowess in French prose and verse was to earn him
considerable renown among his contemporaries, and later the title of
'pere de l'eloquence françoyse'.[11] The verse which accompanies the
woodcut in the preface to the second printed edition of Chartier's
collected works by Pierre Le Caron for Anthoine Vérard (1493–4),
puns on Chartier's name, revealing an apparently solid reputation:

> Hommes mortelz, tant villains que gentilz
> Qui chariez au monde en maint cartier,
> Aprenez tous, autant grans que petis,
> A charier en cestuy charetier.
> Du chariot de luy avez mestier,
> Car c'est celluy qui le veult converser
> Qui charie et va le droit sentier
> Ou nul ne peut chanceller ne verser.[12]

This self-styled 'lointaing immitateur des orateurs'[13] wrote debates
in both Latin and the vernacular, in prose and in verse, as well as

---

[9] Chartier's birth date is assumed to lie somewhere between 1385 and 1395.
Walravens's discussion is inconclusive: see Walravens, *Alain Chartier, études biographiques*
(Amsterdam: Meulenhoff-Didier, 1971), pp. 10–15. Laidlaw simply refers to Walravens's
discussion: see Alain Chartier (1974), p. 2. Similarly: Hoffman, *Alain Chartier, His Works
and Reputation* (Geneva: Slatkine, 1975; 1st edn 1942), pp. 9–12. I am inclined to
put Chartier's birth between 1385 and 1390 in agreement with Joret-Desclosières, *Un
Ecrivain national au XVe siècle: Alain Chartier* (Paris: Fontemoing, 1899, 4th edn), and
Piaget (1901).

[10] The only evidence to support the fact that Chartier served Charles VI as a secretary
is a statement in the prologue of the *Quadrilogue invectif*, written before Charles VI's
death, in which he describes himself as 'Alain Charretier humble secretaire du roy nostre
sire et de mon tresredoubté seigneur monseigneur le regent', Alain Chartier, *Quadrilogue
invectif*, ed. Droz (Paris: Champion, 1950), ll. 3–5, p. 1, also Alain Chartier (1974),
p. 4.

[11] This title is bestowed on Chartier by Pierre Fabri in *Le Grand et Vrai Art de pleine
rhétorique* of 1521. See the three-volume edition by Héron (Rouen: A. l'Estringant,
1889–90), I, p. 72.

[12] This is my transcription from the printed edition. I have modernized the punctuation in accordance with the established rules. See Roques, 'Etablissement de règles
pratiques pour l'édition des anciens textes français et provençaux', *Romania* 52 (1926),
243–9; and Foulet and Speer, *On Editing Old French Texts* (Lawrence: Regents Press of
Kansas, 1979).

[13] See Alain Chartier (1950), l. 6, p. 1.

composing Latin letters and orations as part of his diplomatic business.[14] The early humanist scholars Jean de Montreuil, Nicolas de Clamanges, and Gontier Col, among others, were also part of the chancery milieux at Paris and Avignon in which Chartier operated.[15] When thinking about the interaction of Chartier, his predecessors, and contemporaries, I have found it useful to trace models of social organization from the material (predominantly textual) evidence available. To this end, the methodology that underpins this study is based on a paradigm that I term the *collaborative debating community*. This new model is derived partly from Brian Stock's *textual community*, which is a historical grouping that derives its social coherence from the common reading and interpretation of a text or body of texts.[16] Stock's textual community, however, is essentially non-productive, whereas the collaborative debating community is a productive and dynamic social entity, generating *collaborative fictions*. The collaborative debating community derives its coherence not simply from its reading and interpretation of texts but also from its own written responses to those texts and from the material *loci* in which these responses are gathered. Like the model of the *hermetische Lyrik* which Jörn Gruber develops for the earlier troubadour corpus, the participants in these elaborate poetic or intellectual games are all initiates, playing by certain sets of rules.[17] Expanding on Gruber's more formalistic model, I draw on the sociology of Pierre Bourdieu to suggest a dynamic field of playful and competitive relations between texts and poets, reinforcing my own model. Simon Gaunt and Sarah Kay have previously discussed the significance of Bourdieu's theories of practice for an investigation of practice in medieval literature and culture.[18]

---

[14] See Laidlaw's chronological table of Chartier's documented movements, Alain Chartier (1974), pp. 18–21. For Chartier's Latin works see Alain Chartier, *Les Oeuvres latines*, ed. Bourgain-Hemeryck (Paris: CNRS, 1977).

[15] These scholars were a generation earlier than Chartier, but may have coincided with him at Paris before the Burgundian siege of 1418 forced the Dauphin and his court, including Chartier, to flee to Bourges. See Coville, *Gontier et Pierre Col et l'Humanisme en France au temps de Charles VI* (Paris: Droz, 1934), and Ornato, *Jean Muret et ses amis: Nicolas de Clamanges et Jean de Montreuil* (Geneva: Droz, 1969).

[16] See Stock, *Listening for the Text: On the Uses of the Past* (Baltimore/London: Johns Hopkins University Press, 1990).

[17] See Gruber, *Die Dialektik des Trobar: Untersuchungen zur Struktur und Entwicklung des occitanischen und französischen Minnesangs des 12. Jahrhunderts* (Tübingen: Niemeyer, 1983).

[18] See Gaunt and Kay, *Forum for Modern Language Studies* 33/3 (1997, special issue); and in particular their preface, 'Introduction: theory of practice and practice of theory', 193–203.

They suggest that Bourdieu's models are perhaps ultimately limited for certain objects of study in that they cannot offer the perspective afforded by psychoanalysis. However, the current object of study is particularly well suited to Bourdieu's theories of practice. This approach permits of a deeper and more fruitful investigation into the socio-cultural issues surrounding the participatory literary culture of late medieval France, in particular the transmission and reception of works. Indeed, I follow both Taylor and Armstrong who also draw on Bourdieu in their research into late medieval poetic and literary culture.[19] Taylor refers to a late medieval 'poetics of engagement: debate, response, provocation, competition',[20] and suggests that individual literary works of this period should be situated in their specific cultural context. So, originality and individual authorial prowess are defined in relation to specifically situated socio-cultural fields. Within these late medieval communities of poets and scholars, the literary product is not the single work of an isolated individual, but rather the result of a knowing collaborative effort. Each individual strives to 'trump' his predecessors (and even him/herself) intellectually and artistically in response to previous moves in the game. Engagement in literary debate suggested itself to me (drawing on Bourdieu's notion of the field as game) as an elaborate textual game, in which texts can be seen as moves in a competitive struggle between players to acquire prestige (Bourdieu's symbolic capital). To this end I also draw on Huizinga's and Caillois's sociologies of play and game,[21] suggesting parallels between the game (of love) within the text, the game supposed by the debate form itself, and the wider textual game in which the collaborative debating community participates. I ask to what extent this textual game may have a serious purpose in terms of the transmission of forms of poetic knowledge, particularly in the case of Chartier's French verse.

The Bakhtinian sense of the situatedness of the language utterance is particularly appropriate to the socio-cultural model of literary activity I adopt. For Bakhtin, the utterance is fundamentally dialogic, and thus always assumes a social context of interaction between interlocutors; dialogue is always embodied as discourse, and must always have an author

---

[19] See Taylor, Jane (2001), and Armstrong (forthcoming).
[20] Taylor, Jane (2001), p. 7.
[21] See Huizinga, *Homo ludens: A Study of the Play-Element in Culture*, rev. edn. (London: Routledge & Kegan Paul, 1998), and Caillois, *Les Jeux et les hommes: le masque et le vertige* (Paris: Gallimard, 1967).

(speaker).[22] In the literary debate this oral dialogue is always mediated textually, be it through the figure of the narrator in the text, the jongleur reciting the text, an authorial subjectivity, or through the audience (reader or listener) of the debate. The interplay and slippage of the oral and the textual modes in the literary debate will prove crucial to my discussion. The literary debate, as Badel puts it, is a 'dialogue en récit'.[23] A literary dialogue (direct dialogue minus the narrator) is therefore always staged as a debate situation, with an authorial subjectivity, a reader or listener mediating the characters' utterances. The private forum of the dialogue becomes the public performance of the debate as soon as it is mediated by a third agent. This distinction between the concepts of debate and dialogue is vital to an understanding of the dynamics of the debating climate of early humanist France since private (often epistolary) dialogues are opened up as debates for 'public' enjoyment as soon as they are passed to or otherwise experienced by a third party.

The socio-cultural model I adopt of the collaborative debating community assesses not only actual historical and synchronic communities of scholars and poets but also virtual and often diachronic communities. These virtual communities may be formed by links forged between texts which all respond to an initial text (as in the case of the extended *Querelle de la Belle Dame sans mercy*), even if the poets/scholars involved are operating in different periods and in different places. Further levels of the virtual community assess such texts within their material manuscript context, and examine the phenomenon of fictional collaboration. I am interested in manuscript context as the materialization of the textual collaborative game, and the unique insights it gives into medieval reading practices. Here I follow such scholars as Sylvia Huot, and more recently, Adrian Armstrong, who have emphasized the significance of manuscript production, transmission, and reception for interpretation.[24] Specific examples of the collaborative debating communities I postulate in the later medieval period which relate to prolonged scholarly and literary quarrels are the *Querelle de la Rose* and the *Querelle de la Belle Dame sans*

---

[22] See Bakhtin, *The Dialogic Imagination*, trans. Emerson and Holquist (Austin: University of Texas Press, 1981).
[23] See Badel, 'Le Débat', in *Grundriss der romanischen Literaturen des Mittelalters* VIII/1, ed. Poirion (Heidelberg: Carl Winter, 1988), 95–110, p. 98.
[24] See Huot, *The 'Romance of the Rose' and its Medieval Readers: Interpretation, Reception, Manuscript Transmission* (Cambridge: CUP, 1993), and Armstrong, *Technique and Technology: Script, Print, and Poetics in France, 1470–1550* (Oxford: Clarendon Press, 2000).

mercy. The first of these grew from the controversy occasioned by Jean
de Meun's portrayal of women in his continuation of Guillaume de
Lorris's *Roman de la Rose*.[25] This *Querelle* generated mainly epistolary
responses, exchanged in both Latin and the vernacular, between scholars
at the Paris chancery and the author Christine de Pizan over a period
of a few years at the beginning of the fifteenth century. In contrast,
the later fifteenth-century *Querelle de la Belle Dame sans mercy*, whose
initial exchanges I mentioned earlier, generated further poetic sequels
and imitations of Chartier's original over a period spanning more than
half a century.[26] There has been a flurry of critical interest in this
latter *querelle* over recent years, culminating in David Hult and Joan
E. McRae's important new bilingual French edition of the cycle, edited
from Paris, BnF, fr. 1131.[27] There is now also available an English
translation of the cycle by Joan E. McRae.[28]

My study of Chartier's contribution to a vigorous late medieval poetic
culture in France begins with an investigation of the notion of literary
and poetic community from a historical perspective. Early dialogued
forms from the Virgilian *eclogue* to the troubadour *tenso*, *demande
d'amour*, and northern French *jeu-parti*, combine with the scholastic
disputatio, and the model of the judicial trial, to shape the late medieval
debate poem. These literary and intellectual traditions all foster a vast
enthusiasm for collaborative debate that finds full expression in the
prolonged *querelles*. Jean le Seneschal's allegedly collaborative poem the
Cent Ballades provides a paradigm for the operation and dynamics of
virtual late medieval debating communities in my first chapter. My
close reading of Jean's poem will illustrate how this enthusiasm for
collaborative debate created a new poetic phenomenon: that of the
fictional collaboration.

In my second chapter I move to the intellectual and practical debating
carried out by groups of humanist scholars in the royal chancery at

[25] See Guillaume de Lorris and Jean de Meun, *Le Roman de la Rose*, ed. Strubel (Paris:
Librairie générale française, 1992).
[26] Another essential difference between these two prolonged debates or *querelles* is
that most of the pieces attached to the *Querelle de la Rose* were not themselves in debate
form, but simply epistolary responses (except Jean Gerson's *Traité d'une vision faicte
contre 'Le Ronmant de la Rose'*). By contrast, the responses generated during the *Querelle
de la Belle Dame sans mercy* are themselves debates (mainly of the type *jugement*, see
Chapter 1, p. 30).
[27] See *Le Cycle de La Belle Dame sans Mercy* (2003).
[28] See *The Quarrel of the Belle Dame sans mercy*, ed. and trans. Joan E. McRae
(London/New York: Routledge, 2004).

Paris, and the papal chancery at Avignon in the late fourteenth and early fifteenth centuries. I give an account of the debating climate in early humanist France in which political and religious divisions are expressed through written accounts: diplomatic treatises and debates. In the chanceries, scholars also exercise their epistolary style by indulging in debate with colleagues on literary topics. They adopt what I term debating positions as part of an elaborate intellectual game, often playfully assuming a strong polemical tone. In this way, scholars compete for symbolic capital within chancery milieux. This is very much the milieu in which Chartier was later to operate, though his engagement in contemporary politics through literary debate lends the game a more 'serious' purpose and is part of a contemporary valorization of vernacular verse. It was also in this atmosphere that the *Querelle de la Rose* developed. Here I explore Christine de Pizan's vernacular intervention in the *Querelle*, and her interaction (or lack of it) with Jean de Montreuil and the defenders of Jean de Meun's *Rose*. Christine refuses to conduct the *Querelle* according to Jean de Montreuil's rules and publishes her own edited version of the *Querelle* dossiers.[29] Her new socially motivated debating moves pave the way for the social and political comment that Chartier was later to make through his verse debates.

Chartier is unusual in that he participates in two debate traditions—intellectual and literary—writing debates both in Latin and in the vernacular. In my third chapter, I demonstrate how the two strands combine in Chartier's *oeuvre*. By tracing intertextualities between the Latin and French prose and French verse, I effect a rehabilitation of his French verse. The common critical consensus on Chartier's 'joyeuses escritures'[30] has been that they are conventional courtly poems of little originality or import. I refute this theory, and demonstrate Chartier's rejection of a corrupt courtly discourse from within the confines of the courtly poem through a close rereading of the French verse through the Latin and French prose. I establish, in this chapter, that Chartier

---

[29] For a discussion of the composition of these dossiers, see *Débat sur le 'Roman de la Rose'*, ed. Hicks (Paris: Champion, 1977).

[30] I use Hoffman's term. Hoffman divides Chartier's French verse into two categories: 'joyeuses escritures' and 'serious poems': see Hoffman (1975), 39–43. Hoffman classifies in the 'joyeuses escritures' Chartier's *Lay de plaisance*, *Debat de reveille matin*, *Complainte contre la mort*, *Belle Dame sans mercy*, *Excusacion*, and the *Debat des Deux Fortunés d'amours*. The 'serious poems' are the *Livre des Quatre Dames*, the *Lay de paix*, the *Debat du Herault, du Vassault, et du Villain*, and the *Breviaire des nobles*.

was a leading light in early humanist circles, whose contribution to vernacular eloquence went far beyond that of his contemporaries. I shall suggest that Chartier's works inspired a community of thought and debate about the nature of the poetic voice and mission that helped to promote vernacular verse as a fit medium for the transmission of knowledge and *senefiance*. The new reading of Chartier's French verse works through his Latin and French prose that I propose is supported by the manuscript context of Chartier's French verse: by its transmission and reception. This material context sees Chartier's French verse frequently juxtaposed with his French prose and also with his Latin works the *Dialogus* and the *De vita curiali*. I explore the dialogic links forged through the compilation of these texts in manuscripts of Chartier's work.

Chartier's legacy to the debating culture of late medieval France, the *Querelle de la Belle Dame sans mercy*, is addressed specifically in my fourth chapter. In the first part of my fourth chapter I begin by tracing creative modes within the *Querelle* as a whole and through its various minor cycles. I raise questions about the nature of literary invention and textual relations within this community of texts, and seek to answer them through the application of my model of the collaborative debating community, suggesting the fundamentally collaborative and competitive urge of the *Querelle* poets. The collaborative fictions generated by the interaction of these poets are gathered in forty manuscripts. Part II explores the manuscript context of the *Querelle de la Belle Dame sans mercy* as the materialization of the poetic game engaged in by the *Querelle* poets. Here I engage with the theories of game of Johan Huizinga and Roger Caillois and the sociology of Pierre Bourdieu to suggest a dynamic field of playful dialogic relations between texts, and between poets beyond the texts. These manuscripts often bear traces of coherent planning which are not immediately explicable. The game of chess, an example found in many of the texts collected in this body of manuscripts, provides a useful organizing metaphor. The examination of these contradictory yet complementary texts in material spaces of play gives us a unique insight into reading and compositional practices in the Middle Ages.

Chartier's work, highly esteemed by medieval and Renaissance authors, and in spite of two excellent modern editions of the French verse and Latin works respectively,[31] has been curiously neglected. I hope to reverse that neglect, and to set him firmly at the junction—and pinnacle—of two cultures, Latin and vernacular, learned and literary.

[31] I refer to Alain Chartier (1974) and Alain Chartier (1977). Droz's edition of the *Quadrilogue invectif,* Alain Chartier (1950), is the most recent (there is a new translation by Florence Bouchet, Paris: Champion, 2002); see also Alain Chartier, *Le Livre de l'Esperance*, ed. Rouy (Paris: Champion, 1989).

'JE VOUS DEMANDE PAR LA FORCE DU JEU'
THE LITERARY, LEGAL, AND INTELLECTUAL ANTECEDENTS OF LATE MEDIEVAL DEBATE

Je vous demande par la force du jeu, lequel vaut mieux: joïr sans desirer, ou desirer sans jouyr? Desirer sans jouir.[1]

This *demande d'amour* which appears in London, Westminster Abbey, CA 21[2] presents an interesting parallel between the game constituted by the *demande* itself, and the game of love as played through the *demande* structure, as Margaret Felberg-Levitt remarks in her recent edition.[3] I locate yet a third layer of allusion in these lines, to the broader collaborative poetic game at work in late medieval France which, like the game of love, is played in a constant state of desire for continuation rather than completion; the end of the game (closure) is often deliberately deferred in order to perpetuate the game, and further poetic exchange solicited from within the text, either by virtue of that text's lack of closure,[4] or by specific calls for continuation. The phrase 'la force du jeu' is suggestive of

---

[1] This is edited from London, Westminster Abbey, CA 21. See *Les Demandes d'amour*, ed. Felberg-Levitt (Montreal: CERES, 1995), p. 134.

[2] It is significant, as I shall discuss later, that as well as eighty-seven prose and verse *demandes d'amour*, this manuscript also contains Oton de Granson's *Belle Dame qui eut mercy* (fols. 78^r–80^v), one of the poems linked to Chartier's *Belle Dame sans mercy* (this is probably a earlier poem; the later title links it explicitly to the sequence), listed by Piaget in *Romania* 33 (1904), 200–6; nine *ventes [venditions] d'amour* on fols. 45^r–45^v; Jean de Garencières's *Complainte d'amant* on fols. 14^r–14^v, and in a series of forty-two ballades from fols. 15^r–34^r, a ballade which forms part of the *Concours de Blois* exchange between Charles d'Orléans and others; incipit: 'Je meurs de soif bien près de la fontaine'. There is also a copy of Christine de Pizan's *Epistre au dieu d'Amours*, fols. 52^r–64^v. For a description of this manuscript see Meyer, 'Notice d'un recueil manuscrit de poésies françaises du XIIIe au XVe siècle, appartenant à Westminster Abbey', *Bulletin de la Société des Anciens Textes Français* 1 (1875), 25–36, and also *Les Demandes d'amour* (1995), 50–4.

[3] See *Les Demandes d'amour* (1995), p. 134, n. 29.

[4] Deferral is achieved by a variety of means. In the debate poems of both Chartier and Christine de Pizan, the final judgement is never pronounced, leaving the debates inconclusive. Chartier operates a vocabulary of closure by which he destabilizes the conclusions to his verse debates. See my article, 'Drawing Conclusions: The Poetics of Closure in Alain Chartier's Verse', *Fifteenth-Century Studies* 28 (2003), 51–64; also Armstrong (1997b).

a poetic game which is a highly wrought system, played out according to specific and recognized rules of engagement, on which all collaborators must agree. This particular collaborative poetic debating game is privileged by the debating climate of late medieval France, which fed on earlier intellectual, legal, and literary structures, and in which an economy of exchange was nourished between debating poets. I borrow the term economy of exchange from Bourdieu's study of the economy of linguistic exchange. Bourdieu situates linguistic exchange within the context of markets, asserting that:

les discours ne reçoivent leur valeur (et leur sens) que dans la relation à un marché—la valeur du discours dépend du rapport de forces qui s'établit concrètement entre les compétences linguistiques des locuteurs, entendues à la fois comme capacité de production et capacité d'appropriation et d'appréciation.[5]

In the current chapter, I evaluate the *demande* genre as a structuring element for formal games (*Le Jeu des demandes et responces d'amours, Le Roi qui ne ment, Le Jeu aux rois et aux reines*),[6] for literary texts, and for debate poems (such as Machaut's *Jugement* poems, Christine de Pizan's *Livre du dit de Poissy*), in the context of parallel literary genres such as the *vente* or *vendition d'amour*,[7] and in the wider context of literary debate and exchange in the thirteenth, fourteenth, and fifteenth centuries in France. I engage with Gruber's dialectical model of poetic exchange in the troubadour corpus to show how my model of the late medieval collaborative debating community both feeds off and expands on Gruber's more formalistic model.[8] The latter half of the chapter pivots on my investigation of the *Cent Ballades* (1389),[9] which

[5] Bourdieu, *Ce que parler veut dire* (Paris: Fayard, *1982*), ch. 2, p. 60.

[6] See *Les Demandes d'amour* (1995), and Felberg-Levitt's article, 'Jouer aux *Demandes d'amour*', *Le Moyen Français* 39 (1995), 93–124; Firth Green, '*Le Roi qui ne ment* and Aristocratic Courtship', in *Courtly Literature: Culture and Context*, ed. Busby and Kooper (Amsterdam/Philadelphia: John Benjamins Publishing Company, 1990), 211–25; Hoepffner, 'Les *Voeux du paon* et les *Demandes amoureuses*', *Archivum Romanicum* 4 (1920), 99–104; Langlois, 'Le Jeu du roi qui ne ment et le jeu du roi et de la reine', *Romanische Forschungen* 23 (1902), 163–73.

[7] See Lazard, 'Ventes et demandes d'amour', in *Les Jeux à la Renaissance: Actes du XXIIIᵉ colloque international d'études humanistes, Tours—Juillet 1980*, ed. Ariès and Margolin (Paris: J. Vrin, 1982), 133–49; Bergeron, 'Les Venditions françaises des XIVᵉ et XVᵉ siècles', *Le Moyen Français* 19 (1986), 34–57.

[8] See Gruber (1983).

[9] This work forms a triptych with Christine de Pizan's *Cent Ballades* and the subsequent *Cent Ballades d'amant et de dame* (1409–10), which were very much influenced by and play off Jean le Seneschal's earlier collaborative collection. I am grateful to Kevin Brownlee for his illuminating comments on this literary patterning.

is taken as a model of the operation and dynamics of what I understand by a virtual (in this case probably fictional) collaborative debating community. Jean de Werchin's *Le Songe de la barge* (1404–15), and an exchange of forty-six ballades with his equerry Gilbert de Lannoy (late 1404), are also cited here as examples of actual and virtual poetic collaboration.

The *loci* of such literary debates and contests, which are not only played out at the level of the text or manuscript compilation, but also performed within poetic institutions and groups such as the *puys* of northern France, the *Cour amoureuse* of 1400,[10] or the *Consistoire de la gaie science* of Toulouse (founded in 1324), are of particular significance.[11] Poetic competition was also fostered under the aegis of a proliferation of chivalric and literary orders such as *L'Écu d'or* (founded by Louis de Bourbon), the *Toison d'or* (founded in 1430), or *L'Ordre de la dame blanche à l'escu vert* (founded by Jean le Meingre, or Boucicaut,[12] in 1399), and the fictional *Ordre de la Rose* created by Christine de Pizan in 1402, and championed by the Duc d'Orléans.[13] I suggest how these poetic associations often mirror the practices of intellectual or legal institutions. A survey of such intellectual and legal structures (textual, social, and material) in the medieval period will serve to demonstrate how these structures are absorbed and reproduced in literary texts. The focus in this chapter, then, is on *literary* debate. By tracing the literary, legal, and intellectual antecedents of late medieval literary debate, I show how *demandes* and *ventes d'amour* as well as other literary games and exchanges (predominantly of the thirteenth and fourteenth centuries in France) represent part of a wider pattern of playful and collaborative

[10] See Bozzolo and Loyau, *La Cour amoureuse dite de Charles VI*, 3 vols. (Paris: Léopard d'Or, 1982–92); Piaget, 'La Cour amoureuse dite de Charles VI', *Romania* 20 (1891), 417–54.

[11] See *Les Joies du gai savoir: recueil de poésies couronnées par le Consistoire de la gaie science*, ed. Jeanroy (Toulouse: Édouard Privat, 1914), and *Las Leys d'amors: manuscrit de l'Académie des Jeux Floraux*, ed. Anglade, 4 vols. (Toulouse: Édouard Privat, 1919).

[12] Jean le Meingre, called Boucicaut, was also a member of the *Cour amoureuse* of 1400, and one of the alleged four initial composers of the *Cent Ballades*. See Jean le Seneschal, *Cent Ballades*, ed. Raynaud (Paris: SATF, 1905), and also the anonymous *Livre des faits de Jean le Meingre, dit Boucicaut* (1406/7–1409), ed. Lalande (Geneva: Droz, 1985).

[13] Christine de Pizan's *Dit de la Rose* (1402) describes the founding of this order, essentially for the protection of women from slander. See Christine de Pizan, *Poems of Cupid, God of Love*, ed. Fenster and Erler (Leiden: Brill, 1990).

debate which was to find full expression in later literary contests such as the *Querelle de la Belle Dame sans mercy*. This enthusiastic debating was to continue throughout the fifteenth century with such exchanges as those of the *Concours de Blois* (*c.*1457–60), a series of ballades, initiated by Charles d'Orléans, and inspired by the line 'Je meurs de soif auprès de la fontaine',[14] or the collection entitled *Les Douze Dames de rhétorique* (*c.*1463–64), a partially epistolary collaboration between George Chastelain, Jean Robertet,[15] Jean de Montferrant, and M. de la Rière.[16] I am also concerned with the way in which the manuscript tradition of some of these literary debates[17] engages with that of the *Querelle de la Belle Dame sans mercy*,[18] extending the metaphor of play here to suggest a network of dialogic and playful relations between texts within and across manuscript collections.

Let me start with the intellectual influences on literary debate. The Scholastic tradition of *disputatio*, the intellectual and scientific basis of the late medieval literary debate, is well documented in accounts of medieval university curricula, providing one of the principal methods of teaching and learning in France from the 1150s on. The Theology faculty

[14] This series of ballades is preserved in an autograph manuscript of Charles d'Orléans, Paris, BnF, fr. 25458. See Charles d'Orléans, *Ballades et rondeaux*, ed. Mühlethaler (Paris: Librairie générale française, 1992).

[15] For Jean Robertet's involvement in this epistolary collaboration and others, see Jean Robertet, *Oeuvres*, ed. Zsuppán (Geneva: Droz, 1970).

[16] See Jean Robertet; George Chastelain; Jean de Montferrant, *Les Douze Dames de rhétorique*, ed. Cowling (Geneva: Droz, 2002), and an earlier edition by Louis Batissier (Moulins: Desrosiers, 1838).

[17] I shall be looking in particular at Jean de Werchin's *Songe de la barge*, and the exchange of forty-six ballades between Jean de Werchin, sénéchal de Hainaut, and Gilbert de Lannoy, his equerry, both preserved in a sole manuscript: Chantilly, Musée Condé, 686, which also contains Chartier's *BDSM* and Caulier's *Cruelle Femme en amours*, as well as the manuscripts of the *demandes* and *ventes d'amour*, four of which contain either works by Chartier (Paris, BnF, fr. 1130; Bern, Burgerbibliothek, 205; Turin, Biblioteca Nazionale, L. II. 12), and/or texts of the *Belle Dame sans mercy* cycle (Turin, BN, L. II. 12; London, Westminster Abbey, CA 21). Turin, BN, L. II. 12 also contains a *complainte* by Jean le Seneschal (fols. 148ʳB–149ᵛB), one of the four original authors of the *Cent Ballades*, a late fourteenth-century poetic exchange (1389). Also significant is Paris, BnF, fr. 19139, a manuscript which is the sole witness to the poetry of Jean de Garencières who engaged in poetic exchanges with both Charles d'Orléans, and Jean de Bucy, author of one of the thirteen responses to the *Cent Ballades*. London, Westminster Abbey, CA 21 also contains a version of Garencières's *complainte* XXIX, 'Belle, prenez temps et espace' (fols. 14ʳ–14ᵛ).

[18] See Chapter 4, part II for a discussion of the manuscript context of the *Querelle de la BDSM*.

in Paris, a model for many other faculties across Europe, divided learning into two exercises, studied morning and afternoon respectively.[19] The first of these exercises, *lectio*, involved reading of the *auctoritates*; the second, *disputatio*, was divided into four or five parts: a *quaestio* on a specific topic; a proposition in response; objections to the proposition; a *determinatio* delivered by the master; then possibly answers to the objections.[20] The exercise of *disputatio* is recorded in the statutes from 1215, and was practised in the faculties of Medicine and Law as well as Theology. The *quodlibet*, attributed to Thomas Aquinas, developed from the *disputatio* in the mid-thirteenth century.[21] The main difference between the two seems to have been that the *quodlibet* was not a regular mode of teaching. University lectures on set texts were conducted through *quaestiones*. After a close reading of the text, *quaestiones* would be raised and answered with recourse to various *auctoritates*. The closely argued structure of the *disputatio* would be influenced by the student's grasp of grammar and logic, both of which were studied at Paris (as elsewhere) in the Arts faculty (though rhetoric was excluded from the Paris curriculum in the mid-thirteenth century).[22] The *disputationes* were often copied down for circulation after their public performance, and Bazàn conjectures that some bypassed the performance stage, and were composed purely for copying.[23] The copying of these *disputationes* might have been done by the participants, by the master himself, or by a clerk (*socius*). Many recueils of *disputationes* and *quodlibets* have come down to us, often carefully organized by topic.[24] These recueils would have been circulated among students and masters for practice. The

[19] See Verger, *Les Universités au moyen âge* (Paris: Quadrige/PUF, 1999; 1st edn 1973).

[20] See Murphy, *Rhetoric in the Middle Ages: A History of Rhetorical Theory from Saint Augustine to the Renaissance* (Berkeley/Los Angeles/London: University of California Press, 1974).

[21] See Bazàn, *Les Questions disputées et les questions quodlibétiques dans les facultés de théologie, de droit et de médecine* (Turnhout, Belgium: Brepols, 1985), and also Glorieux, *La Littérature quodlibétique*, 2 vols. (Paris: Kain, 1925–35).

[22] For a more detailed picture of the medieval university and its origins, see Rashdall, *The Universities of Europe in the Middle Ages*, 3 vols. (Oxford: Clarendon Press, 1987); Ferruolo, *The Origins of the University: The Schools of Paris and the Critics 1100–1215* (Stanford, CA: Stanford University Press, 1985).

[23] Bazàn (1985).

[24] Bazàn (1985) mentions Douai 434, which contains 572 disputes of Parisian masters from 1230, as well as Assisi 158 and Worcester MS. Q. 99, which contain *disputationes* held at Oxford and Paris at the end of the thirteenth century. See also Glorieux, 'Les 572 questions du ms de Douai 434', *Recherches de Théologie ancienne et médiévale* 10 (1938), 123–267.

disputatio might be separated from its *determinatio* (judgement) within the body of the collection, mirroring the deferral of judgement that might occur at the end of the oral version of the *disputatio*. The master might give a *determinatio* on the spot, or more likely, deliver his judgement separately, after the public performance of the *disputatio*. A different judge might occasionally have been invited to give the *determinatio*.

The Scholastic method developed from a vogue for dialectic. Hunt, Le Goff, and Murphy concur that this may have been a response to the newly available Latin translations of the *Logica nova*, consisting of Aristotle's *Analytica priora*, the *Analytica posteriora*, the *Topica*, and the *De sophisticis elenchis*.[25] The last two of these four treatises were widely adopted as manuals of dialectic for university students. Book VIII of the *Topica* contains advice for the proper conduct of a *disputatio*. Aristotle here makes a vital distinction between contentious and dialectical argument which will be useful for my later exploration of subjectivity in the debate poem:

> Criticism of an argument when it is taken by itself is not the same thing as when it forms the subject of questions; for often the person questioned is the cause of the argument not being properly discussed, because he does not concede the points which would have enabled the argument against his thesis to have been properly carried out [...] He who asks his questions in a contentious spirit and he who in replying refuses to admit what is apparent and to accept whatever question the questioner wishes to put, are both of them bad dialecticians.[26]

In a seminal article, Tony Hunt traces the influence of dialectic on the development of courtly literature, and particularly the dialectical reasoning set out by Aristotle in his *Topica*.[27] Hunt identifies three main areas of influence. First the concept of *courtly love* itself, which he suggests is fundamentally dialectical in nature, and 'susceptible of dialectical treatment'; then the 'construction of poetic works themselves on the dialectical model of oppositions and correspondences'; and third the 'prominent part played by ratiocination itself in the frequent debates

[25] See Hunt, 'Aristotle, Dialectic and Courtly Literature', *Viator* 10 (1979), 95–129; Le Goff, *Intellectuals in the Middle Ages*, trans. Fagan (Cambridge, MA/Oxford: Blackwell, 1993); Murphy (1974). The Latin translations were made by James of Venice in around 1130; see Minio-Paluello, 'Iacobus Veneticus Grecus, Canonist and Translator of Aristotle', *Traditio* 8 (1952), 265–304; and Aristotle, *Posterior Analytics*; *Topica*, ed. Goold, trans. Tredennick and Forster (Cambridge, MA: Harvard University Press, 1997).

[26] Aristotle, *Topica*: VIII, X–XI, 161a–b, pp. 718–19.

[27] See Hunt (1979) and Aristotle (1997).

found in the romances'.[28] In a recent study of contradiction in twelfth-century courtly literature, Sarah Kay recognizes the pervasiveness of dialectic, but nuances Hunt's argument by asserting that courtly texts adopt the dialectical model in a playful and subjective way that contradicts the scientific and objective spirit of dialectic as practised by the Scholastics:

Although courtly contradictoriness may reflect the views current among twelfth-century dialecticians, it may also contradict—in the sense of flout—the principles of rightful argument which many of them extolled.[29]

Courtly texts of the earlier medieval period often pivot on a series of paradoxes and contradictory discourses (the erotic and religious for example) that Kay suggests disturb the surface of the text, but that need not be reconciled as scholars have attempted. Kay detects a psychoanalytic dimension to these textual disturbances that she explored previously in her study of the interpenetration of the *chanson de geste* and the medieval romance. Following Fredric Jameson, Kay demonstrates how certain aspects of the historical or social context of the text are 'repressed', but struggle to the surface as 'conflicting narratives'.[30] Kay's theories offer an interesting alternative and even complementary angle for my consideration of the dialogic relationship between Chartier's Latin and French works. To adopt Jameson's terminology as mediated through Kay: the Latin and French prose works provide a clue to the 'political unconscious' of the French verse (though I shall suggest in my third chapter that Chartier's moves are largely self-conscious).

The dialectical model of the *disputatio* clearly subtends many of the longer debate poems of the later medieval period in which an initial proposition (equivalent to the *quaestio*) is stated, then argued from two or more points of view (*propositio*), each protagonist refuting the opposing view, and stating his own case. The *determinatio* is reached, often in the form of a judgement, which may be deferred to an extra-textual point in the future.

Alain Chartier's *Debat des Deux Fortunés d'amours* provides an example of the logical progression of the *disputatio* as it becomes embedded in poetic structure. In Chartier's debate poem, the legacy of the *disputatio*

[28] Hunt (1979), pp. 108–9.
[29] See Kay, *Courtly Contradictions: The Emergence of a Literary Object in the Twelfth Century* (Stanford, CA: Stanford University Press, 2001), p. 19.
[30] Kay, *The Chansons de geste in the Age of Romance* (Oxford: Clarendon Press, 1995), and also Jameson, *The Political Unconscious: Narrative as a Socially Symbolic Act* (Ithaca, NY: Cornell University Press, 1981).

combines with the *demande d'amour* and is informed by the more subjective strain of conflictual poetry exemplified by the *jeu-parti*. The scene is set in a castle, where the forlorn narrator figure finds himself amid a noble company of ladies and knights, who are amusing themselves after dinner with questions of love,[31] 'et en parlant a demander se mirent | Que c'est d'amours', vv. 27–8.[32] The debate itself is proposed by one of the ladies present, who asks,

> S'en amours a biens et plaisirs si haulx
> Et d'autre part dueil et mortelx assaulx,
> Duquel y a plus? De biens ou de maulx?
>
> vv. 202–4

This question proposed by the lady, as well as the original, 'Que c'est d'amours', both resemble *demandes* formulae, transcribed in various variant forms in the body of *demande* manuscripts.[33] The *demande* around which the debate balances is similar to that posed in Christine de Pizan's *Livre du debat de deux amans* (1400).[34] Two knights take up the debate in Chartier's poem. The first, whose general appearance reflects his argument, being 'en bon point, sain, alegre et joyeulx', v. 212, argues that 'en amours a plus joye que douleur', v. 670. He is contradicted by a second knight, the antithesis of the first in both appearance and opinion: he is 'pensif et pale', v. 679, and argues that 'en amours a plus de mal que de bien', v. 1110. These two conflicting

---

[31] This after-dinner occupation resembles the courtly game of *demandes d'amour*, usually played in mixed company in order to exploit erotic tension. On this function of the *demandes* see particularly Firth Green (1990).

[32] See Alain Chartier (1974), pp. 158–95.

[33] Felberg-Levitt divides the manuscripts and printed editions of the *demandes* into eight groups based on their content and phrasing. She edits the first *demande* type I cited here (Que c'est d'amours?) from four groups of manuscripts: 1, 2, 4, 6; the formula varies from group to group. In group 2 it appears, 'Beau sire, je vous demande, qu'est amours?', p. 178. The second, used by both Christine de Pizan and Chartier, appears in three groups: 1, 2, and 4. In group 4 it appears, 'Beau sire, je vous demande, duquel loyal amans s'i treuvent plus en amours: du bien, ou du mal?', *Les Demandes d'amour* (1995), p. 214.

[34] Christine de Pizan's debate is set at a party where the guests are amusing themselves with questions of love, asking 'Que c'est d'amer', v. 365. Christine's narrator figure then leaves the party with a *dame*, a *bourgeoise*, and two knights: 'cil qui fu blanc | Et palle ou vis', vv. 317–18, and another, 'joyeux', v. 350, and they begin to debate the narrator's question: 'Dittes, sire, car plus estes rassis | Et le plus sage, | Vo bon avis de l'amoureux servage, | S'il en vient preu, joye, honneur ou dommage', vv. 403–6. See Christine de Pizan, *The Love Debate Poems*, ed. Altmann (Gainesville: University Press of Florida, 1998).

arguments are then followed by a brief recapitulation by each knight, in an attempt to refute the other's claims. A *determinatio* in the form of a judgement is then called for. Jean de Grailli, comte de Foix, is appointed judge, but the conclusion to the debate is projected beyond the end of the text, since the Comte is absent on a campaign, and is to be presented with a written version of the debate on his return.[35] The structure of Chartier's poem, thought previously to be one of his earlier debates,[36] is also greatly influenced by the process of judicial trial, in spite of its courtly setting. The *Querelle de la Belle Dame sans mercy* was later to precipitate the debate genre 'out of the garden and into the courtroom', as Joan E. McRae puts it.[37] These judicial trial models, and earlier poetic forms such as the *demandes*, *joc-partits*, or *tensos* combined with the scholastic model of the *disputatio*, shape the late medieval debate poem.

Bloch's general survey of the relationship between law and medieval French literature gives a picture of the climate in which judicial trial in the twelfth century onwards tended to replace the traditional trial by battle or duel. For him, 'the substitution of an inquisitory procedure for battle transformed the archaic test of martial strength into a test of intellectual strength within the confines of formal debate'.[38] The shift towards judicial debate is understood by Bloch as an attempt to verbalize physical conflicts, in a society increasingly aware of the power of the spoken or written word and in the light of a failing feudal system. He further identifies the three conditions that, from the twelfth century on, will lead to a widespread culture of debate: 'a highly developed system of civil judicial procedure, vernacular debate literature, and philosophical dialectic'.[39] The conclusions reached in

---

[35] There is a further obstacle to closure here: the Comte de Foix is appointed to judge the debate, but Chartier adds the caveat, 's'il lui plaist, son advis en diroit', v. 1230, suggesting that a final *determinatio* may never be given.

[36] See Laidlaw's discussion of the dating of this poem: Alain Chartier (1974), pp. 29–32. I put this debate later than Laidlaw, *c*.1419–20: see Chapter 3, p. 94.

[37] See McRae, 'The Trials of Alain Chartier's "Belle Dame sans mercy": The Poems in Cyclical and Manuscript Context' (unpublished thesis: University of Virginia, 1997), p. 20. I am very grateful to Joan E. McRae for allowing me to read a copy of her thesis.

[38] See Bloch, R. Howard, *Medieval French Literature and Law* (Berkeley/London: University of California Press, 1977), p. 139.

[39] Bloch continues, 'the rise of an inquisitory court system, in which argumentation was practised in the place of battle, along with the increasingly dialectical patterns of Latin and vernacular poetry, attest to the tremendous importance in all areas of cultural life—legal, intellectual, and literary—of what remains the verbal form of violence *par excellence*: the debate', p. 164.

this survey, though, are less than satisfactory, as Lisa Jefferson points out in her study of medieval oaths, vows, and promises.⁴⁰ Bloch does not examine the later Middle Ages in much detail, but concentrates mainly on earlier disputes between troubadours, singling out the *joc-partit* and the *tenso* as verbally competitive forms. The *Querelle de la Rose* and the *Concours de Blois* are mentioned as later examples of verbal conflict, but the omission of Chartier or any reference to the *Querelle de la Belle Dame sans mercy* is rather surprising, particularly given the legal nature of many of the sequels. Jefferson's less ambitious study focuses on specific legal aspects underpinning one text. She reinterprets the first part of the prose *Lancelot* in the light of her thorough investigation of medieval canon and secular law, and concludes that the climate of theological and legal debate in thirteenth-century France influenced and shaped the literary text. One such debate arose over the validity of bonds and oaths sworn under duress and the exercise of free will. Jefferson argues that the writer of the *Lancelot* must have been aware of these legal issues, and makes his characters act accordingly.⁴¹

By the end of the thirteenth century, the *Parlement de Paris* had developed a complex *inquisitio* procedure, a brief exposition of which will clearly show the influence of the judicial trial procedure on medieval literary debate texts.⁴² The plaintiff would plead his case in the *Grand Chambre* before the defendant and the court, after which the defendant might call for an adjournment to seek counsel. The plaintiff would then write a *litis contestatio,* or statement of accusation, which was subsequently delivered to the defendant for his response. *Enquêteurs* were despatched by the judge to seek out witnesses and information, which was then recorded by *greffiers.* The information gathered (compiled in an *inquisitory dossier* by the *greffier*) would be assessed at the *Chambre des Enquêtes,* and finally, in the *Grand Chambre,* an *arrêt* or judgement

⁴⁰ See Jefferson, *Oaths, Vows and Promises in the First Part of the French Prose Lancelot Romance* (Bern: Peter Lang, 1993), p. 27, n. 83.

⁴¹ 'When we look again at our fictional text in the light of our knowledge of this legal and theological dispute, we are drawn to the seemingly inevitable conclusion that whoever wrote it was fully familiar with the issues of debate, and that he is making his characters portray in action the truth of the maxim: *coactus voluit, sed voluit*', Jefferson (1993), p. 212. Jefferson looks at an earlier period, and a different genre of medieval literature than is the focus of my study, but my reference to her work here is intended to provide a precedent for the influence of the legal mode on medieval literary production.

⁴² See Ducoudray, *Les Origines du Parlement de Paris et la justice aux XIIIᵉ et XIVᵉ siècles* (Paris: Hachette, 1902) and Autrand, *Naissance d'un grand corps de l'Etat: les gens du Parlement de Paris 1345–1454* (Paris: Sorbonne, 1981).

would be pronounced in the name of the king. The compilation of these *inquisitory dossiers* is further evidence for the verbalization and textualization of conflicts.

In his recent typology of literary debates, Pierre Bec asserts that the judicial setting functions as a dramatization of the debate poem, staging the poetic competition that generates the text as an actual contest within the text.[43] The performative aspect of literary debate that, as I mentioned in my introduction, is a prerequisite of the genre, allows the author to manipulate a cast of personae. The introduction of judicial structures to literary debate concretizes this sense of theatricality. The appointment of a judge is common both to early debates (such as the *tenso* and *jeu-parti*), and to later *dits* such as Machaut's mirrored *Jugements*[44] or Christine de Pizan's love debate poems.[45] Later, the *cour d'amours* was to move from its traditional bucolic setting to relocate in an actual court of law, as McRae remarks, and so the debate is recast as the fictional image of the medieval trial.[46] The late medieval poetic debate thus draws imaginatively on oral competition as embodied in the legal trial, just as the written versions of the *disputatio* draw on an essentially oral and competitive exercise, without necessarily recording an actual oral performance.[47]

The medieval court *greffier* corresponds to the figure of the narrator-scribe in the debates of Alain Chartier,[48] who observes the dispute, and is called upon to record it, adopting the role of 'simple clerc' (*DDFA*, v. 1245). In the *Livre des Quatre Dames*, Chartier's narrator figure records the debate as a present to be sent to his lady, so that she may judge, and return an oral or written statement: 'Or est arbitre | De ce

---

[43] 'L'intervention d'une tierce personne (haut personnage, cour mondaine ou public populaire) [...] «théatralise» la performance, lui donne la dynamique d'une véritable compétition et [...] finalement, est la seule à en déterminer l'issue', Bec, *La Joute poétique: de la tenson médiévale aux débats chantés traditionnels* (Paris: Les Belles Lettres, 2000), p. 28.

[44] See Guillaume de Machaut (1988), and (1988b).

[45] See Christine de Pizan (1998b).

[46] See McRae (1997), p. 20.

[47] As I mention on p. 16, many of the textual versions of *disputationes* and *quodlibets* were composed straight onto paper without passing through an oral performance stage.

[48] Chartier's two longer debate poems: the *DDFA*, and the *LQD*, draw much of their inspiration from the innovative narrative *dit* form of Machaut's *Le Jugement du roy de Behaigne* (pre 1342) and *Le Jugement du roy de Navarre* (1349), and of Christine de Pizan's debate poems, *Le Livre du debat de deux amans* (1400), *Le Livre des trois jugemens* (1400), and *Le Livre du dit de Poissy* (1401).

debat que j'enregistre | Et qu'a jugier lui administre', vv. 3432–4. In the *Debat de reveille matin*, the narrator figure asserts that he recorded the debate he overheard: 'Si mis en escript ce qu'ilz dirent | Pour mieulx estre de leur butin', vv. 365–6. The narrator of Chartier's *Belle Dame sans mercy* overhears the debate concealed behind a trellis, but does not refer explicitly to the textual recording of the debate, and similarly in the *Excusacion*, though here Chartier's narrator is simultaneously the observer of debate and a participant. The narrator figure of the *Debat du Herault, du Vassault, et du Villain* appears only at the end of the debate, here asserting that he has had the debate recorded by another copyist: 'quant je l'ay fait escripre, | J'ay a l'escripvain deffendu | Du moustrer', vv. 436–8. In later texts, the figure of the *greffier* surfaces in a fictional courtroom, appearing in Baudet Herenc's *Accusations contre la Belle Dame sans mercy*, the first of the *Belle Dame sans mercy* sequels, along with other personifications who exercise legal functions within the court.[49] Further poems in the *Querelle de la Belle Dame sans mercy* explicitly take the judicial trial as their model for a fictitious court of love. *Le Jugement du povre triste amant banny*[50] and *Les Erreurs du jugement du povre triste amant banny*[51] are both set in law courts. The second of these poems, like the *Erreurs du jugement de la Belle Dame sans mercy*, is related entirely by a narrator figure in the third person; there is no direct engagement. This oblique style of narration emphasizes the legal character and formality of the poems, mirroring the composition of the *inquisitory dossier*. A later prose text, the *Arrêts d'amours* (1460–6),[52] which has close intertextual links to the *Querelle* cycle, employs a similar

---

[49] In Chapter 4, I discuss patterns of invention and mimesis in the *Querelle de la Belle Dame sans mercy*. See *Le Cycle de La BDSM* (2003), McRae (1997), and *The Quarrel of the Belle dame sans mercy* (2004), for an edition of the four immediate sequels of the *Belle Dame sans mercy*: Herenc's *Accusations contre la Belle Dame sans mercy*, *La Dame lealle en amours*, Achille Caulier's *La Cruelle Femme en amours*, and *Les Erreurs du jugement de la Belle Dame sans mercy*, all of which involve scenes within a court of love. McRae lists the presence of legal figures in the various sequels: a *dieu d'Amours* who corresponds to the king as the head of the parliament; *les présidens* (whose number varies in the sequels: twelve in the *Accusations* and fifteen in *Dame lealle*); the *procureur* and *avocats du roi* (*Espoir* and *Desir* are the *procureurs* in *Accusations contre la Belle Dame sans mercy*, as in *Dame lealle* and *Cruelle Femme*); a *huissier* (called *Doulx Penser* in *Accusations*; *Dame lealle*; *Cruelle Femme*); a *greffier* (*Accusations*; called *Gracieulx Parler* in *Cruelle Femme*); and the *avocats du deffendeur* (the *Belle Dame* adjourns the court in order to summon these in *Accusations*, they appear as *Loyaulté* and *Verité* in the *Dame lealle*, and *Fiction* and *Faulceté* in the *Cruelle Femme*).

[50] See Piaget's edition in *Romania* 34 (1905), 375–411.

[51] See Piaget's edition in *Romania* 34 (1905), 412–16.

[52] See *Les Arrêts d'amours*, ed. Rychner (Paris: Picard, 1951).

oblique narration through the figure of a clerk who overhears some of the *arrêts* pronounced by a *greffier* in the *parlement d'Amours*. In spite of its legalistic terminology and its court setting, the *Arrêts* is nonetheless a literary text in the *Belle Dame* tradition, and as such subject to the same rules as other literary texts generated by the *Querelle*, and by collaborative poetic exchange in general. These game rules are amply demonstrated in the verse epilogue to the *Arrêts*, when a device ostensibly intended to emphasize the veracity of the account actually undermines the entire structure of the text, and leaves the *Arrêts* inconclusive and unstable.

> Ainsi le greffier s'avança
> De plusieurs autres arrestz dire,
> Mais de tous ceulx qu'il prononça
> Ne peuz rien rapporter ne escripre;
> Il avoit ung peu la voix basse
> Tant qu'on ne le povoit entendre,
> Et puis ma plume estoit fort lasse,
> Par quoy n'eusse sceu rien comprendre
> [...]
> Helas! jugemens sont doubteux,
> Nul n'est pas saige qui s'i fie.
>
> vv. 5–12; 19–20

Not only is the narrator unsure about the other *arrêts* that were pronounced that day, the reader infers that the *arrêts* that have been recorded may be suspect, and subject to reversal (mimicking the frequent reversal of verdicts in appeals procedures).[53]

Two important late medieval debate poems, Martin le Franc's *Le Champion des dames* (1440–2),[54] and Pierre Michault's *Le Procès d'Honneur féminin* (post 1461),[55] adopt the model of the judicial

---

[53] These reversals and unstable endings are characteristic of much debate poetry. The poets engaged in the *Querelle de la Belle Dame sans mercy* use this closural ambiguity as an implicit challenge to solicit further poems. Machaut, Christine de Pizan, and Chartier all employ the technique of deferred judgements (the verdict reached in Machaut's *Jugement du roy de Behaigne* is overturned in his *Jugement du roy de Navarre*). See Armstrong (1997b), 12–14.

[54] See Martin le Franc, *Le Champion des dames*, ed. Deschaux, 5 vols. (Paris: Champion, 1999).

[55] See Pierre Michault, 'Le Procès d'Honneur féminin de Pierre Michault', ed. Folkart in *Le Moyen Français* 2 (1978), special edition. This poem is preserved in a sole manuscript: Paris, Bibliothèque de l'Arsenal, 3521, which also contains imitations of the *Belle Dame sans mercy*.

trial for their defence of the female sex. Martin le Franc's *Le Champion des dames* builds a defence of women on a foundation of virtuous women—literary, historical, and mythical—much in the same way as Christine de Pizan built the edifice of her *Livre de la cité des dames* (1405).[56] In the *Champion des dames*, the judicial trial sequence follows a physical battle (in book I) in which *Franc Vouloir* attempts to defend the *château d'Amours*, which houses the *dames*, and which is being assaulted by *Malebouche* and his followers. The subsequent trial by jury pits *Franc Vouloir* and his supporters (characters such as *Nature* and *Sainte Église*) on the side of the *dames* and *Amours* against *Malebouche* and his five lawyers who are the detractors of women (*Bref Conseil, Vilain Penser, Trop Cuidier, Lourt Entendement*, and *Faux Semblant*). *Verité* finally judges in favour of *Franc Vouloir* and crowns him victor. A significant intertextuality which connects the *Champion des dames* to the *Querelle de la Belle Dame sans mercy*, locates Chartier's *Belle Dame* in Martin le Franc's cemetery of the *chapelle d'Amours*, where she lies, 'en notable et haultain repos', v. 1912; no longer the 'dame au cueur noircy', v. 1904, as Achille Caulier had labelled her in his sequel *La Cruelle Femme en amours*,[57] but waiting to join the *dieu d'Amours* in the *paradis d'Amours*, 'en conclusion finale', v. 1925. Pierre Michault takes Martin le Franc's poem as the model for his *Procès d'Honneur féminin. Honneur féminin*, in the shape of an old man, is accompanied by the narrator to a court at which figures from classical and medieval literature (and particularly those authorities cited in what became known as the *Querelle des femmes*) join the ranks of the allegorical figures. Martin le Franc, Alain Chartier, and Boccaccio[58] support *Honneur féminin*, led by their *procureur, Vray*

---

[56] Gaston Paris records that Martin le Franc's *Le Champion des dames*, dedicated to Philippe le Bon, met with a less than rapturous reception at the court of Burgundy, and provoked le Franc into further poetic activity, writing the poem *Complainte du livre du Champion des dames a maistre Martin le Franc son acteur* shortly after sending the original work to Philippe around 1442. (In writing that his book was ill received, le Franc may have been self-consciously playing with the notion of continuation and response, though, and so should not be taken entirely seriously.) The poem is written in the form of a dialogue between the author and his book, imitating the practice of classical poets such as Ovid and Horace. See Martin le Franc, 'Un poème inédit de Martin le Franc', ed. Gaston Paris, *Romania* 16 (1877), 383–437.

[57] Martin le Franc also refers to the sequel poem *La Dame lealle en amours*, describing the *Belle Dame* as 'la dame leale', v. 1921.

[58] Boccaccio's *De mulieribus claris* (1355–9) was regarded as a profeminine treatise, and discusses famous and virtuous women of the past (biblical/historical/literary), earning its author a place among the other champions of women in Michault's court. It became known widely through the vernacular translation of 1401 by Laurent de Premierfait,

Rapport, while Juvenal,[59] Matheolus,[60] and Jean de Meun[61] form the defence team, led by *Faux Parler*; the defendant is simply known as *l'Inculpé*. It is particularly relevant that the trial sequence in *Le Procès d'Honneur féminin* should consist of a prosecuting side made up of the defenders of women, and a defence made up of detractors, since the traditional medieval pattern was a defence of women against male attack: woman's *responsio* to male *quaestio*, as Solterer would put it.[62] The defence is finally quashed, and *Honneur féminin* declared victorious, while Juvenal, Matheolus, and Jean de Meun are indicted: 'desloyaux, faulx, inicques et mauldis, | dampnez en feu ensemble leurs maulx dis', vv. 99–100. The four parts of Michault's trial — *deductions* (defence pleas), *replicques*, *dupplicques*, and *protestacions* — are mirrored in the structure of the *Arrêts*, and reflect a similar order of statements in the medieval judicial trial.

The theme of the defamation and the concomitant notion of the defence of women is one which runs throughout the later medieval debate tradition, from the early fifteenth-century *Querelle de la Rose*, in which Christine de Pizan, supported by Jean Gerson, accuses Jean de Meun of slandering women in his vastly popular *Roman de la Rose*,[63] to the later *Querelle de la Belle Dame sans mercy*, in which Chartier's heroine is both

---

De cleres et nobles femmes. See *De casibus virorum illustrium* (*Des cas des nobles hommes et femmes*), ed. Gathercole and trans. Laurent de Premierfait (Chapel Hill: University of North Carolina Press, 1968). Ironically though, Boccaccio also wrote antifeminist texts such as *Il Corbaccio* (1355). See Blamires, *Woman Defamed and Woman Defended: An Anthology of Medieval Texts* (Oxford: Clarendon Press, 1992), 166–76; also id., *The Case for Women in Medieval Culture* (Oxford: Clarendon Press, 1997).

[59] The silver age Latin poet Juvenal wrote the virulent antifeminist *Satire VI* (second century AD), and was widely imitated in the medieval period.

[60] Matheolus, also known as Mathieu de Boulogne, wrote the antifeminist *Liber lamentationum Matheoluli* (1295), which became widely known in the later Middle Ages through the vernacular translation of Jean Le Fèvre (1371–2). Le Fèvre subsequently wrote a profeminine text, *Le Livre de leesce*, which refutes Matheolus's antifeminist claims, and which was a source for Christine de Pizan.

[61] Jean de Meun is, of course, cited for his misogynistic continuation of Guillaume de Lorris's *Roman de la Rose* (*c.*1275), which sparked the early fifteenth-century epistolary exchange known as the *Querelle de la Rose*. See Chapter 2.

[62] See Solterer, *The Master and Minerva: Disputing Women in French Medieval Culture* (Berkeley/London: University of California Press, 1995), and also Joan Kelly, 'Early Feminist Theory and the *Querelle des femmes*, 1400–1789', *Signs* 8 (1982), 4–28: 'caught up in opposition to misogyny, the feminists of the *querelle* remained bound by the terms of that dialectic. What they had to say to women and society was largely reactive to what misogynists said about women', p. 27.

[63] In Chapter 2, I discuss the problem of Christine de Pizan's vernacular intervention in what is essentially a male-dominated Latin debate among the humanist secretaries

figuratively and actually put on trial. In the *Querelle de la Rose*, Christine de Pizan is left in the role of respondent, a role that Solterer ascribes to women throughout the debating tradition, from the High Middle Ages onwards:[64]

The response increasingly became a field for challenging the dominant feminine symbols in poetic discourse. […] While the woman's response displayed a contestatory aspect typical of so much of medieval literature, it derived its particular force from the *disputatio*. Moreover, it resembled the set role of *responsio* in these debates as they were conducted in the schools and the universities.[65]

In her fascinating study, Solterer demonstrates how women's response to male discourse, though ostensibly mimetic of the master's work, can weaken the dominant discourse through a coherent system of opposition to it, according to a principle of contrariety and not contradiction.[66] Through the use of accusations of slander—a woman's arsenal—woman's response to male attack finally culminates in the criminal charges of slander purportedly levelled against Chartier for his *Belle Dame sans mercy*.[67]

Although, with Solterer, I agree that women's role in medieval debate was very much that of response, the debate surrounding the *Belle Dame sans mercy*—indisputably intense and long-lived—was played out, I believe, according to other motives than those she attributes to the players. The question of the defence of women was an important part of the *Querelle*,[68] but the motives behind it were twofold, stemming also

and notaries Jean de Montreuil, Gontier, and Pierre Col, and her position outside the patriarchal *jeu*.

[64] However, as I also discuss at greater length in Chapter 2, which focuses on the *Querelle de la Rose*, Christine de Pizan engineers her own version of the *Querelle*, and includes a sequence of the *Querelle* letters in manuscripts of her personally organized and collected works. In this way she is able to re-establish her position, and by selecting and publishing the letters with her own *oeuvre*, achieve control and even authorial status over the material. She even effectively imposes closure on the *Querelle*.

[65] Solterer (1995), intro., pp. 10–11.

[66] Contrariety, according to the Aristotelian square of oppositions, holds two opposite objects in coexistence, whereas in contradiction the two opposing objects cancel one another out. Solterer (1995), pp. 103–4, and also Kay (2001).

[67] See my introduction, pp. 1–2; also *Le Cycle de La BDSM* (2003), pp. 85–9; Alain Chartier (1974), pp. 360–1. Gretchen Angelo explores the woman's responses in Andreas Capellanus's *De amore*, in relation to the uncourtly behaviour of Chartier's *Belle Dame sans mercy* in 'A Most Uncourtly Lady: The Testimony of the *Belle Dame sans mercy*', *Exemplaria* 15/1 (Spring, 2003), 133–57. I am grateful to Gretchen Angelo for sending me this article pre-publication.

[68] As I discuss in Chapter 3, Chartier's motives stemmed from a desire not simply to promote the valorization of female discourse but more importantly to free poetic language from the corrupt influences of a courtly or self-serving discourse.

from a desire for competition and collaboration between poets.[69] It is
to the playful poetic antecedents of medieval literary debate that I now
turn, in a closer investigation of the conditions that nurtured a debating
climate in late medieval France, in which collaboration through debate
was the principal creative mode. This will lead into a reading of Jean
le Seneschal's *Cent Ballades* (*c*.1389) as a paradigm of the medieval
debating community.

The competitive poetry of the troubadours and trouvères has been
addressed in a number of important and relatively recent studies, leading
to a renewal of critical interest in the debate genre (which had been largely
neglected, or only partially addressed).[70] Earlier studies include Hans
Walther's 1920 survey of medieval Latin debate poetry,[71] and Michel-
André Bossy's anthology of medieval debate poetry, which concentrates
on the period up to the fourteenth century.[72] Ito Toshiki produced a
competent thesis in 1974, which attempted to trace the antecedents of
debate to classical times, and to provide a typology of French medieval
debate.[73] Pierre-Yves Badel's chapter on debate in Daniel Poirion's
seminal *GRLMA* survey of fourteenth- and fifteenth-century French
literature is the most often cited authority on the genre, and spans
an impressive area, situating debate in its socio-historical context, and
drawing on rhetorical theory from Plato's *Republic*, to Pierre Fabri's
Grand et Vrai Art de pleine rhétorique[74] in the sixteenth century.[75] Badel
provides a set of distinctions that are initially useful for my consideration
of Chartier's work in the context of his literary contemporaries and
predecessors, and clarify the complex strands of influence shaping the
late medieval debate. Badel recognizes the difficulty in attempting a
typology of the debate since it was not clearly defined as a genre in
medieval rubrics (the term *dialogue* was often substituted for *débat* and

---

[69] This inherent desire for continuation should also be situated within the socio-
economic context of many of these court poets, whose livelihoods depended on the
creative process, and for whom poetic closure would have entailed loss of money,
prestige, and position.

[70] These include Paterson, *Troubadours and Eloquence* (Oxford: Clarendon Press,
1975); Gaunt, *Troubadours and Irony* (Cambridge: CUP, 1989); and Kay, *Subjectivity
in Troubadour Poetry* (Cambridge: CUP, 1990).

[71] See Walther, *Das Streitgedicht in der lateinischen Literatur des Mittelalters* (Munich:
Beck, 1920).

[72] See Bossy, *A Garland Anthology of Medieval Debate Poetry: Vernacular Works* (Paris:
Garland, 1987).

[73] See Toshiki, 'Les Débats dans la littérature française du moyen âge' (unpublished
doctoral thesis, Paris, 1974).

[74] See Pierre Fabri (1889–90).   [75] See Badel (1988), pp. 95–110.

vice versa). He does distinguish, however, between the terms *dialogue*, 'un mode de représentation, le rapport au discours direct d'un entretien à deux', and *débat*, 'un événement, un faire, une situation conflictuelle, un litige'.[76] *Dialogue*, then, refers to the mode of transmission, *débat* to the subject of conflict itself. A debate can be related in *dialogue*, but the term *débat* does not necessarily refer to the poetic mode itself. The medieval *débat* is frequently written in the form of a *dit*.[77] The *dit* is loosely defined in a recent study by Monique Léonard as:

Une oeuvre littéraire rédigée en vers, non chantée, plutôt brève, dont l'auteur cherche à transmettre une senefiance, grâce à quelques procédés stylistiques.[78]

Léonard here builds on Jacqueline Cerquiglini's earlier conclusions. Cerquiglini identifies three conditions that characterize the *dit*: an aesthetic of discontinuity, a first-person enunciation spoken by a *clerc-écrivain* figure (the narrator), and a didactic aim.[79] Alain Chartier's debate poems are typical of what Badel terms 'dialogues en récit', in that they use a first-person narrator who frames and records the debate that unfolds between two or more further characters.[80] I suggest that the mediation of a direct dialogue between two protagonists by the narrator turns the dialogue form (as Badel recognizes it) into a debate, since the narrator acts in some sense as a *locus* for the performance of the conflict between the speakers. On a conceptual level, as I argued in my introduction,[81] the literary dialogue is always already a debate, as it is always mediated by a third agent, be it the authorial subjectivity (possibly in the guise of a narrator) or the reader/listener. In other words, the literary dialogue can only ever be experienced via a performance, either reading or hearing.

[76] Badel (1988), p. 98.
[77] Badel (1988) cites Christine de Pizan who refers to her debate poems as *dits*. The term *livre* frequently precedes *débat* in the titles of her poems as of Chartier's in manuscript rubrics, reinforcing our sense of the debate as the poetic subject rather than the poetic mode, pp. 98–9.
[78] See Léonard, *Le Dit et sa technique littéraire: des origines à 1340* (Paris: Champion, 1996).
[79] Cerquiglini summarizes her position on the 'aesthetic of discontinuity' with a comparison of the *roman* and the *dit*: 'Le roman comme genre est du côté de la conjointure et d'une narration au passé, le dit du côté de la disjonction et d'une énonciation au présent', 'Le Dit,' *Grundriss der romanischen Literaturen des Mittelalters* VIII/1, ed. Poirion (Heidelberg: Carl Winter, 1988), 86–94, p. 87.
[80] Two of Chartier's debate poems fall into the category of *dit*: the DDFA and the LQD. Laidlaw argues that these are both early debates, based on the similarity of their *dit* form compared with the form of late debates such as the BDSM, or DRM. See Chapter 3 for a discussion of Laidlaw's conclusions.
[81] See Introduction, pp. 6–7.

Badel makes a further distinction between what he sees as the three main types of debate literature in the late medieval period: the *dialogue*, *jugement*, and *débat*. The *dialogue*, inspired by classical and patristic models, privileges dialectic over rhetoric, and establishes one interlocutor in a position of dominance over the other. Usually composed in prose, the *dialogue* is focused on the topic of discussion rather than the subjectivities of the debaters, which play no role in the debate. According to Badel, this genre represents 'des points de vue en conflit'.[82] The term *dialogue* is extended by Badel to include debates of more than two interlocutors, such as Alain Chartier's prose works, the *Livre de l'Esperance* and *Quadrilogue invectif.* The *jugement* is calqued on the model of the *jeu-parti* (to which I shall come presently), and is first embodied in Guillaume de Machaut's mirrored *dits*, the *Jugement du roy de Behaigne* and *Jugement du roy de Navarre.*[83] This poetic form sets the dialogue of two or more characters within a narrative frame, and relies more on the exchange of a few long speeches than the more frequently exchanged responses of the *dialogue*. It is usually composed in continuous verse. A request is made by the interlocutors to the clerkly narrator to nominate a judge for the debate, and he is charged with the textual recording of the dialogue. Chartier's *LQD* and *DDFA* would naturally fall into this category of debate. Another sub-category of the *jugement*, not covered by Badel, is the *songe* (or dream vision debate) in which the narrator is transported to a dream landscape where he observes a debate unfolding.[84] A more developed form of *jugement/songe* type sees the dream intrigue unfolding in an allegorical or actual courtroom.[85] The *débat*, by contrast with the *jugement*, organizes dialogue into short responsive stanzas, which tend to emphasize the 'élément conflictuel'.[86] Badel asserts, however, that what he terms *débat* is simply 'une pièce d'un jeu de société' and does not carry *senefiance* as the *dit*, *jugement*, or *dialogue* may. This is particularly obvious, he states, when the *débat* turns on a question of love. Badel gives Chartier's *BDSM* or *DRM* as examples of this more frivolous type of debate, a categorization I

---

[82] Badel (1988), p. 102.

[83] See Guillaume de Machaut (1988) and (1988b).

[84] In this category of *jugement/songe* we could place Chartier's *Quadrilogue invectif* as well as many of the sequels and imitations of the *BDSM*. The *songe* may of course exist independently of the *jugement* genre.

[85] See my earlier discussion of the legal settings of the sequels and imitations of the *BDSM*.

[86] Badel (1988), p. 104.

shall refute in my third chapter. Badel's final category of *débat* seems to be a convenient repository for everything that refuses to fit under *dialogue* or *jugement*. He subdivides *débat* into four categories by theme: amatory, moral (Chartier's *DHVV*), religious, and those inspired by scholarly exercises. Further nuances can be introduced into Badel's classification, however, through a consideration both of subjectivity and of *senefiance* in the *débat*, as I shall suggest.

A new anthology by Pierre Bec is the most complete survey of literary debate to date, spanning a period of almost four thousand years. Bec's anthology is angled towards a typology of the *tenso*, which he defines as:

une composition dialoguée en vers [...] dans laquelle deux (ou plusieurs) interlocuteurs se lancent une sorte de défi sur un sujet quelconque et rivalisent d'adresse et d'ingéniosité pour défendre des points de vue contraires.[87]

Bec makes a useful distinction among the *tenso*, a poetic contest between two players, performed before an audience, with a winner and a loser, the *débat*, a non-musical genre which involves the opposition of personifications or inanimate objects, not necessarily performed before an audience, and the *dialogue amoureux*, a dispute between the sexes.[88] The textual origins of literary debate are, according to Bec, to be found in *adamanduga*, Mesopotamian disputes, preserved in ancient Sumerian and Akkadian texts, in which the various merits of seasons, jobs, objects, animals, trees, and so on were debated in alternating couplets, with a final judgement imposed by a king or divinity. It is likely that this tradition was independent from later debate cultures that developed in Syrian and Arabic literature. The clashes of debating poets, closer to the predominant mode of literary debate in the medieval period, found expression in the *agôn* (struggle/contest) of Euripides and Aeschylus staged in Aristophanes' play *The Frogs* (405 BC),[89] and in the *agôn* of Hesiod and Homer from the popular apocryphal poem written sometime between the second centuries BC and AD. The bucolic contests of shepherds in Theocritus's *Idylls* of the third century BC[90] became

---

[87] See Bec, *La Joute poétique: de la tenson médiévale aux débats chantés traditionnels* (Paris: Les Belles Lettres, 2000), p. 9.

[88] Bec (2000) classifies Chartier's *BDSM* as a *dialogue amoureux*, for example; *Introduction*, p. 23.

[89] See Aristophanes, *The Frogs*, ed. Dover (Oxford: Clarendon Press, 1997).

[90] See Theocritus's *Idyll* V: a confrontation between Comatas and Lacon leads to a singing contest, judged by Morson; *Idyll* VIII stages an *amoebaean* (responsive) singing contest; and *Idyll* X pits the reapers Milon and Bucaeus against one another. See Theocritus, *The Idylls*, ed. Wells (London: Penguin, 1989).

the inspiration for the *amoebaean* (responsive) song of Virgil's Latin *Eclogues*.[91]

The Greek concept of *agôn* is significant for the collaborative poetic endeavours of late medieval poets, and particularly the *Querelle de la Belle Dame sans mercy* poets, since it encompasses the complementary notions of struggle and skill. In his sociological study of games, Roger Caillois appropriates the Greek concept and sets up the categories of *agôn* and *alea*, the first of these denoting games of skill such as chess, the latter games of chance such as dice.[92] This distinction illuminates the skilful, rule-bound, and competitive game played by late medieval poets.

In Europe, the debating mode increasingly manifested itself in a multiplicity of literary forms. The early Latin *conflictus* and *altercatio* both stage disputes over the relative merits of winter and summer,[93] body and soul,[94] flowers,[95] and so on. Twelfth-century goliardic poems such as the *Altercatio Phyllidis et Florae* and the *Concilium romarici moncium* (*Council of Remiremont*) spawned a series of debates known as *Débats du clerc et du chevalier*, in which two *dames* dispute their preference for a clerkly or knightly lover respectively, exemplified in the late twelfth-/early thirteenth-century French poem *Florence et Blanchefor*, also known as the *Jugement d'amour*.[96] These debates, Bec suggests, develop from the *adamanduga* type, and have more in common with

---

[91] See Virgil's third *eclogue* (*c*.42 BC) for the poetic contest between Menalcas and Damoetas with Palaemon in the role of judge. This is an instance of *amoebaean* song, influenced by Theocritus's *Idylls* I, IV, V, and VIII. Virgil's seventh *eclogue* stages a similar contest between the shepherds Corydon and Thyrsis. See Virgil, *The Eclogues and Georgics*, ed. R. D. Williams (Bristol: Bristol Classical Press, 1996).

[92] See Caillois (1967).

[93] An early model of this type of debate is Alcuin's ninth-century *Conflictus veris et hiemis*, which spawned later poems such as the twelfth-century *Altercatio hiemis et aestatis*.

[94] The earliest model is the twelfth-century *Visio Philiberti*, a dream vision in which the sleeper witnesses the dispute of a soul and body. In a later adaptation of this model, the *Pèlerinage de l'âme* (1355–8), Guillaume de Deguileville stages a dispute between a pilgrim's soul and his corpse in Purgatory. See the edition by Stürzinger (London: Nichols & sons, 1895).

[95] Sedulius Scottus's *Rosae liliique certamen* (see *Sedulii Scotti carmina*, ed. Meyers (Turnhout: Brepols, 1991)) is the model for Froissart's *Plaidoirie de la rose et de la violette* (1392–3). See Jean Froissart, '*Dits*' *et* '*débats*', ed. Fourrier (Geneva: Droz, 1979).

[96] Another surviving French poem in this genre is *Hueline et Aiglentine*; in addition there are two Anglo-Norman versions, *Blanflor et Florence* and *Melior et Ydoine*. See *Les Débats du clerc et du chevalier dans la littérature poétique du moyen âge*, ed. Oulmont (Paris: Champion, 1911).

that early form (*débat* in Bec's typology) than with the Greco-Roman poetic singing contests, *Idylls* and *Eclogues* (*tenso* in Bec's typology). I nuance Bec's typology by making a clear distinction between the early literary debates (*débats*) whose subject is the source and focus of conflict (wine v. water; clerk v. knight), and the debate whose subject is largely irrelevant, the focus being instead the opposition and conflict between two or more subjective interlocutors, be they poets, clerks, or lovers (*tenso*). This opposition may manifest itself overtly in the terms of the dialogue, or covertly in the ironic subversion of rival discourses. The second of the categories I identify was practised in the twelfth and thirteenth centuries by Occitan troubadours via the conflictual lyric forms known as *tenso*,[97] *joc-partit/partimen*, double *sirventes*,[98] and *pastorela*,[99] while jongleurs exchanged *coblas*.[100] The earliest *tenso* dates from around 1135, and opposes the Occitan poets Marcabru and Uc Catola, whereas the earliest *partimen* is not recorded until 1190.[101] The distinction between the *tenso* and *partimen* (this latter a term only used much later) seems particularly subtle. In general, the term *tenso* may be used to denote a *partimen*, but not vice versa.[102] In a discussion of the Occitan *tenso* and the Arrageois *jeu-parti*, Michèle Gally identifies the *tenso* as a freer form than the *jeu-parti* or *partimen*.[103]

The French *jeu-parti* (Occitan *partimen/joc-partit*), flourished in the north of France in the second half of the thirteenth century, and was

---

[97] The *tenso* was usually a contest between two interlocutors; a poetic contest between more than two was known as a *tornejament*.

[98] The *sirventes* was satirical in character, and formed the basis for the double *sirventes*: an exchange of opposing and often rhythmically identical verses between two poets. See Jeanroy, 'Un Duel poétique du XIIIᵉ siècle', *Annales du Midi* 27/28 (1915–16), 269–305.

[99] The Occitan *pastorela*, also popular in France (*pastourelle*) from the early twelfth century, was a debate between a knight and a shepherdess or peasant girl, in which the former attempted to woo the latter.

[100] The *cobla* was the basic unit of the *tenso*, but also a genre in its own right. The *cobla esparsa* was a single couplet, which might then be exchanged in longer antithetical sequences. See for example the contest between Peire Bremon Ricas Novas, and Gui de Cavaillon, in Bec (2000), pp. 243–6.

[101] This is a debate between Folquet de Marseille and Tostemps.

[102] Bec (2000).

[103] See Gally, 'Entre sens et non-sens: approches comparatives de la *tenso* d'oc et du *jeu-parti* arrageois', in *Il genere «tenzone» nelle letterature romanze delle origini (atti del convegno internazionale Losanna 13–15 novembre 1997)*, ed. Pedroni and Stäuble (Ravenna: A. Longo, 1999), 223–35.

particularly popular at Arras;[104] the majority of the *jeux-partis* edited in Långfors' comprehensive *recueil* were composed by poets belonging to the *école d'Arras* who are documented in the register of the *Confrérie des jongleurs et bourgeois d'Arras*.[105] The *jeu-parti* and the *demande d'amour* share common elements and often debate identical questions of love. In the traditional *jeu-parti*, one poet suggests the initial topic for debate in the form of a *demande*, the other chooses his preferred response, and debate ensues in the form of alternate stanzas; finally appeals are made to two appointed judges respectively, though the judges' answers are not supplied.[106] Interestingly, Michèle Gally notes that the *jeu-parti* frequently remains unresolved since each interlocutor refuses to alter his arguments in the light of his opponent's response.[107] The term *jeu-parti* itself was used to designate an ineluctable situation both in battle and in the game of chess and may, as Paul Remy argues through H. J. Murray, have developed as a term for poetry from its use in chess.[108] These *jeux-partis* or problems in chess, like their poetic namesakes, were commonly written down and collected in manuscript form for the edification and entertainment of 'princes et damoiselles', this material context literally transcribing play.[109] Each *jeu-parti* (poem or chess game) is inscribed in a wider pattern of play. The stalemate reached in chess naturally gives

---

[104] See *Recueil général des jeux-partis français*, ed. Långfors, Jeanroy, and Brandin (Paris: Champion, 1926).

[105] Jehan Bretel (d. 1270) is one of the most prolific of the authors of *jeux-partis*, and is registered among the members of the *Confrérie*.

[106] Långfors' definition of the *jeu-parti* is widely cited: 'une pièce lyrique de six couplets de deux envois: dans le premier couplet, l'un des deux partenaires propose à l'autre une question dilemmatique et, celui-ci ayant fait son choix, soutient lui-même l'alternative restée disponible. Dans les deux envois, chacun des deux partenaires nomme un juge. Il n'y a dans les textes aucune trace d'un jugement que ceux-ci auraient prononcé', *Recueil général des jeux-partis* (1926), V–VI.

[107] Gally (1999).

[108] Paul Remy explains that the term *jeu-parti* in chess refers to 'un problème, c'est-à-dire une position déterminée des pions qui, par sa difficulté, rend la fin de la partie indécise', in his article 'De l'expression «partir un jeu» dans les textes épiques aux origines du jeu-parti', *Cahiers de Civilisation Médiévale* 17 (1974), 327–33, p. 330. For an exhaustive history of the game of chess in Europe see Murray, *A History of Chess* (Oxford: Clarendon Press, 1913). The analogy of the game of chess (which I shall explore further in Chapter 4, part II) may illuminate the playful dialectical networks through which poems are generated in a *collaborative debating community*.

[109] Murray (1913) mentions 30–40 extant manuscripts of these problems, mostly copied between 1340 and 1450, including Paris, BnF, fr. 1173, and an early printed edition (Denis Janot, Paris: 1530–40) preserved in Vienna, whose incipit reads: 's'ensuit jeux Partis des eschez: Composez nouvellement Pour recrer tous nobles cueurs et pour eviter oysiveté a ceulx qui ont voulenté: desir et affection de le scavoir et aprendre et est appellé ce Livre le jeu des princes et damoiselles'. This is my transcription. I have

rise to a rematch, as the impasse reached in the debate poem solicits future judgement and further debates. In one typical *jeu-parti*, Jehan Bretel poses Jehan de Grieviler an amatory dilemma:

> Grieviler, vostre ensïent
> Me dites d'un ju parti:
> Se vous amés loiaument
> Et on vous aime autresi,
> Li qieus sera mieus vos grés,
> U chele qui vous amés
> Sera bele par raison
> Et sage a tres grant fuison,
> U sage raisnaulement
> Et tres bele outreement?[110]

Variations on this same theme are recorded in Groups 1, 2, 4, 6, and 7 of the *demandes d'amour* manuscripts.[111] It is not necessarily clear which form (*jeu-parti* or *demande*) had the greater influence on the other, as Felberg-Levitt observes,[112] since although the *demandes* were not actually formally collected in manuscripts before the fourteenth century,[113] they were incorporated in both literary texts and society games from the thirteenth and possibly early twelfth centuries.[114] In contrast to the *demande d'amour*, however, the *jeu-parti* is characterized by the subjectivity of the interlocutors, who frequently become personally involved in their contest, each more concerned to discredit the other's arguments than with the topic itself. As Jean-Claude Mühlethaler observes in a recent article:

Le recours à l'injure crée aussi, en focalisant l'intérêt sur les interlocuteurs et les modalités du discours plutôt que sur le sujet posé, l'espace pour une mise en

---

modernized the punctuation in accordance with the established rules. See Roques (1926), and Foulet and Speer (1979).

[110] *Recueil général* (1926): XXVII, pp. 98–102. Jehan de Grieviler follows (or sets) the *demande* pattern by choosing the first option.

[111] *Les Demandes d'amour* (1995), p. 190.

[112] Felberg-Levitt notes many instances of correspondences between the *demandes* and the *jeux-partis* in her edition: *Les Demandes d'amour* (1995).

[113] Felberg-Levitt edits the 363 existing prose and verse *demandes d'amour* from twenty-five fourteenth- and fifteenth-century manuscripts.

[114] Ilvonen suggests that the *juec d'amor* which the troubadour Guillaume IX, comte de Poitiers, evokes in verses dating from the early twelfth century is evidence for the existence of a formal game involving *demandes d'amour*. See Ilvonen, 'Les *demandes d'amour* dans la littérature française du moyen âge', *Neuphilologische Mitteilungen* 14 (1912), 128–44.

scène du moi. Ainsi s'abolit, du moins ponctuellement, la distance esthéthique qu'imposent les conventions formelles du jeu-parti.[115]

This focus on the subjectivity of the interlocutors moves the debate genre away from the more purely scientific *disputatio* or *dialogue* whose goal is to move logically to an objective *determinatio* or conclusion. This notion of a scientific and objective focus on the argument as opposed to a subjective focus on the debater is already addressed in Aristotle's influential treatise on dialectic, the *Topica*, as I mentioned earlier. Kay develops this concept of a poetic subjectivity in her study of the troubadour corpus.[116] Kay argues that a 'sense of *self*' emerges from the very conventions of troubadour poetry, challenging Zumthor's contention that subjectivity has no place in the medieval lyric.[117] In his complementary study, Simon Gaunt identifies irony as the subjective element within troubadour lyric that resists a purely formalistic interpretation, engaging with Gruber's model of the *dialectic* of troubadour poetry.[118] Gruber establishes a pattern of poetic composition based on intertextuality. Each successive troubadour poet absorbs the poetic structures of his contemporaries and predecessors into his own text, and elaborates them, in a consciously competitive move. For Gruber, each troubadour is part of an initiated group, producing highly inflected work: the *hermetische Lyrik*, inaccessible to the non-initiate. In other words, there is an implicit collaboration between the troubadour poets: one that can only be traced through the text itself. Gruber's model, although a challenge to the traditional formalist analysis of medieval lyric, does not take account of the wider socio-cultural implications of these dialectical networks. Gaunt goes further, to suggest that it is specifically *ironic* intertextual play that characterizes troubadour poetry. The troubadour poet playfully ironizes convention and tradition from within its very confines, setting up a competitive dialogue with earlier poets, that establishes a socio-cultural context for his own contribution.[119] It is precisely this socio-cultural

[115] See Mühlethaler, 'Disputer de mariage: débat et subjectivité: des jeux-partis d'Arras à l'échange de ballades et de rondeaux chez Eustache Deschamps et Charles d'Orléans', in *Il genere «tenzone» nelle letterature romanze delle origini (atti del convegno internazionale Losanna 13–15 novembre 1997)*, ed. Pedroni and Stäuble (Ravenna: A. Longo, 1999), 203–21, p. 208.

[116] See Kay (1990).

[117] Kay (1990), p. 5, and Zumthor, *Essai de poétique médiévale* (Paris: Seuil, 1972).

[118] Gruber (1983), and Gaunt (1989).

[119] I discuss in Chapter 3 how Chartier ironizes courtly convention from within a traditional courtly poetic form.

context that is a basis for the late medieval collaborative debating communities I postulate, and which takes account, as Gaunt acknowledges, of the material context within which poetry is transmitted. Jane Taylor engages with Gruber's intertextual dialectic as well as Pierre Bourdieu's model of social dialectic in her study of François Villon's poetry, to trace a pattern of reciprocal poetry in the later Middle Ages into which Villon taps.[120]

The personal, subjective conflict of disputing scholars/poets in the scholastic *disputatio* is irrelevant; conflict in this case is determined by and centred on the initial topic or question. The shift to a more subjective style of argumentation involving the poet's own fragmented subjectivities allows for an authorial engagement in literary debate and situates it in a socio-cultural framework. I suggest that the subjective element apparently lacking in the 'scientific' *demande d'amour* genre is provided through the variety of social and literary contexts into which it is absorbed. The *demandes d'amour* were a popular social pastime, intimately connected with the *jeu-parti*, as we have seen, and reflected in a series of literary debates, ranging from Andreas Capellanus's well-known treatise on courtly love, the *De amore* (1181–6),[121] Richard de Fournival's *Consaus d'amour* and *Li Commens d'amour* (pre 1250), to Machaut's mid fourteenth-century *Jugement* poems, Christine de Pizan's love debate poems, or Chartier's *DDFA* and *LQD*.[122] So the courtly game is reflected in the text, itself part of the wider pattern of poetic game through which the text is generated, creating an effect of mise en abyme. Both *demande* and poetic game must be classified as *agôn*, contests of skill, governed by predetermined rules of engagement. A further mise en abyme is detected in the medieval texts that incorporate

---

[120] See Taylor, Jane (2001), especially chapter 1, 'Painted Eloquence and Serious Games', pp. 6–32.

[121] The *De amore* was dedicated to Capellanus's friend Gautier, and designed to provide instruction in the art of courtly love. Book II contains a series of male–female love disputes, and includes twenty-one judgements pronounced by noble women; see Andreas Capellanus, *On Love*, ed. P. G. Walsh (London: Duckworth, 1993).

[122] See my earlier discussion of Chartier's *DDFA* in the context of its reliance both on the scholastic *disputatio* and on the *demande* form (also Christine de Pizan's *Livre du debat de deux amans*). Chartier's *LQD* (Alain Chartier (1974), pp. 196–304) is structured around the debate of four ladies whose lovers have respectively been killed, been imprisoned, gone missing, or deserted at a recent battle (probably Agincourt). This recalls the dispute in Christine de Pizan's *Livre du dit de Poissy*, between a *dame* and a squire; the squire is forced to see the lady he loves and who rejected him on a regular basis, whereas the *dame's* lover is imprisoned abroad. The challenge here is to elect the unhappier of the two plaintiffs. See Christine de Pizan (1998b), 203–74.

the *demande* within the context of formal game playing. The three games of *Le Jeu des demandes et responces d'amour*, *Le Roi qui ne ment* and *Le Jeu aux rois et aux reines*, are often alluded to in medieval texts.[123] The rules of these formal games, structured around the *demande d'amour* unit, may be established from the various literary sources.[124] The most widely cited is *Le Roi qui ne ment*, of which *Le Jeu aux rois et aux reines* appears simply to be a pastoral version. Evidence suggests that *Le Roi qui ne ment* was played in a group of nobles of mixed gender; a King would be chosen to preside (there might be a crowning ceremony, in an echo of the crowning of victorious poets in the *puys*). The game unfolded as a series of subtle, often delicate questions of love casuistry were posed and answered by the participants, in pairings of opposite sexes. In fact, as Richard Firth Green suggests, *Le Roi qui ne ment* allowed its players to engage in a 'mock courtship'.[125] These three games are staged in Thomas III, Marquis de Saluces's *Le Chevalier errant* (1359),[126] Jacques de Longuyon's *Les Voeux du paon* (1312–13),[127] Jean de Condé's *Le Sentier batu* (1313–40),[128] and Adam de la Halle's *Jeu de Robin et Marion*.[129] Here the game does not generate the text, as for the literary debates mentioned earlier, but may provide a textual mirror that reflects the self-conscious practice of the author.[130] The physical tournament, or duel, expressed in the verbal poetic conflict of the *tenso* or debate, is reflected on a further level in the poeticized contests represented within these texts.

[123] Examples include Jacques Bretel's *Tournoi de Chauvency* (*c*.1285) which mentions both *Le Roi qui ne ment* and *Le Jeu aux rois et aux reines*, and possibly *Le Jeu des demandes et responces d'amour*; see *Les Demandes d'amour* (1995), p. 23. Machaut mentions *Le Roi qui ne ment* in his *Remède de Fortune* and *Voir Dit*; Froissart in *L'Espinette amoureuse*.

[124] *Le Chevalier errant* describes the game of *demandes et responces d'amour*, recording a series of thirty-one *demandes* whose topic is the plight of lovers from mythology, romance, or history. See *Les Demandes d'amour* (1995).

[125] See Firth Green (1990).

[126] This romance stages the game of *demandes et responces d'amour*.

[127] See Hoepffner (1920).

[128] See *Les Demandes d'amour* (1995), p. 19.

[129] Adam de la Halle's *pastourelle* stages the down-market version of *Le Roi qui ne ment*, known as the *Jeu aux rois et aux reines*. See Langlois (1902).

[130] The episode of the game of *Le Roi qui ne ment* in *Les Voeux du paon* is significant in the context of the game of chess that also opposes the protagonists of this text. See Chapter 4, part II for a discussion of chess in the context of debate and game, and Blakeslee, 'Lo Dous Jocx sotils: La partie d'échecs amoureuse dans la poésie des troubadours', *Cahiers de Civilisation Médiévale* 28 (1985), 213–22.

Another game, *ventes* or *venditions d'amour*, seems to have developed later, and was most popular in courtly circles in the fourteenth and fifteenth centuries in France. The *venditions* are preserved in nine manuscripts,[131] and with two exceptions[132] are always collected with *demandes d'amour*.[133] The dialogic ethos is similar to that of the *demande*, and erotic tension between the sexes is again exploited. The game was a poetic female–male exchange, in which a lady or gentleman offered a symbolic flower, bird, or object for sale to her/his fe/male interlocutor, and s/he was expected to respond with another line or lines of verse, respecting the rhyme sequence; failure to respond, or repetition, might result in a forfeit being imposed.[134] The element of skill involved in these verbal exchanges is reminiscent of the *demandes*. Christine de Pizan composed seventy *jeux a vendre*, which are included in copies of her collected works.[135] In choosing to model her poems on these improvised, and essentially performative *venditions*, Christine turns the courtly pastime into an elaborate game of ventriloquism in which she manipulates both female and male speaking voices. Bergeron discusses the oral/textual character of the *venditions*, and suggests that Christine's *jeux a vendre* (as with the anonymous collections of *venditions* transcribed in manuscripts) are primarily a written genre, not mere transcription of oral improvisation: 'que les *Jeux à vendre* de Christine de Pizan soient le produit d'une écriture, nul n'en disconviendra'.[136] In the last of Christine's *jeux a vendre*, she inserts an anagram signature, as she often does elsewhere in her writing, emphasizing their specifically textual character.[137] The anagrams of 'Crestine', and Christine's late

---

[131] See Bergeron (1986), pp. 34–5, n. 2, for all manuscript and printed sources of the *ventes*. On the *ventes* see also Lazard (1982).

[132] Bern, Burgerbibliothek, 218, fols. 102^v–3^r; Paris, Bibliothèque Mazarine, 3636, fols. 228–9^r.

[133] I omit the five manuscripts of Christine de Pizan's *jeux a vendre* from my total. See Bergeron (1986).

[134] For example: 'Je vous vens le vers chapellet. |—Nul amant ne puet estre let, | Mais que ses taches soient bonnes, | De loiaulté suive les bonnes, | Si sera digne que l'en l'aime | Et que sa dame ami le claime', Christine de Pizan, *Jeux a vendre*, 22. The symbol of the courtly *vers chapellet* is part of the network of intertextualities which link the poems of the *Querelle de la BDSM*.

[135] See Christine de Pizan, *Oeuvres poétiques*, ed. Roy, 3 vols. (Paris: Firmin-Didot, 1886–96). For the *jeux a vendre* see vol. I, pp. 187–205.

[136] See Bergeron (1986), p. 54.

[137] See *Le Livre du debat de deux amans* (vv. 2021–3); *Le Livre des trois jugemens* (vv. 1526–31); and *Le Livre du dit de Poissy* (v. 2075), in Christine de Pizan (1998b).

husband 'Estien' (du Castel) are metaphorically contained within the 'escrinet' ('writing' box; emboldened below). From within textuality, gender identities may be thus asserted, and confused:[138]

> Je vous vens l'**escrinet** tout plein.
> —Mon nom y trouverez a plain
> Et de cil qu'oncques plus amay,[139]
> Par qui j'ay souffert maint esmay,
> Se vous y querez proprement;
> Or regardez mon se je ment.
>
> *Jeux a vendre*, 70

Christine's playful use of ventriloquism can also be seen in her *Cent Ballades*, and *Cent Ballades d'amant et de dame* where she engages with Jean le Seneschal's earlier *Cent Ballades* (c.1389). She sets up a knowing reversal of the male-authored dialogue that governs Jean le Seneschal's *Cent Ballades*, where the female interlocutor *la Guignarde* is essentially a puppet in the hands of male creators, by manipulating her own male puppets. A close reading of Jean le Seneschal's poem will reveal a new form of poetic play: the fictional collaboration, which represents the culmination of earlier debating games. This ostensibly collaborative poem will provide a model of the operation and dynamics of virtual (fictional) late medieval debating communities.[140]

Jean le Seneschal's *Cent Ballades* refers to itself in the penultimate ballade as a collaboration between four poets: Jean le Seneschal (sénéchal d'Eu), Philippe d'Artois (comte d'Eu), Jean de Crésecque, and Jean Boucicaut. It remains unclear how far, if at all, each of these historical figures actually contributed to the body of the text, though it emerges in the course of the responses that Jean le Seneschal is the principal narrator.[141] The poetic responses to the *Cent Ballades*, written by

---

[138] It is difficult here to establish the gender of the speaker and the respondent, as in many of the *venditions* (see Bergeron), but Christine perhaps knowingly leaves the ambiguity, in order to challenge the traditional gender roles. It is interesting in this light that her signature and that of her late husband are intertwined in one word, suggesting a fusion of male and female identities within the text, reflected in the ambiguous form of the *jeu a vendre*.

[139] A third word may also be found concealed in the 'escrinet': 'Crestien'. Christine often plays on the similarity of the letters forming both her name and her faith.

[140] See *supra*: Introduction, p. 8.

[141] See Raynaud's discussion of the attribution of authorship: Jean le Seneschal (1905).

thirteen further poets,[142] and transcribed with the *Cent Ballades* in the six extant fourteenth- and fifteenth-century manuscript versions and two eighteenth-century copies,[143] may have been composed for a formal *puy* that took place in Avignon in October–November 1389, at which Jean, duc de Berry, composer of one of the responses, presided.[144] Many of the alleged participants in this poetic collaboration were, around ten years later, to become members of Charles VI's *Cour amoureuse* (1400), whose armorials list two of the named collaborators in the *Cent Ballades*, and at least eight of the authors of the responses.[145] (The *Cour amoureuse* may of course itself be an elaborate literary fabrication, designed to give a social and material context for the poetic endeavours of its members.)

The *Cent Ballades* dramatizes the conflict between the counsels of a *mondain chevalier*, versed in the ways of love and battle (referred to as *Hutin* [de Vermeilles] in the responses), and of a *dame* (referred to as *la Guignarde* in the responses), both of whom seek to instruct a *jeune chevalier*, the narrator of the poem (later identified with Jean le Seneschal in the responses) in amatory matters. The wise *chevalier* urges the narrator to maintain the love of one lady alone, thus espousing *Loiauté*

---

[142] The names of these thirteen, recorded in the manuscripts, are Renaud de Trie; Jean de Chambrillac; Monseigneur de Touraine (Louis d'Orléans); Lionnet de Coesmes; Jacquet d'Orléans; Guillaume de Tignonville; Monseigneur de Berry (Jean, duc de Berry); Jean de Mailly; Charles d'Ivry; François d'Auberchicourt; Guy VI de la Trémoïlle; Jean de Bucy; Raoul, le bâtard de Coucy. MS A preserves a fourteenth response, possibly added by the owner of the manuscript, Charles II d'Albret, after 1421. See Jean le Seneschal (1905), for this later response.

[143] Raynaud lists six manuscript versions, A: Paris, BnF, nouv. acq. fr. 1664; B: Chantilly, Musée Condé, 1680 (491); C: Paris, BnF, fr. 2360 (old 8047); E: Paris, BnF, fr. 826 (old 7211); F: Brussels, Bibliothèque Royale, 11218–11219; G: Paris, BnF, fr. 2201 (old 7999); and two copies: B[1]: Paris, BnF, fr. 759 (18th-century copy of B); F[1]: The Hague, KB, 71 G. 73 (18th-century copy of F). MS A preserves all thirteen responses, as does MS B; MS C has eleven (without XII and XIII); MS E has a lacuna, and lacks most of response X and the following responses; MS F transcribes eleven (without XII and XIII); MS G has a lacuna, and lacks the end of XII, and response XIII.

[144] The idea of the formal *puy* is Raynaud's, and was contested by Barbara Altmann at the Xth triennial ICLS conference, Tübingen, 2001.

[145] Jean le Seneschal is listed as one of the twenty-four *ministres* of the *Cour* and Jean Boucicaut was also a member of the *Cour*, as well as founding his own chivalric order: *La Dame blanche à l'escu vert* (1399). Eight of the authors of the responses to the *Cent Ballades* are listed in the charter: Renaut de Trie (*escuyer* of the court); Jean de Chambrillac (also one of the thirteen *chevaliers* of Boucicaut's order); Louis d'Orléans (one of the eleven *conservateurs* of the *Cour amoureuse*); Jacquet d'Orléans; Charles d'Ivry; Guillaume de Tignonville (*ministre* of the *Cour*); Jean, duc de Berry (*conservateur* of the *Cour*); François d'Auberchicourt (also a *chevalier* of Boucicaut's order).

and rejecting *Fausseté*: 'dessoubz l'ombre de Fausseté ne vous logiez' (XLIX), while the guileful *dame* later attempts to persuade the young *chevalier* to cast his nets wider: 'en maint lieu faciez amie' (XC), since 'qui partout seme, partout queult' (XCI). The narrator rejects her advice: 'pour vous n'en feroie rien' (XCIV), citing the *chevalier*'s arguments. But the *dame* persuades the narrator to embark on a quest to discover 'le plus eüreux conseil' (C). To this end, the narrator consults his companions and throws the debate open to the general public. He creates the fiction of an external poetic collaboration—a 'compagnie d'esbanoy'[146]—from within the text, citing the names of his would-be collaborators in the penultimate ballade of the collection (emboldened below):

> Et depuis,
> Enquestay de cest afaire
> Au **conte d'Eu**, que je truiz
> Prestz et duiz
> A toute loiauté faire
> […]
> Puis volz **Bouciquaut** atraire
> Pour parfaire,
> Et **Creseques** raconduiz,
> Que leur respons volentaire
> Pensse estraire
> De leurs bouches: s'en parçuiz
> Qu'en loiauté sont instruiz
> Et aduiz,
> N'autre amour ne leur peut plaire.
> Par nous fu ce livre estruiz;
> Mais je y luiz:
> A toute loiauté faire!
>
> Ballade XCIX

The narrator figure asserts here that the debate, of which he has been the focus, rather than the simple scribe, has been a collaborative literary project, involving himself, Philippe d'Artois, Jean Boucicaut, and Jean de Crésecque. The veil of fiction is thus torn somewhat, since the narrator figure both claims the veracity of the debate he has participated in, through the use of first-person narrative, and signals its fictionality by referring to it as a literary composition in which others, who did not explicitly belong to the fictional world of the debate, participated: 'par nous fu ce livre estruiz'. The narrator refers to the possible outcome of

---

[146] Ballade XXXII, v. 4.

the debate, explaining that he enlisted the help of these collaborators in order to achieve closure: 'Il m'estoit necessaire | D'a chef traire | La matiere que j'ensuis' (XCIX). However, a further ripping of the fictional veil occurs as the *Cent Ballades* closes without the conclusion solicited from the narrator's collaborators: 'puis vols Bouciquaut atraire | Pour parfaire, | Et Creseques raconduiz' (XCIX). In fact, no written responses are provided to substantiate the narrator's claims that his companions all support the cause of *Loiauté*. Far from concluding the debate, the floor is then opened in the final ballade to other poets. Further ballades are solicited purportedly to resolve the continuing debate:

> Sy **prions** tous les amoureux
> Que chascun seulz
> Par une balade savoir
> **Nous** face lequel des conseulx
> Leur semble entr'eulx
> Mieudre a tenir.
>
> Ballade C

The narrator here uses the first person plural form (emboldened above), supporting his claim for collective authorship in the previous ballade. The plurality of authorship echoes the polyphony of the debate itself, and mirrors the fracturing of textual identities, which are parallel with but not assimilated to the historical identities of the poets. So the framework of collaboration is not only externally imposed on the *Cent Ballades*, it may be seen as part of the poem's deep fictional structure, and intimately linked to the text's lack of closure. This fiction of collaboration is further maintained by the series of responses that, as I mentioned, follow the text of the *Cent Ballades* in all the extant manuscript copies. Barbara Altmann has described the transition from the *Cent Ballades* to these responses in the manuscript tradition in terms of a shift from fictional to actual collaboration. I suggest, however, that these responses bear traces of a coherent planning consistent with the notion of a larger fictional design whose aim is not to achieve closure but to perpetuate debate. Further, in referring to the *Cent Ballades* as a non-fictional debate, the authors of the responses, like the narrator, implicate themselves in the fictional framework of the poem.

Seven of the thirteen responses uphold the cause of *Loiauté*, represented by the chevalier *Hutin*, two are undecided, two ambiguous, and a further two support the promiscuity advocated by *la Guignarde*. A final conclusion or judgement is not imposed. The transmission of these responses with the *Cent Ballades* suggests that they were intended as part of the poetic whole. There is a textual order within the responses which arises from specific intertextualities, and which further implies deliberate compositional design. Renaud de Trie's response, the first in the series, appears to be a direct response to the challenge issued by 'nous' in the last of the *Cent Ballades*; Renaud begins 'Je vous mercie doulcement | Entre vous .iiii. compagnons'. Guillaume de Tignonville (VI) defers to the company of poets to whose challenge he is responding, explicitly naming all four; Jean de Bucy states that he is responding to 'vous [...] seigneurs, qui demander | Avez voulu par si bonne ordenance | Qu'une balade chascun veulle ordenner | Des amoureux' (XII). Jean de Mailly is the only poet to address his challengers in the singular: 'doulx Seneschal, m'alez vous demandant ... ' (VIII).

The responses not only refer back to the *Cent Ballades* by means of explicit semantic, rhythmical, and conceptual reminiscences but also refer to one another, instituting a textual order and coherence later found in the web of semantic and thematic relations drawn between the texts of the *Querelle de la Rose* or the *Querelle de la Belle Dame sans mercy*. These *querelles* stage an intertextual dialogue both with the *Rose* or the *Belle Dame sans mercy* respectively, and with the other texts that form the *querelles* proper. In his response, Louis d'Orléans refers to the previous two in the series by Jean de Chambrillac and Renaud de Trie, both of whom supported *la Guignarde*'s arguments: 'de bon cuer vous pri, | Chambrillac, Regnault, humblement | Que ne soustenez point cecy | Qu'avez soustenu ça devant' (III). Guillaume de Tignonville evokes Charles d'Ivry's response (IX) in the refrain to his ballade (VI) (Raynaud suggests for this reason that the ballade may be out of place in the sequence), as well as referring to the 'folour' of Chambrillac and Renaud de Trie. Jean de Bucy further refers to the sequence of responses solicited by the narrator/s of the *Cent Ballades* (XII). His use of the words 'ordenance' (v. 32) and 'ordenner' (v. 33) here emphasizes the literariness of the enterprise.

The process of collaboration, which is inscribed figuratively in the economy of poetic exchange between poets of the late medieval court, within the material manuscript anthology, and within the physical framework of the poetic compilation or *puy*, may also operate, then, on a fictional level within the literary framework of the text. This notion of a fictional collaboration is suggestive of a complex set of collaborative, competitive exchanges that both arise from, and create debate in and around the text. We might refer to a meta-discourse of debate in the *Cent Ballades* focused on collaborative exchange.

Jean de Werchin, sénéchal de Hainaut (like Jean le Seneschal, a *ministre* of the *Cour amoureuse*), seems with his debate poem, *Le Songe de la barge* (c.1404–15), to engage with Jean le Seneschal's *Cent Ballades*, as I shall suggest. So Werchin writes himself into a medieval tradition of collaborative and responsive poetic exchange. *Le Songe de la barge* was perhaps also intended as a response to Christine de Pizan's earlier request to Werchin as elected judge of her *Livre des trois jugemens*: 'le demourant commet a parfiner | A vo bon sens', vv. 1521–2.[147] Werchin's dream vision, however, far from presenting the 'demourant', and delivering judgement on the cases heard before the court of the *dieu d'Amours*, persists in delaying closure. The narrator, recently rejected by his lady, is transported in a dream from a *barge* to a court of Love in session where he overhears five amatory disputes brought before a *dieu d'Amours* by *chevaliers* and their *dames*. These cases are promised future conclusions by the *dieu d'Amours*: 'tous jugeray', v. 1532. Of the five, one is finally resolved, though the initial judgement of the *dieu d'Amours* is rejected by the plaintiffs, and one is judged by the narrator, but not the *dieu d'Amours*; the others remain unresolved. Finally the narrator prepares to plead his own case before the court, but at this point he is abruptly woken from his vision:

> Lors voul partir
> Pour en aler devant Amours gehir
> Les griefs doulours que j'avoye a souffrir,
> Mais droit alors vint sur ma nef ferir
> Une grant barge.
>
> vv. 3430–4[148]

Le Songe de la barge might be seen as an indirect response to Jean le Seneschal's *Cent Ballades*, in that the struggle of *Loiauté* and *Fausseté* which governs the latter debate poem here pervades the conflicts which are brought for adjudication before the *dieu d'Amours*, and is made explicit in the final debate between a lady and her younger lover who

---

[147] There is some confusion as to whether Jean de Werchin was also the appointed judge of the *Livre du dit de Poissy*, but Altmann suggests that as Werchin was not absent from France, it was more likely to have been Jean Boucicaut or Jean de Châteaumorand (both members of the *Cour amoureuse*). (Christine's nomination of Boucicaut would make sense, particularly in the light of her responses to the *Cent Ballades* on which he allegedly collaborated.) See Christine de Pizan (1998b), pp. 203–74.

[148] See Jean de Werchin, *Le Songe de la barge*, ed. Grenier-Winther (Montreal: CERES, 1996), pp. 3–94.

has left her for another woman.[149] At the close of the lady's speech, the narrator silently berates the lover's infidelity:

> Et a mon cueur parfaictement sembloit
> Que **leaulté** faire ne luy faisoit,
> Mais **faulseté**
> L'avoit ainsy a son acord fermé.

vv. 2988–91

The narrator then delivers his own judgement after the knight has made his defence, in the absence of any reaction by the *dieu d'Amours*:

> Mais lors pensay **faulseté** l'enorta
> A ainsy faire;
> Ne me pourroit pas sembler le contraire.

vv. 3233–5

In choosing to pass judgement on this case, Jean de Werchin, via his constructed textual self, is perhaps adding his response to the sequence inspired by Jean le Seneschal's *Cent Ballades*. So Jean de Werchin, through *Le Songe de la barge*, participates in a debating tradition which involves both virtual (fictional) and actual collaboration. The participants of the fictional debate are involved in a collaborative project of sorts, and beyond the text—through it—the author collaborates with previous texts and poets. While the influence of the *jeu-parti*, *demande d'amour*, and *jugement* can clearly be read through *Le Songe de la barge*, Werchin's poetic exchange of late 1404 with Gilbert de Lannoy (also a member of the *Cour amoureuse*) is calqued on the *tenso* model, the contest (*agôn*) of two or more poets. Werchin's textual self, within the sequence of forty-six ballades, is styled after the *mondain chevalier* type (*Cent Ballades*), experienced in love, who advises a younger *chevalier*, Lannoy's persona, on the necessity of renouncing his love for a lady who has rejected him. Lannoy refuses to accept Werchin's advice, wishing to remain loyal to his lady, but Werchin insists, in terms reminiscent of *la Guignarde*'s exhortations to the *jeune chevalier* of the *Cent Ballades*, and in the course of ballade XVIII suggests that their debate should be judged by Lannoy's lady:[150]

---

[149] The common intertext for *Le Songe de la barge* and the *Cent Ballades* is of course the *Roman de la Rose*; see Taylor, Jane, 'Inescapable Rose: Jean le Seneschal's *Cent Ballades* and the Art of Cheerful Paradox', *Medium Aevum* 67 (1998), 60–84.

[150] Jean de Werchin (1996), ballade XVIII, vv. 21–8, p. 114.

> Mais je vous pry, de voulenté certaine,
> Puis qu'en tel vueil vous estes si ferméz,
> Qu'a vo dame que tenez souveraine
> Nostre debat a loisir remonstrez,
> Et qui tort a d'elle soit condempnéz,
> Puis me faictes savoir ce qu'en dira.
> Ainsy sarons que le droit soustendra.
> De nostre estrif n'a meilleur jugeresse.

Werchin and Lannoy's sequence, like *Le Songe de la barge*, forges semantic and thematic links with the *Cent Ballades*. The conflict of *Loiauté* and *Faussété* is again played out through these ballades, with Lannoy swearing loyalty to his lady, and rejecting Werchin's advice in strong terms, just as *la Guignarde*'s advice is rejected by the *jeune chevalier* of the *Cent Ballades*. Lannoy's lady herself is accorded a voice in ballade XL in which she speaks to encourage the young *chevalier* in his loyalty:

> Si vous pry doncques que bien celee
> Soit vostre amour de vo costé,
> Et **loyaulté** tousjours gardee
> Sans regarder a **faulseté**.

> XL, vv. 21–4

The direct intervention of Lannoy's lady here may approximate a judgement on her part: her continued encouragement of Lannoy's love shows her rejection of Werchin's advice to him. In the penultimate ballade, Lannoy submits his plaint to the jurisdiction of the *dieu d'Amours*, implying that a conclusion to this debate will be imposed:

> Sy pry Amours que ma querelle
> Luy veulle monstrer sans sejour,
> Et que [de] tout mon fait se mesle.

> XLV, vv. 21–3

The final ballade is a direct plea by Lannoy to his lady to end this *querelle*, and 'oste[r] la tristesse' by granting him *mercy*. The proliferation of perspectives set up in this sequence of ballades, spoken through the voices of Werchin, Lannoy, and the lady respectively, is rendered more complex by the references to other poets within the textual body. The figure of Lannoy apostrophizes not only Werchin, the *dieu d'Amours*, and his lady, but also the poets Lourdin de Saligny[151] and Jean de

---

[151] Also recorded in the armorials of the *Cour amoureuse* as a 'chevalier thresorier'. See Piaget (1891). See also Bozzolo and Loyau (1982–92).

Garencières (ballade II), and possibly Pierre de Hauteville, prince of the *Cour amoureuse* (ballade V), to whom he refers as 'Princes', taking as his model the traditional address to the prince of a *puy*. Jean de Werchin thus inscribes himself in an existing tradition of collaborative exchange with his *Songe de la barge* and the ballade sequence, this latter work itself perhaps a fictional collaboration.

The polyphony created by this proliferation of voices operates in various *loci*: within the text itself, through the collaboration that generates the text, within the formalized frame of the *Cour amoureuse* or *puy*, and on the level of the manuscript anthology. It is significant for these layers of poetic collaboration that Jean de Werchin's *Songe de la barge* and the ballade sequence are collected together, and make their sole appearance in a fifteenth-century manuscript (Chantilly, Musée Condé, 686) which also contains Chartier's *Complainte pour la mort*, his *BDSM*, the sequel poems: *Accusations contre la Belle Dame sans mercy* (Baudet Herenc), and Achille Caulier's *La Cruelle Femme en amours*, as well as texts collected in other manuscripts belonging to the *BDSM* cycle. Similarly, four manuscripts which contain *demande d'amour* and *vente d'amour* sequences also collect works by Chartier: Paris, BnF, fr. 1130; Bern, Burgerbibliothek, 205; Turin, BN, L. II. 12, and/or texts of the *Belle Dame sans mercy* cycle: Turin, BN, L. II. 12; London, Westminster Abbey, CA 21. The Turin manuscript also contains a *complainte* by Jean le Seneschal, the probable originator of the *Cent Ballades*. The compilation of these texts in the same manuscript connects the *Querelle de la Belle Dame sans mercy* with this previous literary debate and others, creating a conflictual community within a context of material transmission. London, Westminster Abbey, CA 21 contains a version of Garencières's *complainte* XXIX, 'Belle, prenez temps et espace', as well as *demandes* and *ventes d'amour*, and *La Belle Dame qui eut mercy* (probably by Oton de Granson):[152] a poem attached to the tradition of the *Querelle de la Belle Dame sans mercy*. Of additional significance is Paris, BnF, fr. 19139, a manuscript which is the sole witness to the poetry of Jean de Garencières, the poet apostrophized by Lannoy in the course of his exchange with Werchin, and which also contains poems of the *Belle Dame sans mercy* cycle.[153] Jean de Garencières also engaged in poetical exchange with both Charles d'Orléans, and Jean de Bucy, author of one of the thirteen responses to the *Cent Ballades*.

[152] See Piaget (1904), pp. 203–4.
[153] See also Piaget, 'Jean de Garencières', *Romania* 22 (1893), 422–81.

Connections are thus drawn in this manuscript between poets engaged in three separate poetic collaborations: the *Cent Ballades*, the exchange of ballades between Jean de Werchin and Gilbert de Lannoy, and the *Querelle de la Belle Dame sans mercy*.

What I hope to establish here is a pattern of dialogic exchange between debate texts and the poets beyond those texts, which is reinforced by the organized anthologization of such texts within these manuscripts. The intersection of one debate tradition with another within the manuscript collection points to a network of relations between debating poets and their texts which extends beyond one *querelle* and connects with others; a complex pattern of collaboration is then revealed. This patterning of manuscript compilations may also be observed in Paris, BnF, fr. 9223 (post 1453), a collection of diverse lyric pieces, many attached to specific poetic challenges such as that initiated by Charles d'Orléans, on the verse 'En la forest de longue atente'.[154]

The manuscript collection provides one *locus* for playful poetic collaboration, while the *Cour amoureuse, puy*, or chivalric order provides another conceptual playground within which poetic debate is the habitual mode of communication, and which is informed by legal and intellectual structures. The *Cour amoureuse*, whose charter was established in the *Hôtel d'Artois*, Paris, on St Valentine's Day, 1400, was based on models of poetic competition such as the northern *puys* at Lille, Amiens, Rouen, or Tournai, or the *chambres de rhétorique* that decided on questions of literary style.[155] It was established primarily for the defence and honour of women, a stipulation included in the statutes of many chivalric orders of the period, such as Christine de Pizan's *Ordre de la Rose*,[156] but also for the nurture of a vernacular poetic culture.[157] Another foyer which had been created for the development and reward of a vernacular poetic was the *Consistoire de la gaie science*, established in Toulouse in 1324.[158] This organization was itself born of a poetic challenge, issued by a group of seven troubadours from Toulouse to

---

[154] Charles d'Orléans was involved in a series of poetic exchanges, including the *Concours de Blois*: a series of poems inspired by the verse 'je meurs de soif auprès de la fontaine'. See *Rondeaux et autres poésies du XVe siècle*, ed. Raynaud (Paris: Firmin-Didot, 1889) for an edition of the Paris manuscript (BnF, fr. 9223).

[155] See Cerquiglini-Toulet, *The Colour of Melancholy: The Uses of Books in the Fourteenth Century*, trans. Lydia G. Cochrane (Baltimore/London: Johns Hopkins University Press, 1997), pp. 43–4.

[156] Christine describes the founding of this order in her *Dit de la Rose*, see Christine de Pizan (1990).

[157] See Piaget (1891).   [158] See Jeanroy (1914).

poets from the Languedoc. Annual competitions (the *Jeux Floraux*) were held by the *Consistoire*, at which *joies* or prizes would be awarded. The poetic endeavours of the *Consistoire* were regulated by a book of rules, the *Leys d'amor*, written in 1356 by two prominent lawyers: Guilhem Molinier and Berthomieu Marc. The association modelled itself on the organization of a university with its book of statutes, its chancellor, the practice of sitting exams, and the conferring of mock academic titles (there were two academic ranks to which one might aspire: *Bachelier* or *Docteur en gaie science*). The *Cour amoureuse* was a similar organization with a charter, holding *puys*, and electing winners, though the hierarchy was modelled on that of the court rather than on the intellectual ranking of the university, with a prince of the *puy* at its head (Pierre de Hauteville), *conservateurs, ministres, présidents, conseillers*, and so on. As I have shown, many of the poets involved in literary debate in the late fourteenth and early fifteenth centuries became attached to the *Cour amoureuse* in some capacity. This was a formalized playground that provided a material forum for collaborative debate (even if it only ever existed within the confines of an elaborate collective fiction).[159] A conceptual forum was provided within the debate text itself by the model of the judicial trial or by the intellectual model of the *disputatio*. The judicial model is located in the informal *cour d'amour* settings such as that of Werchin's *Le Songe de la barge*, or the sequels of the *Belle Dame sans mercy* (*Accusations contre la Belle Dame sans mercy*; *La Dame lealle en amours*; *La Cruelle Femme en amours*), as well as the more formal trial settings of later debates attached to this cycle. The *disputatio* fuses with early conflictual literary forms such as the *demande d'amour* or *jeu-parti* to shape the late medieval debate poem formally.

The response to the *demande d'amour* I cited at the beginning of this chapter, 'desirer sans jouir', seems then to represent a fundamental poetic code which operates via the socio-cultural groupings I term collaborative debating communities. For these court poets, closure and hence fulfilment entails not only the end of desire and of the game, but the end of creative endeavour, prestige, and ultimately subsistence. The late medieval poet often operates a deferral of closure by postponing the final *determinatio* or *arrêt* to an extra-textual future. As I have suggested, collaboration is specifically linked to lack of closure.[160] This can be seen

<hr />

[159] I mentioned earlier in this chapter the possibility that the *Cour amoureuse* was merely an elaborate fiction, created in order to perpetuate poetic play: p. 41.
[160] I shall return to the theme of closure in Chapter 3.

in the sequences of continuation and imitation in the literary *querelles* arising from the *Cent Ballades*, or the *Belle Dame sans mercy*, and in the dialectic of the debate poem proper where resolution means the cessation of playful discourse. Finally, in the manuscript anthology, a network of playful and collaborative relations between texts is maintained and thus perpetuated. The tradition of literary exchange in the context of play and competition, as I have shown, is deeply rooted in medieval culture, from the earliest troubadour *tensos* and *joc-partits*, to the French *jeux-partis*, *demandes d'amour*, and *ventes d'amour*. This vernacular culture, together with the formal organization of intellectual learning in the universities and a developing judicial system, created a vogue for debate which flourished throughout the later Middle Ages. Groups of poets collaborate in debating communities—actual or fictionalized—either materially in *loci* such as the court, *puy*, *Cour amoureuse* or manuscript collection, or figuratively through the text itself, and through the intertextual networks traced by the poet.

2

'TU RECITES, JE REPLIQUE; ET QUANT NOUS AVONS FAIT ET FAIT, TOUT NE VAULT RIENS'[1]

EXPLORATIONS OF A *DEBATING CLIMATE* IN EARLY HUMANIST FRANCE

The *Querelle de la Rose* is perhaps the best-known literary debate of the late medieval period.[2] This early fifteenth-century epistolary quarrel was largely provoked by the controversy surrounding Jean de Meun's portrayal of women in his continuation of Guillaume de Lorris's *Roman de la Rose*.[3] As a purportedly 'real' debate, this *Querelle* will provide a contrast with the fictitious literary debates I discussed in Chapter 1. Its development within chancery milieux was fostered by an existing climate of literary and practical debating in contemporary French and Italian court society. I propose here to give an account of this debating climate, focusing on the private exchange and circulation of epistles and treatises among close circles of clerks and scholars in the late fourteenth and early fifteenth centuries. I briefly explore the formal diplomatic and legal debating taking place in these intellectual and literary circles in France, looking particularly at the body of work generated by the disputed English claim to the French throne, often referred to as the *Querelle anglaise*.[4] To this end, I also address the debate over the healing of the Great

[1] See Christine's letter: *Response de Cristine a maistre Pierre Col sur le Romant de la Rose*, in *Débat sur le 'Roman de la Rose'*, ed. Hicks (Paris: Champion, 1977), ll. 363–5, p. 126

[2] All references to the *Querelle* documents are to Hicks's edition, unless otherwise stated.

[3] See Guillaume de Lorris et Jean de Meun (1992).

[4] I refer especially to Craig Taylor, '*La Querelle anglaise*: Diplomatic and Legal Debate during the Hundred Years War, with an Edition of the Polemical Debate *"Pour ce que Plusieurs"* (1464)' (unpublished DPhil thesis, University of Oxford, 1998). I am grateful to Craig Taylor for allowing me to refer to his thesis in my work and also to Peter S. Lewis, of All Souls' College, Oxford, for advice on the socio-historical issues surrounding political debate in early humanist France. See Lewis, *Essays in Later Medieval French History* (London/Ronceverte: The Hambledon Press, 1985).

Schism (1378–1417),[5] and the burning issue of regal as opposed to papal power.[6] I show here both how literary debate feeds off more formal diplomatic debating in chancery circles, and how political and ethical debate may, in certain circumstances, be shaped by literary knowledge.

I base myself on Brian Stock's model of the textual community as an interpretative body that derives its social coherence from common interpretations of a text or body of texts. As Stock explains:

> We can think of a textual community as a group that arises somewhere in the interstices between the imposition of the written word and the articulation of a certain type of social organization. It is an interpretive community, but it is also a social entity.[7]

I also engage with Pierre Bourdieu's categories of social organization to suggest a new socio-cultural model for participatory literary production at this time, which I refer to as the collaborative debating community. As I mention in my introduction, Stock's textual community is largely non-productive, whereas the collaborative debating community I postulate is a generative body, producing what I call collaborative fictions. This community, then, derives its social coherence not only from its interpretations of text/s, but from its production of further text/s in response to those interpretations, forming a network of collaborative relations between texts and poets/authors which corresponds to Bourdieu's notion of field. The collaborative fictions produced are bodies of work whose separate parts are connected through a network of internal intertextual references, like Gruber's concept of the self-referentiality of the troubadour corpus.[8] Debate is often conducted through a system of debating positions whereby the participants adopt a range of personae within the text. These debating positions may be designed specifically to polemicize and thus perpetuate debate. The model of fifteenth-century debate I term the collaborative debating community is examined in this chapter through these notions of debating positions and collaborative fictions. Further on I shall apply the notion of the collaborative debating

---

[5] The standard authority on the Schism is Valois, *La France et le Grand Schisme d'Occident*, 4 vols. (Paris: Picard, 1896–1902). For one of the early humanists involved in the discussions over the healing of the Schism, see Jean Courtecuisse, *L'Oeuvre oratoire française*, ed. di Stefano (Turin: G. Giappichelli, 1969).

[6] See Krynen, *L'Empire du roi: idées et croyances politiques en France, XIIIᵉ–XVᵉ siècle* (Paris: Gallimard, 1993), and id., *Idéal du prince et du pouvoir royal en France à la fin du moyen âge (1380–1440)* (Paris: Picard, 1981).

[7] See Stock (1990), p. 150.   [8] Gruber (1983).

community to such literary exchanges as the series of sequels and imit-ations which Alain Chartier's poem *La Belle Dame sans mercy* inspired. Chartier himself, as I suggest in Chapter 3, is implicated both in this later poetic community, and in the earlier humanist community I investigate here.

I am concerned initially with selected letters exchanged between the two polarized groups of colleagues often associated with the rise of Humanism in France, namely those attached to the chanceries at Paris and Avignon.[9] I look in particular at the literary letters of Jean de Montreuil, Provost of Lille, and secretary and notary to Charles VI (whom Antoine Thomas in 1883 described as the first French humanist),[10] and at his contribution to the *Querelle de la Rose*. I further discuss Jean de Montreuil's earlier literary disputes, and explore his exchanges with Ambrogio dei Migli, a visiting Milanese scholar.[11] Also involved in the *Querelle de la Rose* were the brothers Gontier and Pierre Col, both royal secretaries and notaries as well as ambassadors, attached to the Paris chancery, and Jean Gerson, eminent theologian and Chancellor of the University of Paris. Of those attached to the papal chancery at Avignon (such scholars as Jean Muret, Pierre d'Ailly, Giovanni Moccia, and the prolific translator Laurent de Premierfait),[12] I focus on Nicolas de Clamanges, a bright light in the University of Paris who caused general dismay among his colleagues by accepting a post at Avignon in 1397, following the election of Pope Benedict XIII.[13] Jean Gerson, Nicolas de Clamanges, and Jean de Montreuil were all scholars at the famous *Collège de Navarre* in Paris where they received a

---

[9] Nicole Pons talks of the Paris chanceries in the plural, her term encompassing the entourages of the dukes of Berry, Burgundy, and Orléans, as chancery secretaries might also have worked at these courts. See Pons, 'Les Chancelleries parisiennes sous les règnes de Charles VI et Charles VII', in *Cancelleria e cultura nel medio evo*, ed. Gualdo (Vatican City: Archivio Segreto Vaticano, 1990), 137–68.

[10] I refer to Thomas's comment that Jean de Montreuil was the first French humanist. See Thomas, *De Johannis de Monsterolio vita et operibus* (E. Thorin, 1883). See also Combes, *Jean de Montreuil et le chancelier Gerson* (Paris: J. Vrin, 1942). Combes here lists numerous other scholars who concur with Thomas's assertion (ibid. pp. 13–15).

[11] The epistolary exchanges of French humanists with their Italian models and contemporaries (Petrarch, Coluccio Salutati, Ambrogio dei Migli, and Cardinal Galeotto Tarlati da Pietramala) are fundamental to our discussion of the climate of debate from which the *Querelle de la Rose* sprang.

[12] The humanist circle attached to the papal chancery thrived under Pope Benedict XIII, but was dispersed in 1408 following the assassination of Louis d'Orléans in 1407, and Benedict XIII's excommunication of Charles VI. See Ornato (1969).

[13] Ornato ingeniously plots the complex movements of other members of the two circles in his book (1969).

rigorous formation under the patronage of Charles V, and later Charles VI, that was to shape their literary and political careers. In a recent study, Nathalie Gorochov examines the complex links between the *Collège de Navarre* and the chancery milieux.[14] It is clear that Paris and Avignon, as the two main cultural and intellectual centres in France at this time, were intimately linked, not least through the flow of scholars and diplomats moving between the two. Gorochov describes a constant 'va-et-vient' of *nonces* (embassies) between the royal and papal courts.[15] As a result of the Italian bias of the court at Avignon, compounded by the dispute over royal autonomy from papal obedience, tensions inevitably arose that paradoxically strengthened the literary bonds between the two communities, fostering their written confrontations.

Turning to the prolific author and scholar Christine de Pizan, I examine her part in the *Querelle de la Rose*, and her motives for the publication of the first 1402 dossier of the *Querelle*.[16] I then discuss her role as compiler and editor of this dossier and subsequent collections.[17] The nature and purpose of Christine's intervention in the *Querelle* are vital to an understanding of its mechanics, set within the context of previous literary debates staged by the groups of early humanists in Paris and Avignon. I suggest that there is a 'playfulness' about debate in these circles. Scholars engineer and even fictionalize conflicts in a desire to perpetuate literary play. Christine de Pizan's letters are written in an entirely different spirit from those penned by her male supporters

---

[14] See Nathalie Gorochov's exhaustive study of the *Collège, Le Collège de Navarre de sa fondation (1305) au début du XVᵉ siècle (1418)* (Paris: Champion, 1997). Jean de Montreuil entered the *Collège* in 1374, Nicolas de Clamanges in 1375, Jean Gerson in 1378.

[15] Gorochov (1997), ch. XV, pp. 433–71.

[16] This first dossier was published on 1 February 1402, under the patronage of Queen Isabeau of France and Guillaume de Tignonville, Provost of Paris, and is limited to the epistolary exchanges of Gontier Col and Christine herself, as well as two dedicatory letters addressed to her two patrons respectively. There are no extant witnesses.

[17] This original *querelle* dossier is included by Christine in a recueil of her works finished on 23 June 1402. The original has vanished but three copies survive: Paris, BnF, fr. 12779; Chantilly, Musée Condé, 492–3; BnF, fr. 604. A second dossier, compiled by Pizan after 2 October 1402 contains the original exchange of letters between Col and Pizan, plus Christine's response, *Pour ce que entendement*, to Pierre Col's response (June–September 1402) to both Christine's original letter to Jean de Montreuil (pre 13 September 1401), and to Gerson's treatise against the *Rose* (18 May 1402). This dossier is also preserved in three MSS: Berkeley, University of California, UCB, 109; BnF, fr. 835; London, BL, Harley 4431. Hicks notes that BnF, fr. 1563 is the only witness to Pierre Col's response and may form a third *querelle* dossier compiled by a Jean de Meun sympathizer, *Débat sur le 'Roman de la Rose'* (1977), LVIII–LXIII.

and opponents, all of whom collude in the game of debate by adopting debating positions, often vituperative in their polemic. These positions constitute moves in the literary field of play, and generate collaborative fictions.

In their introduction to a special issue of *Forum for Modern Language Studies*, Simon Gaunt and Sarah Kay explore the work of the sociologist Pierre Bourdieu, and discuss the relevance of his theory of practice for medieval studies, focusing on his rejection of a structuralist hermeneutics in favour of a dialectical methodology expressed through the notions of field, habitus,[18] and symbolic capital.[19] I suggest that the dialectical structures inherent in interpretative groups such as those at Avignon and Paris are appropriate for this model. Socio-cultural competition between individuals is addressed in Pierre Bourdieu's *Logic of Practice*, through his notion of societies as fields of play within which players struggle competitively (but in collusion with one another) to acquire forms of symbolic capital. By symbolic capital, Bourdieu refers to whatever is valued (materially, socially, or intellectually) in any given community and provides its owner with status (material/social/intellectual) in that community: what Bourdieu describes as trump cards.[20] We could think, for example, of publication in the academic field or film credits in the acting world as forms of symbolic capital. Capital is played for, won, and lost by the members of a field much as in a game. The players of this game 'agree, by the mere fact of playing [...] that the game is worth playing [...] and this collusion is the very basis of their competition'.[21] So the collusion between members of a particular community, and hence collaboration, even in the antagonism of competition and debate, is the social glue that enables the perpetuation of the game within a certain field. All

---

[18] Bourdieu defines habitus as 'a system of durable, transposable dispositions, structured structures predisposed to function as structuring structures, that is, as principles which generate and organise practices and representations that can be objectively adapted to their outcomes', in *Le Sens pratique/ The Logic of Practice*, trans. Nice (Cambridge: Polity Press, 1990), p. 53. I discuss habitus in Chapter 4, part II, in the context of the relationship between the text and the manuscript (its means of transmission).

[19] See Gaunt and Kay (1997), 193–203.

[20] As Gaunt and Kay (1997) put it: 'This symbolic capital refers to the honour or prestige derived from certain practices that may be translated into high status or into material gain, or both', pp. 195–6. For a discussion of symbolic capital see Bourdieu (1990).

[21] Bourdieu's sociology, at times complex, is cogently summarized, appropriately enough, in dialogue, with Loïc J. D. Wacquant. See Bourdieu and Wacquant, *An Invitation to Reflexive Sociology* (Cambridge/Oxford: Polity Press, 1996), p. 98.

players must necessarily collude in this group fiction; those who do not are automatically excluded. The success of the game depends on the participation of all its players and their recognition both of the rules and of the particular symbolic capital at stake in the field. Symbolic capital in terms of the *querelles* conducted in chancery circles, for example, might refer to good epistolary style.

The evidence we have of literary letter-writing in the chanceries comes mainly from the surviving epistolary collections of Jean de Montreuil and Nicolas de Clamanges.[22] The relatively closed circulation of chancery letters is no doubt largely to blame for their disappearance, as well as the destruction of archives during the Burgundian assault on Paris in 1418 in which Jean de Montreuil and many of his chancery colleagues, including the Col brothers, were brutally murdered.[23] Jean de Montreuil and his colleagues in chancery circles were frequently involved in literary disputes, worked out on paper, alongside the habitual diplomatic debating that constituted the bulk of their office. The copying and transmission of these literary exchanges, often in epistolary form, attests to what I term the debating climate of early humanist France.[24] Christine de Pizan, although no doubt a political actor as Zimmermann suggests, was not engaged in debate on the same level.[25] An instance of the conflict of Christine's and Montreuil's approaches to debate is seen in a political and legal wrangle known as the *Querelle anglaise*, in which the English claim to the French throne was disputed.[26] Both Jean de Montreuil and Christine de Pizan engage in discussion of a version of the Salic Law (though Christine only indirectly through her *Livre de la cité des dames*),[27] which excluded women and their cognates from ruling. This law rendered invalid the

---

[22] See Jean de Montreuil, *Opera*, ed. Ornato, 4 vols. (Turin: G. Giappichelli, 1963–86), I: *Epistolario*; II: *L'Oeuvre historique et polémique*; III: *Textes divers, appendices et tables*; IV: *Monsteroliana*; Nicolas de Clamanges, *Opera omnia*, ed. Lydius (Farnborough: Gregg Press, 1967), and more recently his *Epistolario*, ed. Cecchetti (typewritten thesis, Turin, 1969). Gorochov also refers to the letters of Gérard Machet which are edited by Santoni: 'Gérard Machet, confesseur de Charles VII et ses lettres' (typewritten thesis, École des Chartes, 1968).

[23] See Ornato (1969), and Lewis (1985).

[24] I shall discuss specific examples of the transmission of these exchanges later on.

[25] See Zimmermann, 'Vox femina, Vox politica: The *Lamentacion sur les maux de la France*', in *Politics, Gender, and Genre: The Political Thought of Christine de Pizan*, ed. Brabant (Boulder/San Francisco/Oxford: Westview Press, 1992), 113–27.

[26] See Taylor, Craig (1998).

[27] See Christine de Pizan, *La Città delle dame*, ed. Caraffi and Richards (Milan: Luni, 1998).

English king Edward III's claim to the French throne, since he stood to inherit through his mother, Isabelle of France. The *Querelle anglaise* is characterized by a series of polemical treatises, including the redaction of two treatises by Montreuil, each in both Latin and French versions: *Regali ex progenie/A toute la chevalerie* (1408/1408–13), and the *Traité contre les Anglais* (1413–16).[28] Montreuil's treatises and others, Taylor asserts, were intended to be used not as political propaganda, but as diplomatic manuals. The medieval custom of compiling sources provided useful diplomatic tools for chancery and governmental use, particularly in terms of aide-mémoires for oral debate, at a time when the French royal archives were in some disorder, and material was not readily accessible.[29] Montreuil himself drew on previous compilations for his treatises, and particularly the *Memore abregé* (1390).[30] One of the arguments against the English claims to the French throne that carried considerable weight in the French political arsenal was the question of Salic Law. Montreuil's discussion of this law in his polemical treatises provided source material for many diplomats, and traced the first set of clear guidelines justifying the exclusion of women from rule (where previously one had only been able to draw on vague customary law as a justification). However, as Sarah Hanley argues, Montreuil's version of the Salic Law was a cunning mixture of truth and invention. Montreuil invokes the authority of Charlemagne and uses a secondary manuscript source (for information on the *De allodio* ordinance of the Salic Law which excludes women from the right to inherit land), which is itself corrupt, while claiming to have read an original Latin law, written in 1328.[31] Crucially, Montreuil included the interpolated phrase 'in

---

[28] See Jean de Montreuil (1975): II; and also Blanchard and Mühlethaler, *Écriture et pouvoir à l'aube des temps modernes* (Paris: PUF, 2002), ch. 2, pp. 34–9, for a discussion of the central role of the 'clerc' in spreading patriotic feeling during the reign of Charles VI

[29] See Taylor, Craig (1998).   [30] See Lewis (1985).

[31] See Hanley, 'Identity Politics and Rulership in France: Female Political Place and the Fraudulent Salic Law in Christine de Pizan and Jean de Montreuil', in *Changing Identities in Early Modern France*, ed. Wolfe (Durham, NC: Duke University Press, 1997), 78–94. The *De allodio* ordinance prohibiting the inheritance of land by females pertained to allodial lands only, and as Hanley explains, this ordinance was 'mediated' by others in the full redaction of the Law. This Salic Law was based on Merovingian (*c*.507–11) and Carolingian (802–3) versions, neither of which mentioned the rights of succession to the throne. Montreuil relied on Brussels, Bibliothèque Royale, 10306 which gives second-hand a fragment of the Salic Law with the interpolation 'in regno': 'Mulier vero nullam in regno habeat portionem' (Indeed, a woman shall have no stake in the kingdom).

regno' (in the kingdom), present in his manuscript source, but not in the original ordinance. In the *Traité contre les Anglais*, Montreuil writes:

Et aussi par coustume et ordonnance faite et approuvee et notoirement tenue et gardee des devant qu'il eust onques roy crestien en France et expressement confermee par Charlemaigne, femme ne masle qui ne vient seulement que de par femme et non descendant de masle de sang royal de France ne succede point ne est habile de succeder a la couronne de France.[32]

Hanley suggests that Montreuil's treatise is a response to Christine's *Livre de la cité des dames* (1405). Christine's city is built in part by fabled female rulers, emphasizing the viability of female rule. Montreuil's support of the Salic Law in successive treatises would thus represent an undermining of Christine's female-led city at its very foundations. Some of the authorities Montreuil relies upon are not only highly suspect but proverbial, supported more by the popular tradition of misogynous attacks on women's capabilities than by the word of the law. Hanley makes a useful distinction between Christine's and Montreuil's contribution to the unfolding *Querelle des femmes*.[33] She observes that while Montreuil adopts a position backed largely by the misogynist *literary* authority of such writers as Ovid, Juvenal, and Jean de Meun, Christine refuses to play the game entirely in a literary sphere, appealing to the highest political and legal authority outside the text to support her arguments.[34] Taylor argues, against Hanley, that Montreuil's treatise was not expressly intended as a response to Christine's *Cité des dames*, with which I concur. I suggest, however, that both these theories are compatible when one looks in the broader sense at the activity of debate, and how it is conceived of by the two authors. Montreuil was engaged in more than one debate in his polemical treatises, dealing first and foremost with the *Querelle anglaise* but, consciously or otherwise, making a move in the slowly evolving *Querelle des femmes*. He used his expertise in debate to fabricate arguments, based partly on a popular and literary misogynist culture, which would refute all female claims to authority, including Christine's. So literary knowledge is seen to

---

[32] See Jean de Montreuil (1975): II, ll. 85–90, p. 164.
[33] On the *Querelle des femmes* see Angenot, *Les Champions des femmes: examen du discours sur la supériorité des femmes 1400–1800* (Montreal: University of Québec, 1977); Joan Kelly, 'Early Feminist Theory and the *Querelle des femmes*, 1400–1789', *Signs* 8 (1982), 4–28.
[34] By publishing and circulating the dossiers of the *Querelle de la Rose* to Queen Isabeau de Bavière and Guillaume de Tignonville, the Provost of Paris, among others, as I shall discuss.

shape and alter political and legal knowledge. Montreuil's version of the Salic Law was widely drawn upon for sources of diplomatic and legal argumentation during the *Querelle anglaise*.[35]

The *Querelle anglaise* and the partition of France into Burgundian and Armagnac/Orléanist factions during the Hundred Years War provide concrete instances of political divisions which are played out in literary form at this time. A well-known later example of this fusion of the literary and the political is the anonymous *Debat des herauts d'armes* (1453–61) in which an English and a French herald present their respective cases before *Dame Prudence*. The debate unfolds as each herald responds in turn to the initial question posed by *Prudence*, 'Qui est le royaume chrestien qui est plus digne d'estre approuché d'Honneur?'[36] This debate, following what appears to be a late medieval device, remains unresolved.[37] *Dame Prudence* instructs the heralds to copy down their arguments in a book which will be both instructive and enjoyable for 'jeune noblesse', and promises to deliver her verdict once other heralds from Christian countries have been heard.[38]

Polemical treatises were written alongside these more literary debate texts, and were popular among diplomatic communities.[39] These treatises were often written in a monophonic complainte form rather than in the polyphonic form of the debate. In the category of polemical complaintes we can place François de Monte-Belluna's *Tragicum argumentum de miserabili statu regni Francie* (1356),[40] Jean de Montreuil's *Regali ex progenie/A toute la chevalerie* (1408/1408–13) and the *Traité contre les Anglais* (1413–16),[41] as well as Christine de Pizan's *Lamentacion sur les maux de la France* (1410).[42] Christine de Pizan's earlier

[35] See Taylor, Craig (1998) and Lewis (1985).

[36] See *Debat des herauts d'armes*, ed. Pannier and Meyer (Paris: Firmin-Didot, 1877).

[37] I discuss closure in late medieval poetry in Chapter 3. See also Armstrong (1997b), 12–14; Reed, *Middle English Debate Poetry and the Aesthetics of Irresolution* (Columbia/London: University of Missouri Press, 1990); and my article, Cayley (2003).

[38] *Debat des herauts*, ch. 142, p. 52.

[39] Taylor, Craig (1998); and Daly, 'Mixing Business with Leisure: Some French Royal Notaries and Secretaries and their Histories of France, *c.*1459–1509', in *Power, Culture, and Religion in France c.1350–c.1550*, ed. Allmand (Bury St Edmunds, Suffolk: The Boydell Press, 1989), 99–115.

[40] See François de Monte-Belluna, *Le Tragicum argumentum de miserabili statu regni Francie*, ed. Vernet, Annuaire-Bulletin de la Société de l'Histoire de France 1962–63 (Paris: C. Klincksieck, 1964), 101–63.

[41] Jean de Montreuil (1975): II.

[42] See Christine de Pizan, *Lamentacion sur les maux de la France*, in *Mélanges de langue et littérature française du Moyen Age et de la Renaissance offerts à Charles Foulon,*

Livre de l'advision Cristine (1399–1405),[43] though, falls in the genre of
polemical dream vision debate, or *songe politique* to borrow Marchello-
Nizia's term.[44] Christine's narrator, 'Cristine', encounters a succession
of allegorical figures in a dream landscape including that of *Libera*
(France), who delivers a long complainte on the state of the nation
before asking 'Cristine' to intervene on her behalf with the princes of
the realm. Alain Chartier's vernacular prose work *Le Quadrilogue invectif*
(1422), a debate between Lady France and the three estates,[45] and his
Livre de l'Esperance (1428–30),[46] a dream vision in which the narrator
discusses the plight of France with a series of allegorical figures, were no
doubt greatly inspired by the polemical complainte (and particularly by
Monte-Belluna and Montreuil), but also drew on a tradition of polemical literary debates (and specifically *songes politiques*) like Christine's, as
I suggest in the next chapter. Chartier's particular use of the medium of
literary debate as a vehicle for political engagement, was to inspire such
figures as Jean Juvénal des Ursins, a lawyer at the *Parlement de Paris*
from 1400 to 1418. In Jean Juvénal's dream vision, *Audite celi* (1435),
the narrator encounters a 'devote creature' who relates her meeting with
the allegorical figures of France, England, and the Church, at Arras.
These personifications have come together to debate the question of the
French crown. The vision ends, however, before the discussions can get
under way.[47] It is significant in the light of Chartier's influence that Jean
Juvénal's debate is collected with five works by Chartier in Paris, BnF,
fr. 1128,[48] and that André Duchesne's collected edition of Chartier's
works from 1617 contains extracts from Jean Juvénal's *Tres reverends*
and *Loquar in tribulacione*.[49] I discuss the significance of manuscript
context as material evidence of collaborative debating communities in
Chapter 4, part II.

ed. Kennedy (Rennes: Institut de français, Université de Haute Bretagne, 1980), vol. 1,
177–85.

[43] See Christine de Pizan, *Le Livre de l'advision Cristine*, ed. Dulac and Reno (Paris:
Champion, 2001).

[44] See Marchello-Nizia, 'Entre l'histoire et la poétique: le *Songe politique*', *Revue des
Sciences humaines*, 55 (1981), 39–53.

[45] See Alain Chartier (1950).   [46] See Alain Chartier (1989).

[47] See Jean Juvénal des Ursins, *Écrits politiques*, ed. Lewis, 3 vols. (Paris: C. Klincksieck,
1978–92), I, pp. 93–281.

[48] These are Chartier's Latin dialogue, *Dialogus familiaris*; the French prose works,
Quadrilogue invectif and *Livre de l'Esperance*; and his French verse, *DDFA* and the *Lay de
paix*. For the French verse see Alain Chartier (1974), 155–95 and 410–20 respectively;
for the Latin dialogue see Alain Chartier (1977), 245–325.

[49] See Alain Chartier, *Les Oeuvres*, ed. Duchesne (Paris: Samuel Thiboust, 1617).

As Krynen asserts, the writers of such polemical works associated the French–English conflict with the division in the Church known as the Great Schism (1378–1417), which saw rival popes establishing obediences from Avignon and Rome respectively.[50] These scholars further believed that Charles VI, as monarch, had a key role to play in the healing of the Schism.[51] The opposition of regal and papal power, debated in Christian political thought since Pope Gelasius I's distinction between the temporal and spiritual kingdoms in the fifth century AD,[52] inspired a series of important debates, often set out as scholastic *disputationes*.[53] These debates were to influence such humanist scholars as Jean Gerson and Pierre d'Ailly (a Master of Theology at the *Collège de Navarre* who was succeeded as Chancellor of the University of Paris by Gerson in 1395), in their discussions over the healing of the Schism. Jean Gerson was involved in diplomatic talks with the antipope Benedict XIII and Gregory XII of Rome during his embassies to Avignon (1403–4), Marseilles, and Rome (1407).[54] In the *De potestate regia et papali* (1303), the Dominican Jean de Paris (Jean Quidort) issued a challenge to the dominance of papal power through his rejection of the concept of the 'plenitude of power' which gave the papacy both temporal and spiritual power over the people.[55] Many thinkers supported the view that the monarchy was itself a divine institution and not subject to papal rule. The role of the monarch was explored in a proliferation of *miroirs des princes* which set him at the head of the political body, or *corpus mysticum*,[56] and established guidelines for good leadership

---

[50] See Oliver O'Donovan and Joan Lockwood O'Donovan, *From Irenaeus to Grotius: A Sourcebook in Christian Political Thought 100–1625* (Michigan/Cambridge, England: William B. Eerdmans Publishing Company, 1999), pp. 389–96.

[51] Krynen (1981).

[52] O'Donovan (1999), pp. 177–9. Gelasius I (pope from 492 to 496), wrote famously in a letter to Emperor Anastasius: 'Two there are, august Emperor, by which this world is ruled: the consecrated authority of priests and the royal power. Of these the priests have the greater responsibility, in that they will have to give account before God's judgement seat for those who have been kings of men', p. 179.

[53] I discuss the *disputatio* in Chapter 1, pp. 15–20. These debates include the *Disputatio inter clericum et militem* (1296), the *Quaestio in utramque partem* (1302) and the *Quaestio de potestate papae* (known as *Rex pacificus*). See Krynen (1993).

[54] For a comprehensive summary of Gerson's religious and political thought see O'Donovan (1999), pp. 517–29.

[55] For a summary of Jean de Paris's contribution to the debate see O'Donovan (1999), pp. 397–412.

[56] See O'Donovan (1999). The notion of the corpus mysticum in late medieval thought is derived from St Paul's notion of the Church as the body of Christ (1 Cor. 10: 17). However, the term was gradually to lose its religious connotations through its

which would ensure the well-being of the whole body. *Ardant Desir*, the principal protagonist of Philippe de Mézières's allegorical *Songe du vieil pelerin* (1389),[57] written for Charles VI, embarks on a tour to examine the state of Christian morals around the world. Mézières employs the two popular political metaphors of the French ship of State, and the chessboard as social hierarchy, to instruct the king in his regal duties.[58]

The divisions inherent in the State and Church and the desire for an autonomous monarchy in France led to a great flourishing in the later Middle Ages of both practical and literary debate. Such scholars as Jean de Montreuil, Christine de Pizan, Jean Gerson, and later Alain Chartier, were to engage both in political and literary debate, the literary often shaping, as well as being shaped by the political. The polyphonic voice within the literary debate form mirrors such external political or social divisions, and promises a remedy with its final judgement or resolution, but one that is not always forthcoming, as I shall suggest.

I now turn to focus on the epistolary and predominantly literary debating which took place in chancery circles at the end of the fourteenth century in France. A quarrel opposing Jean de Montreuil and the Italian Ambrogio dei Migli will illustrate the enthusiasm for debate among these circles, and the collaborative nature of such exchanges.[59] Composed between the autumn of 1397 and the spring of 1398, this epistolary exchange immediately predates the *Querelle de la Rose*, and debates the mastery of two literary giants, Cicero and Virgil.[60] In Epistle 131 (*Querimoniarum seu*),[61] Jean de Montreuil urges his unknown correspondent to give an opinion of an enclosed dossier of letters, all of which are addressed to Nicolas de Clamanges (probably Epistles 129, 130, and 132).[62] Their common topic is the series of disputes

application to the temporal nation, and to the political community. See also John of Salisbury's *Policraticus* (1159); *Policraticus: Of the Frivolities of Courtiers and the Footprints of Philosophers*, ed. and trans. Nederman (Cambridge: CUP, 1990).

[57] See Philippe de Mézières, *Le Songe du vieil pelerin*, ed. Coopland, 2 vols. (Cambridge: CUP, 1969).

[58] I discuss the metaphor of the French ship of State in Chapter 3, and the chessboard as space of poetic play in Chapter 4, part II.

[59] See Ouy, 'Humanisme et propagande politique en France au début du XVe siècle: Ambrogio Migli et les ambitions impériales de Louis d'Orléans', in *Culture et politique en France à l'époque de l'humanisme et de la Renaissance*, ed. Simone (Turin: Accademia delle Scienze, 1974), 13–42.

[60] See Ornato (1969), *appendice* IV, pp. 233–8.

[61] Jean de Montreuil (1963): I, 194.

[62] See Ornato's discussion of these individual epistles: Jean de Montreuil (1986): IV, pp. 209–13.

staged between Jean de Montreuil and the Milanese scholar Ambrogio dei Migli. In this debate, as in the later *Querelle de la Rose*, Jean de Montreuil addresses his opponent indirectly through an intermediary, or series of intermediaries: in the case of Epistles 129, 130, and 132, it is Nicolas de Clamanges to whom Montreuil airs his grievances against Migli. The rhetorical violence of the epistolary debate between Montreuil and Migli was such that Nicolas de Clamanges felt moved to step into the breach, sending conciliatory letters to Montreuil and Migli respectively.[63] However, the letter addressed to Migli from Clamanges, urging him to curb his ingratitude, was sent through Gontier Col, who subsequently refused to forward it to Migli.[64] This occasioned further letters from Montreuil to Col (Epistles 137, 144, and 161), and possibly led to Epistle 106, the most venomous of the series. The three epistles 137, 144, and 161 constitute a new dispute between Montreuil and Gontier Col.

Montreuil's grievances against Ambrogio dei Migli are literary in character; he reproaches him on three counts. Montreuil relates in Epistle 130 how Migli has claimed that Cicero deems the practice of rhetoric useless (and how Migli has himself stated that it *is* quite useless), and in Epistle 132 how Migli has accused Cicero of contradiction. In Epistle 129, Montreuil is indignant that Migli should esteem Ovid more highly than Virgil:

Est hic **quidam degener** in hac parte et futilis **Ambrosius nomine**, familiaris tuus quondam et michi; nunc vero, et quamdiu isto perstiterit in errore, inimicus capitalis, **ausu** qui temerario palam ac vicibus repetitis, dictu mirum et terribile cogitatu, magistrum illum amoris Ovidium, quia forsan illi vacat, prefato **poetarum parente Virgilio**, prothnefas, ingenii excellentioris asseveravit extitisse, Ep. 129: *Mirabilem et.*[65]

Montreuil's later astonishment at Christine de Pizan's judgement of the work of a man he regards as a master (Jean de Meun) is comparable with

---

[63] These are letters VI and VII in *Veterum scriptorum et monumentorum amplissima collectio: tome II*, ed. Martène and Durand (Paris: Montalant, 1724), pp. 31, 33.

[64] See Ornato (1969), *appendice IV*.

[65] 'There is that degenerate round here who goes, oddly enough, by the name of Ambrosius: once your friend and mine; but now, and for as long as he persists in his error of judgement: our arch enemy, who with open and reckless audacity and repeatedly—something astonishing and frightening to contemplate—has asserted quite wrongly, perhaps because he studies him, that it is obvious that Ovid, that master of love, is of greater intelligence than our aforementioned Virgil, father of poets', Jean de Montreuil (1963): I, pp. 187–91.

this earlier clash; Montreuil defends literary excellence and authority in the face of the impudent claims of both Migli and Christine. The classical invective Montreuil employs in Epistle 154 (*Ut sunt mores*), which is part of the later *Querelle de la Rose*, emphasizes the similarity in his approach to his two 'correspondents':[66]

Audies, vir insignis, et videbis pariter in contextu cuiusdam mee rescriptionis in vulgari, quam inique, iniuste et sub ingenti arrogantia nunnulli **in precellentissimum magistrum Johannem de Magduno** invehunt et delatrant, precipue **mulier quedam, nomine Cristina**, ut dehinc iam in publicam scripta sua ediderit: que licet, ut est captus femineus, intellectu non careat, michi tamen audire visum est Leuntium grecam meretricem, ut refert Cicero, que '**contra Theofrastum, philosophum tantum**, scribere **ausa** fuit', Ep. 154.[67]

Montreuil here employs the same technique of oblique reference to the target of his indignation, not addressing Christine directly but through a third party, the recipient of the letter.[68] She is evoked scathingly as 'mulier quedam', just as Ambrogio is referred to in Epistle 129 as 'quidam degener'. 'Real' dialogue is thus thwarted, as the debate is turned aside and reported, rather than taking place directly: it becomes a 'dialogue de sourds', as Badel puts it.[69] This type of obliquely angled epistle seems to indicate an extreme and vituperative debating position adopted by Montreuil in his dealing with Christine de Pizan and Migli, since he addresses himself directly both to Gontier Col and to Cardinal Pietramala in the course of *their* disputes. Migli and Christine effectively become demonized fictional characters in Montreuil's invective, to be manipulated as he chooses. Montreuil however becomes 'reconciled' with Migli, the proof of this being an epistle directly addressed to him (Epistle 109). I shall raise the issue of obliquely addressed epistles and

[66] I have emboldened the words and phrases in this passage which coincide with those of the earlier passage from Epistle 129.

[67] 'O famous man, you will see and hear, in one of my writings in the vernacular, how unfairly, unjustly, and arrogantly some people have accused and attacked the most excellent Master Jean de Meun. I speak especially of a certain woman named Christine, who has just recently published her writings, and who, within feminine limitations, is not, admittedly, lacking in intelligence, but who, nevertheless, sounds to me like "Leontium the Greek whore", as Cicero says, "who dared to criticize the great philosopher Theophrastus" ', *Débat sur le 'Roman de la Rose'* (1977), ll. 2–10, p. 42. English translation: *La Querelle de la Rose: Letters and Documents*, ed. Baird and Kane (Chapel Hill: University of North Carolina Press, 1978).

[68] The recipient has not been identified, but Ornato suggests a well-known poet such as Eustache Deschamps or Honoré Bouvet. Jean de Montreuil (1986): IV, pp. 235–6.

[69] See Badel, *Le 'Roman de la Rose' au XIVᵉ siècle: étude de la réception de l'oeuvre* (Geneva: Droz, 1980), ch. VIII, p. 414.

thwarted dialogue again later in conjunction with discussion of the purpose and form of the correspondence that partially constitutes the *Querelle de la Rose.*

When in the course of Epistle 154 Montreuil compares Christine to 'Leontium, the Greek whore', we cannot but be referred back to his treatment of Ambrogio dei Migli to whom he refers in Epistle 106 (*De Intimatione*) as a venomous snake hidden underground, who emerges into the light:[70]

De intimatione tua regratians, vir insignis ac fidelissime, letor utique et gaudeo, ac magnam michi cedit ad cautionem, quod anguisequus ille ligur non degenerans suum virus amarissimum **introrsus diu latens, tandem evomuit et erupit**, Ep. 106.[71]

This classical metaphor of the snake representing a treacherous individual had previously been adopted in a public letter of 25 May 1390 addressed by Coluccio Salutati, the Florentine Chancellor, to all Italian leaders. Salutati refers to the Milanese prince Giangaleazzo Visconti as 'serpens ille ligusticus' (that Ligurian serpent), hidden in the 'latebris' (shadows). Witt notes that Salutati's metaphor plays also on the Visconti family's crest, a snake, or *biscia*. This letter was a calculated move in the series of conflicts that erupted between Florence and Milan from 1390 on.[72] The two Milanese 'serpents', Migli and Visconti, are further linked by Ambrogio dei Migli's stint as notary in Giangaleazzo Visconti's chancery.[73]

---

[70] In Epistle 106, Montreuil addresses Gontier Col on the subject of a letter sent to Col by Migli, and subsequently passed on to Montreuil by Col: a letter which constituted a virulent invective against Montreuil. Epistle 106 is dated by Ornato to after the spring of 1400, possibly even the spring of 1401, and follows on from Montreuil's Epistles 137, 144, and 161. The last of these appears to have met with a frosty reception from Migli who, Ornato suggests, took Montreuil's flippant tone in this letter quite seriously. It is partly Migli's reaction to this letter (161), addressed to Gontier Col, with which Montreuil takes issue in Epistle 106. Jean de Montreuil (1986): IV, pp. 185–9, 217–21.

[71] My emboldening highlights the vocabulary of concealment and exposure. 'I am most grateful for your communication, most loyal and excellent man, I rejoice and delight in the news, and must now be greatly on my guard, for that Ligurian snake who has long lain hidden with the most bitter poison accumulating inside him, has at last burst forth and spewed it out', Jean de Montreuil (1963): I, pp. 148–59.

[72] See Witt, *Coluccio Salutati and his Public Letters* (Geneva: Droz, 1976), pp. 58–63, and id., *Hercules at the Crossroads: The Life, Works, and Thought of Coluccio Salutati* (Durham, NC: Duke University Press, 1983).

[73] A further voice linking Christine de Pizan to these Milanese serpents is the biblical serpent which in Jean de Meun's *Rose* represents the treachery of woman. Genius uses the metaphor of the snake to warn the lover to avoid women, 'Fuiéz! fuiéz! fuiéz le serpent

Montreuil possessed a copy of Salutati's private correspondence, totalling two hundred letters, which he describes offering as models of style to young scholars (Epistle 93).[74] Montreuil's later use of Salutati's classical image in his invective against Migli suggests his own stylistic debt to the chancellor. In a recent article, Nicole Pons discusses Coluccio Salutati's formative influence on French scholars and on Jean de Montreuil in particular.[75] Salutati, she argues, may have been instrumental in the establishment of literary circles in France within which the *ars dictaminis* was practised through reading and writing. Salutati effectively instigates the type of epistolary 'jeu littéraire' upon which Montreuil embarks with his colleagues at the Paris and Avignon chanceries and which defines many of the exchanges found in his letter collection, including his contribution to the *Querelle de la Rose*, to which I shall return.[76]

The classical metaphor of the snake used by both Salutati and Montreuil derives from the *Aeneid*, a work upon which Montreuil draws extensively in his epistles. The image of the serpent as a portent both of doom and of regeneration is a key motif throughout the epic poem; Virgil often uses the serpent as a symbol of hidden treachery.[77] In Book II, the Greeks lie in wait in the marshes and, later, are concealed within the Wooden Horse. Virgil's use of the metaphor ties the treachery of the Greeks here to the appearance throughout his poem of assorted serpents.[78] Montreuil's comparison of Migli with a snake thus refers us to this series of classical associations with the slippery, treacherous

venimeux.' Christine takes issue with this statement in her letter to Jean de Montreuil, *Reverence, honneur: Débat sur le 'Roman de la Rose'* (1977), ll. 173–4, p. 17.

[74] See Pons (1990), pp. 142–3.

[75] See Pons, 'La Présence de Coluccio Salutati dans le recueil épistolaire de Jean de Montreuil', *Franco-Italica: Serie Storico-Letteraria* 1 (1992), pp. 9–24. See also Ornato (1969), p. 81, no. 47. Pons observes that Montreuil replaced the 'vouvoiement médiéval' with the 'tutoiement classique' in his private correspondence under Salutati's influence. This method of address became standard among humanists of Montreuil's circle.

[76] See Pons (1992), pp. 15–17.

[77] For Virgil's use of the serpent as symbol see Pöschl, *The Art of Vergil: Image and Symbol in the Aeneid* (Ann Arbor: University of Michigan Press, 1962); McAuslan and Walcot, *Virgil* (Oxford: OUP, 1990).

[78] I am thinking here of the twin serpents which come across the sea from Tenedos, the island where the Greeks are waiting in concealment, to devour the priest Laocoön as he attempts to dissuade the Trojans from taking the Wooden Horse, a gift of the Greeks, into their city. These twin serpents symbolize the Greek leaders Agamemnon and Menelaus who will come from the same direction as the serpents, also bringing death in their wake. See Virgil, *Aeneid Bks. I–VI*, ed. R. D. Williams (Surrey: Nelson, 1992), Book II, vv. 199–227, pp. 31–2.

Greeks,[79] and specifically to the Greek whose deceit set the fall of Troy in motion: Sinon, to whom Montreuil compares Migli in Epistle 106:[80]

Fuit alius compatriota valens suus, cuius nomen me auffugit, [...] qui huic nostro Sinoni multas curialites humili mendico et egentissimo impenderat atque fecerat, et [...] de stercore erexerat pauperem, Ep. 106.[81]

The fact that Migli is Italian forges a further link with Sinon. For Virgil, the outsiders are the Greeks, for Montreuil it is the Italians, and specifically the Milanese, who are to be mistrusted. When Montreuil then compares Christine de Pizan to a Greek, and a foreigner, associating her semantically with Migli,[82] there are implications for Christine's presence in the *Querelle de la Rose*, which, at best, is merely tolerated by her interlocutors. Given that Migli is branded Greek for his treachery to Virgil, and for his nationality, one might then say that Christine is branded Greek for her treachery to Jean de Meun (hence to French scholarship) and for her sex. Montreuil thus implicates Christine and Migli within a textual space, setting both up as fictional constructs and as traitors. He attempts to control Christine's intervention in the *Querelle* through his rewriting of her role, a role that she subsequently refuses to play.

The racial tension 'on paper' between the French scholar Montreuil and the Italian Migli may have been exacerbated because of a previous

[79] Montreuil further compares Migli in Epistle 106 (*De Intimatione*) to a 'vipera crudelis', Jean de Montreuil (1963): I, pp. 148–59.

[80] Sinon came as a supplicant into the midst of the Trojans, pretending that he had escaped death at the hands of the Greeks and, falsely having won their sympathy, persuaded them that the Wooden Horse had been built by the Greeks to appease Minerva, and that if the Trojans were to take it within their city walls, it would bring great prosperity to Troy. See Virgil, *Aeneid*, Bk. II, vv. 57–194.

[81] 'There was another excellent compatriot of his, whose name escapes me, [...] who stood by this Sinon of ours when he was a humble beggar and in the greatest need, and did all kinds of courtly services for him, and [...] now rises up from the filth a poor man', Jean de Montreuil (1963): I, ll. 113–17, p. 151.

[82] The semantic and racial link between Migli and Christine is heightened by a mutual connection with Lombardy. Montreuil compares Migli to a Lombard in Epistle 109 (*O quam vere*), composed sometime after spring 1400/1: 'vereor ne in illo Longobardorum numero ascribaris', Jean de Montreuil (1963): I, l. 6, p. 192: 'I am afraid that you might be tarred with the same brush as those Lombards'. Christine states in the *Mutacion* that she was born near Lombardy: 'Je fu nez pres de Lombardie', *Le Livre de la mutacion de Fortune par Christine de Pisan*, ed. Solente (Paris: Picard, 1959), I: v. 166, p. 13. Christine and Migli are linked, not just by their alien status, but by the same region, and to a people connected with the scurrilous occupation of money-lending, 'usuriers'.

heated literary exchange involving Cardinal Galeotto Tarlati da Pietra-mala, in which Nicolas de Clamanges adopted the role of intermediary. The exchange stemmed from a dispute about the superiority of Italian culture. This was a dispute that was to prove crucial for the develop-ment of humanism in France, and to cement the literary bonds between Montreuil and his colleagues at Paris and Avignon. As Dario Cecchetti puts it in his work on this early *querelle*:

Vi sono alcuni fatti, di per sé occasionali, che diventano miti della storiografia e sono assunti come simbolo di situazioni culturali caratterizzanti un'epoca, o addirittura vengono evocati ogniqualvolta si tratti di determinare un periodo o creare una nuovo categoria storica. Tale è il caso della corrispondenza polemica fra Nicolas de Clamanges e il Cardinale da Pietramala.[83]

This particular *querelle* had at its origin a letter penned by Petrarch to Pope Urban V in 1368 in which the infamous phrase 'oratores et poete extra Italiam non querantur' (orators and poets should not be sought outside Italy) appears. Cardinal Pietramala then sparked the later controversy with his public letter of 2 December 1394 (*Sepe alias*) addressed to Nicolas de Clamanges,[84] congratulating him on the style of his previous letters, after all surprisingly well written for a Frenchman. Montreuil and his colleagues at the royal chancery in Paris were riled by the assertion of the Italian contingent at Avignon that a strong literary culture could not exist in France independently of Italian influence. Clamanges's responses to Pietramala: the *Perpulchras pater* and the *Quod in superiori*,[85] the latter constructed in the form of a *disputatio* on the Petrarchan phrase quoted above, argue for the transmission of literary excellence from antiquity, through Italy to France: the translatio studii. The *Quod in superiori* answers Pietramala with lists of French orators and poets who, in Clamanges's view, have inherited great style and ability from the ancients. Montreuil joined the fray with two epistles of his own: 96 (*Non dici*, December 1394–March 1395), and 149 (*Venit ad*, June 1395),[86] both addressed to Cardinal Pietramala.[87] The first of

---

[83] See Dario Cecchetti, *Petrarca, Pietramala e Clamanges: storia di una «querelle» inventata* (Paris: CEMI, 1982).

[84] Ornato (1969), *appendice* IV, pp. 233–8.

[85] These are Epistles IV and V in *Veterum scriptorum et monumentorum amplissima collectio* (1724).

[86] Jean de Montreuil (1963): I, pp. 171–3.

[87] Epistle 138 (*Nichil profecto*), written between September 1397 and July 1398, and addressed to the secretary of an Avignon cardinal, again deals with the Petrarchan pronouncement. Jean de Montreuil (1963): I, pp. 222–3.

these expresses incredulity that Pietramala should subscribe to Petrarch's opinion of French culture:

Ais enim, pater circumspectissime, si rite audita recordor, in Petrarcha legisse (eloquar an sileam?) extra Italiam poetas aut oratores non esse querendos; dicit extra Italiam oratores non esse querendos aut poetas, Ep. 96.[88]

Montreuil and Clamanges here adopt debating positions;[89] their principal concern is the style and disposition of their arguments.[90] Cecchetti argues that the polemical slant to the epistolary exchange of 1394–5 between Clamanges and Pietramala was added later by Clamanges, who revised his letters in the 1430s. This discovery lends weight to the notion of a debating climate in early humanist France. The fabrication of literary collaboration was already in evidence in the work of such authors as Jean le Seneschal. His *Cent Ballades* of 1389, as I discuss in Chapter 1, is a poem in which an alleged collaboration with three others is woven into the fictional framework of the poem, and becomes part of the deep structure of the debate.[91] For these humanist scholars, then, the practice of literary debate becomes more important than the questions or issues at stake; debate becomes an end in itself. For the Paris and Avignon groups, the *forme* was more important than the *fond*, in contrast with the Scholastics who considered style secondary to thought, as Thelma Fenster argues in a recent article. [92]

Colleagues would strive to improve their own epistolary style by emulating their peers, and often debated the finer points. Montreuil engages Laurent de Premierfait of the Avignon chancery in debate on this subject in Epistles 97 and 148 (dated by Ornato to after September/October 1394, and June 1395 respectively). Montreuil criticizes Premierfait for his attack on Clamanges's style in Epistle 97 (*Si thersitem*),[93] and

---

[88] 'For you say, most considered father, if I write correctly what I have heard, that you have read in Petrarch (shall I speak or be silent?) that orators and poets should not be sought outside Italy; he says that one should not seek orators or poets outside Italy', Jean de Montreuil (1963): I, ll. 22–5, p. 136.

[89] See *supra*: p. 53 for a definition of debating positions.

[90] Montreuil refers to Petrarch in Epistle 208 as 'devotissimus catholicus ac celeberrimus philosophus moralis' (most devout catholic and renowned moral philosopher), Jean de Montreuil (1963): I, l. 1, p. 315. Cecchetti (1982) observes that Clamanges's two responses to Pietramala's *Sepe alias* were regarded as antipetrarchist propaganda.

[91] See Chapter 1, pp. 40–4, and Jean le Seneschal (1905).

[92] See Fenster ' "Perdre son latin": Christine de Pizan and Vernacular Humanism', in *Christine de Pizan and the Categories of Difference*, ed. Desmond (Minneapolis/London: University of Minnesota Press, 1998), 91–107, p. 96.

[93] Jean de Montreuil (1963): I, pp. 137–40.

suggests in Epistle 148 (*Quem pleraque*) that Premierfait's silence is a tacit acknowledgement of his error of judgement in condemning Clamanges's style:

Qui tacet consentire videtur. Tu ratiunculis meis, quibus te in metra nostri de Clamengiis minus mature dixisse [...] probavi, non respondes. Ergo, in 'darii' reductive concludendo, rem consentis, aut sillogismo respondeto.[94]

Montreuil and Gontier Col seem to have regarded Clamanges as a master in the art of letter writing, and defer to the 'splendissimus stylus clamenginus'.[95] The epistolary form provided a convenient vehicle for such debate, but was used loosely, following a classical precedent. The 'literary letter' can be traced back to such Latin writers as Cicero, Seneca, or Horace,[96] all of whom wrote sequences of epistles which were subsequently collected and published; there can be no doubt but that Montreuil and his colleagues were heavily influenced by classical thought.[97] In humanist circles addressees were largely irrelevant, since the letters would be circulated freely within and between the chanceries, sometimes reaching their addressee only after having passed through other hands.[98] Letters might also be written obliquely (as I have suggested in the case of Migli's letter to Gontier Col and Montreuil's 'reply' to Migli through Col: Ep. 106), their addressee not necessarily the intended recipient. There is evidence that letters were written in the presence of other chancery colleagues. These open writing sessions were perhaps intended both as instructive as well as enjoyable occasions,

---

[94] *'Keeping quiet is as good as agreeing.* You do not reply to my reasonings, whereby I judged, in metre [...] that you had spoken rather hastily about Clamanges's writings. Therefore, by a process of deduction, you agree with me about the matter, or if not, answer me with a syllogism', Jean de Montreuil (1963): I, ll. 2–5, p. 214.

[95] See Montreuil's Épistle 161 (*Perplexitate nimis*), addressed to Gontier Col, Jean de Montreuil (1963): I, 227–40.

[96] Cicero's letters survive in a number of collections such as the *Epistolae ad familiares*, and *Epistolae ad Atticum*; see Cicero, *Select Letters*, ed. Shackleton Bailey (Cambridge: CUP, 1995). Seneca's *Epistolae morales ad Lucilium* track the conversion of a philosophical novice (Lucilius) to Stoicism, see Seneca, *Select Letters*, ed. Summers (Bristol: Bristol Classical Press, 1990). For a discussion of the collection as fiction, see Seneca, *Letters from a Stoic*, ed. and trans. Campbell (London: Penguin, 1969), p. 21. See also Horace, *Satires, Epistles and Ars poetica*, ed. Fairclough (Cambridge, MA/London: Harvard University Press, 1991).

[97] In a discussion of Clamanges's epistles, Ornato remarks that 'dans tous les cas, la lettre ne constitue qu'un prétexte, et nous n'aurons aucune difficulté à reconnaître, dans le contenu annoncé par la rubrique, un certain nombre de topoi bien connus', Ornato (1969), p. 56, n. 30.

[98] I have discussed how Gontier Col retained the letter meant for Ambrogio dei Migli from Clamanges: VII in the *Amplissima collectio*.

at which colleagues might have had a chance to discuss style and composition. In Epistle 132, addressed by Montreuil to Clamanges on the topic of Migli, Montreuil states that the literary debates with Migli that are the topic of Epistles 129, 130, and 132, were copied down in the presence of such scholars as Jean Gerson, Jean Courtecuisse, and Jacques de Nouvion.⁹⁹ Pons notes that a letter of Gontier Col's implicated in the *Querelle de la Rose* was written in the presence of three colleagues, Jehan de Quatre Mares, Jehan Porchier, and Guillaume de Neauville.¹⁰⁰ What appear to be closed dialogues between two individuals are in fact inscribed in the open collaborative culture of debate at this time, partly by virtue of their theatrical and performative aspects. Dialogue is staged as debate through the participation of the audience/reader. Moreover, there are indications that these literary letters were copied out for circulation, either for more public enjoyment of the exchanges (though probably remaining within chancery circles), or as models of style. In Epistle 121 (*Mee an fuerit*), Jean de Montreuil addresses a church dignitary, requesting that he keep private the accompanying satirical invective:

Rursus igitur subiit mentem meam Paternitati Vestre mittere eam de qua pridie in domo vestra sermonem habuimus, satirice invectionis formam tenentem epistolam: non ut transcribatur—hoc supplicio, posco, obsecro requiroque—sed solum eam Vestra Dominatio pervideat.¹⁰¹

Montreuil's explicit instruction to his addressee suggests that the transcription of such documents and letters for subsequent circulation was common practice, and his hyperbolic pleas attest to the enthusiasm with which colleagues would follow literary discussions and disputes. This enthusiasm for debate spills over into their everyday diplomatic business and is in turn sharpened by practical debating. Alongside these elaborate literary letters, more formulaic diplomatic missives would

---

⁹⁹ Montreuil writes that the debates were delivered 'preter nostrum de Noviano et quam plures multiscios, duos illos sacris in litteris antistes et eloquente sydera Ecclesie Pariensis, videlicet plusquam meritum cancellarium, et alium cui Breviscoxe est nomen', Epistle 132: *Portentuosum Prodigium*, Jean de Montreuil (1963): I, ll. 36–40, pp. 194–5: 'in front of our Nouvion (Jacques de) and many other knowledgeable men, two of them masters in Scripture and stars of eloquence at the Paris Church, namely the highly worthy chancellor (Jean Gerson), and another whose name is Courtecuisse (Jean)'.

¹⁰⁰ Col's '*Femme de hault et eslevé entendement*', see Pons (1990), pp. 147–8.

¹⁰¹ 'It therefore occurred to me to send you this letter which we discussed yesterday in your home, a letter in the form of a satirical invective: not for you to copy out—this I ask, beg, plead and demand—but for Your Eminence's eyes only', *Débat sur le 'Roman de la Rose'* (1977), ll. 14–18, p. 36.

have been written. Formularies were kept at the chanceries containing models of letters and acts which the notaries and secretaries would have had to compose as part of their diplomatic and political duties.[102] These formularies were explicitly designed for the use of chancery notaries and secretaries and often included instructions for use with the models.[103]

The free circulation and copying of letters and tracts was essentially private, in that it operated within the relatively closed circles of colleagues attached to the chanceries and to the University of Paris. In the context of the documents implicated in the *Querelle de la Rose*, though, there are conflicts between private and public circulation. I suggest that Montreuil and Christine de Pizan have entirely divergent views on the conduct of the *Querelle*. Montreuil adopts his customary debating position and attempts to curtail Christine's role in the *Querelle* through his portrayal of her as literary traitor. Christine however refuses to cede her active role as correspondent, and by publishing selected *Querelle* documents she places the debate on unfamiliar territory for Montreuil, leading to his withdrawal from engagement. Christine effectively turns a private, literary game into a public and political one, where the symbolic capital at stake is no longer simply a matter of the style and disposition of arguments. With Rosalind Brown-Grant I suggest that Christine creates a fictional role for herself in the *Querelle*. Brown-Grant identifies this role as that of victim in a debate whose stakes Christine altered to transform what was essentially a literary dispute into a dispute between the sexes.[104] Far from casting herself as victim, though, I shall show how Christine manipulates the material generated by the *Querelle* to promote herself to a prominent and unassailable position.

It is a significant feature of his correspondence that Montreuil never engages directly with Christine, but continues to evoke her

---

[102] See Tessier, 'Le Formulaire d'Odart Morchesne (1427)', in *Mélanges dédiés à la mémoire de Félix Grat*, II (Paris: Pecqueur-Grat, 1949), 75–102. An autograph copy of this formulary is preserved in BnF, fr. 5024. There is evidence of earlier formularies, including BnF, lat. 4641 and 13868. Odart Morchesne, notary and secretary to Charles VII, achieved great success with his formulary, which was copied a number of times in the fifteenth century and survives in three manuscript copies in addition to the autograph copy (BnF, fr. 5318, 6022, and 14371).

[103] Odart Morchesne's formulary contains instructions on fol. 195ᵛ, as well as commentaries on each of his seventeen chapters.

[104] See Brown-Grant, *Christine de Pizan and the Moral Defence of Women: Reading beyond Gender* (Cambridge: CUP, 1999).

obliquely in Epistles 120 (*Scis me*),[105] 122 (*Etsi facundissimus*),[106] and 154. In contrast, in spite of addressing Migli through Clamanges (Epistles 129, 130, 132), and Col (Epistle 106), Montreuil nonetheless engages directly with him. Migli is apostrophized directly in Epistles 129[107] and 106,[108] and is the likely addressee of Epistle 109 (*O quam vere*).[109] This distinction between the two recipients of Montreuil's invective is linked to the nature of Christine's intervention in the *Querelle de la Rose*. I suggest that whereas Montreuil adopts a debating position in his dealings with Migli, Col, Clamanges, or Pietramala, this position is eroded and redundant with Christine, since she refuses to play the game on his terms. For this reason the section of the *Querelle de la Rose* that deals with Christine de Pizan and Jean de Montreuil is particularly unsatisfactory as an epistolary debate. Christine addresses a substantial letter to Montreuil in response to his vernacular pro-*Rose* treatise (of which two copies were sent, to Pierre d'Ailly and Christine de Pizan respectively),[110] but although she

---

[105] 'Male visum perscrutatumque et notatum, ignominiose despiciunt nostri correctores, execrantur et impugnant. O arrogantiam, temeritatem, audaciam', *Débat sur le 'Roman de la Rose'* (1977), ll. 41–4, p. 34: 'Yet they despise, execrate, and impugn him ignominiously, and [...] do so without having thoroughly read and studied the book. O the arrogance, temerity, audacity', English translation: Baird and Kane, see *Querelle de la Rose* (1978). This epistle is addressed to Gontier Col.

[106] 'Que duo maxime iudicium perverterunt ac te precipitem dederunt in errorem,—non fidei quidem, vel iniquitas aut malicie, sed in quem nonnulli predictorum (ipsius de Magduno superficietenus viso pede) tecum ruunt', *Débat sur le 'Roman de la Rose'* (1977), ll. 20–3, p. 38: 'It is these two factors which distorted your judgement and led you into precipitate error, not certainly an error of faith, nor even of deliberate wickedness, but one into which a good number of the supporters of Meun himself have rushed with you, for they too, in their haste, have only a shallow understanding of him', English translation as above. This epistle is addressed to an unidentified lawyer.

[107] 'Et tu Ambrosi, Nasonem tuum, tametsi velocis, acuti ac rapidi fuerit ingenii, Virgili comparabis?' Jean de Montreuil (1963): I, ll. 79–80, p. 191: 'And as for you, Ambrosius, even though your Ovid was a man of swift, acute and quick wit, will you yet compare him to Virgil?'

[108] Ambrogio dei Migli is apostrophized on a number of occasions, his name invoked in the context of animals, classical and biblical traitors, or perverts (those who have committed crimes against nature), for example: 'canis rabidissime' (O, most savage dog); 'Neroneque neronior' (O, more Nero-like than Nero); 'scelestissime Juda' (O, most wicked Judas); 'immanissime Cayn' (O, most monstrous Cain). The use of the superlative adjective in each case (and the comparative in the second example) reinforces Montreuil's rhetorical anger. Jean de Montreuil (1963): I, pp. 148–59.

[109] Jean de Montreuil (1963): I, p. 192.

[110] *Débat sur le 'Roman de la Rose'* (1977), *Épître V*, pp. 11–22.

attempts to engage with Montreuil, and to solicit further debate, he never replies directly to her.[111] The oblique reference to Christine in Epistle 154, which I have mentioned, is the only place in Montreuil's correspondence where Christine is mentioned by name. Elsewhere she is assimilated to the amorphous plurality of the detractors of the *Rose*:

Nichil agimus tamen, frater honoratissime, sed tempus terendo incassum aera verberamus, 'nec est quod speremus posse aliquid impetrare, tanta est hominum pertinacia.' Hi sunt mores, ea dementia! **'Timent** enim ne, a nobis **revicti**, manus dare aliquando, clamante ipsa veritate, **cogantur. Obstrepunt** igitur', ut ait Lactantius, 'et **intercidunt** ne **audiant**', Ep. 120: *Scis me*.[112]

The elegant epigrammatic clause 'tempus terendo incassum aera verberamus' (we beat the air uselessly passing the time), encapsulates the essence of this *Querelle*. The intertext Montreuil uses is St Paul's First Epistle to the Corinthians (9: 26):

Omnia autem facio propter evangelium ut particeps eius efficiar/nescitis quod hii qui in stadio currunt omnes quidem currunt sed unus accipit bravium sic currite ut conprehendatis/omnis autem qui in agone contendit ab omnibus se abstinet et illi quidem ut corruptibilem coronam accipiant nos autem incorruptam/ego igitur sic curro non quasi in incertum sic pugno **non quasi aerem verberans**/sed castigo corpus meum et in servitutem redigo ne forte cum aliis praedicaverim ipse reprobus efficiar.[113]

---

[111] Epistle 103 (*Cum, ut dant*) is a letter addressed to Pierre d'Ailly, intended to accompany Montreuil's lost vernacular treatise. *Débat sur le 'Roman de la Rose'* (1977), p. 28.

[112] I have emboldened any plural verbs which refer to the group of detractors of the *Rose*. 'Yet we can do nothing, most honored (sic) brother, but beat the air uselessly, passing the time. "So great is the obstinacy of man that we cannot hope to obtain anything." This is the temper of the time, this is the madness. "For they fear lest, conquered by us, they are obliged to yield by lamenting Truth herself. Therefore, they clamour", as Lactantius said, "and interrupt lest they hear"', *Débat sur le 'Roman de la Rose'* (1977), ll. 29–34, p. 34, English translation: *Querelle de la Rose* (1978), p. 166.

[113] Vulgate Bible: 1 Corinthians 9: 23–7. 'All this I do for the sake of the Gospel, to bear my part in proclaiming it. You know (do you not?) that at the sports all the runners run the race, though only one wins the prize. Like them, run to win! But every athlete goes into strict training. They do it to win a fading wreath; we, a wreath that never fades. For my part, I run with a clear goal before me; I am like the boxer **who does not beat the air**; I bruise my own body and make it know its master, for fear that after preaching to others I should find myself rejected', *The New English Bible* (Oxford: OUP, 1973). I am grateful to Julia Barrow of Nottingham University for giving me this reference at a conference held there on the Avignon Papacy (22 June 2002).

St Paul here uses the metaphor of a competitive race (or *agôn*) in which all participants must strive to win, not simply punch the air, to describe the struggle for grace and participation in the gospel. Montreuil knowingly appropriates the image to suggest through this religious intertext his dissatisfaction with the conduct of this particular *Querelle*, and with that of certain participants. It is interesting for our discussion of the debate as game that Montreuil himself uses an analogy for the *Querelle* drawn from competitive sport. He conceives of the debating game as it should be played in terms of a competitive struggle, an *agôn*. In another letter implicated in the *Querelle*, Montreuil uses an intertext whose resonances are not only of competition but specifically of literary competition. Epistle 118 (*Quo magis*) evokes Virgil's third *Eclogue* which relates a poetic singing contest between the shepherds Menalcas and Damoetas, judged by fellow shepherd Palaemon: 'sed si amodo serio dixisse fatearis, dic quo pignore certes: veniam, ut ait Virgilius, quocum vocaris.'[114] Interestingly Virgil's third *Eclogue* closes without the prize being awarded to either contender.[115] The ambiguous end to this singing contest has implications for the *Querelle de la Rose*, which itself remains unresolved, although Christine believes that in publishing her dossiers of the *Querelle*, she has brought it to a conclusion: 'si feray fin a mon dittié du debat non hayneux commencié, continué et finé par maniere de soulas sans indignacion a personne'.[116] The *Querelle de la Rose* ceases to have the desired element of competition for Montreuil once Christine becomes involved. The sense of futility he evokes in the passage cited above from Epistle 120 (*Scis me*) is reminiscent of a dream-like state (such as is the premise for Guillaume de Lorris's and

---

[114] *Quo magis*, *Débat sur le 'Roman de la Rose'* (1977), ll. 17–18. Montreuil cites here from lines 31 and 49 of the third *Eclogue*, see Virgil, *The Eclogues and Georgics*, ed. R. D. Williams (Bristol: Bristol Classical Press, 1996). 'But if you confess that you spoke seriously, tell me for what prize you contend; I shall come, as Virgil said, whithersoever you have called', English translation: *Querelle de la Rose* (1978).

[115] 'Non nostrum inter vos tantas componere lites: | Et vitula tu dignus et hic—et quisquis amores | Aut metuet dulcis aut experietur amaros', *Eclogue* III, vv. 108–10: 'It is not for me to settle so high a contest between you. You deserve the heifer, and he also—and whoever shall fear the sweets or taste the bitters of love', Virgil, *Eclogues*; *Georgics*; *Aeneid 1–6*, ed. and trans. Fairclough, rev. edn (Cambridge, MA: Harvard University Press, 1986).

[116] *Pour ce que entendement*, addressed to Pierre Col. *Débat sur le 'Roman de la Rose'* (1977), ll. 1128–30, p. 150. The rubric in all the manuscripts of this letter contains the explicit 'escript et compleit par moy, Cristine de Pizan, le. iie. jour d'octobre, l'an mil .IIII^C. et deux'; the use of 'compleit' here suggests Christine's determination to put a full stop to the debate.

Jean de Meun's *Roman de la Rose*), in which the dreamers are powerless to change the events unfolding before them. Montreuil may have had in mind his recent reading of the *Rose*, a book which Gontier Col had apparently recommended in a previous exchange:[117]

Scis me, consideratissime magister atque frater, iugi hortatu tuo et impulsu nobile illud opus magistri Johannis de Magduno, *Romantium de Rosa* vulgo dictum, vidisse: qui, quia de ammirabili artificio, ingenio ac doctrina tecum sisto—et irrevocabiliter me fateor permansurum, Ep. 120.[118]

Montreuil's language in this passage is uncompromising: from the start he is not prepared to change his opinion of the *Rose*. He may be eager for debate, but on his terms. Montreuil and Christine have fundamentally divergent conceptions of Jean de Meun's work. In so far as they engage with each other at all, the two argue at cross-purposes, rendering the ground of the *Querelle* sterile, as Hicks and Ornato observe:

La polémique entre Christine et Montreuil s'annonçait sans issue, non seulement parce que les jugements portés sur le Roman étaient diamétralement opposés, mais aussi et surtout parce que les deux interlocuteurs ne se plaçaient pas sur le même terrain: Jean de Montreuil voulait mettre en évidence les mérites philosophiques et littéraires du Roman, d'où la nécessité d'en justifier les écarts de langage; Christine, pour sa part, s'interrogeait sur les effets pernicieux de l'ouvrage, que ses qualités formelles n'auraient pu effacer [...] Ce qui était primordial pour l'un était secondaire pour l'autre.[119]

Not only do Christine and Montreuil argue at cross-purposes, but in different languages. Christine's choice of French puts her at an immediate disadvantage, as Montreuil only communicates in Latin, with all the austerity, formality, and prestige *that* language can convey. The

---

[117] The dream world of the *Rose* mirrors that of a long tradition of 'dream' literature: Guillaume de Lorris mentions Macrobius's famous commentary on Scipio's dream in his prologue, Guillaume de Lorris et Jean de Meun (1992), vv. 6–10. Given Montreuil's debt to Virgil, and great familiarity with his *oeuvre*, it is likely that Montreuil was also thinking of the crucial contest in Book XII of the *Aeneid*, in which Turnus is paralysed in his clash against Aeneas, and moves as if in a dream: Virgil *Aeneid*, Bk. XII, vv. 906–12; see Virgil (1992b).

[118] *Débat sur le 'Roman de la Rose'* (1977), 'Most learned master and brother, you know that, thanks to your continual urging and encouragement, I have read that noble work of Master Jean de Meun, commonly called the *Roman de la Rose*. And [...] I stand with you in admiration of his art, ability, and learning—and I assert irrevocably that I will persevere in this belief', English translation: *Querelle de la Rose* (1978).

[119] See Hicks and Ornato, 'Jean de Montreuil et le débat sur le *Roman de la Rose*', *Romania* 98 (1977), 34–64; 186–219, p. 213.

lost vernacular treatise written by Montreuil in support of Jean de Meun's *Rose* seemed to have been a cause of some potential embarrassment to the scholar, as he explains to a church dignitary who has requested a copy:

Huiusmodi nugas vobis mitto, tali pacto, pater mi confidentissime, ne cuiquam communicentur: quoniam ab alio de stili ruditate et incompto, ab alio de materia, [...] aut de levitate scurrilitateve in eo quod vulgari sermone editum est reprehendi possem vel notari, Ep. 119: *Ex quo nugis*.[120]

If Montreuil feared ridicule for the redaction of a treatise in French,[121] it is little wonder that he objected so strongly to Christine's publication of the *Querelle* documents, and that he avoided addressing her directly, in French or in Latin. Christine, from the first, organized the *Querelle de la Rose* on her own terms by choosing a language that would be more widely read on publication; though there is some dispute among scholars as to how well Christine could actually read Latin,[122] and it is not certain that she would have had the option of writing in Latin.[123] So she refused to

---

[120] 'So I am sending you these trifling works with the understanding that they are not made known to anyone: since I could well be blamed or rebuked by some for the bareness of my unadorned style, and by others for the content, [...] or for frivolity and buffoonery because I wrote in the vernacular', Jean de Montreuil (1963): I.

[121] Montreuil seems to have been particularly concerned to keep his writings 'private', that is to keep them within the circulation of select chancery colleagues and other acquaintances attached to the Paris and Avignon courts. As I mentioned earlier, Epistle 121 (*Mee an fuerit*), which was accompanied by another epistle in the form of a satirical invective, and possibly sent to the same recipient as Epistle 119 (see Jean de Montreuil (1963): I, pp. 201–2), also contains a request that the addressee keep its contents to himself.

[122] Christine translated various Latin works into French, see Fenster (1998), but it is also clear that she used the vernacular translations of classical and patristic works in her own writing rather than the originals. Widespread use was made by Christine of texts in translation such as the Hesdin-Gonesse translation of Valerius Maximus's *Facta et dicta memorabilia*, and the medieval French translation of Boccaccio's *De claris mulieribus* by Laurent de Premierfait; see *Des cas des nobles hommes et femmes*, ed. Gathercole (Chapel Hill: University of North Carolina Press, 1968). The influence of this translation of Boccaccio is seen particularly in Christine's *Livre de la cité des dames*; see Jeanroy, 'Boccace et Christine de Pisan. Le *De claris mulieribus* principale source du *Livre de la cité des dames*', *Romania* 48 (1922), 93–105, as well as that of the *Ovide moralisé* (see *Ovide moralisé*, ed. Cornelis de Boer (Amsterdam: North-Holland Pub. Co., 1954)). See Solente's introduction to her edition, Christine de Pizan (1959), xxx–xcviii, for further details of classical, patristic, and medieval sources drawn on by Christine.

[123] Fenster (1998) notes that the *Querelle de la Rose* took place at a critical moment in the development of the vernacular as a literary language, when humanists were returning to the use of Latin after a period under Charles V during which he promoted the use of the French language in political and intellectual life, and commissioned many vernacular translations of classical and medieval texts. The publication at this time, then, of a literary

implicate herself in the male-dominated Latinate world of the papal and royal chanceries at Avignon and Paris, and set a precedent for her inter-locutors which they were more or less obliged to follow. The gendering of Latin and the vernacular may not be as straightforward as the distinction between a feminine French and a masculine Latin. As Fenster explains, a 'feminization' of Latin under Charles V allowed the vernacular cultur-ally to acquire a masculine power, perhaps rendering Christine's choice of French a conscious step into the masculine, a step which she felt that she had taken initially through her decision to write.[124]

Montreuil's almost total refusal to engage with Christine on any level is evidence of his desire to divorce himself from the *Querelle* as Christine conceived of it. Other early humanists from the Paris and Avignon groups were not as eager to withdraw, however. Gontier Col and his brother Pierre supported Jean de Montreuil in his rigid defence of Jean de Meun's *Rose*, but were willing to engage with Christine, and to do so in the vernacular. On Christine's side, Jean Gerson, Chancellor of the University of Paris, intervened, composing a ver-nacular fictional treatise in the form of a *jugement* against the *Rose*: *Traictié d'une vision faicte contre Le Ronmant de la Rose* (May 1402).[125] Gerson sets the scene for his allegorical treatise at the 'court sainte de Crestienté',[126] at which Jean de Meun (*Fol Amoureux*) is tried before *Justice Canonique* by *Chasteté* and *Eloquance Theologienne*. The eight grounds on which the case is predicated are suffused with the legal

---

debate in French—the first of its kind—was to force French intellectuals to recognize once more the appropriateness of the vernacular as a literary vehicle.

[124] Christine's *Livre de la mutacion de Fortune* (1400–3) relates her transformation into a man by Fortune at the age of twenty-five, and articulates Christine's belief that in order to write she had to become a man: 'Vous diray qui je suis, qui parle | Qui de femele devins masle | Par Fortune, qu'ainsy le voult; | Si me mua et corps et voult | En homme naturel parfaict; | Et jadis fus femme, de fait | Homme suis, je ne ment pas, | Assez le demonstrent mes pas', Christine de Pizan (1959), vv. 141–8, p. 12.

[125] *Débat sur le 'Roman de la Rose'* (1977), pp. 58–87. Ward includes a Latin version of this treatise in his collection of the *Querelle* documents: *The Epistles on the 'Romance of the Rose' and Other Documents in the Debate* (Chicago: microfilm, 1911). The Latin version, *Tractatus contra Romantium Rosa*, is a later redaction, and not from Gerson's hand. Langlois suggests that the original French was translated into Latin for Martin Flach's 1494 Strasbourg edition of Gerson's collected works: see Langlois, 'Le Traité de Gerson contre le *Roman de la Rose*', *Romania* 45 (1919), 23–48.

[126] This is an intriguing, and perhaps deliberate, use of the word 'Crestienté', since it contains a partial anagram of 'Cristine' which Christine de Pizan herself uses in an anagram signature at the end of one debate poem: 'S'il le cerche, trouver le peut enté | En tous les lieux ou est Cristïenté', Christine de Pizan (1998b), *Le Livre du debat de deux amans*, vv. 2022–3.

language of slander. This accusation of the defamation of women, literally the removal of their good reputation, initially levelled at the *Rose*, but later at a range of classical, patristic, and medieval texts, was to fuel the protracted *Querelle des femmes*,[127] and would encompass in its scope the fifteenth-century *Querelle de la Belle Dame sans mercy*. Gerson also delivered a series of connected sermons (the *Poenitemini*), based on the seven deadly sins at the church of St Germain l'Auxerrois between December 1402 and March 1403.[128] *Responsio ad scripta cuiusdam errantis de innocentia puerili*, the one letter of Gerson's included with the *Querelle* documents by both Hicks[129] and Ward,[130] is addressed to Pierre Col, and is a response to the epistle with which Col answered both Gerson's vernacular treatise and a letter of Christine's. Interestingly, this epistle, like Montreuil's correspondence, is composed in Latin, effectively reclaiming it for private circulation.

One of the fundamental clashes between the supporters and detractors of Jean de Meun's *Rose* springs from a dispute about authorial responsibility. Rosalind Brown-Grant identifies this as one of four key issues addressed by Christine in her criticism of the *Rose*, along with language, love, and anti-feminism.[131] Baird and Kane refute the view that Christine and Gerson fail to see any distinction between Jean de Meun and his characters, since as authors themselves, they argue, both Gerson and Christine would have been familiar with the concept of authorial distance.[132] The thrust of the detractors' argument seems to be that Jean de Meun does not maintain that authorial distance, nor does he set out a moral framework to guide the reader through his/her interpretation of the characters' words. Gerson and Christine argue that he manipulates his position outside the text in order to excuse the various obscenities and misogynous statements which issue from the mouths of characters such as *Le Jaloux*, *La Vieille*, or *Genius*, as Gerson asserts in his treatise against the *Rose*:

---

[127] See Solterer (1995). Solterer is particularly eloquent on the topic of defamatory language (see chapter 1, pp. 29–31) starting from the phonetic similarities of the couplet: feme/diffame.

[128] *Débat sur le 'Roman de la Rose'* (1977), pp. 177–85. Hicks reproduces the French text of the *Poenitemini* from MSS: BnF, fr. 24842, and BnF, fr. 24840.

[129] *Débat sur le 'Roman de la Rose'* (1977), pp. 161–75.

[130] *Epistles on the 'Romance of the Rose'* (1911), pp. 77–82.

[131] See Brown-Grant (1999).

[132] See Baird and Kane, 'La *Querelle de la Rose*: In Defense of the Opponents', *French Review* 48 (1974), 298–307. See also Baird's later article: 'Pierre Col and the *Querelle de la Rose*', *Philological Quarterly* 60 (1981), 273–86.

Je voulroie bien que ce Fol Amoureulx n'eust usé de ces personnaiges fors ainssy que la sainte Escripture en use, c'est assavoir en reprouvant le mal, et tellement que chascun eust apperceu le reproche du mal et l'aprobacion du bien, et—qui est le principal—que tout se fist sans excés de legiereté. Mais nennin voir. Tout semble estre dit en sa persone; tout semble estre vray come Euvangille.[133]

Christine is subject to similar doubts about Jean de Meun's motives. Her in extenso reply, *Pour ce que entendement* (2 October 1402), to Pierre Col's letter, *Aprés ce que je oÿ* (end of summer, 1402), answers Col's contention that:

Maistre Jehan de Meung en son livre introduisy personnaiges, et fait chascun personnaige parler selonc qui luy appartient: c'est assavoir le Jaloux comme jaloux, la Vielle comme la Vielle, et pareillement des autres.[134]

Christine assiduously picks apart Col's argument point by point in her *replique*. In this case, her response is that although Jean de Meun has created fictional characters, he has chosen these characters specifically to slander women:

Tu respons a dame Eloquance et a moy que maistre Jehan de Meung en son livre introduisy personnages, et fait chascun parler selonc ce que luy appartient. Et vraiement je te confesse bien que **selonc le *gieu* que on vuelt *jouer*** il convient **instrumens propres, mais la voulanté dou *joueur* les appreste telz come il luy fault.** [...] Tu dis que ce fait le Jaloux comme son office. Et je te dis que auques en tous personnaiges ne se peut taire de vituperer les fames.[135]

The reference to game-playing in this citation which I have emboldened above may serve not only as an assessment of Jean de Meun's authorial practice but as Christine's assessment of the *Querelle* as a whole. Christine comes to this debate as an interloper, a woman, and a foreigner to the language and habits of literary debate as it was conducted in chancery circles. However, she then appropriates the *Querelle* for her own purposes, and excludes material hostile to her cause from her publicly circulated dossiers. Christine wields her 'instrumens propres' in the course of the game of debate for different ends from those of her opponents, and ends up playing a different game. To draw on Stock's model of interpretative textual communities, we could say that Christine participates in a different textual community as she

---

[133] *Le Traictié d'une vision faite contre Le Ronmant de la Rose, Débat sur le 'Roman de la Rose'* (1977), ll. 379–86, p. 74.

[134] *Débat sur le 'Roman de la Rose'* (1977), ll. 403–6, p. 100.

[135] See *Débat sur le 'Roman de la Rose'* (1977), ll. 552–7; 565–7, p. 132.

brings different interpretative strategies to bear on her reading of the *Rose*. Disparate readers of the same text who bring the same learned interpretative strategies to bear on their reading are said to be members of the same community, while those who use different interpretative strategies must necessarily belong to different communities, an idea elaborated by Stanley Fish.[136] Christine's use of the language of play: *jouer, gieu*, and *joueur*, is vital to an understanding of the climate in which literary debate operated in early humanist France, and the words in Christine's mouth seem to be directed at her opponents. The debate on their terms could be described as a *gieu*, albeit a fiercely intellectual one: a *gieu* in which the 'instrumens propres' are the debating positions that each participant must adopt.

I suggest that Christine acts in propria persona throughout the *Querelle de la Rose*, fighting her corner with the tenacious conviction of the wronged, conducting a 'debat gracieux et non haineux',[137] perhaps, but none the less serious for that. Her opponents and even her defender, Jean Gerson, on the other hand, assume customary debating positions or personae. They become the participants in a literary game, a collaborative fiction, itself implicated in a longer tradition of epistolary dispute and exchange, and from which Christine must then be excluded. Christine's *Querelle*, and the *Querelle* as her opponents conceive of it, are incompatible and divergent debates. Jean de Montreuil refuses to engage with Christine because she demands that he change the stakes of the debate, that he engage with her on her terms: in the vernacular and with masks cast aside. The phrase of Christine's I cite in the title of this chapter, 'tu recites, je replique', bears within it recognition of the different stances taken by Christine and the other participants in the debate. Neither Jean de Montreuil nor Jean Gerson addresses any material to Christine directly. Gerson's only interlocutor in the *Querelle* is Pierre Col to whom he writes in Latin. Gontier and Pierre Col attempt to engage with Christine, but no actual concessions are made. Christine addresses epistles to each of her opponents, and hence fulfils the second half of the clause, but her own replies are predicated on a rigid conception of Jean de Meun's *Rose*, and so never engage fully with her opponents' arguments. Christine is aware of this lack of proper

---

[136] See Fish, *Is There a Text in this Class?: The Authority of Interpretive Communities* (Cambridge, MA: Harvard University Press, 1980).

[137] This is taken from Christine's dedicatory letter to Guillaume de Tignonville, *A vous mon seigneur: Débat sur le 'Roman de la Rose'* (1977), ll. 9–10, p. 7.

interchange, and in a letter addressed to Pierre Col she talks of the multiple possible readings of the *Rose*. She acknowledges that debate about the text is therefore futile, using a simile drawn from alchemy:

Sés tu comment il va de celle lecture? Ainsy come des livres des arguemistes: les uns les lisent et les entendent d'une maniere, les autres qui les lisent les entendent tout au rebours; et chascun cuide trop bien entendre. Et sur ce ilz œuvrent et apprestent fourniaux, alembis et croisiaux, et soufflent fort, et pour ung petit de sulimacion ou congyeil qui leur appere merveillable, ilz cuident ataindre a merveille. Et puis quant il ont fait et fait et gasté leur temps, ilz y scevent autant comme devant,—mais que coust et despence a la maniere de distiller et d'aucunes congelacions de nulle utilité.[138]

The reference itself is no doubt derived from Christine's reading of the *Rose*, and Jean de Meun's discussion of alchemy in the context of Nature versus Art.[139] The author him/herself is an alchemist, generating fiction based on his/her observations of Nature. One could equally apply the alchemy analogy of reading the *Rose* to a reading of the letters and documents of the *Querelle*. Each participant in this literary game makes their move based not only on their initial interpretation of the *Rose*, but also according to his or her reading of the previous texts (moves). In the light of this popular medieval analogy, Jean de Montreuil's definition of debate from Epistle 118 (*Quo magis*), one of those attached to the *Querelle de la Rose*, is particularly interesting: 'immo, quia altercando scitur veritas, "aurumque probatur in fornace"' (indeed, since truth is discovered through debate, 'as gold is proved in the furnace').[140] Montreuil here equates truth with a substance allegedly produced through alchemy, and by extension then, through writing. The unfolding debate of the *Querelle de la Rose* produces nothing but 'aucunes congelacions de nulle utilité', as Christine asserts. In full knowledge of the sterility of any debate about the *Rose*, Christine prepared dossiers of the *Querelle* which essentially map *her Querelle*; her decision to publish and circulate these dossiers alienated her correspondents and opponents, for whom the activity of literary debating was conceived of rather differently. As a woman and an author, it was a matter of

[138] *Débat sur le 'Roman de la Rose'* (1977), ll. 352–62, p. 126.
[139] Jean de Meun includes a famous passage on alchemy in the *Rose* (vv. 16069–152), as part of a discussion of Nature and Art, and concludes that the works of alchemy can never surpass those of Nature: 'Mais ce ne feroient cil mie | Qui oevrent de sophisterie: | Travaillent tant com il vivront, | Ja nature n'aconsivront', vv. 16149–52.
[140] *Débat sur le 'Roman de la Rose'* (1977), Ep. 118 (*Quo magis*), ll. 24–5, pp. 28–9. (English translation: *Querelle de la Rose* (1978)).

vital importance to Christine that misogynous attitudes expressed by characters in the *Rose* be brought into the public domain. In engaging with the *Rose*, Christine also stakes her claim in the wider *Querelle des femmes*. For Montreuil and his colleagues, this was merely one in a series of literary jousts to be played out within private circles.

It has been shown that Christine not only anthologized her own works for publication, but that she frequently acted as scribe, editor, and glossator of those collections.[141] It is significant that in selecting representative documents for her dossiers, Christine chose to exclude Jean de Montreuil's letters.[142] Montreuil's letters were circulated 'privately'[143] among groups of colleagues at Avignon and Paris, only compiled later into manuscript form,[144] and so never had any place in Christine's published version of the *Querelle*. Montreuil has no voice in Christine's *Querelle*, just as she was not permitted directly to enter the closed male Latinate world of Montreuil's correspondence, except as a fictional construct. There are three manuscript witnesses to the first version of Christine's collected works that include the initial exchange of letters between herself and Gontier Col, the two dedicatory letters to Queen Isabeau and Guillaume de Tignonville, and Christine's letter to Montreuil. Two of these were copied under the supervision of Christine herself: BnF, fr. 12779 and Chantilly, Musée Condé, 492–3; the third, BnF, fr. 604, was copied at some point after 1407. Laidlaw mentions a table of contents found in the Chantilly manuscript that lists twenty-one items beginning with Christine's *Cent Ballades* and ending with the *Quinze Joyes de Nostre Dame rimés*, and fixes the period of composition between 1399 and 23 June 1402.[145] Christine prepared two other major

---

[141] See Laidlaw, 'Christine de Pizan—An Author's Progress', *Modern Language Review* 78 (1980), 532–50, and Ouy and Reno, 'Identification des autographes de Christine de Pizan', *Scriptorium* 34 (1980), 221–38.

[142] *Débat sur le 'Roman de la Rose'* (1977) edits Epistles 103, 118, 119, 120, 121, 122, 152, and 154. Ward includes Epistles 118, 120, and 122 in his appendix: *Epistles on the 'Romance of the Rose'* (1911). Christine also wrote Pierre Col out of her revised second dossier of the *Querelle*, by omitting his response to her initial letter to Montreuil and Gerson's treatise.

[143] As I have suggested, 'privacy' in the circulation of epistolary exchanges among chancery colleagues is a relative term.

[144] Ornato lists the four extant MSS witnesses to Montreuil's letters in his introduction: BnF, lat. 13062; Vatican, Reg. lat. 332; BnF, lat. 18337; Florence, Bib. Riccardiana, 443. The first of these contains 202 letters, the second 43, of which it has 31 in common with the first MS, the third 2 private letters, one of which is common to the first two MSS, and the fourth contains one letter, Jean de Montreuil (1963): I.

[145] Laidlaw (1980).

collections of her collected works for presentation to the Duc de Berry in 1408–9 (the 'Duke's manuscript' survives in five parts: BnF, fr. 835, 606, 836, 605, and 607), and to Queen Isabeau of France in 1410–11 ('The Queen's manuscript': London, BL, Harley 4431).[146] The Harley manuscript and part 835 of the Paris manuscript contain a second version of the *Querelle* documents that Christine revised and added to (Christine's response *Pour ce que entendement* to Pierre Col's letter *Aprés ce que je oÿ* is also present in these manuscripts). As Laidlaw illustrates by comparing different manuscript witnesses of Christine's selected ballades and rondeaux, extensive revision has gone on from manuscript to manuscript, and scholarship has suggested that the revising hand is none other than Christine's.[147] This evidence that Christine edited her own texts for publication, and revised versions progressively, often altering the material to suit the particular manuscript into which it was compiled, puts a new complexion on the *Querelle de la Rose*, which, as we have seen, Christine directed on her own terms and in public. Christine's uncompromisingly serious and engaged approach to this debate was quite alien to Montreuil and his colleagues, as she seemingly made no distinction between the significance of public, political debate and 'private', literary debate. The chancery milieux were already steeped in literary, scholarly, and practical disputes. The humanists of Montreuil's circle would, unlike Christine, distinguish between their diplomatic and political business (*negotium*—business), and their literary disputing (*otium*—leisure). They would be accustomed to adopting debating positions in these literary disputes, and would concentrate on achieving an elegant epistolary style rather than on the content of their argument, considered subordinate to stylistic and rhetorical concerns. These scholars colluded in an elaborate literary game whose aim was to perpetuate dialogue and suspend conclusion, generating collaborative fictions that were to characterize late medieval poetic production. The figure of Christine in Montreuil's correspondence is a fictional construct that he is able to manipulate. Christine's refusal to accept this role or to join the *gieu* using her opponents' *instrumens*, and her automatic exclusion from it as a woman, writing in the vernacular, eventually led to the withdrawal of her opponents. She was to escalate this particular debate

---

[146] Jim Laidlaw is heading up a major AHRC project (2004–8), based at the University of Edinburgh, entitled 'The Making of the Queen's Manuscript'; see http://www.pizan.lib.ed.ac.uk.

[147] See Willard, 'An Autograph Manuscript of Christine de Pizan?', *Studi Francesi* 27 (1965), 452–7.

beyond their control through her publication of their exchanges, and not only publication, but subsequent collation, tailoring, and editing. She exerted authorial control over all the *Querelle* documents, regardless of their respective original authors. Christine created her own fictional *Querelle de la Rose* from which she emerged victorious. Her refusal to adopt a debating position constitutes a new position, unfamiliar to Montreuil and his colleagues. By making this final move, Christine shaped the destiny both of those documents that were included in her dossiers and those she chose to exclude, rewriting the debate on her terms.

3

'CLERC EXCELLENT, ORATEUR MAGNIFIQUE'[1]
ALAIN CHARTIER AND THE RISE OF A VERNACULAR HUMANIST RHETORIC

> 'Ainsi se fait.' 'Quoy?' 'Dyalogue.
> Commë ainsi, faignant deux estre.'
> 'C'est donc autrement que prologue?'
> 'Voire.' 'Qui l'enseigne?' 'Maint maistre,
> Especiaulement en maint estre
> Et lieu: maistre Alain Charretier.'
> 'Est il voir?' 'Oy, s'en fut l'encestre.'
> 'Fut il premier?' 'Non. Mais entier
> Grant maistre fut.' 'En quel science?'
> 'En rethorique que l'on prise.'
> 'Pourquoy?' 'Pour son experience.'
> 'Je m'en doubtes.' 'A tant souffise.'
>
> (L'Infortuné, *Instructif de seconde rhétorique*, 1480)[2]

The lyric manuscript compilation assembled by the anonymous author of this art of poetry, who calls himself *l'Infortuné*, was edited by Anthoine Vérard in his *Jardin de plaisance et fleur de rethorique* (1501), and a further seven times in the sixteenth century. Alain Chartier is here evoked in the capacity of master in the art of rhetoric and dialogue, a position he frequently occupies in works of the fifteenth and sixteenth centuries.

The Grands Rhétoriqueurs often cited Chartier among the ranks of Italian and French masters.[3] In later arts of poetry, Pierre Fabri (*Le Grand*

---

[1] See Octovien de Saint-Gelais, *Le Sejour d'honneur*, ed. Frédéric Duval (Geneva: Droz, 2002), v. 6331.

[2] See *Jardin de Plaisance et fleur de rethorique*, ed. Droz and Piaget (Paris: Firmin-Didot, 1910), vol. I, fols. 2^v–15^r, fol. 5^r (facsimile of Anthoine Vérard's 1501 edition). I have modernized the punctuation in accordance with the established rules. See Roques (1926), and Foulet and Speer (1979).

[3] See Hoffman (1975), see also Meyenberg, *Alain Chartier prosateur et l'art de la parole au XVe siècle* (Bern: Francke, 1992), pp. 38–43.

et Vrai Art de pleine rhétorique, 1521), and Thomas Sebillet (*Art poëtique françois*, 1548),[4] also refer to Chartier as one of the leading rhetoricians of early humanist France. Fabri notably remarks that Chartier's 'beau langage' is more than simply elegant, it is 'substancieux'.[5] Sebillet places Chartier in the illustrious company of Dante, Petrarch, Jean de Meun, and Jean Lemaire de Belges. Chartier is accorded a place of honour among the dead in Achille Caulier's *Ospital d'Amours* (pre 1441), one of the long line of imitations and sequels of Chartier's *Belle Dame sans mercy*, where he lies in state in the *cimitiere* reserved for 'les vrais et loyaulx amoureux': 'Entour sa tombe en lettre d'or | Estoit tout l'art de Rhetorique'.[6] In a later work also attached to the *Querelle de la BDSM*, the *Champion des dames* (1441),[7] Martin le Franc calls upon the poetic authority of Chartier. Another *Querelle* text, Pierre Michault's *Le Procès d'Honneur féminin* (post 1461) later establishes Chartier as a profeminine authority in the trial of *Honneur féminin* versus *l'Inculpé*, where the question of women is to be debated.[8] Chartier forms part of a formidable prosecution side that includes Boccaccio and Martin le Franc.

In spite of such significant medieval and Renaissance acclaim and two excellent recent editions,[9] Chartier's works have not been explored in depth by modern scholars—with some important exceptions[10]—and rarely have his Latin and French prose and verse been examined side by side.[11] Chartier's French verse has long been subject to an artificial division between the 'joyeuses escritures' (deemed of little import) and the 'serious poems',[12] which I propose here to break down through a system of intertextual links I trace between the French verse and the

---

[4] Thomas Sebillet, *Art poëtique françois*, ed. Goyet (Paris: Nizet, 1988).

[5] For Pierre Fabri (1889–90), Chartier is no less than the 'pere de l'eloquence françoyse', I, p. 72. He cites Chartier in a long line of great rhetoricians: 'la science (de rhétorique) a esté amplement magnifiee en nostre langage de plusieurs et grans orateurs, et mesmes de nostre temps, de maistre Arnault Grebon, de Hurion, imitateur de Georges Castelain, maistre Guillaume le Munier, Moulinet, Alexis, le moyne de Lyre, lesquelz tous ensemble donnent le lieu de triumphe a maistre Alain Charestier, normant, lequel a passé en beau langage elegant et substancieux tous ses predecesseurs', I, p. 11.

[6] See Alain Chartier, *Les Oeuvres*, ed. Duchesne (Paris: Samuel Thiboust, 1617), pp. 732–3.

[7] See Martin le Franc (1999).   [8] See Pierre Michault (1978).

[9] Alain Chartier (1974) and (1977).

[10] The main biographical studies are Hoffman (1975) and Walravens (1971). Important full-length critical studies to date are Rouy, *L'Esthétique du traité moral d'après les oeuvres d'Alain Chartier* (Geneva: Droz, 1980) and Meyenberg (1992).

[11] Meyenberg (1992) compares the Latin and French prose works, though not the French verse.

[12] This division is Hoffman's (1975), pp. 43–121.

Latin and French prose. I show how Chartier's poetic capital (to use Bourdieu's terminology) is enhanced through a reading of his works in their specific cultural and material context.

In her technical study of Chartier's Latin and French prose, Regula Meyenberg identifies two levels of rhetoric within the text. The first level is an application of rhetorical procedures in the text, and the second a meta-rhetorical discourse operating across the *Dialogus familiaris amici et sodalis*, the *Quadrilogue invectif* and the *Livre de l'Esperance*. By her use of the term meta-rhetorical discourse, Meyenberg refers to Chartier's self-conscious evaluation of the rhetorical techniques he employs in his texts:

Il est clair que le discours métarhétorique, loin d'être innocent, remplit lui-même une fonction rhétorique à l'intérieur du texte, en lui imprimant une structure et en fortifiant ainsi l'intention communicative de conviction.[13]

Chartier reflects on and characterizes his own rhetorical programme from within his texts, a meta-discourse which Meyenberg suggests is particularly developed in his *Livre de l'Esperance*.[14] I propose an extension of this concept of the meta-rhetorical discourse in Chartier, relating it not only to the internal workings of the prose text, and of the French verse, but also to a conceptual discourse outlining Chartier's poetic and moral mission. I demonstrate how the rhetorical and ethical agenda Chartier proposes in his Latin and French prose works is carried out through the French verse by a close rereading of the verse through the Latin and French prose. Deep textual structures in Chartier's work are informed by what Thomas L. Reed has termed an 'aesthetics of irresolution',[15] common to much late medieval debate poetry, and through which Chartier is able to express an anti-courtly critique. I suggest, through a focus on notions of closure and open-endedness in Chartier's prose and verse works, that he uses a meta-rhetorical discourse to provide both a theory and a practice of debate that are intimately connected to his political, moral, and aesthetic agenda.

I focus initially on rhetorical strategies and discourse in Chartier's French verse debates: the *Belle Dame sans mercy*, the *Livre des Quatre*

[13] Meyenberg (1992), p. 133.
[14] Meyenberg (1992) remarks that the character of *Defiance* in Chartier's *Livre de l'Esperance* employs specifically logical reasoning, whereas *Foy* bases her superior reasoning on the authority of the Scriptures, thereby opposing 'l'éloquence divine et l'éloquence humaine', p. 142. This distinction is interesting in the light of my discussion of Chartier's rejection of logical systems of language in the *Dialogus*.
[15] Reed, *Middle English Debate Poetry and The Aesthetics of Irresolution* (Columbia/London: University of Missouri Press, 1990).

Dames, the *Debat des Deux Fortunés d'amours*, the *Debat de reveille matin*, and the *Debat du Herault, du Vassault, et du Villain* (also known as the *Débat patriotique*).[16] These French texts will be read through Chartier's Latin dialogue, the *Dialogus familiaris amici et sodalis*,[17] as well as the polemical letter addressed by Chartier to a close friend, *De vita curiali*.[18] (I am particularly concerned with these two Latin texts as they are the only ones to be collected with the verse in manuscript collections, a matter I shall discuss.) In the *Dialogus*, Chartier appears to advocate the rejection of a Scholastic logic concerned only with the mastery of language, in favour of the adoption of an engaged humanist rhetoric. It is this informed humanist rhetoric, for example, that will win the debate for the *Belle Dame* against her suitor, his empty dialectic having been exposed as a sham, a 'fol parler', v. 729. This opposition of the language of *mots* and of *choses*—of dialectic and rhetoric—will be situated in the context of Chartier's political and moral engagement, to reveal Chartier's conscious emptying of courtly convention and proverbial wisdom. Through an exploration of Chartier's use of a meta-rhetorical discourse linking his Latin and French prose and verse production, I shall show how Chartier self-consciously participates in two debating cultures: learned and literary, Latin and the vernacular. Chartier's moral and intellectual engagement in literary debate makes a unique contribution to the genre.

A central opposition in Chartier's *Dialogus* is that of *verba* and *res* —words and things—the former embodied by the Scholastic logic of the *Amicus* (Friend); the latter by the humanist rhetoric of the *Sodalis* (Fellow). This picks up Aristotle's opposition of the good and bad dialectician that I addressed in my first chapter in the context of subjectivity in the debate poem.[19] The good dialectician focuses on the logical progress of his argument on a linguistic level whereas the bad dialectician becomes personally involved in the argument and loses his objectivity. However, it is precisely this loss of objectivity that Chartier advocates in order to achieve emotional and not purely intellectual engagement with one's topic. Chartier's mastery of rhetoric,

---

[16] Alain Chartier (1974).   [17] Alain Chartier (1977), pp. 245–325.
[18] Alain Chartier (1977), pp. 345–75. Bourgain-Hemeryck believes the letter to be addressed not to Chartier's brother Guillaume, as recorded in certain of the manuscripts which preserve the French version of Chartier's Latin original, but simply to a close friend. Her argument is persuasive (pp. 67–76).
[19] Aristotle (1997). *Supra*: Chapter 1, p. 17.

remarked upon by Pierre Fabri,[20] marks a conscious move away from the superiority of logic, once thought to include both rhetoric and poetry.[21] The relationship between dialectic and rhetoric (both arts of the trivium with grammar) underwent a sea change in humanist circles in France during the early fifteenth century with the revival of classical rhetorical manuals such as Cicero's *De inventione*.[22] Boethius had demonstrated in his popular *De differentiis topicis* that dialectic and rhetoric were similar arts, both made up of topics (the units of argumentation), but insisted that rhetorical argumentation was subordinate to dialectic.[23] The fourth book of Boethius's *Topica*, which deals with rhetoric, was used separately from the other three as an authority on rhetoric in the Universities of Montpellier, Oxford, and Paris, until the Paris statutes were revised in the mid-thirteenth century to exclude rhetoric from the curriculum.[24] Aristotle, whose treatises on dialectic, *Topica* and *De sophisticis elenchis*,[25] were university set texts, held that rhetoric and dialectic were equal arts. Early humanist scholars such as Nicolas de Clamanges or Jean de Montreuil rejected both these positions to maintain that rhetoric, the art of eloquence, was superior to dialectic. Chartier clearly inherits these humanist values.[26] Rhetoric is regarded in medieval and classical manuals as a political science whose aim is to 'suader ou dissuader en sa matiere'.[27] Chartier's unique contribution to this political science was to practise it in verse form in the debate, rejecting purely formalistic approaches to the dialogued genre, and adopting a more engaged, subjective style. Chartier's amatory verse debates depart from and develop those of his predecessors in that his concealed or meta-discourse throughout is ideological, concealed with

[20] Pierre Fabri (1889), I, p. 11.

[21] Minnis and Scott explain that poetry, rhetoric, and sophistic were all considered subordinate parts of logic in the Scholastic movement. See Minnis and Scott, *Medieval Literary Theory and Criticism c.1100–c.1375: The Commentary Tradition* (Oxford: Clarendon Press, 1991), IX, pp. 373–438.

[22] See Cicero, *De inventione*; *De optimo genere oratorum*; *Topica*, ed. Goold (Cambridge, MA: Harvard University Press, 1993).

[23] See Leff, 'Boethius' *De differentiis topicis*, Book IV', in *Medieval Eloquence: Studies in the Theory and Practice of Medieval Rhetoric*, ed. Murphy (Berkeley/Los Angeles/London: University of California Press, 1978), 3–24.

[24] See my discussion of university teaching in Chapter 1, pp. 15–17.

[25] See Aristotle (1997).

[26] Minnis and Scott (1991) caution, however, against the simplification of the transition from Scholasticism to humanism, noting that in Italy, Scholasticism and humanism developed simultaneously, and that all humanist theory owes a large debt to Scholastic thought, pp. 8–11.

[27] Pierre Fabri (1889), I, p. 15.

an integument of the amatory. I suggest that Chartier is concerned
with the notion of language and discourse, and the search for a poetic
discourse that may more nearly approach that of revealed truth.

Pierre Fabri refers to Boccaccio's influential *De genealogia deorum*
(1350–74)[28] in the prologue to his art of rhetoric (1521). For Fabri, as
for Boccaccio, poetry is a science, and is related to though not subsumed
by rhetoric:

> Rethorique presuppose toultes les aultres sciences estre sceuez et especiallement
> poesie qui contient toultes les fleurs de elegante composition. Et a ceulx qui
> dient mal des poetes en les appellant menteurs, Bocasse au premier de sa
> *Genealogie des Dieux* leur en donne response. [29]

Boccaccio, like many of his humanist contemporaries, considered poetry
a similar art to theology, both of which proceed by allegory, having
an integumental structure beneath which lies a foundation of truth.[30]
He further emphasized the parallel aims of poetry and philosophy,
though he rejected Boethius's classification of poetry or rhetoric as a
system of syllogisms. Significantly, the final two books (XIV and XV)
of Boccaccio's *De genealogia* which propose a defence of poetry are
collected with Chartier's *De vita curiali* in a manuscript that also collects
two letters sent by Ambrogio dei Migli (the Milanese scholar involved
in epistolary debate with Jean de Montreuil) to Gontier Col,[31] and a
response on Col's behalf from Nicolas de Clamanges to Migli. Tours,
BM, 978, copied in 1435/6 shortly after Chartier's *De vita curiali* (1427)
was completed,[32] presents a material community whose dialogic ethos
is based on the art of humanist rhetoric, represented in both theory and
practice. This notion of the material community refers to the material
manifestation of the collaborative debating community, which I shall
discuss further in Chapter 4, part II.

---

[28] See Boccaccio, *Genealogie deorum gentilium libri*, ed. Romano, 2 vols. (Bari: G.
Laterza, 1951), and Minnis and Scott (1991), 373–438, especially pp. 420–38.

[29] Pierre Fabri (1889), I, p. 12.

[30] For a fuller discussion of poetry as allegory see Jung, 'Poetria: Zur Dichtungs-theorie
des ausgehenden Mittelalters in Frankreich', *Vox Romanica* 30–1 (1971), 44–64.

[31] *Supra*: Chapter 2.

[32] There is a date written on fol. 59[v], '*Actum Ambasie, die secunda februarii, anno
domini millesimo quadrigentesimo tricesimo quinto*' (copied at Amboise, on 2 February
1435/6). Fol. 64[v] has a signature by Jean Majoris, confessor of the future Louis XI,
who died at Saint-Martin de Tours, where the manuscript comes from. This same scribe
copied BnF, lat. 6091, which contains works by Sallust, and is dated at Amboise, 30
November 1434. I am grateful to the BnF for providing me with a microfilm of this
manuscript.

Chartier's *Dialogus* is dated by Bourgain-Hemeryck to 1426. She rejects a date of 1422, proposed by E. Droz in her edition of the *Quadrilogue invectif*,[33] citing historical referents to support her argument.[34] I tend to concur that this is a later work, on the basis of parity of expression with Chartier's other mature works, the *De vita curiali* (1427), the *Invectives* (1427–8),[35] or the *Livre de l'Esperance* (1428–30).[36] The codicological evidence also supports this later dating for the *Dialogus*: eight of the twenty-four manuscripts of this work place it in second position between the *Quadrilogue invectif* and the *Livre de l'Esperance*.[37] The *Dialogus*, Chartier's only Latin debate, was the most widely disseminated of his works in Latin, and is the only Latin work to be copied with his French works.[38] The twenty-four extant manuscript copies of the *Dialogus* include seven which also collect Chartier's *Quadrilogue invectif* and *Livre de l'Esperance*, and two others containing both these two prose works as well as Chartier's *Lay de paix*, and the *DDFA*, or *DHVV*.[39] It is significant that the *Dialogus* and *De vita curiali* (in its French translation) are collected with selected

---

[33] Alain Chartier (1950), pp. VII–IX. Droz gives a chronology of Chartier's works, though many of her conclusions have been challenged by the more recent editions of Chartier's works. See Alain Chartier (1974), pp. 28–42 (summary: p. 42), and Alain Chartier (1977), 3–82, especially pp. 81–2.

[34] Alain Chartier (1977), pp. 38–42.

[35] *Invectiva ad ingratum amicum* (invective against an ungrateful friend), and *Invectiva ad invidum et detractorem* (invective against one envious and disparaging). Alain Chartier (1977), pp. 337–40, 341–4.

[36] Even though I am concerned to show Chartier's engagement with contemporary events in France, I think it unwise to locate historical referents in the fictional text, or to suppose a transparent identification between 'acteur' and author. See Regalado's illuminating article on Villon: 'Effet de réel, effet du réel: representation and reference in Villon's *Testament*', *Yale French Studies* 70 (1986), 63–77. Regalado uses Barthes's term from 'Effet de réel', *Communications* 11 (1968), pp. 84–9. See also Taylor, Jane (2001).

[37] These are Paris, BnF, fr. 126; BnF, fr. 1123; BnF, fr. 1124; BnF, fr. 1128; Moulins, BM, 26; Cambridge, MA, Harvard Uni., Houghton Lib., typ. 92; London, BL, Cotton Julius E V; Vatican, Reg. lat. 1338. See Alain Chartier (1977), pp. 112–14.

[38] The original Latin text of the *Dialogus* appears in Berlin, Kupferstichkabinett, 78 C 7 (Hamilton 144), and in Paris, BnF, fr. 1128. The only known French version of Chartier's *Dialogus* is copied in Paris, BnF, fr. 1642, and is edited by Bourgain-Hemeryck alongside the Latin original; Alain Chartier (1977), pp. 120–23, 247–325. Bourgain-Hemeryck surmises from textual variants and paraphrasing of the Latin that the French was a translation, and was not written by Chartier. The *De vita curiali* was more widely read in its later French version, and this was often copied with Chartier's French works.

[39] The *Dialogus* is copied in Paris, BnF, fr. 1128 from fols. 36–47ᵛ, in between the *Quadrilogue invectif* and the *Livre de l'Esperance*, and before the *Lay de paix* and the *DDFA*. In Berlin, Kupferstichkabinett, 78 C 7 (Hamilton 144), it is copied from fols. 75–84, after the *Quadrilogue invectif* and the *Esperance*, and before the *Lay de paix* and the *DHVV* (the only copy of this last debate to survive).

French verse works by Chartier in the light of the meta-discourse I trace here through Chartier's production. Interestingly, the *DDFA*, to which Laidlaw gives an early date of 1412–13 against the previous critical consensus of 1425–6,[40] is collected in Paris, BnF, fr. 1128 with later works whose common theme is the devastation of a France torn apart by internal divisions and moral decline. I shall later suggest how this debate, through an intertextual dialogue with the Latin and French prose works, speaks on a meta-level of this same moral decline which is expressed through the use of deceptive language. For this reason too, I am inclined to suggest a later date for the *DDFA*, not least because it is placed after the *Belle Dame sans mercy* in fifteen out of twenty-three manuscripts. Laidlaw's argument for an earlier date pivots on the style of this debate which he classifies as a *dit*, like the *Livre des Quatre Dames* which he dates to 1415–16, and unlike 'late' debates such as the *Belle Dame sans mercy*, *Debat de reveille matin*, or *Excusacion*, in which Chartier employs octosyllabic eight-line stanzas rhyming ababbcbc. (The *DHVV* is also of this second type, but rhymes ababcdcd.) The two *dit*-style debates were probably written at roughly the same time, but I suggest that the *LQD* was not necessarily written in 1415–16, and may have been a later reflection on Agincourt.[41] Laidlaw's other arguments for an early date for the *DDFA* are perhaps less persuasive, derived from an identification of the narrator of the poem and the historical Chartier. He suggests that the narrator of this debate is inexperienced in matters of love: 'qui parle ainsi d'amours par ouïr dire', v. 1246, and consequently that the author must himself be a young Chartier. I, however, reject this identification of the narrator and author, and suggest rather that Chartier adopts a persona whose modesty and inexperience are merely a topos. The ambivalence of the relationship between narrator/acteur and author in late medieval poetry weakens the case for treating textual indicators as purely autobiographical. This ambivalence is the result of the interplay between 'vertical' (biographical) and 'horizontal' (textual/intertextual) functions of the poetic 'je' identified by Armstrong.[42] If chronology cannot be empirically established through textual indicators, then the positioning

---

[40] See Alain Chartier (1974), pp. 29–31.

[41] However, since publishing his edition of the *LQD*, Laidlaw has uncovered what he believes may be presentation copies of Chartier's *LQD* (Arsenal, 2940 and BL, Additional 21247). He is currently investigating the possibility that these MSS were copied in Paris before the Burgundian assault in 1418.

[42] See Armstrong (2000), pp. 211–13.

Plate 1. Alain Chartier, *Dialogus familiaris amici et sodalis* (the *Amicus* and *Sodalis* meet to debate the plight of France in front of an audience)

Paris, Bibliothèque nationale de France, fr. 126, fol. 210ʳ

of texts within manuscript or printed anthologies, in other words their order of reception, becomes key.[43]

In Chartier's *Dialogus*, the quest for truth takes the form of a dialogue between two companions known for the space of their debate as the *Amicus* (friend) and the *Sodalis* (fellow).[44] The *Amicus* is the first to speak, and asks why the *Sodalis* seems so troubled. The *Sodalis* explains that it is the wretched state of war-torn France that distresses him. The discussion unfolds as the *Amicus* questions the *Sodalis* about the reasons behind the current situation, and possible solutions. The *Sodalis* maintains that it is the morals of the French that are at fault: all men

[43] According to the codicological evidence, the *DDFA* is more likely to appear with the late debates *BDSM* (twenty-three times) and *DRM* (twenty-one times) than with the *LQD* (fifteen times). The *LQD* appears in thirty-two manuscript versions, while the *BDSM* appears in forty-four, the *DRM* in thirty-seven. On the topic of sequences in anthologies see Regalado, 'Gathering the Works: The 'Oeuvres de Villon' and the Intergeneric Passage of the Medieval French Lyric into Single-Author Collections', *L'Esprit Créateur* 33 (1993), 87–100.

[44] I call the *Dialogus* a 'debate' here, as although it is not mediated by a narrator figure, it is conceived of as an open debate in front of an audience. See plate 1.

have become greedy for personal gain and power, and reject the notion of common good. God will abandon the French, the *Sodalis* predicts, because they remain unrepentant. If each man pulled towards the common good for the health of the whole *corps politique* then individual good would result, and ultimately peace. The *Amicus* remains optimistic for the future, but the *Sodalis* is sceptical, leaving the only hope of peace with God at the end of their debate.

The *Sodalis* sums up the fundamental conflict between his reasoning and that of the *Amicus* when he announces 'verba sequeris, ego rem aspicio'.[45] The *Sodalis* argues that he has often been deceived by words, and now seeks the signified rather than the signifier: 'memini et scio quociens nomen illud pacis me fefellit'.[46] The Socratic figure of the *Sodalis* disputes and deflects what he sees as the empty arguments of the *Amicus*. Chartier, through the *Sodalis*, empties Scholastic logic of purpose since it does not engage with a particular context, and advocates instead a humanist rhetoric that will take account of a given context. Context in this case refers to the material circumstances of war-torn France. Rhetoric, making use of a technique of hypothesis (questions relating to particular circumstances, e.g. is *this* war a bad thing?), is shown by Chartier to be superior to dialectic which proceeds by thesis (general questions with no reference to particular circumstances, e.g. is war a bad thing?).[47] Regula Meyenberg demonstrates how, via a meta-rhetorical discourse operating through the arguments of the *Sodalis* and *Amicus*, Chartier rejects the *Amicus*'s logical reasoning and the traditional Scholastic form of the *disputatio*, in favour of reasoning based on classical rhetoric.[48] Both the *Sodalis* and the *Amicus* refer to their exchange as a 'disputacio', but each is frustrated by the techniques employed by the other. The *Dialogus* becomes a 'dialogue de sourds',[49] both parties arguing at cross-purposes. Rhetoric battles dialectic and the desired *sententia* is never delivered:

Amicus: 'Quid igitur expectamus? Quis nos manet exitus? Uno tu verbo
             argumenta conclude.'

---

[45] 'You follow words, and I look at the thing itself', *Dialogus*, 134, p. 320. All references are to Alain Chartier (1977).

[46] 'I remember and know how many times the *name* of peace has deceived me', *Dialogus*, 134, p. 320.

[47] For a comprehensive discussion of the evolution of rhetoric from the classical to the medieval period see Murphy (1978), and particularly Leff (1978).

[48] See Meyenberg (1992), pp. 139–41.

[49] See *supra*: Chapter 2, p. 65.

Sodalis: 'In Deum reffero sentenciam; quod ab eo decretum est, fiat.'[50]

The undelivered or delayed verdict is a late medieval topos, as Armstrong has argued.[51] This delayed closure is a tool in Chartier's rhetorical arsenal. Through a use of what I term his 'vocabulary of closure', Chartier ironizes and empties courtly convention, as I shall discuss later.

Chartier again explores the notion of empty verbosity in his polemical Latin letter *De vita curiali* (probably a late work of around 1427).[52] This text enjoyed widespread popularity in the fifteenth century, as evidenced by the many surviving manuscript witnesses of both the Latin original and the Middle French translation, often erroneously attributed to Chartier.[53] The *De vita curiali* takes the form of a letter written by one experienced in the ways of the court to a close friend who aspires to a life at court. The writer urges his friend to reconsider this ambition, and describes the greed and corruption rife in court society in which he himself is implicated. He combines this invective, the *taedium curiae*, with the topos of the praise of the quiet life his friend is currently enjoying. Chartier emphasizes throughout the contrast between the subservience of the courtier and the freedom of the person who rejects a life at court. The enslavement of the courtier is characterized by the constraints of the discourse to which he subscribes. The corrupt courtier can no longer express himself with freedom, but is restricted to an empty language that touches nothing beyond itself; it is an enclosed and self-perpetuating system:

Et ecce nos curiales effrontes officiorum non jura, sed nomina sequimur! Verbales sumus et voces, non res recipimus.[54]

---

[50]   *Friend*: 'What therefore should we hope for? What way out is left to us? Now finish the argument with a word or two.' *Fellow*: 'I leave the judgement to God; may his will be done', *Dialogus*, 138, p. 322.

[51]   Armstrong (1997b), pp. 12–14, and Cayley (2003).

[52]   Bourgain-Hemeryck does not find any evidence for the dating of this piece other than its maturity of vision and expression, Alain Chartier (1977), p. 69. It is likely that the *De vita curiali* was written after the *Dialogus*, and possibly before the two *Invectives* (late 1427). I agree that this is a late work, and illustrate here the parity of expression and common ground it shares with the *Dialogus*.

[53]   There was a Middle French translation of the Latin original, the *Curial*, which circulated widely in the second half of the fifteenth century and survives in twenty-three MSS and ten printed editions. The *Curial* was translated back into Latin by Robert Gaguin in 1473 and into Middle English by William Caxton in 1484. See Alain Chartier (1977), pp. 67–76, 133–52.

[54]   'We courtiers, however, shamelessly pursue not the duties of offices but their titles! We are wordy and deal in words, not things', *De vita curiali*, 37, p. 362.

Chartier's position here echoes that espoused in the *Dialogus*. From the
perspective of a courtier struggling within the confines of a corrupt court
community he rejects, Chartier is forced to assimilate himself to the first
person plural 'nos curiales'. His self-awareness is what frees him from the
hypocrisy around him, though he is ultimately trapped by membership
of this group.[55] Chartier was almost certainly influenced in both his use
of the classical anti-curial topos and his polemic on the corrupt state of
the nation by the writings of humanist contemporaries such as Nicolas de
Clamanges, Jean de Montreuil, Jean Muret, and Jean Gerson, following
an established French literary tradition of anti-curial satire.[56] These
humanist scholars adopted debating positions, frequently exaggerating
the polemical aspect of their work.[57] Chartier's debating position,
however, as I shall demonstrate, seems to have been more a reflection
of the author's own ethical position; he becomes the 'restaurateur de
l'écriture engagée', as Mühlethaler and Blanchard put it.[58]

Some interesting patterns emerge from the manuscript tradition of the
French version of the *De vita curiali*, and particularly where it is collected
with Chartier's French verse. There are twenty-three recorded copies of
the French translation, as opposed to only eleven of the Latin original.[59]

[55] See also Eustache Deschamps's anti-curial lyrics, including ballade CCVIII (whose
refrain reflects the court poet/satirist's dilemma, 'un pié hors, l'autre ens'), in *Oeuvres
complètes*, ed. Gaston Raynaud and le Marquis de Queux de Saint-Hilaire, 11 vols. (Paris:
Firmin-Didot, 1878–1903). For a discussion of Deschamps and his anti-curial satire in
the context of Chartier, see Blanchard and Mühlethaler (2002), ch. III, pp. 69–78.

[56] Meyenberg and Pons have observed conceptual similarities between Clamanges's
De lapsu et reparacione justicie (1420), Jean de Montreuil's *Traité contre les Anglais*
(1406–17), Jean Muret's *De contemptu mortis* (1386–8), Jean Gerson's *Deploracio
super civitatem aut regionem* (1418), and Chartier's *Quadrilogue invectif* (1422), *Ad
detestacionem belli gallici et suasionem pacis* (c.1423), *Dialogus* (1426–7), and *Livre de
l'Esperance* (1429–30). See Meyenberg (1992), pp. 32–6 and Pons, 'Latin et français
au XVᵉ siècle: le témoignage des traités de propagande', in *Actes du Vᵉ Colloque
International sur le Moyen Français, 6–8 mai 1985*, vol. 2 (Milan, 1986), 67–81.
See *supra*: Chapter 2, pp. 58–63. For the French literary tradition see Smith, *The
Anti-Courtier Trend in Sixteenth-Century French Literature* (Geneva: Droz, 1966), and
Blanchard and Mühlethaler (2002), ch. III.

[57] These scholars had previously been involved in the *Querelle de la Rose*. See Chapter 2
for a discussion of debating positions in epistolary exchanges within chancery circles at
Paris and Avignon, especially pp. 53–6.

[58] See Blanchard and Mühlethaler (2002), p. 37.

[59] Bourgain-Hemeryck records twenty-one copies, but does not include two included
by Laidlaw in his edition: Copenhagen, Royal Library, Ny Kgl. Saml. 1768. 2° (formerly
Ashburnham Place, Barrois 355), and London, Clumber Sale (Sotheby's, 6. XII. 1937),
941 (untraceable); see Alain Chartier (1977), pp. 140–52, and Alain Chartier (1974),
pp. 126–32. Laidlaw does not record the copy of the *Curial* in Reims, BM, 918, listed
by Bourgain-Hemeryck, p. 141.

Twelve versions of the French *Curial* are copied into manuscripts that also contain Chartier's French verse. These include Paris, BnF, fr. 1642, a manuscript in which a French translation of the *Dialogus* makes its sole appearance in collections of Chartier's French verse, and Brussels, BR, 21521–31, in which the *Curial* is collected with Chartier's *Breviaire des nobles*, as well as works by George Chastelain and Jean Molinet. This second manuscript is thought by Bourgain-Hemeryck to have a Burgundian source, and is relatively late (after 1465).[60] Nine of the twelve manuscripts collect the *Curial* with the *Breviaire des nobles* and two place them in juxtaposition.[61] The *Breviaire des nobles*, a series of thirteen ballades devoted to the twelve virtues that define 'noblesse', has the largest number of manuscript witnesses of any of Chartier's texts, appearing in fifty-four copies.[62] Laidlaw finds it impossible to date this text accurately, given the 'theoretical and general' nature of the poem, but puts it somewhere between 1416 and 1426. I suggest that the *Breviaire des nobles* provides a perfect foil for the *De vita curiali*, and Chartier's other polemical Latin works, in its portrayal of the very qualities whose loss is bemoaned in contemporary French court society. In the *Breviaire*, language and action are intimately linked:

> Voz faiz aux moz accordez.
> Se noblement voulez vivre,
> Vostre mestier recordez,
> Nobles hommes, en ce livre.

vv. 451–4

The *Breviaire* provides both the conceptual 'mirouer' where one 'se doit mirer' (v. 90), and a material mirror image of the vices rife at court in the *De vita curiali* through its anthologization in manuscripts with this polemical letter. The *De vita curiali* forges similar dialogic links with an anonymous text, *L'Abuzé en court*,[63] completed in 1473 and probably directly inspired by the anti-courtly polemic of Chartier's text. This prosimetrum text tells of the narrator's encounter with the sorry *Abuzé*,

---

[60] See Alain Chartier (1977), pp. 146–8.

[61] These are Paris, BnF, fr. 924 (*Breviaire*: fols. 262ʳ–71ᵛ; *Curial*: fols. 272ʳ–82ᵛ), and London, Clumber Sale, 941 (*Curial*: fol. 41; *Breviaire*). Laidlaw notes that Bure lists the *Breviaire* as item 5 in the London manuscript though it is not mentioned in the sale catalogue. See *Catalogue des livres de la bibliothèque de feu M. le duc de la Vallière, première partie*, vol. 2 (Paris: de Bure, 1783).

[62] See Alain Chartier (1974), pp. 393–409 also Sion, Supersaxo 97ᵇⁱˢ.

[63] See *L'Abuzé en court*, ed. Dubuis (Geneva: Droz, 1973). Dubuis discusses the possible authorship of this work, often wrongly attributed to René d'Anjou, xxiv–xxxi.

whose years have been wasted in dissolution at court, deceived by the allegorical figures of *Abus, Fol Cuider, Folle Bobance*, and *Madame la Court* herself. *L'Abuzé en court* takes the form of a dialogue between the narrator and the *Abuzé*, into which the *Abuzé* inserts remembered dialogues with his *maistre d'escole* and the various allegorical figures of the court. The *Abuzé*'s story brings the narrator, who himself has spent time at court, to a self-realization:

Et quant je vous ay oy de vous mesmes nommer le povre homme abusé en court, ung doubte m'est entré subitement au cueur, comme si [en] ce cas me touchoit en partie cestuy nom, p. 10.

Like the writer of the *De vita curiali*, the *Abuzé* is disabused of the illusions he once entertained of life at court and warns his interlocutor of the dangers inherent in such a course. The narrator's sudden pang of awareness here suggests that he too has deserved the name of *Abuzé*, only now realizing the full extent of his deception. Paris, BnF, fr. 25293, one of the nine manuscript witnesses to *L'Abuzé en court*, also collects two texts by Chartier: the *Complainte contre la mort* and the *Lay de paix*. Dialogic links are formed between these texts through their anthologization in the material space of play afforded by the codex. Chartier's dissatisfaction with the corruption at court comes across strongly in his *Lay de paix* (pre 1426), in which he sues for peace amid the confusion of war.[64] Chartier associates language and action here as in the *Breviaire*, urging the people to lay aside the 'faulx debaz et faiz malicïeux', v. 13, that are destroying their well-being.[65]

Through his French verse, Chartier attempts to demonstrate the notion of self-awareness and freedom from within the confines of a courtly society. From a close reading of these vernacular poems, a layered meta-discourse can be observed, informed by the Latin works. Chartier writes not only about writing, but also about writing from within confines: textual confines reflect societal boundaries. Chartier's ranks of narrators and debaters are made up both of those who press

---

[64] Laidlaw suggests that the *Lay de paix* may have been written before an embassy that Chartier undertook to the Duke of Burgundy in April 1426, and possibly much earlier than this; *Alain Chartier* (1974). He bases his assumptions on the fact that four manuscript rubrics link this poem with the Duke of Burgundy, and surmises that it was intended for despatch to him; pp. 11, 37. A date somewhere in the 1420s is supported by conceptual and textual similarities between the *Lay de paix* and the *Breviaire des nobles*.

[65] 'Debat' is the technical word for a written debate, as well as encompassing oral dispute. See Godefroy.

for freedom and of those who endorse closure. The debate itself is an irresolvable and unresolved expression of dissent and conflict among the members of one community. The model of the collaborative debating community that I postulate as a dynamic social entity, and which pivots on Bourdieu's principle of collusion within competition,[66] is analogous to Chartier's more negative model of the court in his *De vita curiali*:

Vis modernam curiam descriptiva diffinicione designare: est virorum conventus, qui ad se invicem decipiendum, boni communis simulacione, communicant.[67]

Chartier here compares the court to an assembly of men (*virorum conventus*), whose interdependence is based on a common principle of deceit; their social coherence paradoxically derived from infighting and competition. This deceit may be seen as a linguistic one in the context of debate: a 'fol parler', designed to convince one's opponent, to win an argument, but essentially hollow and insincere. Through correspondences with the *De vita curiali* and the *Dialogus,* the platitudinous arguments of Chartier's French actors are exposed as an empty sham.

In the *Debat des Deux Fortunés d'amours*, the sorrowful narrator relates a debate that takes place between two knights at a gathering in a *chastel*. After dinner, the men and ladies ask each other questions of love casuistry, calqued on the *demande d'amour* model (see Chapter 1). One lady, particularly skilled in the art of debate, poses a dilemma. She asks some of the company whether love brings more pain or pleasure. All refuse to speak, except one, 'en bon point, sain, alegre et joyeulx', v. 212, who comes forward first to give his opinion. This *gras chevalier* speaks to support the argument that 'en amours a plus joye que douleur', v. 670. He rhapsodizes at length on the lover's pursuit of his lady, explaining how he must strive to ingratiate himself with 'ceulx qui sont | D'elle prouchains', v. 441–2. By this method, the lover may attain his goal; his targets are unaware of the real reason for his sudden friendship, and introduce him into the lady's circle:

Ceulx le loent devant elle en appert
Et le blasonnent,

[66] See Chapter 2, p. 56 for a discussion of collusion within competition, also Bourdieu, *Leçon sur la leçon* (Paris: Editions de Minuit, 1982), pp. 41–6 and Bourdieu and Wacquant (1996), p. 98.

[67] 'Let me describe the modern court for you with an exact definition: it is an assembly of men who come together under the pretence of common good in order to deceive one another in turn', *De vita curiali*, 46, p. 368.

> Et de ses faiz lui parlent et raisonnent,
> Et sans savoir a quoy leurs mos s'adonnent
> Devers elle bonne entree lui donnent.
>
> vv. 452–6

Chartier insists upon the ignorance and trust of those the lover is duping: 'Qui pas n'entendent | A quelle fin toutes ses euvres tendent', vv. 461–2. On the surface, the lover is merely using others benignly to reach his lady: the end justifies the means. However, if one compares similar passages from the *De vita curiali*, the lover's deception takes on a sinister character. Chartier cautions his addressee that if he is sought out and greeted by another at court, it is not necessarily a mark of respect:

Non enim virtutes tuas, sed suas commoditates prospicit, ut quod a te querit blande subripiat.[68]

The suspicion with which kindness at court must be regarded is a topos elaborated by Jean de Montreuil in Epistle 38 (*Iamque fere*), addressed to his colleagues Gontier Col and Pierre Manhac. This letter was sent to accompany a pamphlet against the *aulici* (court officials).[69] Montreuil and Chartier both draw on the Roman comic dramatist Terence's portrayal of the figure of the court parasite. The premise for Montreuil's letter is a dream in which the dramatist Terence appears to warn him of the *aulici*, and encourages him to study his (Terence's) comedies. Through the voice of Terence, Montreuil describes how these *aulici* approach and ingratiate themselves with those in power in order to gain influence, attracted as Chartier says not by their 'virtutes' but for the 'commoditates' they might acquire. The *aulici* drop their friends as soon as they fall out of favour, and are no longer of use:

Cum tuum primum exhaustum officium aut beneficium extiterit, nullatenus te agnoscet. Quod si te adversa invadat fortuna et sibi casu obviabis, scito nil verius esse, tibi protinus tergum vertet et posteriora monstrabit.[70]

This theme is again picked up by Chartier in his *Invectiva ad ingratum amicum* (invective against an ungrateful friend), probably written

---

[68] 'It is not on account of your virtues, but with an eye to his own advantage and what he can stealthily seek and take from you', *De vita curiali*, 33, p. 360.

[69] For the letter see Jean de Montreuil (1963): I, pp. 53–63. For details of the contents see Jean de Montreuil (1986): IV, pp. 109–13.

[70] 'Once he (the parasite) has used up and exhausted your kindness and favour, he no longer acknowledges you in any way. For if bad fortune assails you and you meet with disaster, know that nothing is truer than that he will immediately turn and show you his back', Epistle 38, Jean de Montreuil (1963): I, ll. 64–6, p. 55.

during the same period as the *De vita curiali*.[71] Here Chartier addresses
a friend whom he helped when destitute, and who, now wealthy, has
turned his back on his benefactor. Jean de Montreuil's invective against
the Milanese scholar Ambrogio dei Migli is similarly calqued on this
classical model.[72]

The *Invectiva ad ingratum* is found in eighteen manuscript copies,
and is usually copied before Chartier's *Invectiva ad invidum et detractorem* (invective against one envious and disparaging). This second of
Chartier's *Invectives* chastises an 'emulator' (imitator) for mocking
Chartier's pursuit of philosophy and his poverty. Eight of the eleven
appearances of the Latin *De vita curiali* occur in manuscripts with one
or both of the *Invectives* and in seven of these eight manuscripts the *Dialogus* also appears, reinforcing intertextual dialogue by placing the texts
in adjacent material space. These dialogic links within the manuscripts
of Chartier's Latin works extend to encompass the humanist writings of
such scholars as Coluccio Salutati, Petrarch, or Nicolas de Clamanges,
as well as classical pieces by Sallust, Seneca, and Cicero among others.[73]
The anthologization of these groups of texts in manuscripts of Chartier's
Latin texts suggests Chartier's debt to humanist thought and style. The
reception of these combinations of texts encourages us to read Chartier
as part of this early collaborative community. It is by setting him against
this humanist context that we are able to see how Chartier is innovative,
and how he moves away from the detachment of the more intellectu-
alized debating positions adopted by earlier scholars. Chartier engages
directly in political and ethical matters through his reworking of courtly
poetry and discourse. Courtly language and settings are challenged from
the inside by Chartier's protagonists and found wanting.

---

[71] See Alain Chartier (1977), pp. 65–7, pp. 337–40.

[72] See Chapter 2, and particularly Montreuil's Epistle 106 (*De intimatione*), Jean de
Montreuil (1963): I, ll. 113–17, p. 151.

[73] Paris, BnF, lat. 3127 contains, among other texts, the two *Invectives* as well as a
collection of Nicolas de Clamanges's letters to Jean de Montreuil: Alain Chartier (1977),
p. 124; Paris, BnF, lat. 10922 includes the *Invectiva ad ingratum*, the *De vita curiali*, the
Dialogus, as well as poetry by Nicolas de Clamanges and Seneca's *De remediis fortuitorum*:
Alain Chartier (1977), pp. 125–6; Einsiedeln, Monastery Library, 367 includes the two
Invectives, a short and imperfect extract from the *De vita curiali*, works by Petrarch, the
Invectives of Sallust and Cicero, and the *Exclamacio ad Lucreciam* and its response by
Coluccio Salutati: Alain Chartier (1977), pp. 127–8; Giessen, Universitätsbibliothek,
1256 includes the two *Invectives*, Coluccio Salutati's *Exclamacio ad Lucreciam*, and
Sallust's and Cicero's *Invectives*: Alain Chartier (1977), p. 128. For other examples see
Alain Chartier (1977), Chapter VI: *Oeuvres jointes a celles de Chartier dans les manuscrits*,
pp. 155–61.

The court parasites attacked by Montreuil and Chartier via Terence are duplicitous in language as well as action: 'ore suo benedicebant, corde maledicebant', as Montreuil affirms.[74] In the *Invectiva ad invidum*, Chartier urges his addressee to confront him with the accusations he has been storing up, in an echo of Jean de Montreuil's invective against Ambrogio dei Migli: 'si intra te verba continere non potes, efflue, evome quod intus concepisti venenum'.[75] One should not only be wary of duplicity in the speech of others, but should guard one's own words, for fear that they may be misappropriated and used against one, while furthering someone else's agenda:

Nutrit enim curia viros qui de ore hominum aut fraude sermones extorqueant aut simulacione expectent quod in caput loquentis retorqueant, et sibi ex alterius detrimento graciam concilient. Si officio fungaris, ad litem te prepares.[76]

The duality of language is particularly suited to the debating forum, in which speakers use the arguments of others against them, reversing the import of their words. Chartier exploits this duality in his French verse debates, exposing the unstable nature of courtly discourse through the contradictory speeches of his protagonists. The 'gracïeuse chace', v. 636, which the *gras chevalier* advocates in the *Debat des Deux Fortunés d'amours*, is subsequently undermined by the *maigre chevalier*'s account. A *chevalier*, 'pensif et pale', v. 679, comes forward after the *gras chevalier* has finished his argument and contradicts him. This sorry figure argues that love brings more pain than pleasure. The *maigre chevalier* warns of the dangers of trusting those who may turn out to be 'mesdisans', v. 1003, and betray their companions. In this game, he counters, one must be 'en doubte des amis', v. 1012. The *maigre chevalier*'s account is of a 'chace dont le veneur est pris', v. 1060. His use of language often destabilizes and reverses the meaning of the *gras chevalier*'s words. The 'tonnelles a courtine de fueilles', v. 656, that the *gras chevalier* identifies among the 'haulx instrumens' of *amours*, are later evoked by the *maigre chevalier* in a simile for the snares of *amours*:

---

[74] 'While they were praising with their mouths, they were cursing in their hearts', Epistle 38, Jean de Montreuil (1963): I, l. 62, p. 55.

[75] 'If you cannot contain your words inside, spit them out, vomit up the venom you have brewed inside', Alain Chartier (1977), *Invectiva ad invidum*, 4, p. 341. See *supra*: Chapter 2, pp. 66–7 for a discussion of serpent imagery in humanist invective.

[76] 'For the court nurtures those who seek to extract words from men's mouths either by deceit or dissemblance so that they may then turn them against their speaker, and gain favour for themselves at another's expense. If you hold an office, you should prepare yourself for a fight', *De vita curiali*, 41, pp. 364–6.

> Ainsi labeurent
> Comme perdrix qu'en la tonnelle queurent:
> Jouans y vont et tristes y demeurent.

vv. 787–9

Though the debate remains unresolved within the bounds of the text (the conclusion is deferred until the chosen judge, Jean de Grailli, comte de Foix, returns from battle), correspondences identified above with Chartier's *De vita curiali* support the arguments of the *maigre chevalier* who asserts that 'en amours a plus de mal que de bien', v. 1110. The *maigre chevalier*, like Chartier's *Belle Dame*, is the last to speak in the debate, adding his 'dupplique' to the *gras chevalier*'s 'replique'.[77] The force with which the *maigre chevalier* delivers his final brief assault on his interlocutor's 'propos' suggests sympathy on the part of the narrator:

> Quelque chose que dïez au seurplus,
> Dueil est tousjours la fin, l'issue et l'us
> Ou tous les faiz amoureux sont conclus;
> Et plus n'en di.

vv. 1152–5[78]

The narrator, 'un simple clerc que l'en appelle Alain', v. 1245, asks others who may know better to complete his debate, 'le demourant supplie', v. 1242, using a familiar modesty topos.[79] I suggest that the unwritten 'demourant' exists in intertextual form, linking Chartier's French debate with his Latin epistle (*De vita curiali*), the *Invectives*, and the *Dialogus*, and so operates a destabilizing of the courtly convention and language of the 'deduit amoureux'. Parallels can thus be drawn between the *Amicus*'s hollow Scholastic logic in the *Dialogus*, the deceptive political language of the court in *De vita curiali*, and the snares of a courtly love discourse in Chartier's French debates. Chartier discusses the nature of language

---

[77] These terms are often encountered in legal contexts, and correspond to two parts of a trial sequence. See *supra*: Chapter 1, p. 26. Pierre Michault and the author of the *Arrêts d'amours* both make use of the terms later in the fifteenth century. See the *Arrêts d'amours* (1951), and Pierre Michault (1978).

[78] This insistence on the opposition and collusion between 'dit' and 'fait' is significant for my examination of *verba* and *res* (words and things/deeds).

[79] The narrator's professed inexperience in love does not indicate necessarily that this is an early work by Chartier as mentioned before. It is rather a literary topos, and designed to encourage further speculation about the debate, thereby soliciting further responses. See Alain Chartier (1974), p. 30. Christine de Pizan also uses the term 'demourant' as a means of suspending judgement in her *Livre des trois jugemens*: 'Le demourant commet a parfiner | A vo bon sens', vv. 1521–2. See Christine de Pizan (1998b).

through his texts in Latin and in French, advocating a humanist rhetoric free from the false constraints and conventions of a purely intellectual logical language, or those of courtly love discourse. The triumph of this new engaged rhetoric is heralded in Chartier's *Belle Dame sans mercy*. I also suggest that Chartier takes position in the wider *Querelle des femmes* through his treatment of the *Belle Dame* and her suitor.

For Chartier, the corruption of language is inextricably bound up with the ailing State, which the *Sodalis* portrays as a floundering ship in his *Dialogus*:

Sane equidem nauffrage navi predictis destitute nostra res publica par est. Prudenciam, que gubernaculis modum ponit et medium ductu consiliat, nec intus habemus et extra contempnimus audiendam.[80]

The sea and navigation provide a set of classical metaphors for the government of a State and the corruption of court society that Chartier also employs in his *De vita curiali* and *Quadrilogue invectif.*[81] Pauline Smith suggests that the metaphor of shipwreck may have originated with Lucian's *De mercede conductis potentium familiaribus*, though she acknowledges that Chartier and his contemporaries would not have had access to a Latin translation of the Greek original.[82] However, Cicero's rhetorical treatise, the *De inventione*,[83] was extremely influential in the development of medieval rhetoric, and was widely quoted as an authority by the authors of medieval and Renaissance manuals on style. In the *De inventione*, Cicero adopts the metaphor of the ailing ship of State governed by those armed with eloquence, but lacking in a sense of moral duty:

Hinc nimirum non iniuria, cum ad gubernacula rei publicae temerarii atque audaces hominess accesserant, maxima ac miserrima naufragia fiebant.[84]

It is probable that Cicero rather than Lucian served as a model for Chartier in his *Dialogus, De vita curiali*, and the *Quadrilogue invectif.* The

---

[80] 'Indeed our state is exactly like the shipwrecked boat I mentioned before. We do not possess prudence, which is the means of steering and commanding it, and we reject advice from outside', *Dialogus*, 37, p. 268.

[81] The image of the floundering ship of State recurs in the *Quadrilogue invectif*: Alain Chartier (1950), ll. 10–11, p. 13.

[82] See Smith (1966), p. 39, n. 3.

[83] See Cicero, *De inventione*; *De optime genere oratorum*; *Topica*, ed. Goold and trans. Hubbell (Cambridge, MA: Harvard University Press, 1993), pp. 2–346.

[84] 'Therefore it was not undeserved, I am sure, that whenever rash and audacious men had taken the helm of the ship of State great and disastrous wrecks occurred', Cicero (1993), *De inventione*, ch. 4, p. 8.

early humanist scholars Nicolas de Clamanges and Jean de Montreuil who elaborate on the classical topos of the *taedium curiae* (weariness with the court) in their epistolary collections would have had a more immediate influence on Chartier. In a letter addressed to Montreuil, Clamanges develops the metaphor of the court as a treacherous sea whose obstacles must be wisely negotiated, anticipating Chartier's image of the shipwrecked courtier in the *De vita curiali*:

Desine me a quieta littoris statione semel appraehensa rursus in Syrtes & scopulos evocare. Nam si mare magnum & spaciosum (Sacris attestantibus eloquiis) est mundus iste, ubi tantis inhorrescit procellis, tantis flatibus agitatur, tantis fluctibus intumescit, tam saevis exaestuat turbinibus, sicut in Curiis Principum ubi inter Scillam mordacem invidiae canibus ut aiunt succinctam, & rapacem atque insatiabilem avaritiis Charybdim navigare oportet, ubi velut in solio proprio, imperat superbia, regnat ambitio, furit crudelitas, languescit desidia, defluit luxuria, carpit detractio, tradit proditio, ubi nulla pax animi, nulla quies conscientiae, nulla fides, nulla charitas, nulla securitas, ubi blanda assentatio, amicitiae simulatio, iniuriae dissimulatio, ubi latentia odia, fictis verbis, serena fronte, sed fallacies obsequii mendositate adoperta.[85]

Smith argues that Chartier does not associate the corrupt court with the state of the nation,[86] and that he simply adopts a topos developed by his humanist predecessors. However, correspondences between the metaphor of the floundering ship of State Chartier uses both in his *Quadrilogue* and *Dialogus*, and the metaphor of the sea as a corrupt court in the *De vita curiali*, as well as Chartier's debt to Cicero, suggest otherwise:

[85] 'Stop calling me away from the calm shelter of the shore (now I've reached it) back onto the Syrtes and the crags. For if the great wide sea is the world (as the eloquent Scriptures attest), where it bristles with such great gusts, with such great winds is it disturbed, with such great waves it swells, with such savage whirlpools does it seethe, so it is in the Courts of Princes where one must navigate between the gnashing Scylla surrounded as they say by envious parasites, and the rapacious and insatiable Charybdis surrounded by greedy men, where even as on our own territory, pride dictates, ambition rules, cruelty raves, idleness makes us languid, luxury thrives, slander blackens, treachery betrays, where there is no peace of mind, no rest for the conscience, no faith, no charity, no safety, where seductive flattery, pretence of friendship and disguising of injury are found, where hatred hides with false words and a smooth brow, but it is covered up by the compliant deception of the liar.' I am very grateful to Francesca Galligan for her help with this translation. The Latin is transcribed from the early printed edition of Clamanges's collected works. Nicolas de Clamanges, *Opera Omnia*, ed. Lydius (Leyden: Ludovicum Elzevirium & Henr. Laurentium, 1613), p. 58. There is a more recent edition of Lydius's Clamanges (Farnborough: Gregg Press, 1967).

[86] See Smith (1966), p. 40. Court and nation are juxtaposed in Chartier's *Livre de l'Esperance*. The allegorical figure of *Indignation*, appearing to the narrator, delivers a sharp satire on life at court, before her colleague *Defiance* sets out the sorry state of the French nation: see Alain Chartier (1989), pp. 7–17.

Fugite, viri fortes, state procul, si vos bene beateque vixisse delectat et, velut in littore tuti, nos sponte naufragantes despicite.[87]

The flourishing of the State is linked in Chartier's *Dialogus* to the trans-latio studii, whereby eloquence and good governance passed through Greece and Rome to France. Now that Fortune's wheel has turned, both State and language have become corrupt:

Eheu, ex rerum et morum mucacione fortune favorem a nobis evulsum agnoscimus. Parvos etenim corpore homines, sed animo minores, intelligencia terrestres, verbis molles et opera fragiles enutrimus.[88]

It is the *Amicus* who makes the explicit connection between language and morals in the *Dialogus*: 'ut homines vivunt, sic loquuntur', he con-cludes.[89] So falseness in language is assimilated in Chartier to corruption in political and moral life. Here Chartier draws on the classical topos of language as a mirror of morals, found in Cicero (particularly the *De inventione*), and Seneca, and transmitted later by arts of rhetoric such as Fabri's *Le Grand et Vrai Art de pleine rhétorique* (1521).[90] In letter CXIV to Lucilius, Seneca refers to a Greek source for the topos.[91] The flawed logic of the *Amicus* and the empty courtly discourse of the *Belle Dame*'s suitor reflect insincerity and moral turpitude in society. The *Sodalis* suggests in Chartier's *Dialogus* that the vessel of the State is lost because of the decline in morals among the French, and that it is a greed for power that has corrupted them. The *Amicus*'s arguments

---

[87] 'Flee, courageous men, stand far away, if you want to live well and happily and, just like men safe on the shore, watch us as we voluntarily drown', *De vita curiali*, 49, p. 370.

[88] 'Alas, we know now that through the changing of things and morals good fortune has gone away. We are bringing up men with feeble bodies, of inferior spirit, with basic understanding, casual in speech and hopeless in deed', *Dialogus*, 51, p. 276.

[89] 'As men live, so they speak', *Dialogus*, 77, p. 288.

[90] Pierre Fabri (1889) quotes Cicero in his reworking of this topos: 'Tulles dit que rethorique est telle que sans elle loix ne citez ne peuvent ester iustement maintenues. Tout homme donc amy de bien publicque doibt estudier a bien et prudentement parler, pour lequel il acquerra louenge, honneur et dignité; il sera certain refuge de sage conseil', I: p. 7.

[91] 'Talis hominibus fuit oratio qualis vita. Quemadmodum autem unuscuiusque actio dicendi similis est, sic genus dicendi aliquando imitatur publicos mores, si disciplina civitatis laboravit et se in delicias dedit' (1–2). 'People's speech matches their lives. And just as the way in which each individual expresses himself resembles the way he acts, so in the case of a nation of declining morals and given over to luxury, forms of expression at any given time mirror the general behaviour of that society.' See Seneca (1990), pp. 137–44, and Seneca (1969).

proceed from false premises, as the *Sodalis* repeatedly proves.[92] The *Amicus* upholds the cause of the French in a discourse shown by the *Sodalis* to be as flawed as his arguments: a language that concerns itself only with words is a self-contained system, and so cannot have any real purchase on the material events unfolding in a contemporary France. The *Sodalis*'s superior rhetoric dominates the dialogue as his discourse engages with the *res* that lie beyond language, and so breaks away from the self-contained system of language that entraps the *Amicus*.

Peace cannot be obtained, in the *Sodalis*'s opinion, because each man wants it for his own selfish interest and not for the common good. The pursuit of individual interests is what leads men to war in the first place. The quest for peace in Chartier's *Dialogus* has its corollary in the quest for *mercy* in the *Belle Dame sans mercy*. The hapless suitor of this vernacular poem sues for a *mercy* that will never be accorded him since his arguments are fundamentally flawed, like the *Amicus*'s in Chartier's Latin dialogue. The *Belle Dame* takes on the role of the *Sodalis*, reproving the suitor for his 'foul pensement', v. 221. Although ostensibly cast in the traditional and weak female role of respondent to the suitor's advances, the *Belle Dame* forces her interlocutor to retract and rephrase his demands from her position outside the courtly discourse. The two protagonists of Chartier's poem are speaking at cross-purposes, in two incompatible discourses. A similar pattern is observed in the *Dialogus*, as I suggested earlier, in which the *Sodalis* responds to the questioning and arguments of the *Amicus* from a superior position outside the *Amicus*'s logic.

Critical interest in Chartier's work is often limited in scope to his debate poem *La Belle Dame sans mercy* (1424). Chartier's poem is composed of a hundred octosyllabic eight-line stanzas, a poetic form it shares with the *Debat de reveille matin*, the *Excusacion*, and the *Debat du Herault, du Vassault, et du Villain*. A narrative frame is constructed around the debate proper between a despairing suitor and a *Belle Dame*. The debate is presented in the frame by a 'triste et doloreux' narrator who, following the death of his lady, rides aimlessly one day through the countryside, before sheltering in a place both 'coy et privé'. His

---

[92] In a discussion that arises from an attempt to define peace, the *Amicus* argues that the common good is created by many particular goods (what is good for each individual). The *Sodalis* suggests rather that the common good is created by a harmony of individual 'humores' (intentions), which in turn creates particular or individual goods. The *Sodalis* asserts that the *Amicus*'s premise is false: 'silogismum falsigraphum componis, cum in intellectu principiorum deficias', 123: 'you put forward a falsely argued syllogism, because you err in your understanding of principles'.

friends get wind of his whereabouts, however, and arrive to drag him off to a party. As dinner is served, he spots a sorry figure dressed in black, and guesses his torment. The narrator observes how this *chevalier*'s eyes always rest on the same beautiful lady. Grown weary of the festivities, he moves outside where he sits behind a leafy trellis. From this concealed position he observes the same *chevalier* who has come to sit with the object of his affection on the other side of the trellis. The suitor states his suit in stanzas 24 to 27, the lady responds in 28, and thereafter the stanzas alternate between the suitor and his lady; the final four stanzas are spoken by the narrator. The suitor's case is rebuffed and ridiculed throughout by the *Belle Dame* who ultimately rejects his clichéd arguments and refuses to grant him *mercy*. After the final rejection, the suitor leaves the party with death in his heart. The narrator can only offer us a second-hand report of the conclusion to the story in which the *Belle Dame* has apparently forgotten her suitor and returned to the party while the suitor has allegedly died of pique (*courroux*) after tearing out his hair. The narrator then delivers two morals, the first warning lovers to avoid the 'mesdisans' who prejudice their case with ladies, and the second warning ladies not to behave as cruelly as the *Belle Dame* who might well be labelled 'sans mercy'.

The *Belle Dame sans mercy* is the most widely copied of Chartier's French verse debates, collected in forty-four extant manuscript copies as opposed to thirty-seven of the *DRM*, thirty-two of the *LQD*, thirty-one of the *Excusacion*, twenty-seven of the *DDFA*, and only one of the *DHVV*.[93] It provoked considerable contemporary reaction, eliciting a series of sequels, imitations, and translations that span over half a century.[94] I record forty manuscripts containing sequels and/or imitations of the *Belle Dame sans mercy* which I discuss in my final chapter. Of the forty-four manuscripts that contain the *Belle Dame sans mercy* itself, forty collect the poem with other works by Chartier. Chartier's *Excusacion*, a response to two letters allegedly sent to him by women and men of the court to complain about his *Belle Dame sans mercy*, is written in the form of a dialogue between the narrator and the *dieu d'Amours* and is

[93] See Alain Chartier (1974), pp. 43–58.
[94] See Piaget's editions of the poems in *Romania*, 'La Belle Dame sans Merci et ses imitations', *Romania* 30 (1901), 22–48, 317–51; 31 (1902), 315–49; 33 (1904), 179–208; 34 (1905), 375–428, 559–602. See also *Le Cycle de La Belle Dame sans Mercy* (2003).

collected with the *Belle Dame sans mercy* in thirty manuscripts.[95] Laidlaw
uses information about Chartier's absence from court in the letters to
date both the *Belle Dame sans mercy*, which he locates in 1424, and the
Excusacion, which he puts in the spring of 1425. Both Walravens and
Laidlaw conclude from the evidence of diplomatic letters that Chartier
was probably away from court on diplomatic business for most of
1425.[96] Although the literary letters collected with the *Belle Dame sans
mercy* may well be an elaborate invention by Chartier himself to excite
controversy over his poem, and solicit continuations, there seems to be
no reason to dispute Laidlaw's dating. A date of the mid-1420s would
certainly fit in with Chartier's preoccupation with the decline of morals
at court in his later Latin works.

The predominant nineteenth- and early twentieth-century critical
consensus on Chartier's *Belle Dame sans mercy* is summed up by Piaget
in his edition of the sequels and imitations of the poem:

Il est banal de dire que chez Alain Chartier le prosateur vaut mieux que le poète.
On l'a depuis longtemps remarqué, et il n'est pas difficile de voir d'où provient
cette différence. Chartier, qui se faisait de la poésie la même pauvre idée que ses
contemporains, ne voyait en elle qu'un passe-temps à l'usage des hautes classes
de la société: pour plaire à de riches et puissants patrons, les poètes ne traitaient
dans leurs vers que de questions amoureuses, sans personnalité ni sincérité, avec
les mêmes formules et les mêmes situations.[97]

Piaget, like Champion,[98] Hoffman,[99] and more recently, W. B. Kay,[100]
insists on the conventionality of the *Belle Dame sans mercy* and its
divorce from 'les événements extérieurs, les souffrances réelles, les luttes'
(*Romania* 30, p. 23), seeing a clear distinction between Chartier's prose

[95] Laidlaw notes that the only other copy of the *Excusacion* is contained in an
incomplete manuscript: Fribourg-Diesbach. The first twenty-two folios are lost and the
manuscript begins with the *Lettre des dames a Alain*, suggesting that the *Belle Dame sans
mercy* may also originally have been copied here: Alain Chartier (1974), pp. 128, 328.

[96] Walravens (1971), pp. 27–33, and Alain Chartier (1974), pp. 6–8.

[97] See Piaget, '*La Belle Dame sans Merci* et ses imitations', *Romania* 30 (1901), p. 22.

[98] See chapter VI in Pierre Champion, *Histoire poétique du quinzième siècle*, vol. I
(Paris: Champion, 1923), pp. 60–73. Champion subscribes to the school of nineteenth-
and early twentieth-century 'autobiographical' reading, equating Chartier with the
narrator of his fictional text.

[99] See Hoffman (1975), pp. 52–90. Hoffman includes the *Belle Dame sans mercy*
under the heading of 'joyeuses escritures', as opposed to his category of 'serious poems'.

[100] See W. B. Kay, '*La Belle Dame sans mercy* and the Success of Failure', *Romance
Notes*, 6 (1964), 69–73. Kay writes: 'The fact that he (Chartier) was unable to make the
framework of conventional courtly love poetry fully serve his personal vision is borne out
by his later choice of prose as the instrument of his greatest works', p. 73.

and verse works. In his 1970 study of fifteenth-century poetry, C. S. Shapley expresses concern with the customary division of Chartier's works into two categories: 'serious' (prose) and 'frivolous' (poetry). Shapley is the first to suggest that Chartier's *Belle Dame sans mercy* represents 'a moral indictment as devastating as the *Quatre Dames* or the *Quadrilogue*'.[101] He asserts that the game of love is analogous to the game of life, and that in choosing this conventional theme for his verse, Chartier is able to make social comment from within the 'felt emotion' of his characters.[102] In his edition of the French verse, Laidlaw notes that contemporary debate about the poem may have been a reaction to Chartier's criticism within the poem of courtly attitudes and conventions through the figure of the *Belle Dame*.[103] Dietmar Rieger goes further to suggest that the death of the *Belle Dame*'s suitor represents the death of courtly values, figuratively rejected through the *Belle Dame*'s rejection of the suitor.[104] Both Daniel Poirion[105] and William Kibler[106] make a case for Chartier's identification with the suitor, who, they argue, represents old feudal values. For Poirion and Kibler the *Belle Dame* represents the corruption of these values and a new bourgeois mentality in her refusal to grant *mercy*. Poirion talks of the 'scepticisme et l'égoïsme' of the *Belle Dame*, which he says destabilizes the exchange of courtly service (based on a principle drawn from feudal service). Kibler adopts Poirion's image of a *Belle Dame* who represents a seductive, commercial world far from the feudal and courtly values mourned by the suitor. The *Belle Dame*, according to Poirion and Kibler, is herself the target of Chartier's polemic. Kibler dismisses critics who claim that Chartier is sympathetic to the *Belle Dame* because of the parallels he sees between Chartier and the lovelorn suitor, also citing the double moral at the end of the poem as an indictment of the *Belle Dame*. I, however, read this double moral

---

[101] See Shapley, *Studies in French Poetry of the Fifteenth Century* (The Hague: Nijhoff, 1970), chapter 2, 32–120, p. 116.

[102] Shapley (1970), p. 78.

[103] Alain Chartier (1974), pp. 39–40.

[104] See Rieger, 'Alain Chartier's *Belle Dame sans Mercy* oder der Tod des höfischen Liebhabers: Überlegungen zu einer Dichtung des ausgehenden Mittelalters', in *Sprachen der Lyrik: Festschrift für Hugo Friedrich zum 70. Geburtstag* (Frankfurt am Main: Vittorio Klostermann, 1975), 683–706.

[105] See Poirion, 'Lectures de la *Belle Dame sans mercy*', in *Mélanges de langue et de littérature médiévales offerts à Pierre Le Gentil* (Paris: SEDES et CDU réunis, 1973), 691–705.

[106] See Kibler, 'The Narrator as Key to Alain Chartier's *Belle Dame sans mercy*', *French Review* 52 (1979), 714–23.

as an ironic device to perpetuate textual play, and to render closure deliberately ambiguous, as I shall later explain. Kibler builds on the new critical current, begun by Shapley, to suggest in his article that there is an ideological link between Chartier's *Belle Dame sans mercy*, the *Quadrilogue invectif* and the Latin works: *Ad detestacionem belli gallici* and the *Dialogus*. He identifies a level on which the *Belle Dame* and her suitor represent a conflict between a modern and old-fashioned view of the state of society, an issue also addressed in the other works stated above. The *Belle Dame*, he argues, refuses to play because 'the courtly game has become degraded and lost its meaning', whereas the suitor still believes that a return to ideal courtly values is possible. On this basis, Kibler reads the suitor's death[107] as an attempt on Chartier's part to demonstrate his sympathy with the lover against the *Belle Dame*, since he asserts that Chartier also supports a return to the old values, citing the double moral at the end of the poem as evidence of his claim. Although I agree with Kibler that this poem is indeed linked to Chartier's political and ethical agenda as expressed through his Latin and French prose works, I use this argument to proceed to a different conclusion, namely that what Chartier supports here is neither explicitly the suitor nor the *Belle Dame*, but the *Belle Dame*'s rejection of an insincere courtly discourse. Kibler's own arguments betray a certain male flippancy with regard to women that itself seems almost derived from the medieval *Querelle des femmes*, preferring a solution which has Chartier siding with the male protagonist.[108] As I suggest later on, the *Belle Dame*, far from Kibler's portrait of a flirtatious young woman, is a symbol of France (also feminized in Chartier's *Quadrilogue invectif*), assailed and betrayed by the corruption around her, a corruption which is intimately connected to language systems in Chartier's work. The suitor's alleged death is treated by Chartier in an ironic way and at one remove, dismissing Kibler's sympathy theory. The death is only reported later to the narrator, and so remains speculative.[109] More recently Giuseppe Sansone has addressed a critique of the 'substrat courtois' that he identifies in Chartier's *Belle*

[107] Kibler does not dispute the fact that the lover dies, whereas it is in fact made deliberately unclear in Chartier's text.

[108] I am thinking of the paragraph in which Kibler (1979) talks of an 'us' who I can only assume to be an entirely male critical audience: 'One must certainly concede that to *us* today there is nothing quite so appealing as a young woman who vivaciously states that her eyes are for looking, that she may flirt openly with whom she wishes, and that she is free and intends to remain so', p. 716.

[109] See Alain Chartier (1974), *La Belle Dame sans mercy*, XCVIII, vv. 777–84, p. 359.

Dame sans mercy.[110] Sansone moves away from the idea of a courtly critique centred on the male figure as the representative of traditional courtly values which are degraded by the *Belle Dame*, interpreting Chartier's moral message instead through the female character. Chartier, according to Sansone, proposes a 'revendication de la liberté de la femme, l'indépendance du choix par rapport aux pièges de règles vétustes'.[111] In other words, Chartier defends the woman's right to say 'no', in defiance of courtly convention. Gretchen Angelo builds on Sansone's theories to demonstrate how Chartier's *Belle Dame* rejects not only her suitor but a courtly discourse that is synonymous with the silencing of the woman's individual voice.[112] Angelo suggests that Chartier's *Belle Dame* refuses to be a sounding board against which the male interlocutor displays his verbal agility as in the courtly love dialogues of Andreas Capellanus's *De amore*. The *Belle Dame*'s rejection of the suitor is effectively shown to be a 'challenge to male hegemony over courtly discourse'. I suggest, with Angelo, that Chartier's *Belle Dame* rejects a courtly discourse that is shown to be flawed, self-absorbed, and self-contained. I see this rejection both as a move on Chartier's part in the wider *Querelle des femmes*, as Angelo argues, and moreover, as a thorough rejection of falseness and constraint in language which go hand in hand with the moral corruption of the State. Through correspondences with the *Dialogus*, we can further suggest that the *Belle Dame* rejects the tyranny of courtly discourse in favour of the verbal freedom offered by the humanist rhetoric espoused by the *Sodalis*. The universal application of this ideal discourse, however, remains beyond her reach, trapped as she is in the very realm she wishes to escape. Through his debates, Chartier advocates a language system, which, like the value system that will achieve peace, can come about only through the sacrifice of personal interest to the common good. One must avoid a slavish and selfish devotion to style, and rather subordinate style to *materia* (subject matter). Geoffrey of Vinsauf's *Poetria nova* of 1210, one of the best known arts of poetry in the Middle Ages, describes style as the ornament of *materia*: organization is secondary to the invention of the subject matter.[113] Chartier exposes courtly discourse as self-serving, and dialectic as concerned only with its own propositions and proofs. It is in this light that I examine the poetics of closure in Chartier's verse.

[110] Sansone, '*La Belle Dame sans merci* et le langage courtois', *Le Moyen Français* 39–40–41 (1995–6), 513–26.
[111] Sansone (1995), p. 520.   [112] Angelo (2003).
[113] See Gallo, 'The *Poetria nova* of Geoffrey of Vinsauf', in Murphy (1978), pp. 68–84.

Resistance to closure in Chartier's works is part of a meta-rhetorical discourse in which he rejects the closure enforced by the language systems of courtly discourse and dialectic. Instead Chartier champions an ethically and politically engaged rhetoric that reaches beyond the confines of the text. The 'vocabulary of closure' which Chartier employs points to images of closure and openness within the courtly sphere that represent, on a meta-textual level, constraint and release in language.

The *Belle Dame*, like the *Sodalis* of Chartier's *Dialogus*, attacks not merely what the suitor says but the whole discourse from which his words proceed, challenging the conventional metaphors of courtly love. The metaphor of dying for love used by the suitor, for example, is utterly rejected by the *Belle Dame*:

> Si gracïeuse maladie
> Ne met gaires de gens a mort
> Mais il siet bien que l'on le die
> Pour plus tost actraire confort.
>
> vv. 265–8

Here the *Belle Dame* cuts through the convention; the words themselves do not refer to an actual physical death and are thus divorced from that which they ostensibly signify. The suitor's discourse is hollow and unreliable: 'en telz sermens n'a riens ferme', v. 350. The import of his words lasts only as long as it takes to speak them. In response to the suitor's condemnation of bad lovers, the *Belle Dame* reiterates her conviction that—good or bad—men simply do not expire from love:

> Sur tel meffait n'a court ne juge
> A qui on puisse recourir.
> L'un les maudit, l'autre les juge,
> Mais je n'en ay veu nul mourir.
>
> vv. 585–8

In his article on Sir Richard Roos's Middle English translation of Chartier's original poem, Ashby Kinch explores the rhetorical figure of dying for love, and the impact this has on the terms of erotic exchange.[114] He identifies crucial differences in the language used by the

---

[114] I am grateful to Ashby Kinch for allowing me to read a pre-publication version of his article, 'Richard Roos' *La Belle Dame sans merci* and the Politics of Translation', forthcoming in the *Journal of English and Germanic Philology*.

interlocutors that point towards differences in their value systems. We have already seen how language and ethical systems may be intimately connected. Here I suggest that the suitor's desire to be enclosed by *Amours* refers us to the constraints of his self-serving courtly discourse, while the *Belle Dame*'s desire for autonomy is reflected in her rejection of this 'gouliardye'. The suitor attempts to make the *Belle Dame* solely responsible for his happiness, submitting his will to hers:

> Car ma volenté s'est soubzmise
> En voustre gré, non pas au mien,
> Pour plus asservir ma franchise.
>
> vv. 206–8

This *franchise* is a false autonomy: the individual will is enslaved to the whims of another, just as Chartier observes at court in his *De vita curiali*: 'nos servientes sub alieno statuto victimamus'.[115] The *Belle Dame* refuses to be held responsible for the suitor, thus refusing to accept the servitude of the court and the closure imposed by *Amours*. She asserts her autonomy from the courtly discourse:

> Choisisse qui vouldra choisir.
> Je suis france et france vueil estre,
> Sans moy de mon cuer dessaisir
> Pour en faire un autre le maistre.
>
> vv. 285–8

The chiastic line at 286 resonates through Chartier's poem. The *Belle Dame* confirms her position of autonomy beyond the courtly discourse, and asserts her will independent of any other. It is perhaps no coincidence that Chartier uses the adjective 'franc(h)e' here, evoking both freedom and country. Solterer asks the same question about the relationship of franc(h)e and France; of the political freedom of women and of the motherland, in a recent article.[116] The *Belle Dame*'s declaration of 'franchise', as Solterer argues, would have touched a number of chords in 1424, evoking the dispute over the Salic Law and women's political role.[117] Solterer's study, like the present one, identifies a convergence

---

[115] 'We who serve at the court live by another's rules', *De vita curiali*, 24, pp. 356–8.
[116] See Solterer, 'The Freedoms of Fiction for Gender in Premodern France', in *Gender in Debate from the Early Middle Ages to the Renaissance*, ed. Thelma S. Fenster and Clare A. Lees (New York: Palgrave, 2002), 135–63.
[117] Solterer (2002), pp. 151–3.

between literary and political debating. In it, she refers to seventeenth-century French statutes, the *Institutes coustumieres* of 1611, which contain a decree, supposedly by Chartier, depriving women and their progeny of all rights of succession and feudal property: the words of the Salic Law.[118] I am in agreement with Solterer that this association of Chartier and the Salic Law is likely to have emerged from the repercussions of the *Querelle*, and is entirely spurious.[119]

The contemporary political connotations of 'franchise' thus transform the *Belle Dame* into the figure of the motherland on an allegorical level, besieged by those who would enslave her through violence and suppress her political autonomy. The erotic struggle then assumes undertones of rape, recalling the allegorical figure of France who appears to the narrator in a dream in Chartier's vernacular prose debate, the *Quadrilogue invectif*.[120] The sumptuous robes of this figure are torn and dirtied, suggesting some violent tussle, and even the aggressive possession of France by some foreign body:[121]

Cellui mantel, assemblé par la souveraine industrie des predecesseurs, estoit desja par violentes mains froissez et derompuz et aucunes pieces violentement arrachees, si que la partie de dessus se monstroit obscurcie et pou de fleurs de liz y apparissoient qui ne fussent debrisees ou salies, p. 8.

These 'violentes mains' assail France from both outside and inside. The 'vous' she addresses wage war on her through 'couvoitises et mauvaises ambitions', p. 12, much as the courtiers whose thirst for power leads, as we have seen, to their abuse and misappropriation of language.

Here the suitor's case has been prejudiced by the 'cuers travers', v. 573, who the *Belle Dame* asserts have clouded the sincerity of all lovers' suits:

> Assez est il de cuers travers
> Qu'avoir bien fait toust empirer
> Et loyauté mectre a l'envers,
> Dont ilz soloient souspirer.
>
> vv. 573–6

These same 'cuers travers' are reprimanded by the narrator in one of two morals at the close of the poem. The 'mesdisans' (in the sense of

---

[118] Antoine Loisel, *Institutes coustumieres* (Paris: Abel L'Angelier, 1611, 3rd edn, transcription and facsimile (Mayenne: Floch, 1935), no. 310), p. 54.
[119] See also Hanley (1997) on this question.   [120] Alain Chartier (1950).
[121] See plates 2 and 3.

Plate 2. Alain Chartier, *Quadrilogue invectif* (France addresses her children, Chevalier, Clergé, and Peuple)

Paris, BnF, Rothschild 2796, fol. 5ᵛ

Plate 3. Alain Chartier, *Quadrilogue invectif* (the House of France in disarray)
Paris, BnF, fr. 24441, fol. 5ᵛ

'slanderers'), recalling the *maigre chevalier*'s term in the *DDFA*, must be shunned in order to restore sincerity to the love discourse. The fundamental importance of sincerity in speech is debated throughout the *Belle Dame sans mercy*, the *Belle Dame* repeatedly trumping the verbal ingenuity of the lover, and exposing his speech as 'faulx semblant'.[122] The *Belle Dame* speaks 'amesureement', while her interlocutor in desperation resorts to hyperbole and exclamation. It is all to no avail though, as the *Belle Dame* rejects not only the suitor but his love discourse. 'Ostez vous hors de ce propos', she demands, v. 649. He remains 'escondit', along with his words: 'De tant redire m'ennoyez, | Car je vous en ay assez dit, vv. 767–8. So the *Belle Dame* has the last word.[123] While she has thoroughly rejected the lover's speeches, he is forced finally to recognize the truth of her discourse, and marks this recognition by removing himself physically from her presence. The weaker argumentation of the *Amicus* in Chartier's *Dialogus* similarly concedes defeat, and the last word is given to the *Sodalis* who then projects the final *sententia* beyond the textual close of the dialogue. This delaying of closure is a tactic Chartier also employs in his *Belle Dame sans mercy*. The conclusion to this poem is left in ambiguous irresolution. The narrator admits his initial ignorance of the lover's fate, and then relates a second-hand report which may be spurious:

> Depuis je ne sceu qu'il devint
> Ne quel part il se transporta;
> Mais a sa dame n'en souvint
> Qui aux dances se deporta.
> Et depuis on me rapporta
> Qu'il avoit ses cheveux desroux,
> Et que tant se desconforta
> Qu'il en estoit mort de courroux.

vv. 777–84

---

[122] See Taylor's fascinating discussion of *Faux Semblant* in the context of Chartier's use of the *Roman de la Rose* as intertext for his poem. The *Belle Dame* as anti-rose, asserting her rights as a speaking subject, presents a further angle to my arguments here. Taylor, 'Embodying the Rose: An Intertextual Reading of Alain Chartier's *La Belle Dame sans mercy*', in *The Court Reconvenes: Courtly Literature across the Disciplines*, ed. Barbara K. Altmann and Carleton W. Carroll (Cambridge: D. S. Brewer, 2003), 325–33.

[123] The suitor does speak after the *Belle Dame* at the close of the debate, though he is clearly speaking to himself, rather than replying to the *Belle Dame*: 'Mort, vien a moy courant | Ains que mon sens se descongnoisse, | Et m'abrege le demourant | De ma vie plaine d'engoisse', Alain Chartier (1974), vv. 773–6, p. 359.

The actual fates of both lover and *Belle Dame* are thus left uncertain. The *Belle Dame* forgets her suitor, and returns to the dancing, perhaps suggesting a return to the courtly life. The picture of the lover tearing out his hair, on the other hand, seems more ridiculous than tragic. As I mentioned earlier, the *Belle Dame*, like Chartier, may reject an insincere courtly discourse and assert her autonomy from it, but she is ultimately trapped within the courtly system, and figuratively bound by the confines of the text. By delaying closure, by leaving the narrative unfinished and uncertain, Chartier frees his text from the constraints of poetic convention.

Chartier's *Excusacion aux dames* answers the accusations which purport to have been levelled at the *Belle Dame sans mercy*,[124] and acts as a continuation of this poem. In the *Excusacion*, Chartier in the persona of the narrator, a 'humble serviteur' named Alain, is also one of the two interlocutors of the debate. The narrator relates a dream he had at dawn in which the *dieu d'Amours* appeared to him to chastise him for writing 'nouveaulx livres contre [ses] droiz', v. 24. 'Le maleureux livre', v. 27, referred to here is presumably Chartier's *Belle Dame sans mercy*. The *dieu d'Amours* threatens in no uncertain terms to burn the book and kill the narrator unless he repents of accusing women of showing no *mercy*. The responsive stanzas of the *Belle Dame sans mercy* are replaced here by two long stanzaic sections in which the *dieu d'Amours* and the narrator speak in turn. The narrator defends his postion in the book in question, stating that if one were to read it carefully, one would see that he in fact supports women, rather than slandering them.[125] He further excuses himself, somewhat disingenuously, on the grounds that he is the mere 'escripvain' (in this context, perhaps 'scribe, copyist') of the book, and that the book itself ('qui peu vault et monte', v. 193) has no other purpose than to record the suitor's complaints: 'et qui autre chose y entent | Il y voit trop ou n'y voit goute', vv. 199–200.[126] The *dieu d'Amours* decides to leave the final judgement to the *dames*, to whose court the narrator

---

[124] Two letters follow the *Belle Dame sans mercy* in the majority of manuscripts containing texts of the *Querelle de la Belle Dame sans mercy* cycle, expressing the violent reactions of 'dames' and 'amants' respectively to Chartier's poem. (A *Responce des dames*, answering Chartier's *Excusacion aux dames*, is found in four of these manuscripts.) For editions of the two letters see Alain Chartier (1974), pp. 360–2. See Piaget's edition in *Romania* 30 (1901), 31–5; also *Le Cycle de La Belle Dame sans Mercy* (2003), pp. 493–9.

[125] This admission supports my argument for Chartier's sympathy with the *Belle Dame* against Poirion and Kibler.

[126] I read a certain deliberate irony in this statement. The narrator and Chartier are not one and the same.

pledges to adjourn, thus deferring closure. Literary continuations and responses tend to emphasize the irresolution of the text they continue, and were a frequent medieval phenomenon, from the *Continuations du conte du graal*,[127] or Jean de Meun's section of the *Roman de la Rose*, to the series of sequels and imitations provoked by the *Belle Dame sans mercy*.[128] The debate form provides a platform for this type of ongoing literary revision with its particular brand of polemic, and its potential for inconclusiveness. So Chartier in his *Excusacion aux dames*, proposing to conclude the quarrel that his initial text has caused, actually points to the incompleteness of that text, and perpetuates the quarrel.

Through the *Belle Dame*'s strong rejection of courtly convention in which the lady, as I mentioned, is frequently a mere prop responding to, concurring with, and conceding to male argument, Chartier seems to take a stance in the long-running medieval debate on women.[129] Chartier's *Livre des Quatre Dames* similarly explores the tensions between male and female positions within a courtly discourse. In the *Livre des Quatre Dames*, the narrator, 'pour oublïer melencolie', v. 1, walks through the spring countryside, 'tout seulet', v. 7, pondering the treachery of *Amours*. In the distance he sees four noble ladies and finally approaches them at v. 350 after a long digression on his sorrow. The ladies relate their stories to the narrator in turn, each attempting to trump the others. All four have been affected by the wars with the English. The lover of the first lady has been killed, the lover of the second imprisoned, the third lady's lover is missing, and the fourth lady's lover is a deserter. They ask the narrator to judge which of them has the greatest grief. On hearing the moving speech of the second lady, Chartier's narrator challenges the detractors of women:

> ... Hommes tiennent leurs fables
> De ce que femmes sont müables,

---

[127] There were two principal verse continuations of Chrétien de Troyes's *Conte du graal* (*Perceval*), each of which survives in a number of versions. See Chrétien de Troyes, *The Continuations of the Old French Perceval of Chrétien de Troyes*, ed. Roach, Foulet, Ivy, 4 vols. (Philadelphia: University of Pennsylvania Press, 1949–71).

[128] See Piaget's editions and commentaries in *Romania*; *Le Cycle de La Belle Dame sans Mercy* (2003); and my Chapter 4, part I.

[129] For a discussion of the *Querelle des femmes* in the Middle Ages and Renaissance see Blamires (1992) and (1997); Bock and Zimmermann, 'Die *Querelle des femmes* in Europa: Eine begriffs- und forschungsgeschichtliche Einführung', in *Querelles. Jahrbuch für Frauenforschung 1997 Band 2: Die europäische 'Querelle des femmes': Geschlechterdebatten seit dem 15. Jahrhundert*, ed. G. Bock; M. Zimmermann (Stuttgart/Weimar: Verlag J. B. Metzler, 1997), 9–38, and also Angenot (1977).

Maiz monstrez se sont varïables
Trop plus que dames,
Et de conscïences et d'ames,
Puis dix ans dont ilz sont infames
Et trouvez moins fermes que fames
En leur devoir.

vv. 3293–300

The inconstancy of men is a challenge to the received 'fables'. Here Chartier, through his narrator, suggests that male discourse is subject to fluctuation. The 'fables', like proverbial wisdom, arise from a conventional discourse on women.[130] They represent generalizations that Chartier exposes as divorced from truth. The reference to 'dix ans' may evoke the ten years of civil war between the Burgundians and the Orléanists, which began in 1405.[131] Laidlaw uses this reference to date the *Livre des Quatre Dames* to 1415/16, and concludes that the battle with the English in which the second lady's lover has been captured must refer to the battle of Agincourt in 1415. The battle described in the *Livre des Quatre Dames* may well be the battle of Agincourt, but one cannot always rely on historical referents to date fictional works, as I argued earlier. I suggest a later date for this text of around 1420–2 which still takes account of the reference to the battle of Agincourt and places it in close proximity to Chartier's prose work, the *Quadrilogue invectif*, with which it shares an ethical agenda. This debate is probably posterior to the *Debat des Deux Fortunés d'amours*, as Laidlaw also assumes. A similar reference to time is found in the *Belle Dame sans mercy* in the penultimate moral issued to all lovers, warning them to avoid the 'mesdisans': 'Car ilz ont trop mis puis dix ans | Le païs d'Amours a pastiz', vv. 791–2.

Men's inconstancy in speech and action is first explored in the *Livre des Quatre Dames* through the dilemma of the loyal narrator who has

---

[130] In the *DDFA*, Chartier's *gras chevalier* evinces one of the arguments frequently cited in the case for women: 'Se nous tenons | Que de fame nous naissons et venons | Et par elles noz joyes maintenons, | Grans et nourris et bons en devenons, | Et que Nature | Nous en donne naissance et nourreture, | Amendement, joye et bonne aventure, | Dont devons nous les amer par droitture; | Et sommes faulx, | Desnaturez, vilains et desloyaulx | Desvergondez, mauvais et bestïaulx | S'en fait n'en dit nous pourchassons leurs maulx', vv. 613–24.

[131] See Alain Chartier (1974), pp. 35–36.

suffered rejection at the hands of his lady.[132] She perhaps mistrusted him because of the falseness of his fellows:

> J'ay pour loyauté le rebours
> De ceulx qui usent des faulx tours,
> Et bien leur vient.

vv. 310–12

The first lady, like the narrator's lady and the *Belle Dame*, is sceptical of courtly convention in speech. She questions the rhetorical figure of dying for love, and rejects it as 'loberie':

> … Pou s'en dourroient
> Garde que telz gens secourroient,
> Quant ilz diroient qu'ilz mourroient
> Pour amours fines,
> Et feroient si tristes signes,
> Manieres humbles et benignes,
> Pour rober ce dont ne sont dignes.
> [...]
> Helaz, mon cuer a tant fouÿ
> D'eulx les paroles
> Et leurs grans loberies foles,
> Leurs decevans blandices moles!
> Moult ay deprisié telz frivoles.

vv. 786–92, 796–800

The first lady, however, finds a lover whom she judges 'bon et loyal', and devotes herself to him until his sudden death. Thus by entering into the 'gracïeuse chace' (*DDFA*, v. 636), the woman finds herself trapped. Left alone, her only way out is death. Similarly, each of the four ladies is caught in an untenable situation. The treachery of convention is suggested by the comparison of the ladies' voices to the birds the narrator overhears singing in the prologue to the debate:

> L'un chantoit, les autres doubloient
> De leurs gorgetes qui verbloient
> Le chant que Nature a apris;
> Et puis l'un de l'autre s'embloient,

vv. 26–9

---

[132] The narrator mentions two ladies: the first rejected his suit after two years; the second is his current love. See Alain Chartier (1974), vv. 320–33, pp. 207–8.

The birds' song is a natural one, and contrasts sharply with the 'fol parler' of courtly love discourse that the ladies struggle to escape. The birds are 'hors de cage', v. 103, and may sing freely: 'Dieu scet s'ilz estoient taisant', v. 104. Courtly discourse, as I have suggested, acts as a gag for women, forcing them into the position of respondent to male advance.[133] The third lady asserts that her case is stronger than that of either of the first two speakers. She compares herself to a 'tour minee | Dont la prise n'est pas finee', vv. 2140–1.[134] The image of the falling tower refers us to the popular medieval metaphor of the body as building.[135] Could Chartier be taking as an intertext here Christine de Pizan's *Livre de la cité des dames*? Christine's prose work (1405) is the definitive example of freedom within enclosure; the women form a metaphorical structure, which, far from restricting them, is represented as a symbol of female autonomy and liberation.[136] The tower in Chartier's debate is on the verge of collapse, assailed by the misfortunes of courtly love. The woman's suffering is described in terms of an assault on and possession ('prise') of her body, as in the *Quadrilogue invectif*. She is constrained by the terms of *Amours*:

> Or est encloz
> Mon cuer en l'amoureux encloz,
> De hayes d'espines tout cloz,
> Par quoy le partir m'est forcloz.
>
> vv. 2451–4

Here Chartier employs what I term his 'vocabulary of closure', in other words, a semantic reservoir of terms relating to closure and openness which feeds his verse corpus. Combined with the deliberate postponing or abandoning of judgement in his debates, Chartier effects an undermining of the concept of closure. We have seen how Chartier postpones a final judgement in his *Dialogus* and his *Belle Dame sans mercy*. The final judgement of the ladies' debate in the *Livre des Quatre Dames* is also projected to an extratextual and hypothetical future:

---

[133] For woman's position as the respondent in debate, see Solterer (1995), and my discussion in Chapter 1, pp. 27–8.

[134] This would seem to refer to *Le Jaloux*'s speech in the *Roman de la Rose*: 'Car tours de toutes parz assise, | Enviz eschape d'estre prise', vv. 8599–600, Guillaume de Lorris and Jean de Meun (1992), p. 468.

[135] See Cowling, *Building the Text: Architecture as Metaphor in Late Medieval and Early Modern France* (Oxford: Clarendon Press, 1998).

[136] The conclusion to the work sees the city finished and closed on itself. See Christine de Pizan (1998).

> Pourtant ce livre,
> Pour estre de charge delivre,
> A ma dame transmet et livre,
> Par qui je puis mourir ou vivre.
> El le lira
> Et pas ne les escondira,
> Et puis son avis en dira;
> Si sarons comme il en ira.
> Mais pour enqueste
> Faire du fait de quoy j'enqueste
> Et trouver voie plus honneste,
> Lui envoie ceste requeste
> Qu'escripte avoie.
>
> vv. 3452–64

The use of the future tense here introduces an element of doubt. The lady may well reject the narrator along with his 'livre', and never deliver her judgement. In a direct appeal to his lady, the narrator asks her to read the account of this 'querele', but only 's'il [lui] plaist', v. 3485, and further urges her: 'faictes du vostre a vostre guise', v. 3531. Chartier again introduces elements of uncertainty in his *Debat des Deux Fortunés d'amours*. The chosen judge of the debate, Jean de Grailli, comte de Foix, is absent on a military campaign. The judgement is therefore postponed until his return, upon which: 's'il lui plaist, son advis en diroit', v. 1230. Chartier further destabilizes the ending of his debate by introducing a modesty topos: 'qui mieulx sçaira, le demourant supplie', v. 1242, encouraging further debate and speculation on the topic. In the same vein, the exhortation by Chartier's narrator in his *Belle Dame sans mercy* points to the poem's lack of resolution, and to future continuation, as Armstrong observes in his discussion of the *Querelle de la Belle Dame sans mercy*:[137]

> Desormais est temps de moy tayre,
> Car de dire suis je lassé.
> Je vueil laissier aux autres faire:
> Leur temps est; le mien est passé.
>
> vv. 33–6

---

[137] Armstrong, ' "Leur temps est; le mien est passé": Poetic Ingenuity and Competition in the *Querelle de la Belle Dame sans mercy*' (to appear as a chapter in his forthcoming book on late medieval poetic competition).

The artificial closure of a text was discussed in classical and medieval manuals on style.[138] The literary device of bilateral symmetry, advocated in these treatises, supposes an intimate connection between the beginning and end of a text and hence imposes an inner structure on the literary work, reinforced in the case of fixed form poetry by an outer structure of metrical and rhythmic constraints. Closure is thus related to the frame or structure of a text, and is seen to mirror the aspirations of the artist, in his quest for a perfected, unified object. The author must impose closure artificially, lending his text a contrived circularity perceived retrospectively through its end: a circularity which David Lee Rubin terms 'the knot of artifice' in his study of seventeenth-century French lyric poetry.[139] The work whose beginning is thus encompassed within its end is likened by Geoffrey of Vinsauf in his *Poetria nova* to an arrow that flies back to the bow, an image later adopted by Dante in the *Divine Comedy*.[140] The ending of a text, in returning to its initial proposition, presented a recapitulation and amplification of the work's themes or arguments. Certain conventions might be imposed in order to indicate that the work had reached an end. These closural procedures were prescribed to a greater or lesser extent by the genre or genres that characterized the text, so that fixed form poems, for example, such as the rondeau or ballade, would pivot around the repetition of a refrain, literally writing the end as a beginning.[141] Conventions such as the revelation of the author's identity in a final verse or anagram,

[138] Cicero's treatise *De inventione* (46–44 BC) was a widely cited classical source. Important medieval treatises on style included the *Institutiones divinarum et humanarum lectionum* (Cassiodorus); *Ars versificatoria* (Matthew of Vendôme, 1170); *Documentum de modo et arte dictandi et versificandi*, and *Poetria nova* (Geoffrey of Vinsauf, 1210); *Li livres dou tresor* (Brunetto Latini, 1260–6); *De vulgari eloquentia* (Dante, 1304–6); *Forma praedicandi* (Robert of Basevorn, 1322).

[139] See Rubin, *The Knot of Artifice: A Poetic of the French Lyric in the Early Seventeenth Century* (Columbus: Ohio State University Press, 1981).

[140] 'E forse in tanto in quanto un quadrel posa | e vola e da la noce si dischiava' ('And in such space perchance as strikes a bolt | And flies, and from the notch unlocks itself'). See Dante, *The Divine Comedy*, ed. Bickersteth (Oxford: Basil Blackwell, 1965), *Paradiso*: Canto 2, vv. 23–4, p. 524 (the English translation is by Henry W. Longfellow and is available online at http://www.gutenberg.org/etext1004).

[141] In her article, 'Medieval Concepts of Literary Closure: Theory and Practice', *Exemplaria* 1 (1989), 149–79, McGerr cites a rondeau by Guillaume de Machaut which explicitly illustrates the circularity inherent in the form: 'Ma fin est mon commencement | Et mon commencement ma fin | Et teneüre vraiement. | Ma fin est mon commencement. | Mes tiers chans .iij. fois seulement | Se retrograde et einsi fin. | Ma fin est mon commencement | Et mon commencement ma fin'. McGerr further notes that the two halves of the tenor part accompanying the lyric are mirror images.

or calls for emendation and continuation of the work were equally common.

While a medieval understanding of the interconnection of alpha and omega, the beginning and the end, influenced artists in their quest for earthly perfection that mirrored the divine, medieval methods of education also tended towards a utopian ideal of perfect closure, exemplified in the Scholastic *disputatio*. Debate poetry, as I have suggested, ostensibly embodies the spirit of the *disputatio* in its presentation of conflicting arguments by two or more protagonists, and in the quest for a definitive resolution, to be delivered in the form of a judgement. However, the irresolution of a number of debate poems leads us to question the parameters of the genre, and to search for precedents. Michèle Perret has constructed a typology of closural practice in French fiction of the eleventh to fifteenth centuries.[142] Within the category of explicitly finished works, Perret identifies a certain type of fiction whose closure is deliberately deferred or falsified, an 'achèvement inachevé'.[143] She refers particularly to the double ending of Renaut de Beaujeu's *Le Bel Inconnu*, whose dénouement is projected beyond the physical closure of the romance. The narrator, identified as 'Renals de Biauju', v. 6249, leaves the fate of his protagonist Guinglain in the balance, transferring control over the outcome to his lady.[144] Beyond the physical closure of the romance, imposed by the cessation of writing and the completion of metrical requirements, an unknown dramatic dénouement is projected. In his account of Middle English debate poetry, Reed attributes such 'playfulness about closure' to a satirical reaction on the part of the poet to the perceived necessity of reaching 'reductive certainty' in an argument.[145]

I suggest that Chartier deliberately avoids delivering a *sententia* or final judgement in rejection of the empty Scholastic logic espoused by the *Amicus*, or the hollow courtly discourse of the *Belle Dame*'s suitor. In delaying ending, Chartier reaches beyond the constraints of these

---

[142] Perret, 'Typologie des fins dans les oeuvres de fiction (XIᵉ–XVᵉ siècles)', *PRIS-MA* 14/2 (1998), 155–74.

[143] Perret borrows Dragonetti's term. See Dragonetti, *Le Gai Savoir dans la rhétorique courtoise* (Paris: Seuil, 1982), p. 82.

[144] 'Mais por un biau sanblant mostrer | vos feroit Guinglain retrover | s'amie que il a perdue, | qu'entre ses bras le tenroit nue. | Se de çou li faites delai, | si ert Guinglains en tel esmai | que ja mais n'avera s'amie; | d'autre vengance n'a il mie', vv. 6255–62; Renaut de Beaujeu, *Le Bel Inconnu*, ed. Fresco (New York/London: Garland, 1992). See also Colby-Hall, 'Frustration and Fulfillment: The Double Ending of the *Bel Inconnu*', *Yale French Studies* 67 (1984), 120–34.

[145] See Reed (1990).

self-contained discourses, and strives for the openness of an engaged and sincere discourse. In suspending closure by opening his work to be judged and continued by others, Chartier encourages the perpetuation of the wider debate. He uses the medium of the debate poem, therefore, as a vehicle for ethical and moral instruction. In soliciting further poems, Chartier effectively nurtures and valorizes a participatory vernacular poetic culture. Chartier's 'vocabulary of closure' is strongly linked to the ethical agenda subtending his *oeuvre* as we have seen. I now return to examine this ethical agenda in the light of Chartier's lesser-known debate poems.

Through correspondences with the *De vita curiali* and the *Belle Dame sans mercy*, the platitudes uttered by the desperate *Amoureux* in Chartier's *Debat de reveille matin* are exposed, and his fate left in the balance. The manuscript tradition of this debate is closely bound up with that of the *Belle Dame sans mercy*. The *Debat de reveille matin* is collected in thirty-seven manuscripts, all of which contain other verse works by Chartier. It is collected with the *Belle Dame sans mercy* in thirty-four of these, and the two debates are placed in juxtaposition in fourteen manuscripts.[146] Champion and Laidlaw both suggest that the *Debat de reveille matin* is earlier than the *Belle Dame sans mercy*, against E. Droz, who puts it in 1425.[147] The codicological evidence both supports an earlier date and suggests that the two were written within a short period of time of each other. Intertextual links and similarity of form (responsive octosyllabic huitains) also strengthen this argument.

The premise for the *Debat de reveille matin* is derived from a proverb recorded by Morawski: 'Ami pour aultre veille'.[148] The narrator is lying awake after midnight, when he overhears a lover trying to rouse a sleeper: the two interlocutors of the debate. The *Dormeur* tries to resist striking up conversation, insisting that he must be allowed to sleep if he so chooses: 'face chascun a son plaisir', v. 32. The *Amoureux* counters this argument with recourse to proverbial wisdom:

> Tel voulsist veiller qui sommeille;
> Tel ploure qui voulsist bien rire;

[146] In each case the *Debat de reveille matin* precedes the *Belle Dame sans mercy*. In Pierre Le Caron's printed edition of 1489 the two are also placed in this order in juxtaposition. See Alain Chartier (1974), pp. 142–4.

[147] See Champion (1923), pp. 63–4, Alain Chartier (1950), p. VIII, and Alain Chartier (1974), pp. 38–9.

[148] See Morawski, *Proverbes français antérieurs au XVᵉ siècle* (Paris: Champion, 1925), no. 81.

Tel cuide dormir qui s'esveille.
Non pourtant, Bonne Amour conseille—
Et moult souvent le dit on bien—
Q'un bon amy pour l'autre veille
Au gré d'autruy, non pas au sien.

vv. 34–40

Each man, the *Amoureux* argues, must sacrifice his own desires and will to those of others. This echoes Chartier's description of the slavishness of a life at court in his *De vita curiali*, in which each man must live a servile existence and submit to another's rules and wishes:

Adde quod semper hospes est qui curie servit et aliene domus habitator, alterius in fame alienoque appetitui comedit, cum famelicis sine fame vescitur, cum saturatis curis occupatus esuriem sustinet. Alieno voto vigilat cum jam obsompnuisse cepisset. Et quid servilius est quam nature vires et vitalia jura Fortune subegisse, cum nichil in homine liberius sit quam naturaliter vivere? Nos servientes sub alieno statuto victitamus.[149]

The loss of freedom experienced by the *Dormeur*, forced to stay awake by the *Amoureux*, ostensibly out of friendship, becomes far more sinister through this intertext. The *Dormeur*, like the *Belle Dame*, attempts to reject the courtly convention that dictates this loss of freedom, and subjugation to another's will. Chartier uses the *Dormeur* as an ironic device to ridicule and empty the *Amoureux*'s conventional love discourse. The *Dormeur* uses humour to devalue the *Amoureux*'s desire: 'Dormez, et aprés en somme | Faites ce dont vous avez soing', vv. 63–4.

This crude humour gives way to gentle remonstrating; the *Dormeur* warns the *Amoureux* of the dangers involved in committing oneself to *Amours* in an echo of Chartier's caveat to his young friend:

Dya, compains, qui se veult soubmectre
Desoubz l'amoureuse maistrise,
Il se fault de son cuer desmectre
Et n'estre plus en sa franchise.

vv. 137–40

---

[149] 'Remember that he who serves at court is always a guest, and lives in another's house. He eats according to another's appetite, supping with ravenous people when he is not hungry and, wracked by worries, endures hunger among those who are already satiated. He stays awake at another's request when he had already begun to fall asleep. For what is more servile than to submit natural strength and the laws of life to Fortune, when nothing in man is freer than a natural life? We who serve at the court live by another's rules', *De vita curiali*, 23–4, pp. 356–8.

The *Amoureux*, like the *Belle Dame*'s suitor, and in spite of the *Dormeur*'s warnings, persists in his quest for his lady's *mercy*. The *Dormeur*, in order to get some peace, finally reassures the *Amoureux* that his suit will be successful in the end:

> Qui bien a commencié parface
> Qui bien a choisy ne se meuve;
> Car a la ffin [sic], quoy qu'on pourchace,
> Qui desert le bien, il le treuve.

vv. 153–6

This passage participates in what I have called Chartier's 'vocabulary of closure'. The *Dormeur* utters a string of commonplaces that are revealed as insufficient propositions by recourse to Chartier's meta-rhetorical discourse on closure, as I shall explain. Chartier's ballade XXVIII, 'Il n'est danger que de villain', consists of a similar string of commonplaces or proverbs. Chartier demonstrates the circularity of these empty phrases through his arrangement of them in the ballade form whose refrain is repeated at the end of each eight-line stanza. The circularity inherent in this fixed form verse reflects and compounds the meaningless courtly discourse it encloses. The force of the line 'il n'est parler que gracïeux', v. 26, is particularly relevant to our current discussion. Chartier demonstrates through his Latin and French works that there is indeed a 'parler' outside the courtly discourse, and one that he espouses through the figures of the *Sodalis* or the *Belle Dame*. Each of the propositions of the ballade is revealed as only partially true: true within a discourse that Chartier rejects. Villon takes this satire a step further in his imitation of Chartier's ballade, 'Il n'est soing que quant on a fain', known as the *Ballade des contre-vérités*.[150] Collections of Chartier's ballades appear in twenty-six manuscript copies. Of these, seventeen contain ballade XXVIII. Ten of these seventeen are exclusively lyric collections while seven contain lyrics as well as other verse works by Chartier. Walravens dates ballade XXVIII to 1429, which would make it one of Chartier's last works before his death, documented in 1430.[151] I am inclined to agree that this is a late ballade, and a late date would support my interpretation of this piece as an ironic take on proverbial wisdom.

Beginning does not necessarily entail ending, as we have seen through Chartier's subversion of closure in his verse debates. The *Dormeur* of the

---

[150] See François Villon, *Poésies Complètes*, ed. Rychner and Henry, 3 vols. (Geneva: Droz, 1977).

[151] See Walravens's chronology of Chartier's works (1971), pp. 92–3.

Debat de reveille matin continues to reassure the *Amoureux* by appealing to the *usual* behaviour of women at court:

> Dame n'est mie si legiere
> Que pour son droit ne se deffende;
> Mais combien que Durté soit fiere,
> A la fin fault il qu'el se rende.
>
> vv. 189–92

However unmerciful a woman may seem, having put up the obligatory fight, she must give way in the end, the *Dormeur* concludes. This passage bears a striking resemblance to lines from Chartier's *Belle Dame sans mercy*, setting up an intertextual correspondence that destabilizes the *Dormeur*'s assurances:

> Dames ne sont mye si lourdes,
> Si mal entendans ne si foles
> Que, pour un peu de plaisans bourdes
> Confites en belles parolles,
> Dont vous autres tenés escoles
> Pour leur faire croire merveilles,
> Elles changent si tost leurs coles:
> A beau parler closes oreilles. *BDSM*:
>
> vv. 297–304[152]

Here the same initial proposition leads to a different conclusion. Women remain unmoved by pretty speeches: they will not be won over. Through this intertextual reference, the outcome of the *Amoureux*'s quest to win his lady is rendered uncertain, and the ending of the poem left unresolved, since at the close of the *Belle Dame sans mercy*, the *Belle Dame* remains unmoved even by her suitor's most strenuous pleas. Even the *Amoureux* despairs of his own cause, finding only insincerity and artifice where he hoped for truth: 'Et puis n'y treuve je riens fors | Courtois parler et beau semblant', vv. 215–16. He conceives of the pursuit of his lady as a game in which the stakes are high. The notion of game-playing reinforces the artificiality of the lover's suit. His lady is implicated in this game by default, and on two levels: 'fault qu'el soit juge et partie', v. 263. The lady must play the game on the lover's terms, and yet stand outside the confines of the game to judge it dispassionately. The *Belle Dame* refuses either to join the game or to pass judgement on it, a double refusal to enter into the realm of courtly play.

---

[152] I have emboldened the parallel phrases in each passage.

There is no conclusion supplied in the *Debat de reveille matin*. Before falling asleep, the *Amoureux* leaves his suit in the hands of God, praying that he will influence the lady to make the right choice. So the solution is again deferred to a point in the future beyond the textual close of Chartier's poem and, like the *Dialogus*, the protagonist puts his hope in divine judgement alone. The ending of the *Debat de reveille matin* presents an ironic reversal of traditional dream visions, in which dawn heralds awakening from sleep: 'Ainsi l'aube du jour creva | Et les compaignons s'endormirent', vv. 361–2.

Chartier again exercises his penchant for satire in the *Debat du Herault, du Vassault, et du Villain* in which the representatives of three estates discuss the plight of France, overheard by Chartier's narrator, 'Alain', who only emerges in person at the end of the debate. This debate survives in only one manuscript: Berlin, Kupferstichkabinett, 78 C 7, where it is collected with the *Lay de paix*, the *Quadrilogue invectif,* the *Livre de l'Esperance*, and the only Latin text to be copied with Chartier's French verse, the *Dialogus*. The *Herault* and the *Vassault* dominate the debate, which is joined finally by the *Villain* who has overheard their discussion. The *Herault* and the *Vassault* refuse to address the *Villain* directly, ignoring his presence. The *Villain* in this sense may be seen as yet a further projection of the author in his work, a means by which Chartier is able to pass comment on the debate from within its fictional confines. One of Chartier's most effective satirical tools is the differentiation of dialect within the debate.[153] The *Villain*'s colloquial language is indicative of his low social status, and operates as the instrument within the text by means of which Chartier undermines the noble, yet empty courtly language of the *Herault*, just as the *Dormeur* mocks the unhappy *Amoureux* in the *Debat de reveille matin*. The *Villain*, like the *Belle Dame*, delivers a stinging attack on the other speakers at the textual close of the poem:

> 'Perdra? Mais est il ja perdu!
> Que le deable en soit adouré!'
> Leur a le villain respondu,
> Qui loing d'eulx estoit demouré.
> 'A la bataille, a la bataille,

---

[153] This stratification of language might usefully be compared with Bakhtin's concept of *heteroglossia*. See 'Discourse in the Novel', in *The Dialogic Imagination: Four Essays by M. M. Bakhtin*, ed. Holquist (Austin: University of Texas Press, 1981), pp. 259–422.

> Entre vous aultres gentillastres;
> Non pas au roy tollir sa taille
> Et vous groppir gardant voz astres!'.

vv. 393–400[154]

Chartier continues in the same vein of satire in his colophon to the poem, challenging fellow-poet Pierre Nesson to write a poem 'de pire taille', v. 440. So a further poem is solicited, and closure is again deferred.

Finally, we turn briefly to Chartier's *Lay de paix*. This fixed form poem provides an intertext for Chartier's entire *oeuvre*. The *Lay de paix* (pre 1426) is one of Chartier's most widely copied poems, appearing in no fewer than forty-nine manuscripts, forty-two of which contain other works by Chartier.[155] Within the symmetrical and harmonious form of the *Lay de paix* lurk warring elements that resist closure. The poem concludes with the demise and ascension of worthy souls to God: mortal demise is the final human closure, but beyond this end, Chartier introduces hope of eternal life in God, thus opening the poem to a possible afterlife. On a metaphorical level, the image of peace, foregrounded in this work, and sought in many of his other works, represents a unifying force, tending towards perfect closure, against which the chaos of war and discord is thrown into stark relief:

> Dieux, quelz maulx et quelz dommages,
> Quelz meschiefs et quelz oultrages,
> Quelz ouvrages,
> Quelz pillages
> Et forsaiges,
> Et quans petis avantages
> Sont venuz par voz debas!

vv. 85–91

The use of the word 'debas' in this passage, referring to the quarrels that triggered the civil wars, may be extended to apply to Chartier's debate poetry. The open-endedness of his debates is thus related to the fragmentation and discontinuity effected by war. As peace is always desired in his poetry, and never attained, like the unconcluded debates,

---

[154] The *Villain* is the last to speak in the body of the debate, though the narrator records a final speech by the *Vassault* to the *Herault* after the *Villain*'s words, vv. 420–4.

[155] See my earlier discussion of the anthologization of the *Lay de paix* in Paris, BnF, fr. 25293, with *L'Abuzé en court* for the dating of this poem, p. 99, n. 63.

closure is always deferred. The fragmentation and disharmony of language, represented by dissenting voices raised in debate, is synonymous in the *Lay de paix*, as in Chartier's other Latin and French debates, with a self-serving courtly discourse which is the antithesis of sincere speech. We have seen how a meta-rhetorical discourse working through Chartier's *Dialogus, De vita curiali*, and the vernacular debates, operates an emptying of courtly discourse and conventions. Chartier focuses on the conflict between *verba* and *res*: the first of these categories refers to an intellectual language that is an end in itself, and thus closed, like the courtly game of love played out through words. The second refers to the application of a humanist rhetoric towards which Chartier strives through the agency of his debaters and narrators. This new vernacular rhetoric is a language that is engaged in ethical and political life, and one that reaches beyond artifice and closure. Through this new discourse, Chartier is able to engage with the particular *contexts* of the *Querelle des femmes* and the civil wars devastating France. By reading Chartier's vernacular debates through his *Dialogus* and *De vita curiali* and in the light of his meta-rhetorical discourse, I have suggested how the conventions and commonplaces of courtly life rendered in language are exposed and rejected. In a departure from the literary practice of his intellectual humanist predecessors, Chartier demonstrates that the game of the poetic text may have a 'serious' aim.

4

'LA VÉRITÉ DU JEU'[1]

COLLABORATIVE DEBATING COMMUNITIES IN LATE MEDIEVAL FRANCE

PART I

Text and Context

COLLABORATIVE INVENTION AND CREATIVE MODES IN THE *QUERELLE DE LA BELLE DAME SANS MERCY*

> Et me semble que vous moqués,
> Ou que ce soit esbatement
> Qu'on passe ainsi legiérement;
> Mais, quant a moy, point ne m'en loue,
> Car l'en treuve assez largement
> D'autres esbas, ou mieulx l'en joue.
>
> (*L'Amant rendu cordelier a*
> *l'observance d'amours*, vv. 771–6)[2]

The figure of the *Amant* in this anonymous[3] poem (*c.*1440) from the cycle known as the *Querelle de la Belle Dame sans mercy* expresses his

---

[1] Jacobus de Cessolis, *Le Jeu des eschaz moralisé*, ed. Collet (Paris: Champion, 1999), l. 28, p. 128

[2] *L'Amant rendu cordelier a l'observance d'amours*, ed. Montaiglon (Paris: Firmin-Didot, 1881), p. 35.

[3] *L'Amant rendu cordelier* (1881). This poem was attributed to Martial d'Auvergne by Lenglet-Dufresnoy in the 1731 Amsterdam edition of the *Arrêts d'amours*, and subsequently by Montaiglon and Söderhjelm, *Anteckningar om Martial d'Auvergne och hans Kärleksdommar* (Helsingfors, 1889); but see Piaget (1905), 416–23. The claim for authorship based solely on the similarities of expression of *arrêt* XXXVII and *l'Amant rendu cordelier* is suspect given the common reservoir of images drawn on by poets of the the *BDSM* cycle, and the fact that Martial d'Auvergne is probably not the author of the *Arrêts*.

disillusionment[4] with the game within which he is implicated—namely the game governed by *Amours*—and his desire to leave that particular sphere of play, by taking religious vows. In these lines, the *Amant*'s severe interlocutor, *Damp Prieur*, is accused of 'esbatement' at the former's expense, and advised by him to find alternative entertainment. There are further voices, and 'd'autres esbas', at play in these lines, though, as I shall suggest through a close reading of the poems that constitute the *Belle Dame sans mercy* cycle. My discussion in part I is focused on textual images of the *game*, which I shall relate to the creative and collaborative game beyond the text, by means of which the text, or body of texts forming the *Querelle* as a whole, is generated. In an extension of this game metaphor in part II, I explore the manuscript context of the *Querelle de la BDSM*, identifying common patterns of anthologization across the physical spaces of play provided by the manuscripts, and develop further the notion of the material community.

A brief description of the sequels and imitation poems that form the *Querelle de la Belle Dame sans mercy* will prove useful here for subsequent discussion. Chartier's *Belle Dame sans mercy* presents the debate between a *Belle Dame* and her suitor, overheard by the narrator-poet, in which the suitor woos his lady in vain, while she rejects him throughout in no uncertain terms. This poem, as previously discussed, provoked a long series of literary responses and imitations, starting with letters of outrage, allegedly written by ladies and men of the court, to which Chartier wrote an apology, the *Excusacion aux dames*. This was followed by the bitter *Responce des dames* in which the ladies of the court refuse to pardon Chartier for his alleged defamation of women through the heartless *Belle Dame*. A second cycle of works then joined the growing *Querelle*, consisting of fictional, poetic responses to Chartier's original in which the *Belle Dame* is tried before a series of courts of law. She

---

[4] I use this word as a self-conscious reference to the term 'illusio' used by both Huizinga and Bourdieu. Huizinga explores the semantic field of the Latin 'ludus' or 'play' (*illudere/alludere/colludere*), and suggests that one of the properties of play is the common 'illusio' or 'in-play' it establishes within a community of players. See Huizinga (rev. edn: 1998). Bourdieu's 'illusio' or 'interest' has a similar function: '*illusio* is [...] to be invested, taken in and by the game. To be interested is to accord a given social game that what happens in it matters, that its stakes are important [...] and worth pursuing', Bourdieu and Wacquant (1996), p. 116. In this sense then, the 'disillusioned' *Amant* must abandon the game since he is no longer part of the group illusion; he has become disinterested.

is alternately accused (in Baudet Herenc's *Accusations contre la Belle Dame sans mercy*),[5] pardoned (in *La Dame lealle en amours*), and finally sentenced to death (in Achille Caulier's *Cruelle Femme en amours*). A further poem, *Les Erreurs du jugement de la Belle Dame sans mercy*, presents a posthumous appeal on the part of the *Belle Dame*'s relatives, who insist unsuccessfully that her trial has been misconducted. This second cycle presents the sequels proper; the third cycle of works I refer to as imitations (Piaget's term) as they no longer concern Chartier's original characters. The third cycle of works concerns the fate of a *povre amant* figure who is rejected by his lady, and loses his case against her in court in *Le Jugement du povre triste amant banny*; his relatives later win an appeal against this verdict in *Les Erreurs du jugement du povre triste amant banny*. There follows a sequel in which the *povre amant* seeks refuge in the Church, *L'Amant rendu cordelier a l'observance d'amours*, and a final *Confession et testament de l'amant trespassé de deuil*. In addition, there are numerous debate texts written in imitation of Chartier's *Belle Dame sans mercy*, and texts which renew the theme of love trials, from Martin le Franc's *Champion des dames* to the *Arrêts d'amours*.

Here I propose to analyse the dynamics of the collaborative community formed by the *Querelle* poets in the light of Pierre Bourdieu's notions of field, habitus, and symbolic capital.[6] In my discussion of poetic play I shall also draw on the sociological studies of cultural play by Johan Huizinga,[7] and more recently by Roger Caillois.[8] (I draw on Caillois indirectly here through the application of his notion of games of *agôn* or skill to the skill of the *Querelle* poets, but will develop this parallel more explicitly in part II.) I further suggest a new classification of the poems of the *Querelle de la BDSM* into minor cycles, plumbing the semantic reservoir of images and literary patterning through which each minor cycle both finds its internal coherence and feeds into the major cycle. Recent interest in the literary debate known as the *Querelle de la BDSM* has resulted in some important contributions from Adrian Armstrong, David Hult, Joan E. McRae, and Helen Solterer,

<hr/>

[5] This is the title that occurs most frequently in the manuscript tradition, along with *Le Jugement de la BDSM*. The titles *La Dame lealle en amours* and *La Cruelle Femme en amours* are attested in the MSS tradition, and are both used in Arsenal, 3521, a manuscript central to my discussion in part II.

[6] For a definition of these terms, see my Chapter 2, pp. 56–7. See also Gaunt and Kay (1997), Bourdieu (1990) and his *Homo academicus* (Cambridge: Polity Press, 1988), particularly chapter III: 'Types of Capital and Forms of Power'.

[7] Huizinga (rev. edn: 1998).

[8] See Caillois (1967).

among others.[9] A new bilingual French edition by David Hult and Joan E. McRae presents the two cycles of sequels to the *Belle Dame sans mercy* that appear in Paris, BnF, fr. 1131.[10] McRae has produced a further edition with facing English translation.[11] Any study of the *Querelle* owes a vast debt to the scholar Arthur Piaget, whose editions of, and commentaries on, many of the poems implicated in the *Querelle de la BDSM* have helped to define its boundaries and scope.[12] For the purposes of this discussion, I shall be concerned with those poems that fall within Piaget's selection. The first cycle I identify within the *Querelle* body consists of two prose epistles,[13] *Coppie de la requeste baillee aux dames contre Alain* and *Coppie des lectres envoyees par les dames a Alain* (31 January 1425); the *Excusacion aux dames* (spring 1425),[14] written by Chartier in answer to accusations levelled at him in these letters; and a response from the *dames* to Chartier's *apologia* (*La Responce des dames faicte a maistre Allain*).[15] I label this initial cycle *Chartier on trial*, since although the texts of this cycle do not portray fictional trials as do those of the second cycle, they are pervaded by the legal language of the

---

[9] I refer to Armstrong's forthcoming book on late medieval poetic competition in France, and Solterer (1995), particularly chapter VII. Taylor, Jane (2001) also discusses poetic competition in the *Querelle* in her study of Villon, particularly chapter I, pp. 6–32 ; see also Taylor, Jane (2003). Bill Calin's article (*Fifteenth-Century Studies* 31, 2006, 31–46), 'Intertextual Play and the Game of Love: The *Belle Dame sans mercy* Cycle', touches on the *Querelle* and game theory. I am grateful to him for sending me a pre-publication version after my chapter was completed.

[10] See *Cycle de La BDSM* (2003). This new edition includes the *BDSM* sequels (*Lettre des dames*; *Lettre des amants*; *Excusacion*; *Accusations contre la BDSM*; *La Dame lealle en amours*; *La Cruelle Femme en amours*) edited from one base manuscript, BnF, fr. 1131, as well as Chartier's *Complainte*, *DRM*, and Achille Caulier's *Ospital d'Amours*; a dossier contains *Les Erreurs du jugement de la BDSM*.

[11] See *The Quarrel of the Belle Dame sans mercy* (2004).

[12] See Piaget, '*La Belle Dame sans merci* et ses imitations', *Romania* 30 (1901), 22–48, 317–51; 31 (1902), 315–49; 33 (1904), 179–208; 34 (1905), 375–428, 559–602.

[13] In manuscripts and editions of Chartier's collected *oeuvre*, these letters appear in prose form, but were versified during the fifteenth century. *La Copie de la lettre envoyee aux dames par rithme contre ledict maistre Alain, en maniere de supplication* and *Copie des lettres des dames en rithme envoyees a maistre Allain* appear in two manuscripts alongside their prose counterparts (Besançon, BM, 554; Arnhem, Bibliotheek, 79); one verse letter appears in Fribourg-Diesbach (there is no shelfmark for this manuscript as Mme. de Diesbach, owner of the Diesbach manuscripts, has now died; the collection has been dispersed, and can no longer be traced). For further details see Piaget's account in *Romania* 30 (1901), pp. 27–30, and Alain Chartier (1974), p. 328.

[14] All three works are edited in Alain Chartier (1974), pp. 360–70.

[15] See Piaget's edition of this poem in *Romania* 30 (1901), 31–5. It is found in four manuscripts, three identified by Piaget: Paris, Arsenal, 3521, fols. 74–5ᵛ; Besançon, BM, 554, fols. 77–9; Fribourg-Diesbach, fols. 30–30ᵛ; and one identified by Armstrong: Arnhem, Bibliotheek, 79, fols. 45–6ᵛ.

courtroom and can be constructed in the form of a trial.[16] The letter
from the *dames* to Alain sets out the case for the prosecution, Chartier's
Excusacion provides his defence, and the final response of the *dames*
gives their judgement, advising Chartier to make an appeal to the court
of *Amours*[17] if he is dissatisfied with the verdict.[18] The *dames* accuse
Chartier of defamation through the agency of his *Belle Dame*; but it is
he, and not his character, or his 'faulx mensongier livre'[19] that is on trial
here.[20] The *dames* point out, following Horace, that Chartier's texts,
once written, cannot be taken back, but they imply with their call for
the correction of Chartier's poem that further writing may reverse or
even efface what has gone before:

> Or escrips ce quë escripre vouldras,
> Car en tout ce que tu savras escripre
> Le jugement a raison ne touldras
> De ton meffait que nostre loz empire.
> [...]
> Sy t'en desdiz et humblement demandes
> Grace et pardon, et ton faulx livre amendes.
> En ce faisant tu respites la mort.[21]

The final sentences on Chartier, his original poem, and his characters are
never pronounced, though. Chartier himself leaves the fates of his *Belle
Dame* and her suitor in doubt, closing his text on a note of ironic ambiguity. We never discover whether Chartier does demand a second opinion from *Amours*, or whether he corrects his original poem at the ladies'
behest. This inconclusiveness is exploited by the poets of the second cycle,

[16] For an account of defamatory language in these initial texts, see Solterer (1995),
pp. 176–99.
[17] This is a reference to the institution of the *Cour amoureuse*, which may or may not
actually have existed. See my first chapter, pp. 41,50; Piaget (1891); and Bozzolo and
Loyau (1982–92).
[18] 'Riens plus n'auras de nous, c'est somme toute. | Mais s'il t'appert qu'on te face
injustice | Par trop vëoir ou par n'y vëoir goutte, | Comme dit as glosant ton mallefice,
| Requiers Amours qu'il t'en face justice, | Par devant lui appellant en cas tel, | Et nous
ferons pour moustrer ton mallice | Nos advocatz Dessarteaulx et Chastel', vv. 97–104,
Responce des dames, Cycle de La BDSM (2003), p. 499.
[19] *Responce des dames, Cycle de La BDSM* (2003), v. 42, p. 495.
[20] This long-running debate about the liability of the author arises in the earlier
Querelle de la Rose. Christine de Pizan and Jean Gerson argue that the author bears
responsibility for his texts and characters, while Pierre Col argues for the autonomy of
the characters from authorial control. See my second chapter, pp. 80–1, Baird and Kane
(1974), and also Baird (1981).
[21] *Responce des dames, Cycle de La BDSM* (2003), vv. 81–4, 92–4, p. 498.

who accept the challenge implicit in the lively debate surrounding the existing collection of texts, and choose to try Chartier's *Belle Dame* at a series of fictitious courts.

In the second cycle I collect, under the heading of the *Belle Dame on trial*, four poems: *Accusations contre la Belle Dame sans mercy*, attributed to Baudet Herenc (1425–6),[22] *La Dame lealle en amours* (1426–30),[23] *La Cruelle Femme en amours*, attributed to Achille Caulier (1430),[24] and *Les Erreurs du jugement de la Belle Dame sans mercy*.[25] (Two further poems, *Le Jugement du povre triste amant banny*,[26] and *Les Erreurs du jugement de l'amant banny*,[27] which have extensive thematic and conceptual similarities with these four texts I nonetheless collect in a third cycle, for reasons that will become apparent.) This second 'cycle' of four texts, three of which appear together in at least ten manuscripts, is identified by Hult and McRae as the *Cycle de La Belle Dame sans mercy*.[28] Like Piaget, Hult and McRae distinguish between sequels (*suites*) and imitations. In their 2003 edition, they omit 'imitations' from their definition of the *Cycle de La BDSM* proper, thus restricting it to what I have called my second cycle.[29]

The question of authorial liability debated in the first cycle is at issue in the second cycle too, but becomes part of the fiction of the trial; Chartier's original text is cited as additional evidence, either for the prosecution or for the defence. Chartier is eclipsed during Herenc's trial in the *Accusations contre la Belle Dame sans mercy*, but in *La Dame*

---

[22] Baudet Herenc, *Accusations contre la BDSM*, in *Jardin de Plaisance et fleur de rethorique*, ed. in facsimile Droz and Piaget (Paris: Firmin-Didot, 1910): I, fols. 139–42; *Cycle de La BDSM* (2003), pp. 116–67. Hult and McRae identify eighteen fifteenth- and sixteenth-century MSS, two of which are no longer consultable, *Cycle de La BDSM* (2003), p. 115. See Armstrong, whose discussion of the *Querelle* covers the cycles I have called *Chartier on trial* and the *Belle Dame on trial*.

[23] See Piaget's edition in *Romania* 30 (1901), 321–51; *Cycle de La BDSM* (2003), pp. 169–243. This poem is preserved in thirteen manuscripts; see ibid. (2003), p. 169.

[24] See Piaget's edition in *Romania* 31 (1902), 315–49; *Cycle de La BDSM* (2003), pp. 245–325. This poem is preserved in sixteen manuscripts; see ibid. (2003), p. 245.

[25] See Piaget's edition: *Romania* 33 (1904), 179–99; *Cycle de La BDSM* (2003), pp. 501–23. This poem is preserved in three manuscripts; see ibid. (2003), p. 501.

[26] See Piaget's edition: *Romania* 34 (1905), 375–411. Piaget records four manuscript witnesses: BnF, fr. 1661; Paris, Arsenal, 3523; Rome, Vat. Reg. 1363; Rome, Vat. Reg. 1720, p. 375.

[27] I refer to Piaget's edition: *Romania* 34 (1905), 412–16. Piaget records one manuscript witness: Rome, Vat. Reg. 1363.

[28] *Cycle de La BDSM* (2003), LXVII–LXXI.

[29] Hult and McRae nonetheless include an edition of the *Ospital d'Amours* and other pieces related to the *Querelle*.

lealle en amours, *Vérité* cites Chartier in her defence of the *Belle Dame*, accusing the poet not of slandering women (as did the *dames* of the first cycle texts), but specifically of slandering the *Belle Dame*:

> Car tout ala en escript mectre
> Ce que ot veü et escouté,
> Et tant par bouce que par lectre,
> Publiquement l'a raconté.
> Et oultre, de sa voulenté,
> Pour ce qu'elle l'autre escondy,
> I l'a par son escript nommé:
> 'La belle dame sans mercy'.[30]

The character of *Vérité* resurfaces in Achille Caulier's *Cruelle Femme en amours*: a poem which reverses the judgement passed in *La Dame lealle en amours* and presents a mirror image of this earlier poem. In Caulier's text, *Vérité* exculpates Chartier in order to strengthen her case against the *Belle Dame*:

> Je suis de tout bien informé
> Par ung tresnotable escripvain,
> Bien congneü et renommé,
> Qui vit et ouÿ tout aplain
> Comme l'amant, de doullour plain,
> Prioit et estoit reffusé.[31]

The relationship of author to authorial creation is rendered complex through Caulier's multi-layered fiction; the *Belle Dame* is referred to as Chartier's fictional character, and yet she appears in physical manifestation within the poem alongside her creator, who is evoked by *Vérité*, and thus himself becomes part of Caulier's fiction. As Armstrong observes, *Vérité*'s exposition of the 'poetic lie' of *La Dame lealle* reflects a similar uncertainty back onto Caulier's text.

In *Les Erreurs du jugement de la Belle Dame sans mercy*, the *Belle Dame*'s next of kin take issue with her treatment in Caulier's *Cruelle Femme*, identifying twelve 'erreurs' they allege were made in that trial, one of which is Chartier's gross exaggeration of her bad character:

> *Quarto*: la court aroit erré
> Car touchant le cas principal
> Elle adjoustoit foy au narré

---

[30] *La Dame lealle en amours, Cycle de La BDSM* (2003), vv. 513–20, p. 212.
[31] *La Cruelle Femme en amours, Cycle de La BDSM* (2003), vv. 465–70, p. 284.

> D'un tel quel livre ferïal,
> Fait par ung escripvain fiscal,
> Qui y avoit du sien bouté,
> Et d'elle dit cent fois de mal
> Plus que jamais n'avoit esté.[32]

However, within the same text, the relatives of the late *povre amant* refute this claim, defending Chartier's portrayal of the *Belle Dame*:

> Au quart erreur touchant le livre
> Qu'ilz disoient estre controuvé,
> Leur entendement estoit yvre
> […]
> L'escripvain si estoit entier,
> Et fut de ce livre facteur
> Le noble maistre Alain Chartier,
> Jadis excellent orateur
> Et si parfait explanateur
> Des comedies et faiz d'amours
> Qu'il n'a seigneur ne serviteur,
> Qu'il ne prie pour lui tousjours.[33]

These perpetual reversals raise wider questions about the stability of the community of *Querelle* texts, questions first addressed by Chartier and the *dames* of the first *Querelle* cycle, and then in subsequent cycles, culminating in the epilogue to the *Arrêts d'amours*:

> Et ceulx qu'i cuidoient pour eulx
> Eurent contre eulx, je vous affie:
> Helas! jugemens sont doubteux,
> Nul n'est pas saige qui s'i fie.[34]

In a single stanza, the author effectively undermines the fifty-one *arrêts* that constitute the text, in accordance with the rules of the game in which this same text implicates him. The accusation the *dames* level at Chartier in the *Responce des dames* could equally stand for the reversals and rewriting practised by the *Querelle* poets: 'tu dis le bien, tu l'escrips, tu l'effaces', v. 28. I suggest that this apparent instability or duality within the textual body of the *Querelle* is in fact a source of internal coherence

---

[32] *Les Erreurs du jugement de la BDSM, Cycle de La BDSM* (2003), vv. 161–68, p. 512.

[33] Ibid., *Cycle de La BDSM* (2003), vv. 489–91, vv. 497–504, p. 520.

[34] I use this same citation in expanded form in my first chapter, p. 24. See the *Arrêts d'amours* (1951), vv. 17–20, pp. 220–1.

feeding this collaborative debating community[35] whose balance derives precisely from the very dichotomies and contrarieties inherent in debate, as I suggested in my second chapter.[36] Bourdieu's concept of the collusion between opponents illuminates well the interdependence of the competing authors of the *Querelle* texts:

Each of the two camps finds the better justification of its limits within the limits of the opponent. [...] We should not [...] allow ourselves to forget the solidarities and complicities which are affirmed even in antagonism. [...] Here too there is no absolute domination of a principle of domination, but the rival coexistence of several relatively independent principles of hierarchization. The different powers are both competitive and complementary.[37]

Each individual trial sequence in each of the four texts of the second cycle is itself incomplete. Successive authors deliberately leave their poems open to future continuation and elaboration, thereby both perpetuating the community of *Querelle* texts and establishing themselves as players in a larger game. It is a game whose boundaries are repeatedly redrawn as each author adds new elements, not merely imitating or continuing other texts, but striving to outplay his/her fellow players in terms of literary inventiveness and rhetorical prowess.[38] The ambiguous conclusion to each of these poems of the second cycle inscribes them in a larger trial sequence. As I demonstrated with the texts of the first cycle, the poems of the second cycle together form a trial scenario. The *Accusations* sets out the case for the prosecution of the *Belle Dame*, while in the *Dame lealle* the *Belle Dame* is accorded counsel, defended, and duly acquitted. New evidence comes to light in the *Cruelle Femme*, the previous verdict is declared unsound, and the *Belle Dame* retried, condemned, and executed. *Les Erreurs du jugement de la Belle Dame sans mercy* constitutes a posthumous, though unsuccessful appeal on the part of the relatives.[39]

[35] When I talk about the collaborative debating community, I do not necessarily refer to a group of contemporary poets/authors. My community may also be a *virtual* community: a diachronic grouping, as is the case here with the *Querelle de la BDSM*. See my introduction, p. 7.
[36] See Chapter 2, p. 56.
[37] Bourdieu (1988), p. 113.
[38] See Gruber's study of competition and intertextuality in the troubadour corpus (1983), and Taylor, Jane (2001). Armstrong is also concerned to emphasize this spirit of rhetorical play and competition in the later medieval period and early modern period (see his forthcoming book on late medieval poetic competition).
[39] McRae also likens the structure of this sequence of poems to a trial (1997), p. 25.

The works I organize into a third cycle, the cycle of the *povre amant on trial*, share new common threads of invention, and although they take up the theme of the conflict between a *Belle Dame* and a *povre amant* figure, these figures are no longer specifically identified with Chartier's original characters, as in poems of the second cycle. In this group I include *Le Jugement du povre triste amant banny, Les Erreurs du jugement de l'amant banny, L'Amant rendu cordelier* (1440), *La Confession et testament de l'amant trespassé de deuil* attributed to Pierre de Hauteville (pre 1447),[40] and the *Arrêts d'amours* (1460–6).[41] In this third cycle, the *povre amant* takes centre stage, bringing a case before the *auditoire d'Amours* in *Le jugement du povre triste amant banny* against his absent *dame*,[42] whom his lawyer *Pitié* claims encouraged his attentions with 'ung soubzris au coin de l'ueil', v. 165. The courtroom setting of this poem mimics that of the texts of the second cycle. The poem's opening scene also draws extensively on these texts, in its portrayal of a lovelorn narrator figure who, dazed by 'ung grant escler de tonnerre', v. 5, is suddenly 'transportez et ravis', v. 19,[43] in a vision to 'la plus belle cité qu'on pourroit souhaiter', vv. 21–2, where he encounters a *povre amant*.

The sorrowing narrator of Herenc's *Accusations contre la Belle Dame sans mercy* is likewise transported in a dream to a pleasant *vergier*, at whose centre he finds an *audictoire*. The equally miserable narrator of *La Dame lealle en amours* is out hunting when his *esprevier* takes off

---

[40] *Jardin de plaisance* (1910–25): I, fols. 247–58ᵛ. Bidler has published more recent editions: *La Confession et testament de l'amant trespassé de deuil* (Montreal: CERES, 1982); 'La Complainte de l'amant trespassé de deuil; L'Inventaire des biens demourez du decés de l'amant trespassé de deuil', *Le Moyen Français* 18 (1986), 11–104. Vérard bases his edition on Arsenal, 3523, and Rome, Vat. Reg. 1728, which do not contain the *Complainte* or the *Inventaire*. These two poems precede and follow respectively the version of the *Confession* in Rome, Vat. Reg. 1363 and 1720. A fifth manuscript version of the poem is found in Rome, Vat. Reg. 1723. For a partial edition of the *Complainte*, see *Jardin de plaisance* (1910–25): II, p. 313; also pp. 306–18 for further discussion of the poem. For a partial edition of the *Inventaire* see Piaget, *Romania* 34 (1905), 427–8, and Von Keller, *Romvart: Beiträge zur Kunde Mittelalterlicher Dichtung aus italienischen Bibliotheken* (Mannheim: F. Bassermann, 1844), pp. 180–2. See Piaget's discussion of the attribution to Pierre de Hauteville in *Romania* 34 (1905), pp. 424–7.

[41] *Arrêts d'amours* (1951). For manuscripts and editions see Rychner's introduction, XLVI–LV.

[42] The use of *auditoire* here recalls Herenc's *Accusations*: 'Et eu milieu, une audictoire | Je y vys, de verte marjolainne', *Cycle de La BDSM* (2003), vv. 65–6, p. 120.

[43] The poems of the third cycle share specific elements in common, but remain linked to the first and second cycles by the semantic reservoir that feeds the entire *Querelle de la BDSM*.

after some prey,[44] and leads the narrator to a deserted valley where he encounters Chartier's *Belle Dame*, and the pair are 'ravis', v. 185, in a trance-like state, and led through a series of visions to the throne of *Amours* where fifteen personifications preside over the *Belle Dame*'s case (Herenc's *audictoire* is attended by twelve *presidens*). We find the narrator of Caulier's *Cruelle Femme en amours* in a similarly parlous condition, 'moitié en vie, moitié mort', v. 2, and hovering 'entre leesce et desconfort', v. 4. Caulier's narrator figure is out riding when he too comes across a deserted valley. So affected by his misery that he is 'ravis', v. 79, by a vision, he comes to a great palace whose walls, like the *audictoire* in the *Accusations*, are inscribed with 'ystoires', 'de ditz et de vers', v. 93.[45] He is subsequently transported for a second time, and finds himself, like the narrator of the *Jugement du povre triste amant banny*, in 'la plus belle cyté | Que onques regardast crëature', vv. 141–2. Caulier draws on previous poems of the second cycle for inspiration, but the allegorical setting of his *Cruelle Femme*, as Armstrong has observed, is far more involved than that of the *Accusations* or the *Dame lealle*, reflecting levels of poetic complexity which increase as the *Querelle* evolves.[46]

The *Erreurs du jugement de l'amant banny* draw much of their inspiration from the *Erreurs du jugement de la BDSM*, though the opening of this former poem is more closely tied to other poems of the second cycle

---

[44] This use of *esprevier* is noted subsequently in *Les Erreurs du jugement de la BDSM*, when the *parlement* is disrupted by the arrival of young men and women with their *espreviers* who wreak havoc and cause the session to be abandoned, leaving the sentence only partially pronounced: 'Le president lors se courça | Aigrement a tous les huissiers | Et en prison les menaça | Faire tenir trois moys entiers, | Deffendant que nulz espreviers | N'entrassent plus ou parlement', Piaget (1904), vv. 1033–8, p. 199. Hult and McRae give a partial edition, *Cycle de La BDSM* (2003), 501–23.

[45] 'Et eu milieu, une audictoire | Je y vys de verte marjolainne, | Ou de maintes flours vys l'ystoire | Faicte de Paris et de Helainne, | Et de Vergy la Chastelainne', *Cycle de La BDSM* (2003), vv. 65–9, p. 120; also *Le Jugement du povre triste amant banny*, 'estoient escripz a grant largesse | Virlais et rondeaux gracieux | Des fais d'amours et de noblesse', Piaget (1905), vv. 86–8, pp. 380–1. *Ekphrasis* of this sort is employed in the description of the walls of *Deduit*'s 'verger' in the *Roman de la Rose*, where various personifications are engraved: 'Si vi un vergier grant et lé, | Tout clos de haut mur bataillié, | Portrait et dehors entaillié | A maintes riches escritures', Guillaume de Lorris and Jean de Meun (1992), vv. 130–3, p. 48. Virgil's description of the images engraved on the temple of Juno in Carthage in book I of the *Aeneid* may well provide a classical source of inspiration for this medieval topos. See also Homer's description of Achilles' shield: *Iliad*, Bk.18, and Virgil's description of Aeneas's shield: *Aeneid*, Bk. 8, Virgil (1992).

[46] Armstrong discusses Caulier's practice in the *Cruelle Femme*, identifying allegorical elements in the poem drawn from previous texts of the second cycle, and ascribing Caulier's amplification of these elements to the *Querelle* poets' competitive urge in his forthcoming study of late medieval competition.

in its exploitation of the *songe* genre (one of the sub-categories of debate, and specifically of *jugement*, that I mention in my first chapter).[47] Here too a forlorn narrator, 'ravis' by the force of his introspection to the *pays d'Amours*, v. 8, finds himself before the *parlement d'Amours*, vv. 43–4. The proceedings are related by the narrator figure in the third person; there is no direct dialogue as in the other poems of the second and third cycles (the *Arrêts d'amours* follow the two *Erreurs* texts with their oblique 'legalistic' narration of events). Similarly in the *Erreurs du jugement de la BDSM*, the entire poem is related by a third party, though here we are not made aware of his existence until the final verses when the personal pronoun is unexpectedly employed:

> Si diz a par moy qu'y seroye
> Quoy que coutast le sejourner,
> **Car de tout mon cueur desiroye**
> **Ouyr lesditz arrestz donner,**
> Affin qu'aprés, au retourner,
> J'en peusse parler seurement;
> Et a tant **m'en allay disner,**
> **Car l'en ferma le parlement.**[48]

On this bathetic note, the author of this text leaves his *Erreurs* uncon-cluded, with a promise of future resolution. The *Jugement du povre triste amant banny* mimics the *Erreurs*'s delayed sentencing in the long adjournment of the *amant*'s trial (though in this poem a verdict is finally reached), adopting virtually identical patterns of language:

> Ainsy aprèz la plaidorie
> **Chascun pour disner s'en ala,**
> [...]
> Trois jours aprèz veiz le procèz
> Par le greffier en court porter,
> **Que pleust a Dieu qu'eusse eu accèz**
> **De l'ouyr au long rapporter;**
> **Onques chose plus escouter**
> **Ne desiray que ceste la,**
> Se j'eusse eu lieu ou me bouter,
> **Mais tout estoit cloz çà et la.**[49]

---

[47] See Chapter 1, p. 30.
[48] *Erreurs du jugement de la BDSM*, Piaget (1904), vv. 1049–56, p. 199. I have emboldened the language that corresponds with the subsequent passage cited from *Le Jugement du povre triste amant banny*.
[49] *Jugement du povre triste amant banny*, Piaget (1905), vv. 1193–4, 1201–8, p. 407.

In the *Erreurs du jugement de l'amant banny*, the author undermines his text by suggesting that the narrator's transcription of the *arrêts* may be unreliable. The narrator tells us that he was only able to catch one of the three or four that the judge pronounced (speaking in such a way that 'sembloit [qu'il] se voulsist *esbatre*',[50] v. 79).[51] In its reversal of the judgement passed on the *povre amant* in the *Jugement du povre triste amant banny*, *Les Erreurs du jugement de l'amant banny* mimics the technique that Caulier employs earlier in the cycle in his *Cruelle Femme*.[52] The prosecution's case in the *Jugement du povre triste amant banny* is discredited in this second *Erreurs* poem of the *Querelle*:

> [...]L'en a trouvé
> Ou premier procès ung rapport
> Falsifié et reprouvé
> D'un conseiller nommé Discord
> Qui par hayne, faveur ou port,
> Y avoit usé de malice.[53]

The reflexivity of the two pairs of poems, *Dame lealle/Cruelle Femme* and *Cruelle Femme/Les Erreurs du jugement de la BDSM*, refers us back to Bourdieu's theory of the collusion of opponents: each poem exists in

---

[50] My emphasis. The lexemes of *esbatre* are used throughout the *Querelle* body, in contexts fundamentally related to the play in which the *Querelle* poets are implicated by the creation of these texts. See part II for further exploration of the semantic field of *esbatre* and its frequent partner *combatre*.

[51] 'Onques ne veiz plus grant memoire | Ne si parfait entendement; | Si prins lors mon escriptoure | Pour les rediger rondement. | Assez parloit legerement | Par quoy tout ne pouoie escripre | Ne n'en rapportay seulement | Que ce que vous orrez cy dire', *Les Erreurs du jugement de l'amant banny*, Piaget (1905), vv. 81–8, p. 413.

[52] The author of *Les Erreurs du jugement de l'amant banny* uses the *Dame lealle/Cruelle Femme* pairing as a model for the reflexivity of his poem with the *Jugement du povre triste amant banny* rather than the *Cruelle Femme/Erreurs du jugement de la BDSM* pairing since, as Piaget remarks in *Romania* 33 (1904), 179–80, the first *Erreurs* poem does not reject and reverse the sentence passed in the *Cruelle Femme*, but merely attempts to show that it was flawed.

[53] *Erreurs du jugement de l'amant banny*, Piaget (1905), vv. 241–6, p. 416. Compare *Vérité*'s assertion in the *Cruelle Femme* that she and fellow defence lawyer *Loyauté* have been falsely represented by *Fiction* and *Fausseté* in the *Dame lealle*: '«Moy, dist elle, ne Loyaulté | Ne savons rien de tout ce cy, | Se ce n'est ce qu'en a conté | Cest escuyer qui est droyt cy. | Celle qui se mist en mon non | Pour ceste cause soustenir | Ne fu aultre que Fiction: | Poëtrie luy fist venir | En ma semblance devenir; | Et se transmüa Faulceté | Pour la traÿson parfournir | En la semblance Loyaulté', *Cruelle Femme en amours, Cycle de La BDSM* (2003), vv. 325–6, p. 272.

a space delimited by the boundaries of the other poem.[54] The material *mise en page* of these texts frequently reinforces this sense of collusion and competition. Rubrics in Paris, BnF, fr. 1169, for example, direct us to read *Dame lealle/Cruelle femme* against each other. The poems run on in the manuscript, with the explicit of one facing the incipit of the other (fol. 126ᵛ, fol. 127); the second poem bears the title, *Le Jugement contraire a la leale dame en amours*. This notion of interdependence may account for the stability and coherence of the *Querelle* texts within their own particular literary framework, and for their instability and incompleteness as separate texts.

Instability is introduced at the textual close of *Le Jugement du povre triste amant banny* in the uncertain fate ascribed to the *povre amant*:

> Et comme tout homme desvé
> **Ses cheveulx aux ongles tira**
> **Disant: 'Ma vie tost finera!**
> Ma personne sy est mauldite
> N'amours jamais ne servira.
> Adieu! je m'en vois rendre hermite!'
> **Sy ne sçay dès lors qu'il devint.**
> **La veue a ceste heure en perdy.**[55]

The continuing influence of Chartier's original poem can be directly observed in this passage that the poet of *l'Amant rendu cordelier* will later adapt as the premise for his own text. This next sequel to the *povre amant's* tribulations is set in the narratorial frame we have now come to recognize as typical of the *Querelle*. The narrator, lulled to sleep by the sound of a chambermaid singing and playing a *bastouer clicquant*, dreams that he is transported (*ravit*) by 'un grant boullon d'eaue', vv. 9–10, and carried by 'ung estourbillon de vent', vv. 11–12, to the *forest de Desesperance*. At this point *Amours*, answering his call for help, leads him, with the

---

[54] A similar interdependence can be observed in Guillaume de Machaut's two *Jugement* poems, the latter a reversal of the sentence passed in the former. See Machaut (1988) and (1988b).

[55] *Jugement du povre triste amant banny*, Piaget (1905), vv. 1363–70, p. 411. I have emboldened the language which most closely reproduces Chartier's text: 'Adont le dolent se leva | […] Et dist: 'Mort, vien a moy courant | Ains que mon sens se descongnoisse, | Et m'abrege le demourant | De ma vie plaine d'engoisse'. | Depuis je ne sceu qu'il devint | Ne quel part il se transporta; | […] Et depuis on me rapporta | Qu'il avoit ses cheveux desroux, | Et que tant se desconforta | Qu'il en estoit mort de courroux', *BDSM*, Alain Chartier (1974), vv. 769, 773–8, 781–4, p. 359.

help of a shining arrow,[56] to a magnificent *chapelle* where he encounters the sorrowing lover, and observes the gradual process of the lover's conversion by the austere *Damp Prieur*. Although this text does not specifically fall into the category of trial fictions, the *povre amant* remains on trial here too: obliged to make a choice between the passionate, yet unstable, world of *Amours* and the relative stability and sobriety of a life devoted to God, he must choose whether to play the game or to renounce it. Both *l'Amant rendu cordelier* and Pierre de Hauteville's *La Confession et testament de l'amant trespassé de deuil* are considerably less derivative than the previous *Querelle* poems, constituting new potential narrative directions rather than imitations or reversals of existing texts. The latter poem in particular seems to introduce a new frame of invention, composed virtually entirely in the first person by a narrator figure fused with the *povre amant* figure of the third cycle.

In the *Inventaire des biens demourez du decez de l'amant trespassé de deuil*, which follows the *Confession et testament de l'amant trespassé de deuil* in two manuscripts, the contents of the late *amant*'s library set up explicit intertextual references to a number of other poems in the *Querelle*, reinforcing our sense of the interdependence of texts:

> Item sur ung faitiz pulpitre
> Estoit tendue sa librairie,
> [...]
> Le livre des *Joies et Doulours*
> *Du Jenne Amoureux Sans Soucy*,
> **La Belle Dame Sans Mercy**
> Et aussi *l'Ospital d'Amours*.
> *Passe temps Michault* y estoit,[57]

---

[56] It is 'une sajecte ardant et plaine de **clarté**', vv. 43–4, recalling the '**clarté**' which 'aönda droyt | Sus nous' in the *Dame Lealle*, vv. 147–8; or *Amours* himself who 'tant fut de clere couleur | Avironné', vv. 245–6. There is also an insistence on clarity in the *Cruelle Femme*: the palace is paved 'de matiere **clere** et dure', v. 109. The various palaces and courts of the *Querelle* texts are often made of 'cristal' and encrusted with bright jewels. References to clarity within the domain of *Amours* present a foil to the images of darkness outside the realm of *Amours*, and of those banned from that realm; the *povre amant* is frequently portrayed wearing black: 'le noir portoit et sans devise', *BDSM*, v. 102; 'ce jour de noir se revety', *Le Jugement du povre triste amant banny*, vv. 53; 'un povre amant [...] | Portant le noir et sans devise', *L'Amant rendu cordelier*, vv. 82–3. Green, by contrast, is the colour of *Amours* par excellence; the wearing of green is woven into the network of images of song, music, dance, and play running through the *Querelle*.

[57] It is interesting to find Michault Taillevent's *Passe temps* in the *amant*'s library, as this is a text that frequently appears in the manuscripts that collect poems of the *BDSM* cycle, as I shall discuss in part II. As well as the library and other goods, the *amant* also

> *L'Amoureux rendu cordelier*,
> Et d'autres livres ung millier
> Ou le Defunct **si s'esbatoit**.[58]

Three of the texts cited here form part of the *Querelle* proper; I have included Achille Caulier's *Ospital d'Amours* in the fourth cycle of texts, as I shall explain,[59] although it is closely linked with both the poems of the second and third cycles, and pre-dates the latter cycle.[60] The description of the *esbatement* the 'defunct' used to derive from his library is significant for our model of the competitive, collaborative game of invention played in the *Querelle* and its system of internal references to game-playing.[61] A previous internal reference to the *Querelle* body comes in the *Cruelle Femme*, when *Amours* mentions the trial of the *Belle Dame* held in the *Dame lealle*, referring to it as 'le tiers livre',[62] thus drawing attention to the fictionality of both trials, and to the external organizing principles of that fiction which are the rules of the *Querelle*.

The *Arrêts d'amours* represents, in a sense, the culmination of the *Querelle*. Composed between 1460 and 1466, this is one of the last works within the textual body, and as such has access to images and structures from poems of the first, second, and third cycle, as well as from fourth cycle texts. Jean Rychner attributes the *Arrêts d'amours* to Martial d'Auvergne in his 1951 edition of the poem, citing Martial's library in support of his claim since, like the fictional library of the late *povre amant*, it may have contained previous *Querelle* texts. Rychner suggests that Martial may have owned the manuscript, now Rome, Bibliotheca

leaves behind a chessboard, another arena for skilled play that I shall investigate further in part II; see *Complainte de l'amant trespassé de deuil* (1986), v. 421, p. 70.

[58]   See *Complainte de l'amant trespassé de deuil* (1986), vv. 425–6, 437–44, pp. 70–1.

[59]   This poem, often wrongly attributed to Alain Chartier, enjoyed enormous popularity, appearing in twenty-three manuscripts, and all early editions of Chartier's works. See Piaget, *Romania* 34 (1905), 559–60; *Cycle de La BDSM* (2003), pp. 327–437. Piaget notes that Achille Caulier leaves an acrostic signature: ACILES, which can be read at the beginnings of the first six lines of the first six huitains of the *Ospital*. Caulier also leaves an acrostic signature in the final huitain of his *Cruelle Femme*; see Piaget, *Romania* 31 (1902), 349.

[60]   Piaget dates *L'Ospital* post-*Cruelle Femme*, since the *Belle Dame*, 'nouvellement noÿe en plours', appears in *L'Ospital d'Amours* in a corner of the cemetery reserved for those who are banished by *Amours*: *Cycle de La BDSM* (2003), v. 470, p. 368; Alain Chartier (1617), p. 734.

[61]   See also the passage from *l'Amant rendu cordelier* quoted at the beginning of this chapter.

[62]   In the sequence of *BDSM*, *Accusations*, *Dame lealle* and *Cruelle Femme*, the *Dame lealle* is the 'tiers livre', as Piaget observes in *Romania* 31 (1902), 332, n. 1.

Apostolica Vaticana, Reg. 1363,[63] which contains the *Querelle* poems whose influence can be most closely traced in the *Arrêts*.[64] It seems unlikely that Martial d'Auvergne is the author of this text, but there is no doubt that the author was greatly influenced by these poems of the third cycle of imitations of the *Belle Dame sans mercy*. The legal language of the previous trial cycle reaches a climax in the *Arrêts*, whose clipped prose and oratio obliqua imitate the style of the two *Erreurs* texts. The author adopts the convention of the narrator turned scribe, who records the fifty-one *arrêts* that are to be pronounced. Through our reading of the two *Erreurs* poems, we are aware of the fallibility of this scribal figure and the limitations of his record of events. In the *Erreurs du jugement de la BDSM*, we are subject to the whims of the narrator, who goes off to dinner after the *parlement* closes, hoping to return to hear the pronouncement of the *arrêts*. The text ends at this point, however, and so, within the fictional frame, we must assume either that the narrator did not hear the sentences, or that he neglected to record them, leaving his account unfinished. In the *Erreurs du jugement de l'amant banny*, as mentioned above, the narrator-scribe is only able to record the single *arrêt* he overhears, leading us to question even the reliability of this account.

As we have seen, the author undermines the substance of his *Arrêts* in the epilogue to his work, highlighting not just its own instability but, by implication, that of each of the discrete *Querelle* texts. It is only in the context of the *Querelle* and its relational networks of metaphor and language that these texts gain coherence. The *Arrêts* vary in length, though their structure remains constant. First the appellant or *demandeur* sets out his/her case, which is then refuted by the *deffendeur*; either a verdict is pronounced by the court after this first exchange, or a further set of appeals is made on both sides. Each *arrêt* rehearses the same set of legalistic formulae. *Arrêts* I–XVI are held first before minor tribunals, and then before the *parlement d'Amours*, while *arrêts* XVII–LI take place directly before the *parlement d'Amours*. The fictional courtroom setting, discarded in *L'Amant rendu cordelier* and the *Confession et testament*, is here restored. The *povre amant* of the other third cycle texts is to be seen in a multitude of manifestations, pleading his case against a merciless

---

[63] *Arrêts* (1951), XXXV–XXXVI.
[64] This MS contains *La Confession et testament de l'amant trespassé de deuil* (preceded by the *Complainte de l'amant trespassé de deuil*, and followed by the *Inventaire*), fols. 1–84^v; *l'Amant rendu cordelier*, fols. 105–64^v; *Le Jugement du povre triste amant banny*, fols. 165–208^v; *Les Erreurs du jugement de l'amant banny*, fols. 209–16^v; and *Les Erreurs du jugement de la BDSM*, fols. 217–49^v.

Belle Dame figure. The trial configurations of the *Arrêts* also include *Belle Dame* figures pleading against disloyal lovers, relatives pleading on behalf of late *Belle Dame/povre amant* figures, and frivolous cases such as the accusation brought against the 'gauffriers et patissiers' by the 'galans amoureux' who complain that the former obscure the exits of common lovers' meeting places with their smoke (XLVII). Of the fifty-one *arrêts*,[65] five specifically draw their setting from texts within the *Querelle* body: one is inspired by the *Belle Dame sans mercy* itself (XXV), while another four are inspired by texts collected within Rome, Vat. Reg. 1363.[66] A central theme tying the *Arrêts* to the *Querelle* body is that of banishment from the *pays d'Amours* for betrayal of its codes of conduct, a theme that can also be traced in the practice of the *Querelle* poets and their production of text, as I shall later suggest.[67]

The fourth cycle I label the *Belle Dame sans mercy on trial*—to be distinguished from the second and third cycles (the *Belle Dame* and *povre amant on trial* respectively)—since the poems I categorize here no longer deal with Chartier's characters *per se*, but present reversals and imitations of his original poem, and are usually constructed in the form of debates between a lover and his lady. I have organized the minor cycles according to a principle of common thematic content rather than chronologically, to produce a complex relational network compatible with Bourdieu's model of field. In this cycle I include three poems originally attributed to Chartier, *La Belle Dame qui eut merci*,[68] the *Dialogue d'un Amoureux et de sa Dame*,[69] and Caulier's *Ospital d'Amours*, as well as a series of

---

[65] There are, in addition, two apocryphal *arrêts*. See *Arrêts* (1951), XLI–XLII.

[66] See *arrêt* XXXVI (*Les Erreurs du jugement de la BDSM*); *arrêt* XVII (*Le Jugement du povre triste amant banny*); *arrêt* XXXVII (*L'Amant rendu cordelier*) and *arrêt* XXXIV (*Confession et testament*).

[67] In *arrêt* XXV, modelled after the *BDSM*, sentence is passed on the *defenderesse* that she be 'bannie et privee a tousjours du roiaume d'Amours et des biens qui y sont', vv. 109–10, pp. 121–2. Likewise, in the *Jugement du povre triste amant banny*, the court bans the *amant* from seeing his *dame*, and prohibits all lovers from dancing the infamous 'dance du chappellet'.

[68] Piaget places the composition of this poem before Chartier's *BDSM*; see *Romania* 33, pp. 200–6. But see Joan Grenier-Winther's online edition of the poem at http://www.catchwords.org/belledame.

[69] See Alain Chartier (1617), pp. 684–94 and 782–92 respectively. See also Piaget, *Romania* 33 (1904), 200–6, 206–8, and Joan Grenier-Winther (ibid.) for manuscripts, editions, and discussion of attribution. Piaget attributes *La Belle Dame qui eut merci* to the poet Oton de Granson. There are eighteen manuscript versions of *La Belle Dame qui eut merci*. *Le Dialogue d'un Amoureux et de sa Dame* appears in only four (possibly six with Arnhem and Copenhagen) MSS; it was usually copied with *La Belle Dame qui eut merci*, and in Arsenal, 3523, it follows this poem.

minor poems partially edited by Piaget:[70] *Le Traité de Réveille qui dort*;[71] *Le Débat sans conclusion*;[72] *Le Desconseillé d'Amours* (c.1442) attributed to Henri Anctil;[73] *Le Loyal Amant refusé* (and its counterpart *Le Desloyal Amy*);[74] *La Desserte du desloyal*;[75] *La Sépulture d'Amours*;[76] *Le Martyr d'Amours* (1464), attributed to Franci;[77] and *Le Débat de la Dame et de l'Écuyer* (c.1440).[78]

Caulier's *Ospital d'Amours* is an innovative text, which, while adopting many of the conventions of previous *Querelle* poems,[79] introduces a number of new metaphors, notably the *ospital d'Amours* of the title and the *cimetière d'Amours*,[80] subsequently incorporated into the metaphorical framework of the *Querelle* by later poets. The opening of the *Ospital* runs along familiar lines. The narrator, refused by his lady, enters a trance-like state, and finds himself on a grim path called 'Trop Dure Responce', which opens onto a deserted place. However, within the narrative landscape, Caulier's narrator-lover records only events in which he is the main player, rather than passively observing the fates of others, as the narrator-figures of poems of the second and

---

[70] Piaget (1905) identifies a series of other minor poems connected to the *Querelle*, which I leave out of my discussion, since those poems Piaget chooses to edit, or partially edit, seem adequate representation, pp. 589–97. Piaget's list comprises the following: *Procès du banny a jamais du jardin d'Amours* (attributed to Aimé de Montfaucon); *Le Serviteur sans guerdon*; *L'Amoureux transy sans espoir* (Jean Bouchet); *L'Amant refusé*; *L'Amoureux desconforté*; *L'Epistre envoyée a une damoyselle sans pitié amoureuse*; *La Rigueur ou la Cruaulté d'Amours* (attributed to René le Peletier); and two obscene parodies of the BDSM, edited in *Jardin de plaisance* (1910–25): I, fols. 126–9, 132–6.

[71] See Piaget (1905), pp. 565–70. Piaget lists two manuscripts: Paris, BnF, fr. 1131, fols. 173–83ᵛ, and Paris, BnF, fr. 2264, fols. 85–98ᵛ.

[72] Piaget (1905), pp. 570–4, and *Jardin de plaisance* (1910–25): I, fols. 148–53ᵛ. Piaget lists three manuscripts: Paris, Arsenal, 3523, fols. 793–818; Brussels, BR, 10969, fols. 153–71; Turin, L. IV. 3, fols. 118ᵛ–24ᵛ.

[73] Id., pp. 574–7. Piaget lists one manuscript: Turin, L. IV. 3, fols. 140ᵛ–7ᵛ.

[74] Id., pp. 577–9. Piaget locates *Le Loyal Amant refusé* in Besançon, BM, 554 (fols. 141–60ᵛ), and *Le Desloyal Amy* in Turin, L. IV. 3 (fols. 50ᵛ–63ᵛ).

[75] Id., pp. 579–81. Piaget lists four manuscripts: Paris, BnF, fr. 924, fols. 155–71; Paris, Arsenal, 3523, fols. 219–46; The Hague, T. 328, fol. 106 ff.; Turin, L. IV. 3, fol. 147ᵛff.

[76] Id., pp. 581–2. Piaget lists two manuscripts: BnF, fr. 924, fols. 139–54ᵛ; BnF, fr. 2264, fols. 64–78.

[77] Id., pp. 583–5. Piaget lists one manuscript: BnF, fr. 1661, fols. 12ᵛ–27.

[78] Id., pp. 585–9. I refer to the version in the *Recueil de poésies françoises des XV et XVI siècles*, ed. Montaiglon (Paris: P. Jannet, 1856): IV, pp. 151–79. Piaget lists one manuscript: Besançon, BM, 554, fols. 95ᵛ–106ᵛ.

[79] See *La Requeste baillee aux dames contre Alain*: 'en un pas qui se nomme Dure Response', Alain Chartier (1974), p. 361.

[80] The narrator of Caulier's *Cruelle Femme* also comes upon a 'cymentiere | Ou estoyent les trespassés', *Cycle de La BDSM* (2003), vv. 211–12, p. 262.

third cycles do. Like the majority of the *Querelle* texts, Caulier's poem ends in uncertainty. The lover is finally accorded a 'franc baiser' by his lady within the dream sequence. The poem then ends as the lover awakes, hoping to obtain his lady's embrace in reality.[81] The deserted place which Caulier's narrator stumbles upon, full of the hanging, drowned, or burning corpses of lovers past, forms part of the language of banishment which informs the *Querelle* body, and which serves as a metaphor for the rules of the *Querelle* itself:

> Ce desert estoit hors des termes
> De droit et contraire a nature:
> La ne pleut que pluye de lermes,
> La ne peust vivre crëature.[82]

The notion of a place beyond the jurisdiction of *Amours* where there is no *verdure*,[83] flowers,[84] music,[85] or dancing (the conventional accompaniments of *Amours*), necessarily reinforces the contrary and complementary notion of a circumscribed area in which *Amours* holds sway, an area of play which I assimilate to the textual play of the *Querelle* as a whole. Those fictional lovers who choose to stay within the *pays d'Amours* and abide by the rules of play can be likened to the poets of the *Querelle* who choose to abide by the rules of the game, and hence become a part of the collaborative network of players.

[81] 'Si luy requier a jointes mains | Que le songe veulle averir; | Et je ne requier plus ne mains, | Ne plus hault ne veul advenir: | C'est mon plus grant bien a venir, | C'est tout le plus hault de mon veul, | C'est mon sollas, mon souvenir, | Et la fin de ce que je veul', *Ospital, Cycle de La BDSM* (2003), vv. 1273–80, p. 436.

[82] *Cycle de La BDSM* (2003), vv. 137–40, p. 340.

[83] A complex of references to the colour green accompanies descriptions of lovers and the court of *Amours*; its absence from a place or a person suggests their existence outside the realm of *Amours*. For example: 'ce lieu desplaisant | Ou nulle verdure n'avoit', *Dame lealle, Cycle de La BDSM* (2003), vv. 69–70, p. 174; 'En ceste vallee diverse | N'avoit herbe, fleur, ne verdure', *Cruelle Femme*, ibid. (2003), vv. 41–2, p. 248; 'd'amours plus ne parlerés | Ne de telles folies mondaines; | Que vert ne vermeil porterés, | Bouqués, roses ne marjolaines', *L'Amant rendu cordelier* (1881), vv. 1397–400, p. 61. The *amant* of the *Confession et testament* asks that 'ceulx qui les dueilz meneront | Se jour de vert se vestiront', Pierre de Hauteville (1982), vv. 1153–4, p. 70.

[84] The flowers liberally scattered throughout the *Querelle* texts are bound to the realm of *Amours* by a long literary tradition, but also evoke the medieval metaphor of 'flowers of rhetoric'. Specifically named flowers often set up intertextualities: 'marjolaines' are repeatedly cited both independently and in locutions such as 'les marjolaines querre', *Le Jugement du povre triste amant banny*, Piaget (1905), v. 2, p. 379; 'marjolaines [...] arouser', *L'Amant rendu cordelier* (1881), vv. 413–14, p. 20, or 'reveiller les potz de marjolaine', *Arrêts* (1951), XXI, v. 45.

[85] See Gaunt and Kay (1999); Gaunt (1989); and Kay (1990) for discussion of music and troubadour debate.

Music and song lie at the origins of the debate genre in France; and are fused with it, for example, in the *tensos* of the troubadours.[86] The frequent allusions to the making of music within the *Querelle* provide an internal frame of reference, which, by association, comes to represent the creation of the *Querelle* itself. The self-referentiality set up by this network of allusions to music and song within the *Querelle* is particularly well illustrated by the *Inventaire* of the *povre amant* whose library we are told included:

> Ung caier noté de leçons
> De basses dances nouveletes,
> Et ung autre plein de chançons
> De pastoureaux et bergeretes.[87]

We note also the restrictions imposed on the *povre amant* by *Damp Prieur* in *L'Amant rendu cordelier* as he is instructed to leave the realm of *Amours* behind him. The *povre amant* must renounce all music, song, poetry, dance, or celebration:

> Item, qu'en logis de plaisance,
> Sur vostre vie, n'aviserés,
> N'en lieu ou ait feste ne dance.
> […]
> Que, quant menestriés vous orrez,
> Fleutes, doucines ou vielles,
> Vous grain ne les escouterés,
> Mais metrés voz dois aux oreilles.[88]

Similarly, in the *Jugement du povre triste amant banny*, the notorious 'dance du chappellet' is outlawed for lewdness, while in the *Erreurs du jugement de l'amant banny* this indictment of the 'chappellet' is reversed.

The minor poems draw their inspiration in the main from Chartier's *Belle Dame sans mercy*, and from poems of the second or fourth cycles, introducing little new material into the *Querelle*. Against Piaget who dismisses these pieces out of hand, I argue that they participate in the competitive and skilful game (Caillois's category of *agôn*) of the *Querelle*, adding some ingenious new elements to the mix.[89] In the *Débat sans*

---

[86] See Huizinga's reflections on the semantic roots of the French 'jouer' and 'jongleur': Huizinga (rev. edn: 1998).

[87] *Complainte de l'amant* (1986), vv. 433–6, p. 71.

[88] *L'Amant rendu cordelier* (1881), vv. 1385–7, 1389–92, p. 61.

[89] Piaget is damning of these minor poems, as of the *Querelle* poems in general, failing to see that it is precisely the similarities and reflexivities at play between texts which

conclusion for example, the author, as the title suggests, leaves his poem ostensibly incomplete. In an echo of the original *Belle Dame*'s suitor, the lover issues an ultimatum to his lady, asking for her 'final response', 'mort ou mercy'. Just as she is about to answer, the attention of the narrator shifts to a deer hunt. The narrator leaves the reader with the ironic juxtaposition of a deer which has been caught, and an as yet free *dame*, whose lover is still in pursuit of *his* 'gibier d'Amours':

> La dame avoit bouche ouverte
> A respondre quant la survint
> Le serf tout a la descouverte
> Lors fut la maniere couverte
> Car prestement aller convint
> Au lac ou la chasse parvint
> Illec fut la beste tenue
> Et prinse a force devenue.[90]

La Sépulture d'Amours introduces a conventional image that, in a wider context, hints at the individual poet's engagement in the space of play governed by the rules of the *Querelle*:

> Habandonné et despourveu,
> Ne servant aucune maistresse,
> Si me volut en la forteresse
> D'esbatement et de deduit,
> Pour avoir joyë ou destresse,
> Faire entrer soubz son sauconduit.[91]

Images of games and game-playing pervade the *Querelle* body.[92] This network of references sets up a field of play within the fiction of the

---

characterize this body of work as a crucial, collaborative late medieval literary enterprise: 'Toute cette production littéraire est d'une grande pauvreté. *La Belle Dame sans merci* mise à part, avec l'*Amant rendu cordelier* et quelques fragments de deux ou trois autres poèmes, tout le reste est sans originalité et sans esprit', Piaget (1905), p. 593.

[90] There is a further conversation between the lover and his *dame* at the close of the text, but the narrator cannot hear them: 'Veoye bien qu'ilz devisoient | Mais je ne scay ce qu'ilz disoient', *Jardin de plaisance* (1910–25), fol. 153.

[91] *Sépulture*, Piaget (1905), vv. 11–16, p. 582.

[92] I collect here a representative sample of references to both actual and metaphorical games; to collect them all would take a full-length study: ' ... car ceste femme adés | Le faisoit jouer mal appoint, | Pour ce qu'elle changeit les dés', *Accusations, Cycle de La BDSM* (2003), vv. 506–8, p. 158; 'Item a ses jolys verbois | Je laisse abatre blé et bois, | Courir, saulter, saillir en haines, | Frainguer et dancer «hault le bois», | «Tire t'arriere, je m'en vois», | Et faire cent mille fredaines', *Confession et testament*, Pierre de Hauteville (1982), vv. 871–6, p. 57; 'Item, et sy ne jouerez | Au siron ne a cligne mussettes, | Au jeu de *Mon amour aurés*, | A la queuleuleu, aux billettes, | Au tiers, au perier, aux buchettes, |

Querelle texts, which finds its corollary in the field of play constituted by the texts themselves. Similar complexes of references, such as those to the colour green as representative of *Amours*, to music and dance, or to the deceptive power of language,[93] engage both at the level of the text, through intertextuality and self-referentiality, and on the level of the *Querelle* poets, whose web of self-reflexive invention implicates them in a social network of relations with one another:

> Aussy souvent vous esbatrés
> A lire dans ce petit livre
> Ou nostre rigle trouverés
> Et comment l'en doit ceans vivre.[94]

The text of *L'Amant rendu cordelier* is particularly rich in the language of play, giving deeper insights into the complex processes of collaborative invention at work in the *Querelle* through its position in the more self-consciously imitative third cycle, itself fed by first, second, and in some cases, fourth cycle texts. In the passage cited above, *Damp Prieur*, continuing his conversion of the *povre amant*, encourages him to read the rules of the Church in order to attain a profound knowledge of its workings, and so adapt himself to their way of life. This 'petit livre' is analogous to the textual body of the *Querelle*; through its perusal and adoption of the 'rigle' contained therein, the lover-poet may find *esbatement*, and he may himself enjoy the game of invention. Huizinga's definition of the

---

A gecter au sain et dos l'erbe, | Au propos, pour dire sornettes, | Ne *Que paist on*, ne *Qui paist herbe*', *L'Amant rendu cordelier* (1881), vv. 1729–36, p. 75; 'Hier sur le tart, soubz l'ombre d'un tapis | En passant temps, comme souvent m'esbas | Ainsi que les gens sont cachés et tapis | Pour mieulx ouïr et voir jeus et esbas', *Le Débat de la Dame et de l'Écuyer*, *Recueil de poésies françoises*, vol. IV, p. 151.

[93] This is a recurrent *Querelle* topos and significant in the light of my Chapter 3. It originates with the *Belle Dame*'s rejection of her suitor's courtly 'beau parler', v. 304, and 'plaisans bourdes', v. 299, which are nothing more than 'fol parler', v. 729; see Alain Chartier (1974), pp. 342, 357. The *Requeste baillee aux dames contre Alain* speaks of a 'langaige afaictié', v. 25, id., p. 362; the *Belle Dame* is accused of 'rudes parlers rigoreux' in the *Accusations*, *Cycle de La BDSM* (2003), v. 394, p. 148; the *amant* in the *Erreurs du jugement de la BDSM* is a 'beau bailleur de parabolles', Piaget (1904), v. 20, p. 183. In the *Jugement du povre triste amant banny*, *Pitié* accuses *Justice* and *Raison* of using a 'faux langaige pervers', v. 740, and again, 'langaige perdu', v. 765, 'superflu langaige', v. 794, 'mauvaiz langage', v. 999, Piaget (1905), pp. 395, 396, 401. The *povre amant* of *L'Amant rendu cordelier* (1881) uses a paraphrase of the *Belle Dame*'s speech in Chartier's poem, v. 38, 'pour ung peu de plaisans langaiges', v. 340, p. 17. The foolish lover of *Amours*'s speech in the *Ospital d'Amours* hides his deception 'en ung beau langage', *Cycle de La BDSM* (2003), v. 1052, p. 418; the lover of *Le Débat sans conclusion* is accused of 'parler tout en ambage', *Jardin de plaisance* (1910–25), fol. 150.

[94] *L'Amant rendu cordelier* (1881), vv. 997–1000, p. 44.

particular conditions necessary for play will further illuminate the organization of the play community as formed by the *Querelle* poets:

We might call it [play] a free activity standing quite consciously outside
'ordinary' life as being 'not serious', but at the same time absorbing the player
intensely and utterly. [...] It proceeds within its own proper boundaries of
time and space according to fixed rules and in an orderly manner. It promotes
the formation of social groupings which tend to surround themselves with
secrecy and to stress their difference from the common world by disguise or
other means.[95]

The notion of the poetic play of the *Querelle* existing in a space beyond
the boundaries of 'ordinary' life, as a 'non-serious' occupation is illustrated by the *povre amant*'s punishment at the hands of the other 'cordeliers' who discover him engaged in the illicit enjoyment of ballades:[96]

> Le galant fut prins, a l'escart,
> Au pré de recreation,
> Ou la, pour consolacion,
> Sy faisoit bien ses espenades
> En lisant, par devocion,
> Ung livre tout plain de ballades.[97]

We note the description of the *amant*, 'a l'escart', separated both spatially
and ideologically from the 'cordeliers' by his choice of pursuit. He is found
'au pré de recreation', enjoying his illicit reading in a space delimited specifically for play, recalling Huizinga's concept of the playground.[98] The
povre amant makes his 'devocion' to *Amours*, 'intensely and utterly' caught
up in the game that unfolds within the service of this god. The 'livre tout
plain de ballades' might again be interpreted as the ensemble of poetry in
the *Querelle* that the lover-poet reads assiduously in order himself to enter
into the game as an initiate.[99]

---

[95] Huizinga (rev. edn: 1998), p. 13.

[96] I assert in my third chapter, however, that Chartier's particular poetic game has a
'serious' aim, in that he attempts to engage with a social, moral, and even political context
through his debates. The game of the *Querelle* too may be seen to have a 'serious' purpose,
in that poetry becomes the means by which one acquires socio-economic stability and
prestige in this field.

[97] *L'Amant rendu cordelier* (1881), vv. 1035–40, p. 46.

[98] 'All play moves and has its being within a playground marked off beforehand either
materially or ideally, deliberately or as a matter of course', Huizinga (rev. edn: 1998),
p. 10.

[99] I intend this analogy in the loose sense of poetic form since the poems of the
Querelle are not necessarily composed in ballade form.

The spatial boundaries imposed on this poetic game are implied by the network of references throughout the *Querelle* to the wilderness beyond the realm of *Amours*, and the banishment from the privileged domain (playground) of those who transgress the rules laid down by *Amours*, as we have seen. Bourdieu's concept of field as a relational network within which various types of capital operate and gain dominance according to the nature of the field, can usefully be applied to the relational networks operating between the poets of the *Querelle*.[100] Using Bourdieu's model, we can define this poetic community in terms of the space of play the poets occupy through participation in the creative game. We can further see how each poet struggles to attain dominance over the field by extending his symbolic capital, producing ever more sophisticated, allusive work. Within the community of the *Querelle* then, skill in poetic composition is the desired form of symbolic capital:

In analytic terms, a field may be defined as a network, or a configuration, of objective relations between positions. These positions are objectively defined, in their existence and in the determinations they impose upon their occupants, agents or institutions, by their present and potential situation (situs) in the structure of distribution of species of power (or capital) whose possession commands access to the specific profits that are at stake in the field.[101]

Bourdieu frequently alludes to play when defining his notion of field, explaining that the agents/players within the field/game may acquire capital/trump cards through the application of certain competitive strategies. Unlike Huizinga's game, though, Bourdieu's field has:

Dynamic borders which are the stake of struggles within the field itself. A field is a game devoid of inventor and much more fluid and complex than any game that one might ever design.[102]

Similarly, the boundaries of the creative game of the *Querelle* are not fixed, but, within the rules of the game, are subject to variation from text to text. Bourdieu's concept of shifting borders allows both for individual innovation within the *Querelle* (which can be observed across its four cycles in terms of new networks of metaphor and narrative direction), and for the endless perpetuation of the game. Huizinga's notion of play as formative of exclusive 'social groupings' can be applied to the literary

---

[100] Bourdieu identifies the dominant types of capital as economic, social, cultural, and symbolic, Bourdieu and Wacquant (1996), p. 118–20.

[101] Bourdieu and Wacquant (1996), p. 97.

[102] Bourdieu and Wacquant (1996), p. 104.

confréries of northern France from within whose circles of influence certain *Querelle* texts were produced.[103] However, our concept of the collaborative debating community is formulated from the starting point of the *Querelle* body, rather than the inverse; the social is here defined through the textual.

Damp Prieur's burning of the 'chapel vert' at the end of *L'Amant rendu cordelier*, symbolic both of the lover's past attachment to the domain of *Amours*, and of the literary society of the *Chapel vert*, provides a fusion of the metaphorical layers of game-playing present within the confines of the textual *Querelle* which I have related to the community of players, external to the text, through whose play the text is generated:

> Et, pour l'oster de vaine gloire
> Et qu'il n'eust l'oeil au monde ouvert,
> Damp prieur a son gré fist faire
> Ung chappeau de roumarin vert,
> Lequel, de feu ardant couvert,
> Devant ses yeux le respandist;
> 'Voiés,' dist il, 'la fumée pert;
> *Sic transit gloria mundi.*'[104]

The 'chapel vert', itself part of a pattern of allusion across the *Querelle* texts, is representative of the playful networks of related structures, images, and language I have identified here throughout the *Querelle de la Belle Dame sans mercy*.[105] Through the increasingly sophisticated manipulation of these intertextual networks, each successive poet both inscribes himself in an existing space of play (field), and struggles to dominate that field, his poetic capital enhanced in relation to the

---

[103] See Chapter 1, pp. 14–15. I refer to such societies as the *Chapel vert*, or the *Verde Prioré*, grouped around the *prince d'Amour*, Pierre de Hauteville, to whom the *Confession et testament de l'amant trespassé de deuil* is attributed. These companies centred on the northern French town of Tournai; the *Chapel vert* may have involved the *Querelle* poet Achille Caulier, a native of Tournai (*Cruelle Femme*; *Ospital d'Amours*). See Piaget (1902), pp. 317–18. There is little biographical information about the other known *Querelle* poets. Baudet Herenc, author of the *Accusations*, a native of Chalon-sur-Saône, also composed a *Doctrinal de la seconde rhéthorique* (1432); see Langlois, *De artibus rhetoricae rhythmicae* (Paris: Émile Bouillon, 1890), pp. 36–46, and also *Recueil d'arts de seconde rhétorique*, ed. Langlois (Paris: Imprimerie Nationale, 1902).

[104] *L'Amant rendu cordelier* (1881), vv. 1793–800, p. 78.

[105] 'Lui mis ung vert chappel au col', *Cruelle Femme, Cycle de La BDSM* (2003), v. 206, p. 262; 'En pensant a mes biens passés | Et au romarin vert donné', *Le Jugement du povre triste amant banny*, Piaget (1905), vv. 26–7, p. 379; 'Leur laisse mes bonnes matines | Avec deux cordelieres fines | A houpe de rommarin verd', *Confession et testament*, an extra stanza from Rome, Vat. Reg. 1363, Pierre de Hauteville (1982), p. 62.

measure of his skill. The model of the collaborative debating community exemplified here in the *Querelle de la BDSM* will prove invaluable for further investigation of the collaborative and creative modes at play in late medieval literary communities. In part II, I extend this model to apply to the community of manuscripts that collect the texts of the *Querelle de la BDSM*.

PART II

'Le jeu des eschaz'

PLAYERS AND SPACES OF PLAY IN THE *BELLE DAME SANS MERCY* CYCLE MANUSCRIPTS

In my first two chapters I introduced the concept of a debating climate in early humanist France, in which intellectuals and poets engage one another in dialogue through a pattern of responsive textual moves, which they conceive as a dynamic and skilful game. We saw in my third chapter how Alain Chartier pioneers a new socially engaged style of debate in his French verse, lending this poetic game a 'serious' aim. In the first part of this chapter, I showed how poets collaborate creatively in the *Querelle de la Belle Dame sans mercy* to build on this ideal of social engagement in the spaces of play created within and between their texts. Through the perpetuation of the poetic game, poet-players acquire a socio-economic stability and prestige in court circles that may be equated with Bourdieu's notion of the acquisition of capital. The evidence of this enthusiasm for collaborative poetic play is preserved in material form in the various manuscripts and early printed editions. I identify a body of forty manuscripts which collect the numerous sequels and imitations of Alain Chartier's controversial poem *La Belle Dame sans mercy*.[106] Contained within

---

[106] Laidlaw lists thirty-two *Querelle de la BDSM* manuscripts, Alain Chartier (1974), pp. 99–137. McRae (1997) lists a further three not mentioned by Laidlaw since they do not contain any of Chartier's own works: Rome, Vat. Reg. 1363; Paris, BnF, fr. 1169; Turin L. IV. 3. McRae does not include eleven of the *BDSM* manuscripts discussed by Laidlaw as they do not contain the four sequels which are the focus of her study: *Accusations; La Dame lealle en amours; La Cruelle Femme en amours; Les Erreurs du jugement de la BDSM*. Four further manuscripts, not documented by McRae, were mentioned by Arthur Piaget in his editions of the sequels and imitations of the *BDSM*, namely London, Westminster Abbey, CA 21; Rome, Vat. Reg. 1720; Rome, Vat. Reg. 1728; BnF, nouv. acq. fr. 4237. There is a further manuscript mentioned by Laidlaw [Oo]: Geneva, library of Mlle. Droz, which contains five items, of which two

this community of manuscripts we find a number of other texts that have close semantic and conceptual links with the *Belle Dame sans mercy* cycle. Here I propose a reading of the *Querelle de la Belle Dame sans mercy* in manuscript context, focusing on the individual manuscript as a space of play in which texts, and poets behind the texts, conduct a dialogue and compete with one another. I shall discuss patterns of anthologization both within and across manuscript collections, following common threads of invention through the *Querelle* manuscripts, and applying theoretical models drawn from theories of game and sociology in order to trace more clearly the coherent planning of certain *Querelle* manuscripts. Initially I propose a reading of the Paris manuscript BnF, fr. 1169 which seeks to trace a larger pattern of collaboration through groups of texts collected in the *Belle Dame sans mercy* manuscripts,[107] turning later to look at two sizeable anthologies: Paris, Bibliothèque de l'Arsenal, 3521 and Arsenal, 3523. Such patterning at the level of the manuscript collection will in turn provide a paradigm of collaborative poetic practice in the fourteenth and fifteenth centuries in France.

I shall follow common threads through the four texts collected in BnF, fr. 1169, namely *Le Jeu des eschaz moralisé* in a mid-fourteenth-century vernacular translation of Jacobus de Cessolis's Latin treatise by Jean de Vignay;[108] the two *Belle Dame* sequels: *La Dame lealle en*

---

are imitations, *L'Amant rendu cordelier*, and the sole witness to an imitation entitled *Le Renoncement d'Amours* by Huet de Vignes. The IRHT *Querelle de la BDSM* dossier, and Laidlaw, record a further fifteen manuscripts containing Chartier's *BDSM*; Alain Chartier (1974), pp. 43–144. These fifteen manuscripts also collect many other texts in common with the forty *BDSM* cycle manuscripts mentioned above.

[107] This manuscript is signed on fol. 106^r by the scribe, 'Et fu escript de raoulet d'orliens l'an de grace mil iij^c lx et vij'. This is a fifteenth-century copy of a fourteenth-century colophon attached to an exemplar of Vignay's *Jeu des eschaz moralisé*, copied by Raoulet d'Orléans, which is now lost. Raoulet d'Orléans was one of the four *écrivains du roi* at the court of Charles V, and collaborated on, or single-handedly copied, over twenty manuscripts during his career, the majority signed. See Richard H. Rouse and Mary A. Rouse, *Manuscripts and their Makers: Commercial Book Producers in Medieval Paris 1200–1500*, 2 vols. (Turnhout, Belgium: Harvey Miller Publishers, 2000). As the Rouses note (pp. 273–9), several copies of the *Jeu des eschaz moralisé* found their way into Charles V's library.

[108] There were three vernacular translations of roughly the same date. Jean Ferron's translation is considered the best, and is reproduced in Alain Collet's new edition. All references are to Jacobus de Cessolis, *Le Jeu des eschaz moralisé*, ed. Collet (Paris: Champion, 1999), medieval French translation by Jean Ferron (1347). Medieval readers preferred Jean de Vignay's version, and in many cases Jean Ferron's text has been contaminated with interpolated passages from Jean de Vignay. BnF, fr. 1169 appears to be the only one of the *Querelle* manuscripts that contains a version of the *Eschaz*.

amours,[109] and Achille Caulier's *La Cruelle Femme en amours*;[110] and Michault Taillevent's *Le Debat du cuer et de l'oeil*.[111] I show how the relational patterns drawn between the texts of this manuscript may provide a useful model for investigation both of other *Belle Dame sans mercy* manuscripts, and of the collaborative community of poets whose texts occupy the spaces of play and competition instituted within and across manuscript compilations. Pairings of corresponding poems throughout the *Querelle* body will be highlighted as the embodiment of the dialectical and agonistic movement of the debate.

Roger Caillois's theories on the classification of games, from his *Les Jeux et les hommes*, provide useful boundaries for discussion of the poetic game at work in the *Querelle*, in conjunction with Pierre Bourdieu's categories of social organization. Bourdieu, as I discussed in my second chapter, rejects a structuralist hermeneutics in favour of a dialectical methodology expressed through the notions of habitus and symbolic capital.[112] Bourdieu's notion of habitus refers to the intimate relationship of products and the socio-historical practices whereby they are produced. In textual terms, this relationship may be seen as that between the text and its mode of transmission, here the physical manuscript.[113] I engage with Bourdieu's theory of practice in my study of the practice of the *Querelle* poets and their texts, situating the individual text/poet in the context of a dialectical struggle with others to gain capital, to map a field of collaborative relations operating across manuscript collections. The manuscript as space of play, the poet as player, and the text as move within the game will further provide a set of guiding metaphors for the *Querelle*. The chessboard, an image located in several of the texts collected in

[109] See *Cycle de La BDSM* (2003), pp. 169–243; McRae (1997), pp. 153–221; and Piaget (1901), pp. 321–51, based on our manuscript, BnF, fr. 1169.

[110] See *Cycle de La BDSM* (2003), pp. 245–325; McRae (1997), pp. 222–95, and Piaget (1902), pp. 315–49. In BnF, fr. 1169, this poem is explicitly set up as a response to *Dame lealle* by its rubric, see *supra*, part I, p. 149.

[111] All references are to Deschaux's edition, based on Arsenal, 3521, in *Un poète bourguignon du XVe siècle: Michault Taillevent: édition et étude* (Geneva: Droz, 1975), pp. 190–229. There are sixteen manuscript witnesses to this poem, eleven of which are listed by Laidlaw, McRae, or Piaget as containing imitations of the *BDSM*. As I shall discuss, three other poems by Michault Taillevent are also, more or less frequently, collected with the imitations of the *BDSM*: *Le Psaultier des villains*, *Le Passe temps Michault*, and *Le Regime de Fortune*.

[112] For a definition of symbolic capital see my second chapter, pp. 56–7, and also Gaunt and Kay (1997).

[113] See Armstrong's discussion of Bourdieu's *connaissance praxéologique* in *Forum for Modern Language Studies* 33 (1997), 'The Practice of Textual Transmission: Jean Molinet's *Ressource du Petit Peuple*', 270–82.

the *Querelle* manuscripts, materializes this notion of a space of play, within whose confines the players are guided both by the rules of the game and by the pattern of previous moves. The metaphor of chess will help to illustrate and clarify both the individual patterning of *Querelle* manuscripts, and the dialogic play staged across their boundaries. This metaphor is particularly appropriate for a study of late medieval debate, given the wealth of references to the game in medieval literature, from *chansons de geste* and troubadour lyric, to later works such as Christine de Pizan's *Mutacion de Fortune*, whose third part is inspired by Jean de Vignay's vernacular translation of *Le Jeu des eschaz moralisé*.[114] However, an even more explicit connection links the game of chess and the game of debate. As we saw in Chapter 1, '*jeu-parti*' probably developed as a term for a debate from its use in chess where it denoted a stalemate: a game that could not be concluded. The *jeu-parti* in chess leads to rematches, just as the deferred conclusion of the *jeu-parti* and, by extension, of the late medieval debate poem, leads to the production of further texts.[115]

The enormous popularity of chess in the Middle Ages is clear from the multitude of linguistic expressions in which it is used. The phrase 'estre maté en l'eschequier', for example, means to be beaten (in a game) or be beaten/conquered in life (similarly 'eschac et mat'); chess stands here both as the universal game, and as the game of life. If chess is the 'jeu' par excellence, then debate and chess are two sides of the same coin. 'Se mettre en jeu'; 'mettre en jeu'; 'ouvrir le jeu'; 'faire venir en jeu'; 'ne savoir de qui jouer': these medieval expressions are all found in the context of debate.[116] Interestingly, three of these phrases are attested by a work attached to the *Querelle*, Martin le Franc's *Champion des Dames*, once more linking the game of debate explicitly to the game of love.[117] In part I, I identified a vast network of allusions to games and game-playing that feeds the *Querelle* and gives it an internal coherence, justifying and supporting its very existence. 'Jeu' stands for the game of love, the game of poetic creation, and the game of the debate. The *Belle*

---

[114] See *Les Aventures merveilleuses de Huon de Bordeaux, chanson de geste du XIIIe siècle*, ed. Audiau (Paris: E. de Boccard, 1926); Christine de Pizan (1959); Blakeslee (1985); Lecoy, 'Guillaume de Saint-André et son jeu des échecs moralisés', *Romania* 67 (1942–3), 491–503; id., 'Le *Jeu des échecs* d'Engreban d'Arras', *Le Moyen Français* 12 (1983), 37–42; Murray (1913); Évrart de Conty, *Le Livre des échecs amoureux moralisés* (c.1400), ed. Legaré, Tesson, and Roy (Paris: Éditions du Chêne, 1991).

[115] See *supra*: Chapter 1, p. 34.

[116] See 'echiquier'; 'echec', 'jeu' in Di Stefano, *Dictionnaire des locutions en moyen français* (Montreal: CERES, 1991).

[117] Ibid., and Martin le Franc (1999).

Dame is aware of the implications of operating within the courtly game while resisting it, just like the virtual Chartier of the *De vita curiali* (Deschamps's 'un pié hors, l'autre ens', ballade CCVIII), and, like Christine de Pizan, she refuses to play the game by a set of rules which compromise her 'franchise'. The *Belle Dame* herself uses the metaphor of game in a lingustic expression (cf. Di Stefano) as she recognizes the suitor's advances as a set of moves in a game that he cannot win, since she has changed the rules: 'Et cellui pert le jeu d'actente | Qui ne scet faire son point double', vv. 495–6.[118] So the association of the actual game (such as chess, or dice), the courtly game (of love), the debate, and the game of life, is already attested both in medieval literature and in the *BDSM* cycle. The Hague miniature, reproduced on the jacket cover and here (plate 4), which illustrates Chartier's *Belle Dame sans mercy* in this MS, provides a concrete medieval pictorial example of the association of chess, courtly love, and debate.[119] The *Belle Dame* and her suitor sit on either side of a chessboard within the larger physical space of a room (whose floor itself resembles the squares of the chessboard, suggesting the larger space of play the characters inhabit); their physical moves on the board parallel the verbal moves each makes in the debate poem proper. Although the miniature itself appears rather damaged, and it is in particular difficult to see exactly what is happening on the chessboard, or to read the *Belle Dame*'s expression, we can assume that she may be winning the game, as she seems to have moved her pieces further towards the suitor's side of the board than he to hers. (As far as one can tell, the *Belle Dame* is playing white to the suitor's black.) This fifteenth-century depiction, if indeed it does show the *Belle Dame* winning or gaining the upper hand in the game, may have far-reaching implications both for our interpretation of her portrayal, and for our interpretation of the contemporary reaction towards Chartier's poem.[120] In particular, it would support an account of Chartier's poem where the *Belle Dame* gains an advantage by her skilful play to the detriment of the less skilled suitor, who is left 'eschac et mat' at the close of their game. This miniature, then, would seem both to offer us a material illustration

[118] Alain Chartier (1974), p. 349.

[119] I am immensely grateful to Joan E. McRae for pointing me in the direction of this miniature, which I discovered after most of this chapter had already been written, and which provides a most convincing medieval support for my thesis here.

[120] See the description of this MS in Brayer, *Catalogue of the French-language Medieval Manuscripts in the Koninklijke Bibliotheek (Royal Library) The Hague* (Paris: IRHT, 1954–6).

Plate 4. Alain Chartier, *La Belle Dame sans mercy* (the *Belle Dame* and her suitor play chess)

The Hague, Koninklijke Bibliotheek, 71 E 49, fol. 9ʳ

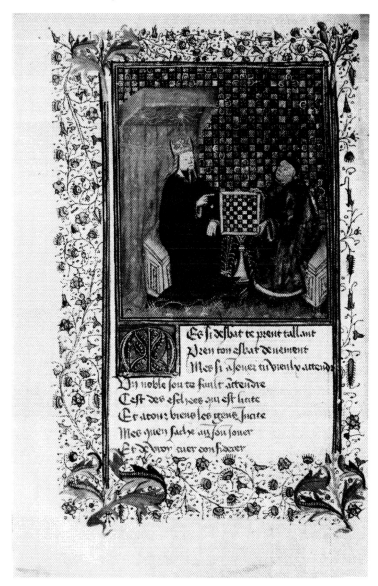

Plate 5. Guillaume de Saint-André, verse adaptation of Jacobus de Cessolis's *Le jeu des eschaz moralisé* (the King and a philosopher play chess)

Paris, BnF, fr. 14978, fol. 3ᵛ

of the metaphor of chess game as love debate, and to support a positive interpretation of Chartier's *Belle Dame*.

Turning now to text, Jacobus de Cessolis's chess treatise, collected in Paris, BnF, fr. 1169, presents a portrait of an ideal hierarchy of contemporary society projected through the confines and rules of the game of chess.[121] The socio-cultural competition between individuals implied by this medieval metaphor is addressed, as I mentioned earlier, in Pierre Bourdieu's *Logic of Practice*. Bourdieu's notion of field, in the context of Jacobus's treatise, might refer us to the physical space of play defined by the chessboard, on which each piece is restricted in its movements by a set of predetermined and absolute rules (and by extension, to a society in which subjects are restricted by the moves appropriate to their rank). Symbolic capital might then refer us to the advantages won and lost by moves played on the board (or by social manoeuvring). In the vernacular translations of Jacobus's treatise, Jean Ferron and Jean de Vignay describe the moves ascribed to the *eschaz nobles* (*le roy, la royne*, two *alphins*, two *chevaliers*, and two *roz*), and to the eight *pietons* (*paonnets*—Vignay), representative of the *commun du pueple* (*le laboureur, le fevre, le notaire* or *le laneur* (*tabellion*—Vignay), *le marchant, le phisicien* (*medecin*—Vignay), *le tavernier, la garde*, and *le ribaut*). So the human pawn (and by extension the poet) must move according to the rules of the creative game defined both by the moves (poems) which have preceded his own, and by a set of ground rules to which he must adhere if he is to enter the field.

Si les amoneste et fais assavoir que se il retieingnent bien en leur cuer la forme et la façon des eschaz, de legier il sauront par eulz le jeu et la verité du jeu.[122]

The *freres* and *seculiers*, at whose request Jacobus composes his treatise, hope to learn 'par le jeu des eschaz comment on se doit en bones meurs gouverner et en bataille maintenir'.[123] In other words, the game is to have

---

[121] See plate 5.

[122] *Jeu des eschaz*, Jacobus de Cessolis (1999), ll. 26–8, p. 128. This quotation comes in Ferron's prologue under the heading: 'C'est le jeu des eschaz appliqué et torné aus bounes meurs des persounes.' Jacobus de Cessolis's prologue (rendered by Ferron in his translation of 1347) is only partially translated by Jean de Vignay. In BnF, fr. 1169, after a short dedication on fol. 2 to 'Jehan de France, duc de Normandie', and a table of contents on fols. 2ᵛ–3, Jean de Vignay begins his translation on fol. 3ʳ with the section entitled: 'Soubz quel roy le gieu fu trouvé' (corresponding to Ferron's first chapter: 'En quel temps ce jeu fu trové'). I refer to Jean Ferron's vernacular translation in Jacobus de Cessolis (1999), but also give transcriptions of Jean de Vignay's translation from BnF, fr. 1169, where the texts coincide.

[123] Jacobus de Cessolis (1999), ll. 20–1, p. 128. This passage also comes from part of Ferron's prologue not rendered by Vignay.

a serious didactic and moral aim, potentially revealing truth to its players; but only full participation and adherence to its rules will yield success.

The game of chess as allegory of society in *Le Jeu des eschaz moralisé* will serve to demonstrate how the notion of game-playing may be applied to textual debating communities such as that formed by the *Querelle de la Belle Dame sans mercy*, and to the collaborative community of poets beyond the texts. To this end, the opposition that Roger Caillois sets up in his sociological study of games between those games that belong to the category of *agôn* or competition and those belonging to *alea* or chance provides a useful distinction, as I suggest in my first chapter.[124] Chess is classified in *agôn*, a term that Caillois applies to games of skill in which players compete to assert their dominance.

> Le ressort du jeu est pour chaque concurrent le désir de voir reconnue son excellence dans un domaine donné. [...] la pratique de l'*agôn* [...] laisse le champion à ses seules ressources, l'invite à en tirer le meilleur parti possible, l'oblige enfin à s'en servir loyalement et dans des limites fixées, qui, égales pour tous, aboutissent en revanche à rendre indiscutable la supériorité du vainqueur. L'*agôn* se présente comme la forme pure du mérite personnel et sert à le manifester.[125]

By extension the verbal jousting of Michault Taillevent's *Le Debat du cuer et de l'oeil*, or the mirrored judgements delivered in *La Dame lealle en amours* and *La Cruelle Femme en amours*, collected with Jacobus's chess treatise, might also be classified in this category of game. The reversal of the judgement reached in *La Dame lealle en amours* by its counterpart, *La Cruelle Femme en amours*, institutes a competitive dialogue between the texts. The poet of *Le Debat du cuer et de l'oeil* creates a similar competition or debate within his text, which is to be judged by Venus. The four texts collected in BnF, fr. 1169 thus find an intracodical coherence which balances on the tension of the game, as represented within each individual text itself by the game of chess, the debate or judgement, and across the codex as a whole conceived of as a wider space of play. There is also a coherence derived from the relation of the individual game of the text to the wider collaborative game of the *Querelle*. Within the physical confines of the manuscript, each text is in turn confined within a nominal space of play: the chessboard in *Le Jeu des eschaz*; the *cour d'Amours* in *La Dame lealle en amours*; the *palais de Justice* in *La Cruelle Femme en amours*; and the *champ d'Amours* in *Le Debat du cuer et de l'oeil*.

---

[124] See my Chapter 1, p. 32.
[125] Caillois (1967), *Classification des jeux*, pp. 52–3.

Caillois draws a specific parallel between the space represented by the chessboard and the circumscribed space within which debates and judgements are carried out, spaces which recall Huizinga's notion of the playground:[126]

> Les débats sont conduits et le jugement rendu dans une enceinte de justice, selon un cérémonial invariable [...] champ clos, piste ou arène, damier ou échiquier.[127]

It seems more than coincidental that the image of the chessboard which I suggest as a guiding metaphor for BnF, fr. 1169, and which refers us to the individual manuscript as a space of play and *agôn*, recurs in other texts collected in the *Querelle* manuscripts, and notably in two poems: *L'Echiquier d'Amours* or *Le Debat de la Damoiselle et de la Bourgoise*[128] by Blosseville (this appears in five manuscripts of the cycle),[129] and *Comment l'estat du monde puet estre comparé au jeu des eschecz* (witnessed only by Arsenal, 3521). There are further occurrences of the *echiquier* throughout the *Querelle* body, for example, in Pierre Michault's *Le Procès de Honneur féminin*, where it is evoked in its primary sense as a game board: 'sur mon corps j'ay plus de playes que ung eschequier n'a de poins',[130] or in the *Arrêts d'amours* where it takes on the secondary meaning of court/parliament as listed by Godefroy: 'les gens tenans l'eschiquier d'amours au profit d'une damoiselle'.[131] The two most frequently attested meanings of *echiquier/eschequier* in Godefroy point precisely to the two fields of relations that are the focus of the current discussion: the *echiquier* as space of play (for debates as for games), and the *echiquier* as a space of judgement where the outcome of games/debates is decided.[132]

---

[126] *Supra*, part I, p. 159, n. 98. See Huizinga (rev. edn: 1998).

[127] Caillois (1967), *Introduction*, p. 17.

[128] This poem was edited by Montaiglon in his *Recueil de poésies françoises des XVe et XVIe siècles* (Paris: P. Jannet, 1856), V: pp. 5–33. For the attribution of this work to Blosseville, see Montaiglon's introduction to his edition of *Le Debat du Viel et du Jeune* (attributed to Blosseville by l'Abbé de la Rue in his *Jongleurs et trouvères*), *Recueil de poésies françoises* (Paris: A. Franck, 1865), IX: pp. 216–20.

[129] These are as follows: BnF, fr. 1661 (fols. 1–12); Arsenal, 3523 (fols. 51–70); The Hague, Koninklijke Bibliotheek, 71 E 49 (fols. 296–306ᵛ); Rome, Vat. Reg. 1363 (fols. 85–104ᵛ); and Rome, Vat. Reg. 1720 (fols. 116–26).

[130] Pierre Michault (1978), l. 32, p. 44.

[131] *Arrêts d'amours* (1951), p. 715.

[132] Godefroy further notes medieval uses of the term that refer to a certain region, to the duration of parliamentary sessions, and to a musical instrument ('l'echiquier d'Angleterre', from Machaut). The sense of *echiquier* as *exchequer* or *treasury* developed from the medieval practice of laying out a chequered cloth for counting money.

In the *Debat de la Damoiselle et de la Bourgoise*, whose alternative title is *L'Echiquier d'Amours*,[133] the poet uses *echiquier* to refer to a space of debate, like the *cour* or *parlement d'Amours* of the *Belle Dame on trial* cycle poems:[134]

> Volay en ung palais de flours,
> Où là, par journées compassées,
> On tenoit l'echiquier d'Amours.[135]

The *gens d'Amours*, who are the players within this *echiquier*, are all well versed in the rules of the debating game:

> Car gens d'Amours, qui là estoient,
> Savoient les drois sans reciter
> Et sur le champ en disputoient.
> Là ne gaignoient rien advocas,
> Par ce que les parties proposent
> Et plaident de bouche leur cas.[136]

The debate itself, a traditional dream sequence witnessed and subsequently transcribed by the narrator-poet, arises from a quarrel between two women, the *Damoiselle* and the *Bourgoise*, as to whether age and experience or youth and beauty should take precedence in matters of love.[137] Jane Taylor suggests that the premise for the debate provides a courtly cover for a debate that is rather less than courtly. The two women, Taylor argues, actually engage in a quarrel about their sexual

---

[133] Montaiglon suggests in the introduction to his *Debat du Viel et du Jeune* that *l'Echiquier d'Amours* was the original title of this debate poem, and that subsequent titles: *Le Plaidoié de la Damoiselle a l'encontre de la Bourgeoise* (Arsenal, 3523), or *Le Debat de la Damoiselle et de la Bourgoise* (the graphies *bourgoise/bourgeoise* both appear in the manuscript tradition of this poem), were later attempts at popularizing the text within the context of manuscript collections of debate poetry; *Recueil de poésies françoises*, IX: p. 216–20.

[134] See my classification of the sequels and imitations of the *BDSM* into four distinct cycles in part I.

[135] *Debat de la Damoiselle et de la Bourgoise*, *Recueil de poésies françoises*, V: p. 5. Montaiglon adds a note to the effect that *echiquier* here is an equivalent of *cour* or *parlement d'Amours*, observing that the *parlement de Normandie* was referred to as the *Echiquier de Normandie*, and that in London, the *cour de l'Echiquier* still went by the same name at the time of publication of the *recueil*.

[136] *Recueil de poésies françoises* (1856), V: p. 6.

[137] Another poem attributed to Blosseville, on a similar theme, *Le Debat du Viel et du Jeune*, appears in BnF, fr. 1661, and Besançon, BM, 554 (both from the manuscripts of the *Querelle de la BDSM*). In the latter manuscript this text is not collected with *Le Debat de la Damoiselle et de la Bourgoise*, though both appear in the former manuscript (*Damoiselle/Bourgoise*, fols. 2–12; *Viel/Jeune*, fol. 106).

integrity which sets up dialogic links with Villon's *Testament* and *Lais*, both collected in the same manuscript as this debate poem: Arsenal, 3523.[138] The affair is aired before the *president* of the *echiquier d'Amours*, who sits in the *parc de l'auditoire*, and who initially delivers a judgement in favour of the *Damoiselle*, though a final decision is projected beyond the textual end of the poem. In the final two stanzas, the poet returns to the original *cadre* of the poem, and to a state of consciousness in which he is able to record his dream:

> Ainsi vous voyez le Debat
> De la Bourgoise et Damoiselle,
> Que j'ay recité par esbat.[139]

The fictional frame of the poem figuratively encloses the *debat/esbat* sequence, just as the space of play within the poem, the *echiquier d'Amours*, physically encloses the game of debate, trial and judgement, played through to its conclusion by the *gens d'Amours*, the *Damoiselle*, and the *Bourgoise*. The second of the poems collected in the *Querelle* body that uses the image of the chessboard as a social metaphor is *Comment l'estat du monde puet estre comparé au jeu des eschecz*. This short poem, inspired by early troubadour lyric,[140] uses the game of chess to represent a hierarchical vision of contemporary society, like Vignay's *Le Jeu des eschaz moralisé*. Here, though, the emphasis is on the end of the game and on Death the leveller of all estates, in keeping with the sombre mood of Arsenal, 3521, to which I shall come later. A passage from this same poem sets up a direct parallel between *esbatre* and *combatre* (play/struggle): two interdependent concepts within the context of *agôn* that together evoke a third, *debatre*:

> Et veult prendre en cel aquest heur
> Les deux personnes qui s'esbatent
> Au dit jeu mais qu'ilz se combatent,
> Car pour verité l'un ne tire
> Qu'a l'autre vaincre et desconfire.[141]

Esbatre and *combatre* are guiding principles for the poetic game or *debatre* that unfolds within and between texts of the *Belle Dame sans mercy* cycle.

---

138 See Taylor, Jane (2001), pp. 27–30.
139 *Debat de la Damoiselle et de la Bourgoise, Recueil de poésies françoises* (1856), V: p. 33.
140 Particularly by Engreban d'Arras's poem, *Le Jus des esquès*. See Lecoy (1983).
141 See my forthcoming edition of *Comment l'estat du monde puet estre comparé au jeu des eschecz*, vv. 121–5, fol. 266ʳ.

In his *Contre passe temps* (*Le Temps perdu*, 1440), Pierre Chastellain responds to Michault Taillevent's *Passe temps* (pre 1440), which is collected with Chastellain's response in Arsenal, 3523. Chastellain uses this metaphor of *combatre*, ostensibly to describe a fight against the onslaught of time, but indicates in the last verse that his poem has been a verbal assault on Michault Taillevent's earlier work:

> Je Pierre Chastellain me nomme
> Qui contre temps perdu bataille,
> Nuyt et jour pour sauver mon ame.
> Le glaive qui me combat taille;
> Et craint comme son debat aille
> Qui sa char en bataille vend
> Prens en gré, Michault Taillevent.[142]

Later I shall discuss how these texts may be organized within Arsenal, 3523, by the *combatre/esbatre* pairing, and the *sacq commun* image, culminating in the insertion of Pierre de Hauteville's *Confession et testament du povre amant trespassé de deuil*,[143] and Villon's *Grand Testament*. This *combatre/esbatre* pairing highlighted above is embodied in the allegorical chessboard of Vignay's *Le Jeu des eschaz moralisé* in BnF, fr. 1169, and finds expression in the antagonistic diptych presented by *La Dame lealle en amours* and *La Cruelle Femme en amours* in the same manuscript. The text in last position, *Le Debat du cuer et de l'oeil*, presents a highly allegorized version of the poetic debate. The *esbatre* element seems more in evidence here, since the outcome of the trial at the court of *Venus* does not prove fatal for either plaintiff, unlike the death sentence pronounced on the *Belle Dame* in *La Cruelle Femme en amours*. In one sequence, though, the *combatre* element in Taillevent's

---

[142] This is a transcription of Chastellain's poem from Arsenal, 3523 (which also appears in Arsenal, 3521, fols. 238ʳ–46ᵛ), fol. 140. See Pierre Chastellain; Vaillant, *Les Oeuvres de Pierre Chastellain et de Vaillant: poètes du XVᵉ siècle*, ed. Deschaux (Geneva: Droz, 1982), pp. 17–41. In both Arsenal manuscripts, Chastellain's *Contre passe temps* is transcribed directly after Taillevent's *Passe temps* (3523: fols. 99–122, fols. 123–40; 3521: fols. 227ʳ–37ᵛ, fols. 238ʳ–46ᵛ). In Arsenal, 3521, both poems are clearly transcribed by the same hand, whereas in Arsenal, 3523, the hands are different (a variety of scribal hands within the same manuscript may be suggestive of a collaborative scribal practice which reflects the collaborative inventive practice of the *Querelle* poets themselves). Arsenal, 3523, is copied by many different hands but as I later suggest is a single manuscript rather than a composite. The IRHT notice on this manuscript identifies two contemporary signatures, 'Jehan Maciot' and 'Claude Maciot', and one sixteenth-century signature, 'Gilbert Coquille' on fol. 818.

[143] Bidler takes Arsenal, 3523, as the base manuscript for her edition of the *Confession et testament*, Pierre de Hauteville (1982).

poem becomes overt with the staging of a physical contest in which the personified *cuer* and *oeil* take up arms and duel:

> Le cuer vint pour combatre l'ueil
> Sur ung destrier couvert de lermes
> Armé de harnais fait de dueil;
> Six souspirs estoient ses armes.[144]

However, the debate between the *cuer* and the *oeil* is finally resolved through a verbal contest whose conclusion is an agreement between the two parties, neither of whom actually wins the debate as such. As in many other debate poems throughout the *Querelle de la Belle Dame sans mercy*, it is precisely the calculated ambiguity of the unconcluded debate that perpetuates poetic dialogue.[145] The narrator-poet adds a postscript to his debate, encouraging further speculation, and perhaps soliciting responses to his text. In his postscript he evokes the image of the winner's *chappel*, the traditional crown worn by the winners of poetic competitions such as the northern French *puys*, and a leitmotif in the *Belle Dame sans mercy* cycle.[146] So Taillevent implicitly issues a poetic challenge to his fellow poets, with the promise of a metaphorical *chappel* as their prize:

> Sy pry ceulx ou Joye s'esbat
> Et qui d'amer sont en la voye
> Que du cuer et l'ueil le debat
> Chascun endroit soy le cas voye
> Et que son opinion envoye
> A Venus et qui le chappel
> Gaignera, Amours le pourvoye
> De tous ses desirs sans rappel.[147]

This debate poem by Taillevent is frequently collected in the manuscripts of the sequels and imitations of the *Belle Dame sans mercy*, counting eleven of its sixteen appearances in these manuscripts. Of these eleven

[144] Michault Taillevent (1975), vv. 457–60, p. 211.
[145] For a discussion of closural practice in Chartier, see Chapter 3, and Cayley (2003).
[146] This image occurs, for example, in Pierre Chastellain's *Le Temps recouvert* (1451), counterpart to his *Temps perdu* (1440), in turn a response to Taillevent's *Passe temps* (pre 1440): 'tirer ne doit a ung hault pris | Qui oncques n'eut le chappellet | S'il a trop bas ne trop hault pris | Ou que son trait eschappe let. | A peine ung seul meschant pelet | De laine ou de coton a taindre | Pourroit au chappellet attaindre', Pierre Chastellain (1982), vv. 729–35, p. 68. Deschaux notes that these lines refer to a game that consisted of aiming a *pelet* (ball) at a *chappellet* (garland); the game of skill and the poetic game coincide here again; id. (1982), p. 111.
[147] Michault Taillevent (1975), vv. 817–24, p. 226.

appearances, all except that in BnF, fr. 1169, occur in compilations that include Chartier's original *Belle Dame sans mercy*, and eight occur with at least one sequel or imitation.

We have seen how *agôn*, the notion of competitive play, acting within the space provided by the *echiquier* of the first text, links the four texts in BnF, fr. 1169, and how the relational field it creates refers us to the collaborative poetic game beyond the text. A second field of relations can be identified in the theme of trial and judgement which runs throughout the manuscript, acting within the space provided by the *echiquier* as *cour* or *parlement d'Amours* in the final three texts. The third chapter of *Le Jeu des eschaz moralisé* points to this set of relations through its description of the third pawn, the *notaire* (*tabellion*—Vignay), whose task it is to sit in front of the *alphin* or judge, and faithfully record the quarrels played out before him:

Le .IIIe. pieton qui est a la destre devant le alphin est ainsi fait. Moult souvent avient que telz gens dont nous avons parlé tancent et noisent et pour ce convient que leurs riotes soient finees par le alphin qui en est juges et qu'il soit escript en lectres autentiques par un notaire et c'est l'office a cellui qui est devant lui. […] Leur office si est estre devant les juges, faire et escrire instrumens autentiques, reciter les condempnacions et les condonacions recevoir, et tout ce represente la penne.[148]

Within the fiction of the *Debat du cuer et de l'oeil*, the narrator-poet figure adopts the role of *notaire*, and records word for word the quarrel he witnesses. He himself is merely the pen of a judge who will actually deliver sentence, and here makes a conventional claim for the veracity of his words:[149]

[148] Jacobus de Cessolis (1999), p. 171. 'Ce tiers paonnet qui est assis devant le destre alphin doit estre figuré comme clerc car il est de raison pour ce que entre les populaires des quiex nous parlons en cest livre les contens, distensions, plaideries muevent aucune fois lesquelles il convient sentencier par les alphins qui sont juges. Si est raison que cellui alphin ait son noctaire par qui les proces soient escrips […] Et ce sont les instrumens et les offices de ceulx par qui les instrumens sont fais et mis en escrits autentiques et doivent estre passez devant les juges si comme libelles, condempnacions, scentences et ce est senefié par l'escriptoire et par la pane' (this is my transcription of Vignay's rendering of the same passage from BnF, fr. 1169, fols. 57ᵛ–58).

[149] The judges appointed to preside over proceedings in the three later texts collected in BnF, fr. 1169 are prefigured by the *alphins* of *Le Jeu des eschaz moralisé* : 'Il est assavoir que les alphins sont fourniez en la maniere de juges et sont accessoires du roy, et sont assis en chaiere, un livre tout ouvert devant eulx, et pour ce que les unes causes sont crimineles et les autres civilles doivent il estre deux, l'un au blanc et l'autre au noir', *Le Jeu des eschaz* (transcription from Vignay's translation in BnF, fr. 1169, fol. 23 bis).

> Lors prestement trouvay descloses
> Les pensees qu'avoye en songe
> Lesquelz sans y adjouster gloses
> Escripvy au net sans mensonge.[150]

The truth upon which Taillevent's narrator-poet insists here is the *poetic* truth that underpins the game of the text. In *La Dame lealle en amours*, the *Belle Dame*'s prosecutor, *Desir*, supports his accusations by referring to 'faiz' stated in previous poems of the *Belle Dame sans mercy* cycle:

> Nous avons proposés nos faiz,
> Qui se preuvent sans nulle erreur
> Par les livres qui en sont faiz.[151]

So the quest for truth in the debate poem is revealed to be subject to the rules of the game, based not on external criteria but on previous moves played. Each successive poet seeks to join the game, and so subscribes to a set of intertextual criteria that direct his moves: like the *notaire* who must move only in the directions dictated by the rules of the game.[152]

I now propose a reading of two anthology manuscripts, Arsenal, 3521 and 3523,[153] in which I consider the manuscript as a space of play, with an emphasis on certain dynamic pairings of texts within the collections.

---

[150] Michault Taillevent (1975), vv. 813–16, p. 226. The narrator-poet figure of *La Cruelle Femme en amours* similarly stresses the veracity of his account by assuring the reader that he has recorded: 'Tout le fait', sans rien oublïer', *Cycle de La BDSM* (2003), v. 940, p. 324.

[151] *La Dame lealle en amours*, ibid., vv. 806–8, p. 236. A later passage in this same poem again refers to the *auctoritas* of previous poems in the cycle: 'Adonc se mistrent tous ensemble, | En conseil et lonc temps parlerent | A Amours, si comme il me semble, | Et pluseurs livres retournerent', ibid., vv. 833–36, p. 238.

[152] So the moral message of Jacobus's text, the truth which must be sought at all levels of society, is acquired through a regulated 'esbatement', allegorically through the rigours and pleasures (*esbatre/combatre*) of the moves of chess: 'Et que celui roy qui convoitoit a aprendre le gieu meist en son memoire et entendist en soy les meurs et les natures devisées en la personne du roy de l'eschequier si que il amendast sa vie, ses meurs, et encore adjousta il que il avoit trouvé ce gieu pour ce que les nobles habondans en richesces et en delices et joissoient de la pais temporele eschevassent oysiveté par ce gieu tant comme il se deliteroient en jouant et pour donner matiere de pourpenser sus ce diverses manieres et diverses raisons tant de jouer comme de parler et d'escrire', *Le Jeu des eschaz* (transcription from Vignay's translation in BnF, fr. 1169, fols. 105ᵛ–6).

[153] For descriptions of these two manuscripts see Alain Chartier (1974), pp. 115–18; McRae (1997), pp. 64–70 and *Catalogue des manuscrits de la bibliothèque de l'Arsenal* (Paris: Plon, 1900), III: pp. 413–15, pp. 415–17. See also Jeanroy and Droz, 'Deux manuscrits de François Villon', in *Documents artistiques du XVᵉ siècle* (Paris: Droz, 1932), VI, vii–ix, and more recently, Di Stefano, *De Villon à Villon: Le Lais François Villon, Ms. Arsenal, 3523* (Montreal: CERES, 1988). Laidlaw's descriptions of the manuscripts list only the works by Chartier; Alain Chartier (1974), pp. 115–18.

The parallel study of this pair of manuscripts will represent a wider collaborative dialogue between manuscripts of the *Querelle de la Belle Dame sans mercy*, between pairings of poets and poems. Both manuscripts once belonged to the library of the Marquis de Paulmy, founder of the Bibliothèque de l'Arsenal. Arsenal, 3521, dates from the fifteenth century; Laidlaw likens one of the watermarks to Briquet 14239, from 1478–83.[154] Arsenal, 3523, has also been dated to the late fifteenth century: Bijvanck, Jeanroy, and Droz[155] suggest a date of ten years after the copying of Stockholm, Royal Library, V. u. 22 (post 1477),[156] but Laidlaw suggests that the watermarks point to an earlier date.[157]

Arsenal, 3521, collects forty-three texts, all of which are copied by the same hand, and is therefore probably a single manuscript. Arsenal, 3523, collects thirty-five texts,[158] in a variety of scribal hands.[159] It is likely, in spite of the multiple copyists working on Arsenal, 3523, that it is a single rather than a composite manuscript, as Jane Taylor asserts in her recent study of Villon.[160] Neither manuscript is illuminated; the hands are cursive and often scrappy, suggesting that these manuscripts were not presentation copies, but were commissioned out of a readerly enjoyment of the poems themselves. An undated note scribbled on one of the fly-leaves of Arsenal, 3521,[161] attributes the majority of the contents of the manuscript to Alain Chartier (probably a common misconception, since the 1900 Paris catalogue makes similar errors of attribution to Alain Chartier).[162]

---

[154] See Briquet, *Les Filigranes. Dictionnaire historique des marques de papier*, 4 vols. (Leipzig: Hiersemann, 1923). The mark Laidlaw identifies is 'an ox-head surmounted by a cross, between lightly sewn chain-lines 38mm apart; 60 or 65mm long over-all'; Alain Chartier (1974), p. 115.

[155] See Laidlaw's discussion of the dating of Arsenal, 3523, in Alain Chartier (1974), p. 117, also Bijvanck, *Spécimen d'un essai critique sur les oeuvres de François Villon* (Leyde: De Brauk & Smits, 1882); Jeanroy and Droz (1932).

[156] In addition to the *BDSM* and other works by Chartier, this manuscript contains Villon's works. For a description, see Piaget and Droz, 'Recherches sur la tradition manuscrite de Villon. I. Le manuscrit de Stockholm', *Romania* 58 (1932), 238–54.

[157] Laidlaw identifies eight watermarks in his description of Arsenal, 3523, five of which he likens to marks in Briquet; the earliest ranges from 1445–52, and the latest 1458–80. See Alain Chartier (1974), pp. 116–17.

[158] See Appendix A for a list of the contents of these two manuscripts.

[159] See note 142 for a list of signatures on fol. 818 of this manuscript.

[160] See Taylor, Jane (2001), pp. 25–6, and especially note 67.

[161] This would appear to be in the Marquis de Paulmy's hand. Arsenal, 3650, has notation in an identical hand on the inside folio, signed 'Paulmy'.

[162] 'Tout ce volume mss me paroit etre d'Alain Chartier, a l'exception du 1ᵉʳ morceau que j'ay d'ailleurs seul dans un beau mss sur velin avec miniature que j'ay placé a la morale. Il est de Georges Chatelain, flamand, mort en 1475, attaché au duc de Bourgogne.' This is a transcription from Arsenal, 3521.

The first two texts in Arsenal, 3523, both transcribed by the same hand, form a pair frequently found together: Alain Chartier's *Le Breviaire des nobles*,[163] and Michault Taillevent's *Le Psaultier des villains*.[164] Taillevent's poem is a mirror image of Chartier's earlier portrait of the ideal qualities of the nobility, explicitly engaging with and amplifying its themes. Each of the thirteen ballades of Chartier's poem that represent the virtues desirable in the nobility is answered by one of the thirteen ballades of Taillevent's response.[165] In Paris, BnF, fr. 1642, we find the sole example within the manuscripts of the *Querelle* of a poem inspired by these two texts: Guillaume Alexis's *L'ABC des doubles* (1451). Both Chartier's and Taillevent's poems are also transcribed in this manuscript. Alexis cites both Chartier's *Breviaire* and Taillevent's *Psaultier* in his prologue, and so tightens the intertextual field of reference operating across the *Querelle* manuscripts:

> Ce qui m'attraict
> Comme en fait le poisson a l'ain
> Si est le *Breviaire* Alain
> Et le beau *Psaultier* a Michault
> Qui fut de Raison amy chault.[166]

Chartier's *Breviaire des nobles* and Taillevent's *Psaultier des villains* both also appear in Arsenal, 3521. They are transcribed separately in the Arsenal manuscript, but by the same hand (fols. 30–37ᵛ; fols. 48–56 respectively).[167] The two poems both occur in a further five of the *Querelle* manuscripts.[168]

---

[163] Laidlaw does not date this poem in his edition of Chartier, but notes that Droz gives a date of around 1424 in her edition of the *Quadrilogue invectif*; Alain Chartier (1950), viii.

[164] See Rice, 'Deux poèmes sur la chevalerie. *Le Breviaire des nobles* d'Alain Chartier et *Le Psaultier des villains* de Michault Taillevent', *Romania* 75 (1954), 55–65; editions: 66–97.

[165] Taillevent's poem includes an introductory ballade: 'Ceux sont villains qui font les villonies', which corresponds to Chartier's first ballade, spoken by *Dame Noblesce*. Deschaux notes, however, that only ballades I, V, and XIII are identical in form in both Chartier and Taillevent's poems; Michault Taillevent (1975), p. 129.

[166] See Guillaume Alexis, *Oeuvres poétiques*, ed. Piaget and Picot (Paris: Firmin-Didot, 1896): I, vv. 20–4, p. 10.

[167] The *Psaultier des villains* occurs in seven manuscripts in the *Querelle* body, always collected with Chartier's *Breviaire des nobles* (though not necessarily following it). The *Breviaire des nobles* occurs in twenty-six of the forty manuscripts I have classified as belonging to the *Querelle de la BDSM*.

[168] Namely BnF, fr. 1642 (fols. 117–23ᵛ; fols. 297–302 respectively); Paris, Musée Jacquemart-André, 11 (fols. 93–108; fols. 109–22 respectively); Carpentras, Bibliothèque Municipale, 390 (*Le Psaultier des villains*, fols. 11–20, most probably originally

Just as Chartier's *Breviaire des nobles* is answered by Taillevent's *Psaultier des villains*, so the *Lay de paix* (Chartier) is answered by Pierre de Nesson's *Lay de guerre*, collected in two of the *Querelle* manuscripts: BnF, fr. 1131 (where it follows the *Lay de paix*, fols. 80–3ᵛ), fols. 84–7ᵛ; and BnF, fr. 1727, fols. 179–88ᵛ (this manuscript does not contain the *Lay de paix*). In the final stanza of his *DHVV*, Chartier had challenged fellow poet Pierre de Nesson to write a response:

> On pourroit avoir souspeczon
> Que je voulsisse cecy dire
> Pour mon bon compaignon Neczon.
> Pour ce, quant je l'ay fait escripre,
> J'ay a l'escripvain deffendu
> Du moustrer. Au fort, s'on lui baille,
> Bien assailly, bien deffendu;
> Face, s'il scet, de pire taille![169]

Chartier figures in numerous other poetic pairings within the manuscript context of the *Querelle*. His *BDSM* is followed by a *Lettre des dames a Alain* and a *Requeste baillee aux dames contre Alain* in twenty-four (and possibly twenty-six) manuscripts.[170] His *Excusacion aux dames*, allegedly written as a response to these letters, is collected with the *Lettre des*

preceded by the *Breviaire des nobles*, but the first quire of the manuscript has been lost); St. Petersburg, National Library of Russia, f.f.v. xiv. 7 (fols. 144ᵛ ff.); and Vienna, Nation-albibliothek, 2619 (fols. 86a–8c; fols. 146–8ᵛ respectively). McRae (1997) does not include *Le Psaultier des villains* in her list of the contents of Vienna, Nationalbibliothek, 2619, but Deschaux lists it: Michault Taillevent (1975), p. 13.

[169] *DHVV*, Alain Chartier (1974), vv. 433–40, p. 435. Laidlaw remarks that in the only extant manuscript of this debate poem, Berlin, Kupferstichkabinett, 78 C 7 [Hamilton 144], two of Nesson's poems are copied directly after it. Chartier's *Lay de paix* is copied directly before the *DHVV* in this MS (fols. 84b–86b). In Arsenal, 3523, Pierre de Nesson's *Priere a la vierge* appears directly before Chartier's *Lay de paix*, fols. 399–410. This poem is immediately preceded in the MS by another of Chartier's works: *Complainte*, fols. 391–8. In BnF, fr. 1642, a further work attributed to Pierre de Nesson appears: *L'Omage fait par maistre Pierre de Nesson*, fols. 326–8ᵛ.

[170] Laidlaw lists thirty-one copies of the *Excusacion*, twenty-four of which occur in manuscripts that also collect both the *BDSM* and the two letters, Alain Chartier (1974), pp. 328–31. The two other possible copies are Fribourg, Diesbach [Qj] which contains a verse copy of the *Lettre des dames a Alain* as well as the *Excusacion* (there are twenty-two missing leaves at the beginning of the manuscript which may have contained the *BDSM* and versions of both letters, see Alain Chartier (1974), p. 128); likewise, Turin, Bibl. Naz. Univ., L. II. 12 [Qp] which contains the *BDSM*, was badly damaged by fire. Piaget and Laidlaw suggest that item 8 which contains the *Requeste baillee aux dames* may contain the two prose letters and the *Excusacion* as well as the imitation poem, *La Belle Dame qui eut mercy*. See Piaget (1904), pp. 200–6, and Alain Chartier (1974), pp. 133–4.

dames and *Requeste baillee aux dames* and the *Belle Dame sans mercy* in all twenty-four (and possibly twenty-six) manuscripts and is followed by a *Responce des dames* in four manuscripts. The second group of sequels, in which Chartier's *Belle Dame* is put on trial, draws on reservoirs of language and image from this first group. New elements are introduced into the *Querelle* by the poets of the second cycle and are then, in turn, picked up by the poets of the third cycle of imitations.

Michault Taillevent, already mentioned as a respondent to Chartier, plays an important role in the two major Arsenal collections and other *Querelle* manuscripts.[171] In addition to his response to Chartier's *Breviaire des nobles* (*Le Psaultier des villains*), both Arsenal, 3521, and 3523 contain his *Passe temps* (pre 1440), and *Le Debat du cuer et de l'oeil* (1444). Arsenal, 3521, also contains Taillevent's *Regime de Fortune* (1445), *Lay fait sur le trespas de Madame Marguerite fille du roy de France contesse de charollois* (1446), *Le Congié d'Amours*, *La Bien Allée* (post *Congié*),[172] and the diptych formed by *L'Ediffice de l'ostel dolloureux d'Amours* and *La Resourse et reliefvement du dolloureux hostel* (post *Bien Allée*).[173] Both these Arsenal manuscripts contain Pierre Chastellain's response to Taillevent's *Passe temps*, known as the *Contre passe temps* or *Le Temps perdu* (1440), which follows Taillevent's poem in both manuscripts. The two poems are also found together in BnF, fr. 1642 (fols. 397–406; fols. 406ᵛ–12ᵛ).[174] Pierre Chastellain explicitly sets up

---

[171] The *Passe temps* is also collected in BnF, fr. 1642 and Besançon, BM, 554 (thirteen manuscripts in total; four from the *Querelle* body, and a further one: Stockholm, Royal Library, V. u. 22, which also contains Chartier's *BDSM*). *Le Regime de Fortune* also appears in BnF, fr. 833 (six manuscripts, two from the *Querelle* body, and Stockholm, Royal Library, V. u. 22 as above).

[172] Taillevent's *Le Congié d'Amours* and *La Bien Allée* form a complementary pair, and follow on in Arsenal, 3521. Two poems entitled *Le Congié d'Amours* (fols. 321–38), probably not by Taillevent, are found directly after Achille Caulier's *l'Ospital d'Amours* (fols. 281–320) in Arsenal, 3523, and come after the *Passe temps* and *Le Contre passe temps* (fols. 99–122; fols. 123–40); see J. W. Gossner, 'Two Medieval French *Congés d'Amour*', *Symposium* 9 (1955), 106–14. In his *Bien Allée*, Taillevent again takes up the theme of *temps perdu*, addressing both poems to the *Prince d'Amours* (as *l'Ediffice* and *La Resource*). The poet renounces the pains and pleasures of love, demanding a respite from the game 'pour ce qu'il a la barbe grise', *La Bien Allée*, Michault Taillevent (1975), v. 188, p. 263.

[173] See Appendix A for a list of the contents of these manuscripts.

[174] Deschaux lists ten manuscripts of Chastellain's *Contre passe temps*, of which three are *Querelle* manuscripts. All three versions follow on directly in the manuscript from Taillevent's *Passe temps*. Of the other seven manuscript versions of this poem, five appear with Taillevent's *Passe temps*, and the other two are found in manuscripts which only contain Chastellain's *Contre passe temps* [*Le Temps perdu*] and its sequel *Le Temps recouvert* (1454): BnF, fr. 2266; BnF, nouv. acq. fr. 6217.

his poem as a response to Taillevent's *Passe temps*, thus locating the poetic game in a textual space of play:

> En contemplant mon temps passé
> Et le *passe temps* de Michaut,
> J'ay mon *temps perdu* compassé
> Duquel a present bien m'y chault.
> Car point ne me suis demy chault
> Trouvé tousjours a grant froidure,
> Mais tousjours froit tant que froit dure.[175]

The manuscript tradition conserves this game by collecting the poems together and, in the majority of instances, actually placing them in adjacent positions within the manuscript.[176] Michault Taillevent is apostrophized frequently throughout the course of the *Contre passe temps*,[177] further creating the impression of a poetic dialogue between the two poets, conducted through the text itself. Deschaux remarks in his edition of Chastellain's *Le Temps recouvert* that the central theme of this poem, taken up from *Le Temps perdu*, and from the *Passe temps*, may actually originate with Chartier in a short passage of the *Breviaire des nobles*, with which Taillevent was certainly familiar (given his response to Chartier in the *Psaultier des villains*).[178] All three titles (*Passe temps/Temps perdu/Temps recouvert*) can be located within these few lines of Chartier's *Breviaire*. Thus the threads of collective invention are shown to start with Chartier, his *Belle Dame sans mercy* beginning one cycle of sequels and imitations, and his *Breviaire des nobles* initiating another, both of which are juxtaposed within the manuscript collections. It is significant, then, that every time Taillevent's *Passe temps* and Chastellain's *Temps perdu* are collected within a *Querelle* manuscript, Chartier's *Breviaire des nobles* also appears.

[175] *Le Temps perdu* [*Contre passe temps*], Pierre Chastellain (1982), vv. 1–7, p. 19.
[176] The two poems are adjacent in BnF, fr. 1642; BnF, fr. 24442; Arsenal, 3145; Arsenal, 3521; Arsenal, 3523; Chantilly, Musée Condé, 499 (1404); London, BL, Harley 4397; and Stockholm, Royal Library, V. u. 23. Refer to Appendix A for the contents of the two Arsenal collections (3521, 3523).
[177] Chastellain addresses Taillevent directly in verses III–XI: 'Mychault, Michault, quel vent te mayne? | Considere la vie humaine' (III); and from XL–end, 'Comment je me suis maintenu, | A! Michault, mon amy, escoute' (XL), Pierre Chastellain (1982), pp. 19–22, 29–39.
[178] See Pierre Chastellain (1982), p. 109. The passage Deschaux refers to occurs in the ballade of *Diligence*: 'Que vault homme qui muse et se pourmaine, | Et veult avoir mol lit et pance plaine | Et demourer en repos a couvert; | Et passe temps sepmaine aprés sepmaine | Et ne lui chault en quel point tout se maine—| Qui soit perdu ne qui soit recouvert', Alain Chartier (1974), vv. 280–5, p. 404.

Chastellain's *Le Temps recouvert* (1454), a sequel to his *Le Temps perdu*, is witnessed by only three manuscripts, not classified within the *Querelle* body. However, like the dialogue initiated between Taillevent's *Passe temps* and Chastellain's *Contre passe temps* across manuscript collections, *Le Temps recouvert* always appears in tandem with its predecessor, the *Contre passe temps* [*Le Temps perdu*], and is always transcribed after the previous text in manuscripts.[179] As Chastellain refers to Taillevent's *Passe temps* from within the *Contre passe temps*, so he refers to his own *Contre passe temps* [*Le Temps perdu*], from within *Le Temps recouvert*, weaving further intertextual threads:

> Dix ans davant ce temps de grace
> Avoye mis en mes escrips
> Comment oncques mes souppe grace
> Ne fis, fors mes plains et mes cris
> Faire, donc ung livre en escrips
> A ceulx qui leur temps passent ens
> Par maniere d'un passe temps.
> 'Mon temps perdu' ot nom ce livre
> Qui pour ma vie infortunee
> A ung checun lire se livre.[180]

This seems to indicate a self-trumping move by Chastellain, which can be explained in the overall economy of the collaborative debating community in terms of the field of objective relationships between positions. If texts are moves, one must not only trump others in order to stay ahead of the game, but also trump oneself. One could think of it in terms of authors producing sequels to their own work, for example. Another medieval instance of this would be Machaut's mirrored *Jugement* poems.[181]

Taillevent again takes up the theme of lost time in his poem *l'Ediffice de l'ostel dolloureux d'Amours*, and its response and remedy *La Resourse et reliefvement du dolloureux hostel*. Just as the theme of *temps perdu* and the substance of Pierre Chastellain's original poem is taken up, remembered and recovered ten years on in his sequel, *Le Temps recouvert*, so Taillevent

---

[179] *Le Temps recouvert* appears in three manuscripts, twice with *Le Temps perdu* alone: BnF, fr. 2266 (fols. 1–11, fols. 11ᵛ–48ᵛ), BnF, nouv. acq. fr. 6217 (fols. 1–11; 11–43), and in a larger collection: Stockholm, Royal Library, V. u. 23 (fols. 72–81, 82–113ᵛ). In this last manuscript, the diptych becomes a triptych with the inclusion of Taillevent's *Passe temps* (fols. 57–69ᵛ).
[180] Pierre Chastellain (1982), vv. 85–94, pp. 46–7.
[181] Guillaume de Machaut (1988) and (1988b).

recovers, restores, and shores up the crumbling *ostel dolloureux* of his original poem in the *Resourse*:

> On doit courir tost au reliefvement
> De sa maison et l'aidier de tous sens
> Par bon advis et bon gouvernement.[182]

In the *Resourse*, Taillevent adopts a didactic tone; the restoration of his *ostel*, or in other words, success in the game, is to be achieved through 'bon advis et bon gouvernement'. As in *Le Jeu des eschaz moralisé*, each *paonnet* must follow certain rules of conduct. The presence of Taillevent's reflexive poems, the *Ediffice* and *Resourse*, within Arsenal, 3521, is in keeping with the introspective tone of many of the texts transcribed here. One of the central organizing metaphors running through the texts collected in this manuscript is decay; the decay of buildings stands for human decay. Time passed in 'esbatement' within the space of play afforded by Amours, often represented as a building or enclosure, like Taillevent's *ostel dolloureux*, gives way to decline, melancholy, and a claustrophobic sense of entrapment. The game of love balances between these two extremes. It is only by perpetuating the game, in other words, by writing further poems or making further moves, that the poet/player may swing the game in his favour, and thus cheat Death who waits at the margins of the game holding open the *sacq commun*. This striking image of the *sacq commun*, the bag into which all the chess pieces are thrown after the game, is likened in *Comment l'estat du monde puet estre comparé au jeu des eschecz* to the earth in which all humans end, irrespective of rank or wealth:

> Lors sont en ung sacq mis arriere
> Pietons et roy comme en biere.
> Le grant sacq commun c'est la terre
> Que tous nous enclot et enserre;
> S'est bien drois que nous retourniesmes
> A la terre de qui nous sommes.
> Quant on a des eschecz joué,
> Ilz sont remis et alloué
> En ung sacq, ou en une bourse,
> Tous ensemble et tout d'une course,
> Sans faire honneur ne reverence
> Au roy, n'a la roÿne en ce

---

[182] Michault Taillevent (1975), vv. 80–2, p. 275.

> Non plus qu'on fait a pyon,
> Car on les prend et les gette on
> Ou sac, cul dessus (et) cul desseure.[183]

The *sacq commun*, then, is a space around the margins of play, where the rules of the game, and by extension of society, can no longer be enforced, and where the distinctions won and moves played during the game have no currency.

The chessboard as space of play, guiding metaphor for BnF, fr. 1169, recurs, as I have discussed, in Arsenal, 3521. The division of the chessboard into white and black squares, the divisions of players into white and black sides, maintain the set of contradictions on which the game balances, the colours suggestive respectively of the joys and sorrows of love, of winning and losing in the game. Taillevent evokes this black versus white metaphor in his *Ediffice de l'ostel dolloureux*, referring to reversals of fortune in his life that prefigure the reversal of this poem in the *Resourse*:

> Tout le rebours de ce que je queroye
> Es biens d'Amours que je cuidoye avoir
> Et le revers de ce que j'esperoye
> Ay en l'ostel ou il me fault manoir,
> Car j'ay trouvé, en lieu de blanc, tout noir.[184]

Such reversals dominate Taillevent's *Regime de Fortune*, which also appears in BnF, fr. 833 and anticipates the theme of Fortune's wheel in the poem *Comment l'estat de ce monde puet estre comparé au jeu des eschecz*. The *sacq commun* awaits all players, both winners and losers. Fortune's caprices are compared in the *Regime* to a roll of the dice (*alea*):

> Les plus grans fait trebuchier et cheoir,
> Et ceulx qui sont de petit lieu venu
> Aucunes fois es haulx sieges seoir
> Puis tout a coup, dont ilz sont esperdu,
> Sans dire qui l'a gaigné ne perdu,
> Cheoir les fait aussi bas qu'emmy Loire
> Et aussitost ung roy qu'ung populaire.[185]

[183] This is my transcription of the poem from Arsenal, 3521, vv. 148–62, fol. 266ᵛ, p. 232. I have added diacritical marks and modernized the punctuation, distinguished between i and j, u and v, and expanded all abbreviations. This poem has not been edited before, save a small section of it; see Murray (1913), p. 558. See my forthcoming edition.

[184] Michault Taillevent (1975), vv. 141–5, p. 270.

[185] Michault Taillevent (1975), vv. 49–55, p. 233.

The poem which immediately follows the *Regime de Fortune* in Arsenal, 3521, is Taillevent's *Lay fait sur le trespas de Madame Marguerite fille du roy de France*, a fitting illustration of Fortune's impartiality. A similar poem, under the title of *Complainte pour la mort de mme. Marguarite d'escosse*, and its counterpart, *La Response et consolation de la complainte cy dessuss escripte*, appear together in a sequence of texts from items twenty-four to thirty in Arsenal, 3523, which are interlinked by the notion of *trespas*.[186] These include the *Epitaphe ou lamentacion du roy derrain trespassé* (Charles VII, by Simon Gréban),[187] *La Confession et testament de l'amant trespassé de deuil*,[188] and Villon's *Grand Testament*.[189]

Other texts within the two Arsenal manuscripts pick up threads left by previous poets. The language of judgement and trial, for example, is renewed in Pierre Michault's *Le Procès de Honneur féminin* (Arsenal, 3521, fols. 195–218).[190] The metaphor of building as text (hence space of play/struggle)[191] is located in the anonymous *l'Ostelerie de joye* (Arsenal, 3521, fol. 147ᵛ), and also in Jean Molinet's allegorical *Temple de Mars* (Arsenal, 3521, fol. 289; BnF, fr. 1642, fol. 456), where it is deconstructed, this deconstruction suggestive of war as the death of art: 'guerre nuisible […] faicte sans art'.[192] Folliant Jonval's *Instruction d'un josne prince pour soy bien gouverner envers Dieu et le monde* with which Arsenal, 3521, begins, and George Chastelain's *Pas de la mort* transcribed towards the end (fol. 268ʳ), together with other didactic texts collected here (*Breviaire des nobles/Psaultier des villains*; *Le Regime de Fortune*; *Le Passe temps*; *Contre passe temps*; *Comment l'estat du monde*), create within the manuscript a space of moral reflection about the game and the end of the game. Similarly, in Arsenal, 3523, the sequence of texts from items twenty-four to thirty, linked by the notion of *trespas* as I mentioned,

---

[186] See Appendix A.

[187] This text also appears in BnF, fr. 1642 (fols. 414–23ᵛ) where it is followed by a similar eulogy: *Exclamacion en la mort pour marye d'anjou, Royne de France* (fols. 424–42ᵛ), and shortly thereafter by *La Complainte du feu roys Loys* (fol. 460); and in BnF, fr. 1661 (fols. 112–21).

[188] This poem is extant in four *Querelle* manuscripts (the sole witnesses): Arsenal, 3523; Rome, Vat. Reg. 1363 (fols. 1–84); Rome, Vat. Reg. 1720 (fols. 1–54); Rome, Vat. Reg. 1728 (fols. 135–9).

[189] This poem is also collected in BnF, fr. 1661 (fol. 236).

[190] Pierre Michault (1978).

[191] See Cowling (1998).

[192] See Jean Molinet, *Faictz et dictz*, ed. Dupire, 3 vols. (Paris: SATF, 1937). For a discussion of war as the death of art in Molinet's text, see Cornilliat, '*Or ne mens*': *Couleurs de l'éloge et du blâme chez les Grands Rhétoriqueurs* (Paris: Champion, 1994), pp. 660–75.

incites reflection about the margins of the game, and the precariousness of worldly positions. The poetic strategy within these manuscripts and throughout the body of *Querelle de la Belle Dame sans mercy* manuscripts seems, like Taillevent's *Resourse et reliefvement*, to consist in shoring up against the passing of time and the inevitability of Death; in perpetuation of play and suspension of conclusion. The manuscript collections, then, pivot around the antithetical yet complementary pairings of poets,[193] and poems,[194] around the interdependence of *esbatre* and *combatre*, to create spaces of play or *debatre* that confront and collaborate with one another. The creation of the individual codex might be compared to a game of chess: it provides a conceptual and material space of play where poets/compilers/scribes are players, making their moves within certain prescribed limits, and responding to the previous moves in the game. The individual poet/player operates in an economy of poetic exchange, accumulating symbolic capital through the moves s/he makes, and so engages in wider collaborative and dialogic play staged at the level both of the text and of the manuscript collection. The material community formed by the texts collected in the body of *Querelle de la Belle Dame sans mercy* manuscripts provides an illustration of how poetic expression in the fifteenth century was influenced and shaped by its mode of transmission or *habitus*, to use Bourdieu's term. Poets compete to trump one another and themselves,[195] building on existing tradition, in a climate of collaborative debate and literary exchange. They engage in a contest of wills and invention within the groupings I term collaborative debating communities, where the desire to perpetuate play is greater than the desire for victory, since victory or failure would necessarily

---

[193] The poets Michault Taillevent and Pierre Michault were often confused, and their works attributed to a single poet, but as Piaget clarifies in his article, 'Pierre Michault et Michault Taillevent', *Romania* 18 (1889), 439–52, these were two distinct poets both working at the court of the dukes of Burgundy. Pierre Michault was the *secretaire* of the Comte de Charolais, writing in the second half of the fifteenth century; Michault Taillevent (dit Le Caron) was the *valet de chambre* of Phillipe le Bon, writing in the first half of the fifteenth century, also referred to in the financial archives of the court of Burgundy as a 'joueur de farses'; see Michault Taillevent (1975), pp. 22–38. Pierre Chastellain was also confused with the poet Vaillant, partly because of a signature in the now destroyed Turin L. IV. 3 on fol. 33ᵛ, 'Pierre Chastellain dit Vaillant'. In Pierre Chastellain (1982), Deschaux separates the two. Both Chastellain and Vaillant worked sometime at the court of René d'Anjou in the Touraine area; see Pierre Chastellain (1982), pp. 11–13.

[194] See for example the palindromic poem, *Maistresse lealle ay d'amours* by Vaillant found in BnF, fr. 2230 (fol. 240ᵛ), Pierre Chastellain (1982), pp. 200–1.

[195] See this chapter, p. 183.

entail poetic closure, the end of the game and of social coherence. Unlike the earlier *Querelle de la Rose* to which Christine de Pizan put a stop with her publication of the *Rose* dossiers, the *Querelle de la Belle Dame sans mercy* rumbled on, inspiring generations of poets. '*La Belle Dame sans Merci* | Thee hath in thrall', announces a nineteenth-century version of Chartier's original poem by the Romantic poet John Keats.[196] The continuing legacy of the *Belle Dame sans mercy* attests not only to Chartier's mastery of the debate genre but to the lasting importance of his valorization of a vernacular poetic.

[196] See Keats (1999), vv. 39–40, pp. 160–2.

Conclusion

Tous ensemble donnent le lieu de triumphe a maistre Alain Charestier, normant, lequel a passé en beau langage elegant et substancieux tous ses predecesseurs. Et depuis, homme ne s'est faict second a luy, ainsy comme ceulx qui verroient ses oeuvres qui sont plusieurs, pourront congnoistre la doulceur de son langage. Et conseille a tous facteurs qu'ilz ensuivent sa doctrine tant en prose qu'en rithme pour tous docteurs.[1]

Fabri's *Le Grand et Vrai Art de pleine rhétorique* (1521) is one in a series of late medieval and early Renaissance arts of poetry and rhetoric that emphasize the significance of vernacular poetry both as an art form and as a means of transmitting *senefiance*.[2] 'Beau parler sans sentence n'est que vent sans science', as Fabri asserts.[3] In this study for the first time, Alain Chartier's unique contribution to vernacular eloquence is framed in the socio-cultural context of his predecessors and contemporaries, and shown to be crucial to the development of a debating climate in late medieval France. Chartier is a central participant in several of the collaborative debating communities I model here, both through his material position in manuscript collections, and through the legacy of such social and poetic engagements as the *Querelle de la Belle Dame sans mercy*.

Previous studies have either dismissed Chartier's French verse as 'joyeuses escritures',[4] viewing only the prose and Latin works as 'serious', or focused their interpretative efforts mainly on the *BDSM* and the French verse to the detriment of the prose and Latin works, or vice versa.[5] Through a meticulous rereading of the French verse against the Latin and French prose, and a consideration of its reception with the

---

[1] Pierre Fabri (1889), I: p. 11.

[2] See *Recueil d'arts de seconde rhétorique* (1902).

[3] See Pierre Fabri (1889), I: p. 21.

[4] See Hoffman (1975); Piaget (1901); Champion (1923); W. B. Kay (1964).

[5] See Chapter 3, pp. 111–14, for a survey of critical work on the *BDSM*. Blanchard and Mühlethaler (2002) acknowledge that Chartier is the 'restaurateur de l'écriture engagée', p. 37; their study does not consider the French verse (with the exception of the *LQD*).

prose in manuscript and early printed collections, I offer a new and productive interpretation of the works of this unfairly sidelined court poet.

In the first couple of decades of the fifteenth century, Chartier thrived in what was already a vigorous debating climate with established communities of scholars and poets. Social, literary, and intellectual conditions combine in the late medieval period to foster and harness this endless enthusiasm for (non-ending) debate among members of these communities. This enthusiasm leads to a material collaboration between the participants in debate that manifests itself in the *locus* of debate, be it the competitive arena of the *puys*, or the manuscript collection itself in which texts, and authors beyond the texts, engage with one another. One of the most important achievements of the current study is the reconstruction of social competition and collaboration between individuals in late medieval France through the metaphor of the text as game. In Chapter 1, I suggest how this metaphor is particularly appropriate for an examination of the debate—which itself represents a competitive game within the text—by applying Roger Caillois's category of *agôn* or skilful games to the game of the text, *eclogue, tenso, jeu-parti, demande d'amour, jugement,* or *débat,* to suggest both the high level of intricacy and poetic skill brought to the debate genre, and the inherent competitive element.[6] The game is played in the perpetual suspension of conclusion, and this suspension of conclusion is manifested in the frequent non-closure of the late medieval debate poem.[7] Pierre Bourdieu's sociological study of field, habitus, and the symbolic capital at stake in the field provides a model for and an explanation of the non-ending debate poem, and the wider poetic context it engages with. The existence of the field supposes the pre-existence of antagonistic yet complementary relations between positions in the field. These sets of relations are only perpetuated as long as the game/struggle for symbolic capital continues, and social cohesion dictates the continuation of the game. I engage with Bourdieu's dialectical methodology in order to view medieval debate poetry from a position that takes into account the inevitable distortion of the modern gaze. Bourdieu rejects the structuralist criticism of such sociologists as Lévi-Strauss, as this method cannot account for the prejudiced gaze of the onlooker. Bourdieu's notion of habitus bridges the gap between the objective structures identified by the structuralist and the necessity

---

[6] Caillois (1967).   [7] Armstrong (1997b); Cayley (2003).

of situating these structures in their original context. Habitus, for Bourdieu, represents the socio-cultural and historical processes whereby these objective structures are reproduced.[8] In the same way, with the help of my new model—the collaborative debating community—I show how these late medieval societies themselves derive value and coherence through literary imitation and competition and how their compositional and reading patterns can be traced through material evidence of collaboration. The significance of this sociological approach for medieval studies is confirmed by recent interest in Bourdieu from scholars such as Sarah Kay, Simon Gaunt, Jane Taylor, and Adrian Armstrong.[9]

I gave a working example of what I mean by the collaborative debating community in Chapter 2, through a close re-examination and theorization of the literary quarrel known as the *Querelle de la Rose*. Groups of early humanists at Paris and Avignon were frequently engaged in literary and mainly epistolary debate in Latin as a complement to their diplomatic and political chancery activities. For these groups, the need to cultivate an elegant epistolary style outweighed the importance of the subject they were debating. To adopt Bourdieu's terminology, acquiring a polished epistolary style for this community of scholars might represent a means of amassing symbolic capital. They would often adopt exaggeratedly polemical debating positions within their texts, following classical models of invective, in order to sharpen the sense of competition. Some, like Nicolas de Clamanges, even added the polemical element to their letters after the event, creating fictional quarrels, such was the enthusiasm for conflict.[10] Both Jean de Montreuil and Christine de Pizan use the metaphor of the debating game as an actual game/competition in the letters that constitute their contribution to the *Querelle de la Rose*. Montreuil compares the *Querelle* both to a competitive race and to the specifically literary competition staged in Virgil's third *Eclogue*,[11] while Christine talks of a *gieu*.[12] My discussion of the vernacular intervention of Christine de Pizan in the *Querelle de la Rose* provides a contrast between the literary debating game as conceived of by these early humanists and that played by Christine de Pizan and Alain

[8] Bourdieu (1990).

[9] Gaunt and Kay (1997); Taylor, Jane (2001); Armstrong (1997) and his forthcoming book on poetic competition. See *supra*: Introduction, pp. 3–4, 6, for a discussion of my position relative to Taylor and Armstrong.

[10] See Chapter 2, p. 70.   [11] See Chapter 2, pp. 75–6.

[12] See Chapter 2, pp. 81–2.

Chartier. Christine's desire for moral engagement and publicity shapes her contribution to the *Querelle*, just as Chartier's social and ethical engagement was to form the subtext for his vernacular verse debates. In this sense, I suggest that the clash of approaches to debate could be explained as the conflict between different types of capital at stake in the field. While early humanist scholars seek to enhance their standing with contemporaries by honing their epistolary style, Christine de Pizan and Alain Chartier play the game for other symbolic capital. Christine seeks public recognition of her cause through the publication of judiciously edited versions of the *Querelle*. Chartier, on the other hand, seeks to reject a corrupt set of courtly morals through the medium of debate, and so doing reinvests vernacular poetry with a *senefiance* long denied it.

I set Chartier here at the convergent point of two debate cultures, intellectual and literary. I reject the conventional division of Chartier's verse into the 'joyeuses escritures' and the 'serious poems',[13] by suggesting that a *meta-rhetorical discourse* informs all the French verse. A thorough rereading of the French verse through Chartier's Latin works, supported by the frequent juxtaposition of these works in manuscript collections, reveals a network of allusions to the interconnectedness of language, discourse, and morals. By means of this dialectical network informing Chartier's *oeuvre*, the vernacular verse debate is invested with *senefiance*. Chartier's protagonists represent the conflict of different subject positions and competing discourses. I demonstrate how Chartier effects an ironic emptying of conventional courtly discourse through the figure of the *Belle Dame* in his poem the *Belle Dame sans mercy*, much as the *Sodalis* of his Latin *Dialogus* rejects the logical discourse represented by the *Amicus*. Chartier makes a distinction between *verba* and *res* (words and things), espousing a discourse which I have called a new humanist rhetoric. This new humanist rhetoric addresses a social context beyond language itself (*res*), and so breaks free from the constraints of a purely logical discourse (*verba*). My focus on the poetics of closure in Chartier's *oeuvre* shows how deliberate non-closure or deferral of ending is part of a moral and ethical agenda through which Chartier asserts his freedom from corruption. The notion of textual closure is connected to self-serving and self-contained systems of language like the courtly discourse the *Belle Dame* renounces. By leaving his poems unresolved

---

[13] Hoffman (1975), pp. 43–121. See Chapter 3, p. 88–9, and my introduction, p. 9.

and open to future resolution, Chartier not only perpetuates the game of the text but mirrors an external quest for peace and emancipation from oppression. Anti-closure is used as a rhetorical device in the late medieval debate poem; I conclude from my study of Chartier's debates that this device has two main effects which are more or less demonstrated in debate poems of this period. First, it encourages socio-cultural competition (thus cohesion) by perpetuating textual play, and second, it suggests an ethical engagement on the part of the poet.

In addressing Chartier's poetic legacy, I focus on his *oeuvre* in its social and material context. I was concerned in Chapter 4 to trace the operation of a later collaborative debating community in text and context. In part I, I looked specifically at the collaboration between the poets who continued and imitated Chartier's *Belle Dame sans mercy*. Complex intertextual threads weave through the four cycles of sequels and imitations of the *Querelle*, generated through the competitive game-playing of the *Querelle* poets. I elaborate a theory of the self-reflexivity of the *Querelle*, based particularly on texts from the later cycles, such as the *Amant rendu cordelier*. My work in turn feeds into a rich research context which includes Jane Taylor's work on intertextuality in Villon, and Armstrong's forthcoming study of poetic competition from the late Middle Ages up to *c.*1530.

The current study is underpinned by a firm belief in the significance of manuscript context, hence reception, as material evidence of the collaborative debating community, in line with major new research being carried out in this area. Manuscript context is specifically explored here in Chapter 4, part II, where I trace patterns of anthologization in the forty manuscripts identified as witnesses to the *Querelle de la Belle Dame sans mercy*. Within these codices, I came across a series of texts not specifically linked to Alain Chartier's original poem, but which nonetheless regularly appeared with its sequels and imitations. The fruitful metaphor of the manuscript as a space of play that materializes the conceptual playground in which the *Querelle* poets make their moves was developed in order to organize this body of texts. I identified a series of allusions to the game of chess as a mirror for social structures in the *Querelle* body, and used this medieval political metaphor myself to suggest the organization, interaction, and skill of the community of *Querelle* poets. Roger Caillois, as I mentioned, includes chess in his category of *agôn* or skilful games. The chessboard on which the game is played within the text provides a parallel for the individual arena in which the debate of each text takes place, as well as for the larger space of play of the manuscript collection. If the poetic game ends, social coherence is destroyed, since the players will no longer derive their social identity from competition with others. This phenomenon is suggested by the image of the *sacq commun* into which all the chess pieces are thrown after the game. A short poem from one of the *Querelle* manuscripts compares the hierarchy of medieval French society to the organization of pieces on a chessboard. After the end of the game, lying in the sack, the pieces are no longer distinguished from one another, as they are no longer in play. It is the play that defines their social position rather than any innate characteristics.[14] This analogy works well for the poets of the *Querelle*, and indeed for my model of the collaborative debating community in late medieval France. Play is perpetuated and closure is deferred not just as a matter of whim, but as a matter of necessity. It is through their collaborative play that these poets and scholars distinguish themselves, in a competitive struggle to gain symbolic capital. This capital translates into prestige and position in a period during which vernacular poetry is undergoing re-evaluation not only as a means of transmitting knowledge but as a method of social and political advancement. Alain Chartier is located firmly at the centre of this socio-cultural movement by this new study.

I highlight and strengthen here, in addition, the case for a 'profeminine' prise de position by Chartier in the long-running *Querelle des femmes*,[15] firmly replacing him on the prosecution bench, where Pierre Michault sat him alongside Boccaccio and Martin le Franc, in the trial of *Honneur féminin* v. *L'Inculpé* (at which the traditional female defensive role was finally exchanged for one of attack).[16] A spate of recent articles and editions have argued the case for Chartier's sympathy with the *Belle Dame*, and her political significance in terms of women's 'franchise',

---

[14] The characteristics which distinguish the pieces during play are a positive hindrance once the game ends. The poem *Comment l'estat du monde puet estre comparé au jeu des eschecz* found in Arsenal, 3521, describes how the king lies at the bottom of the sack as he is the heaviest piece, a reversal of his fortunes on the chessboard: 'Sicom trouveroit chascune heure | Au fons du sac le roy gisant, | Et dessoubx sont ly plus pesant; | C'est raison [que] cilz qui plus poise | Soit au dessoubx qui plus en poise', vv. 163–7 (see my forthcoming edition).

[15] I use the term profeminine here following Blamires (1997): 'Since there is by now some consensus that "feminine" and "masculine" are best used to express cultural constructions of gender, I believe that pre-modern texts which develop constructions of "woman" which are positive according to the cultural ideology of their period ought logically to be called not "profeminist" but profeminine', p. 12.

[16] See *supra*: Chapter 3, p. 88; Pierre Michault (1978).

or political and social autonomy.[17] However, the current study goes much further, to establish a profeminine discourse running throughout Chartier's production, centred around the powerful female figures of *La France* in *Le Quadrilogue Invectif*, the *Belle Dame*, and the ladies of the *Livre des Quatre Dames*, but also read through the speeches of the male interlocutors and narrators of Chartier's debates. This is a discourse that is supported by the reception of Chartier's works in manuscript collections where the question of women is the unifying theme. Not only is Chartier's *BDSM* already the central piece in the majority of the forty manuscripts I classify within the *Querelle* body, but I have recently traced dynamic patterns which see the manuscript tradition of Chartier's French verse frequently intersect with the manuscript tradition of other profeminine debates and treatises.[18] A full-scale research project is now needed to look into how the manuscript tradition of Chartier's works amplifies and responds to the expression of an anti-courtly and profeminine discourse in those works, and to establish a definitive stemma.

The question of the reception of Chartier's works opens up fertile future research paths in this relatively untrodden field of late medieval debate poetry. It is significant, for example, that I uncovered a manuscript containing Chartier's *Breviaire des nobles*, the *Lay de paix* and ballade XXVIII, not listed by Laidlaw in his 1974 edition of Chartier's French verse, while researching the manuscript tradition of the *Songe de la Pucelle*, a fifteenth-century debate poem.[19] The *Songe de la Pucelle* pits *Amours* and *Honte* against each other in their attempts to convince a *pucelle* of their respective cases: *Amours* urges her to join love's game, while *Honte* warns of the deceptions inherent within courtly love and language. The debate typically remains unconcluded, but through correspondences with the other pieces in the manuscript, and particularly those by Chartier, *Honte* emerges as the likely victor.[20] The *Embusche Vaillant*, otherwise known as the *Debat des deux seurs*,[21] by the fifteenth-century Tourangeau poet Vaillant, appears in seven out of its ten manuscripts with Chartier's *Belle Dame sans mercy* and

[17] Particularly Solterer (2002); but also Sansone (1995); Angelo (2003); Kinch (forthcoming).
[18] See Cayley, 'Debating Communities: Revealing Meaning in Late Medieval French Manuscript Collections', *Neuphilologische Mitteilungen* 2 (2004), 191–201.
[19] The manuscript in question is Sion, Bibliothèque Cantonale du Valais, Supersaxo 97bis. See also Aebischer, 'Le manuscrit Supersaxo 97bis de la Bibliothèque cantonale du Valais; le roman de "Ponthus et la belle Sidoine". Textes en vers', *Vallesia* 14 (1959), 245–69.
[20] Cayley (2004).   [21] See Pierre Chastellain (1982), pp. 113–57.

its sequels and imitations,[22] and twice with the *Songe de la Pucelle*.[23] The debate framework is by now familiar: the narrator, returning from a party, overhears two sisters in the corridor talking about love, and hides to listen.[24] The younger sister is in love, but is afraid to declare herself and join love's game. She voices the same concerns about courtly and specifically male deception that can be seen both in Chartier and in the *Songe de la Pucelle*. Other debate poems which problematize gender are often collected with Chartier's works, or occur within the *Querelle* body. The *Debat de la Damoiselle et de la Bourgoise*, which was mentioned earlier, for example, always appears either with Chartier's *Belle Dame sans mercy* or with its imitations,[25] or the *Debat du marié et du non marié* (also known as the *Nouveau marié*), which makes all seven of its appearances in manuscripts with the *Belle Dame sans mercy*, its sequels and imitations, and other verse by Chartier.[26] The manuscript tradition of Chartier seems then to associate his works with a defence of women and moral values; with anti-courtly invective coupled with a call for the renewal of poetic language. The Supersaxo manuscript, which I have now added to the manuscript tradition of Chartier's French works, as well as other fifteenth-century anthologies mentioned here, provide a useful concrete model for the socio-cultural interaction of poets in fourteenth- and fifteenth-century France. This is a model I have termed the collaborative debating community.

Alain Chartier's works are assessed here, then, for the first time both within their socio-cultural context and in the material context provided by their anthologization in manuscript collections. With an investigation

---

[22] In Paris, BnF, fr. 1642 (fols. 384–96); Paris, BnF, fr. 2230 (fols. 211–33); Paris, BnF, fr. 2264 (fols. 127–58ᵛ); Paris, BnF, fr. 25553 (fols. 28–49); Paris, BnF, nouv. acq. fr. 6639 (fols. 132–43ᵛ); Paris, Arsenal, 3523 (fols. 759–92); Valenciennes, BM, 417 (fols. 63–81); Berlin, Staatsbibliothek, Phillipps 1928 (fols. 2–32); Dresden, Sächsische Landesbibliothek, Oc. 68 (fols. 1–33); and The Hague, KB, 71 E 49 (fols. 607–38).

[23] In Paris, BnF, fr. 25553 (fols. 28–49); Paris, Arsenal, 3523 (fols. 759–92).

[24] See plate 6. The curious character hiding behind the room in which the sisters are pictured is not mentioned in the text, but if the figure in the foreground is the virtual acteur/narrator, we could imagine this fourth figure as a portrait of the actual author behind the text.

[25] See *Recueil de poésies françoises*, V: 5–33. It appears in Paris, BnF, fr. 1661 (fols. 2–12); Paris, Arsenal, 3523 (fols. 51–70); The Hague, Koninklijke Bibliotheek, 71 E 49 (fols. 296ʳ–306ᵛ); Rome, Vat. Reg. 1363 (fols. 85ʳ–104ᵛ); and Rome, Vat. Reg. 1720 (fols. 116ʳ–26ʳ).

[26] See *Recueil de poésies françoises*, IX: 148–63. These are Paris, BnF, fr. 924 (221 ff.); BnF, fr. 1661 (fols. 100–5); BnF, fr. 2264 (fols. 159–69ᵛ); Arsenal, 3523 (fols. 83–99); Chantilly, Musée Condé, 685 (fols. 158–66); The Hague, KB, 71 E 49 (fols. 139 ff.); and St Petersburg, National Library, F. V. XIV. 7 (fols. 161–8).

Figure 6. Vaillant, *Debat des deux seurs* [*L'Embusche Vaillant*] (the *acteur* overhears the sisters' debate)

Paris, BnF, fr. 2230, fol. 211ᵛ

centred around one poet's practice, I have demonstrated the many possibilities that would be opened up by the widespread application of this dialectical methodology to medieval studies, specifically in the field of codicology. We must consider medieval texts in dialogue and collaboration with one another as part of material and conceptual debating communities, rather than isolating each poet in his/her own anthology, as in many modern editions. This dynamic interdisciplinary approach offers us unique and fascinating insights into the many vagaries of late medieval composition, transmission, and reception.

APPENDIX A

Table of Contents of Paris, Bibliothèque de l'Arsenal, 3521, and 3523

PARIS, ARSENAL, 3521
(LATE-FIFTEENTH CENTURY)[1]

1. Fol. 1, *L'Instruction d'un josne prince pour soy bien gouverner envers Dieu et le monde* [Folliant de Jonval, but attributed in catalogue to George Chastelain].
2. Fol. 30, *S'ensuit le Breviaire des nobles que fist maistre Allain Charretier.*
3. Fol. 38, *Lay de paix fait par maistre Allain Chartier.*
4. Fol. 43, *Autre lay.*
5. Fol. 46, *Ethimologisation de Paris* [Jean Munier, 1418].
6. Fol. 47, *Lay de Nostre Dame* [Guillaume Alexis ?].
7. Fol. 48, *Le Psaultier des villains* [Michault Taillevent].
8. Fol. 56ᵛ, *Complainte de maistre Allain Charretier.*
9. Fol. 59ᵛ, *S'ensuit la Belle Dame sans mercy* [Alain Chartier].
10. Fol. 72, *Lettre des dames a Alain.*
11. Fol. 72ʳ⁻ᵛ, *La Requeste baillee aux dames contre Alain.*
12. Fol. 73, *L'Excusacion aux dames* [Alain Chartier].
13. Fol. 77, *La Responce des dames, faite a maistre Alain.*
14. Fol. 79, *Traitté fait par Baudart Hereng, correspondant a la Belle Dame sans mercy* [*Accusations*].
15. Fol. 89, *S'ensuit la Dame lealle en amours.*
16. Fol. 103, *La Cruelle Femme en amours* [Achille Caulier].
17. Fol. 118, *L'Ospital d'Amours* [Achille Caulier].
18. Fol. 138, *S'ensuit le Debat resveille matin* [Alain Chartier].
19. Fol. 144, *Lay de plaisance* [Alain Chartier].
20. Fol. 147ᵛ, *L'Ostelerie de joye.*
21. Fol. 149, *Le Debat du cuer et de l'oeil* [Michault Taillevent].

---

[1] There are three foliations for this MS. The most recent, in pencil, numbers two consecutive folios as 57. I therefore follow the original ink foliation, which is accurate. The roman numerals are occasionally cut off the top of the folios, but can be found listed on the first three folios (letters A, B, and C) in the original table of contents. There are 300 fols in this MS: 296 + 4 (A, B, C, D)

22. Fol. 162, *La Confession d'Amours*.
23. Fol. 169ᵛ, *Passio cuyusdam monachi*.
24. Fol. 171, *Le Debat de deux chevaliers sur les plaisirs et dolleurs qui poevent estre en amours fait par maistre Allain Chartier* [DDFA].
25. Fol. 187, *La Lamentacion de Gresse, oppressée des Turcs, et la consolation que lui donnent France et Angleterre* [debate between Greece, France, and England, by Jean Molinet].
26. Fol. 195, *La Deduccion du process de honneur femenin* [Pierre Michault].
27. Fol. 219, *Le Regime de Fortune, fait par Michault Taillevent*.
28. Fol. 223, *Lay fait par Michault Taillevent sur le trespas de Madame Marguerite fille du roy de France contesse de charollois*.
29. Fol. 227, *Le Passe temps de Michault Taillevent*.
30. Fol. 238, *Le Temps perdu de Pierre Chastellain*.
31. Fol. 247, *Le Congié d'Amours, fait par Michault Taillevent*.
32. Fol. 250, *La Bien Allée* [Michault Taillevent].
33. Fol. 253ᵛ, *L'Ediffice de l'ostel dollereux d'Amours, fait par ledit Michault Taillevent*.
34. Fol. 256ᵛ, *La Resourse et reliefvement du dollereux hostel d'Amours* [Michault Taillevent].
35. Fol. 259ᵛ, *Lay fait par Achilles Caulier a l'onneur de la vierge Marie*.
36. Fol. 261ᵛ, *Exhortacion pour le salut de creature humaine*.
37. Fol. 264ᵛ, *Comment l'estat du monde puet estre comparé au jeu des eschecz*.
38. Fol. 267ᵛ, *Meditation a l'ymage du crucefix*.
39. Fol. 268, *Le Pas de la mort fait par George l'aventurier* [George Chastelain].
40. Fol. 276, *Vers a la louange des seigneurs illustres en France* [Simon Gréban].
41. Fol. 285, *Plusieurs bonnes ballades*.
42. Fol. 289, *Temple de Mars* [Jean Molinet].
43. Fol. 294, *Piece de vers ajoutée* [added in later hand].

PARIS, ARSENAL, 3523
(LATE-FIFTEENTH CENTURY)

1. Fol. 1, *Le Breviaire des nobles* [Alain Chartier].
2. Fol. 17, *Le Psaultier des villains* [Michault Taillevent].
3. Fol. 33, *Le Songe de la pucelle*.
4. Fol. 51, *Le Plaidoié de la Damoiselle a l'encontre de la Bourgoise* [Blosseville, *Echiquier d'Amours*].
5. Fol. 71, *Le Debat reveille matin* [Alain Chartier].
6. Fol. 83, *Le Nouvel Marié* [*Debat du marié et du non marié*].
7. Fol. 99, *Le Passetemps de Michault*.
8. Fol. 123, *Le Contrepassetemps* [Pierre Chastellain, *Le Temps perdu*].
9. Fol. 141, *La Belle Dame sans mercy* [Alain Chartier].

10. Fol. 165, *La Response de la Belle Dame* [Baudet Herenc, *Accusations*].
11. Fol. 187, *Les Erreurs contraires a la Belle Dame en amours* [Achille Caulier, *La Cruelle Femme en amours*].
12. Fol. 219, *La Deserte du desloyal*.
13. Fol. 247, *Le Mirouer des dames* [vernacular translation of Durand de Champagne's *Speculum dominarum*].
14. Fol. 281, *L'Ospital d'Amours* [Achille Caulier].
15. Fol. 321, *Le Congié d'Amours*.[2]
16. Fol. 339, *Dialogue entre l'amant et la dame* [Oton de Granson, *La Belle Dame qui eut mercy*].
17. Fol. 351, *D'un amoureux parlant a sa dame par amours*.
18. Fol. 359, *La Confession d'Amours*.
19. Fol. 378, *La Grant Garde derriere*.
20. Fol. 391, *La Complainte maistre Alain Chartier*.
21. Fol. 399, *Priere a la vierge par Pierre Nesson*.
22. Fol. 411, *Le Lay de paix* [Alain Chartier].
23. Fol. 421, *Le Banquet du boys*.
24. Fol. 437, *Epitaphe ou lamentation du roy derrain trespassé* [Charles VII, by Simon Gréban].
25. Fol. 461, *Complainte pour la mort de mme. Marguarite d'escosse daulphin de vennoys*.
26. Fol. 467, *Cy apres s'ensuit la Responce et consolation de la complainte cy dessuss escripte*.
27. Fol. 475, *Le Jugement du povre triste amant banny*.
28. Fol. 519, *La Confession et testament de l'amant trespassé de deuil* [Pierre de Hauteville, 'prince d'Amours'].
29. Fol. 589, *Le Livre de l'amant rendu cordellier a l'observance d'amours*.
30. Fol. 647, *Grand Testament* [François Villon].
31. Fol. 719, *La Ballade de Fortune* [François Villon].
32. Fol. 721, *Le Lais François Villon*.
33. Fol. 735, *Le Debat du cuer et de l'oeil* [Michault Taillevent].
34. Fol. 759, *Le Debat des deux seurs ou l'Embusche Vaillant* [Vaillant].
35. Fol. 793, *La Conclusion du debat sans relacion*.

---

[2] There are two separate poems contained within this item; see Gossner (1955).

Manuscript Tables

MSS CONTAINING MORE THAN ONE FRENCH VERSE WORK BY CHARTIER

MSS	LPl	DDFA	LQD	DHVV	BN	LP	DRM	Com	BDSM	Ex	B/R
BnF, fr. 833[1]	X		X		X	X	X	X	X	X	
BnF, fr. 924	X	X			X	X	X	X	X	X	
BnF, fr. 1127	X	X	X		X	X	X	X	X	X	X
BnF, fr. 1128		X				X					
BnF, fr. 1130	X		X		X	X		X			X[2]
BnF, fr. 1131		X	X		X	X	X	X	X	X	
BnF, fr. 1642		X	X		X	X	X	X	X	X	

[1] I have italicized those manuscripts that also contain Chartier's French prose or Latin works.
[2] X marks those manuscripts that contain Chartier's ballade XXVIII, 'Il n'est dangier que de villain', Alain Chartier (1974), pp. 391–2.

	1	2	3	4	5	6	7	8	9	10	11
BnF, fr. 1727	X	X	X		X	X	X	X	X	X	
BnF, fr. 2230	X	X	X		X	X	X	X	X	X	
BnF, fr. 2249					X	X					
BnF, fr. 2263					X	X					
BnF, fr. 2264							X		X	X	
BnF, fr. 19139	X	X	X		X	X	X	X	X	X	X
BnF, fr. 20026	X	X	X			X	X	X	X	X	
BnF, fr. 24440	X	X	X		X	X	X	X	X	X	
BnF, fr. 25293						X		X			
BnF, fr. 25435			X		X	X	X		X		
BnF, nouv. acq. fr. 4511–13	X	X	X						X		
BnF, nouv. acq. fr. 6220–4					X	X					
BnF, Rothschild, 440			X		X	X	X	X	X	X	
BnF, Rothschild, 2796	X				X	X					X
Paris, Bibl. de l'Arsenal, 3521	X	X	X		X	X	X	X	X	X	
Paris, Bibl. de l'Arsenal, 3523					X	X		X	X		

(continued overleaf)

MSS	LPI	DDFA	LQD	DHVV	BN	LP	DRM	Com	BDSM	Ex	B/R
Paris, Musée Jacquemart-André, 11			X		X	X	X		X		X
Aix-en-Provence, Bibl. Méjanes, 168	X	X			X	X	X	X	X	X	X
Besançon, BM, 554					X		X	X	X	X	X
Carpentras, BM, 390							X	X	X	X	
Chantilly, Musée Condé, 685							X		X		
Chantilly, Musée Condé, 686								X	X		
Clermont-Ferrand. BM, 249					X	X					X
Clermont-Ferrand, Archives du Puy-de-Dôme, 28	X	X					X	X	X	X	
Grenoble, BM, 874	X	X			X	X	X	X	X	X	X
Poitiers, BM, 214					X	X					
Rodez, BM, 57					X	X					
Toulouse, BM, 826		X			X	X	X	X	X	X	X
Valenciennes, BM, 417					X		X				

	1	2	3	4	5	6	7	8	9	10
Arnhem, Bibliotheek, 79	X	X	X							
Berlin, Kupferstichkabinett, 78 C 7					X	X		X		
Bern, Burgerbibliothek, 473	X	X	X	X	X	X			X	X
Brussels, BR, 10961–70	X		X	X	X				X	
Brussels, BR, 21521–31							X			
Copenhagen, RL, 1768		X	X	X		X			X	X
Escorial, O. I. 14							X			
Fribourg-Diesbach		X			X				X	
Geneva, Lib. of E. Droz						X	X			
The Hague, KB, 71 E 49		X	X	X	X	X	X		X	X
Karlsruhe, Badische Landesbibliothek, 410					X				X	
Lausanne, Bibl. Universitaire, 350		X	X			X				

MSS	LPI	DDFA	LQD	DHVV	BN	LP	DRM	Com	BDSM	Ex	B/R
London, BL, Harley 4402					X						
London, BL, Royal 19 A iii					X				X		
London, Clumber Sale, 941	X	X	X		X	X	X	X	X	X	
Madrid, BN, 10307		X					X		X	X	
Manchester, Chetham's Lib., Muniment A.6.91		X			X	X			X	X	
Milan, Bibl. Trivulziana, 971	X		X		X	X	X	X	X	X	
Munich, Bayerische Staatsbibliothek Cod. Gall. 10			X								
Oxford, Bod., E.D. Clarke 34						X		X			X

Manuscript	LPl	DDFA	LQD	DHVV	LP	DRM	Com	BN	BDSM	Ex	R/B
Sion, Supersaxo 97 bis[3]							X	X			X
Stockholm, RL., V. u. 22							X	X		X	X
St. Petersburg, Nat. Lib., F.V.XIV.7			X				X		X	X	
Turin, BN, L II 12	X	X					X	X	X		
Vatican, Reg. lat., 1323							X	X	X		
Vatican, Vat. lat., 4794	X	X	X				X	X	X	X	
Vienna, NB, 2619	X	X	X				X	X	X	X	X
Vienna, NB, 3391							X				X
P. Le Caron (printed 1489)	X		X				X	X	X	X	

Key (in approx. chronological order):

LPl	*Lay de plaisance* (1412–15)
DDFA	*Debat des Deux Fortunés d'amours* (1419–20)
LQD	*Livre des Quatre Dames* (1419–22)
DHVV	*Debat du Herault, du Vassault, et du Villain* (1420–4)
LP	*Lay de paix* (pre 1426)
DRM	*Debat de reveille matin* (1423–4)
Com	*Complainte pour la mort* (1424)
BN	*Breviaire des nobles* (1424–6)
BDSM	*La Belle Dame sans merry* (1424)
Ex	*Excusacion* (1425)
R/B	*Rondeaux et ballades* (1410–25)

[3] Sion (Switzerland), Bibliothèque cantonale du Valais, Supersaxo 97bis, was overlooked by Laidlaw, and hence not listed in his 1974 edition. In addition to the *Breviaire* (fols. 122–31), the *Lay de Paix* (fols. 131v–6v), and ballade XXVIII (fol. 148v–9), it also contains the *Roman de Ponthus et de Sidoine* (fols. 1–122), the *Songe de la Pucelle* (fols. 137–45), and five other ballades, 'a pleysance et de bon advis' (fols. 145v–8). See P. Aebischer, 'Le manuscrit Supersaxo 97bis de la Bibliothèque cantonale du Valais; le roman de "Ponthus et la belle Sidoine". Textes en vers', *Vallesia* 14 (1959), 245–69; and id. (1961); also Cayley (2004).

Appendix B

MSS CONTAINING CHARTIER'S FRENCH PROSE WORKS

MSS	Quadrilogue	Esperance	Curial[4]
BnF, fr. 126[5]	X	X	
BnF, fr. 832		X	
BnF, fr. 833	X	X	X
BnF, fr. 924			X
BnF, fr. 1123	X	X	
BnF, fr. 1124	X	X	
BnF, fr. 1125	X	X	
BnF, fr. 1127	X		
BnF, fr. 1128	X	X	
BnF, fr. 1130	X		
BnF, fr. 1132		X	
BnF, fr. 1133	X	X	
BnF, fr. 1549	X	X	
BnF, fr. 1642	X	X	X
BnF, fr. 1727	X		X
BnF, fr. 2263	X		
BnF, fr. 2265		X	X
BnF, fr. 2861			X
BnF, fr. 5339			X
BnF, fr. 12435		X	
BnF, fr. 12436	X	X	
BnF, fr. 12437	X	X	
BnF, fr. 20055			X
BnF, fr. 24440	X	X	
BnF, fr. 24441	X	X	
BnF, nouv. acq. fr. 6535		X	
BnF, lat. 18583		X	

[4] I include the French prose translation of Chartier's Latin original *De vita curiali* in this table, as although it is most unlikely that Chartier was the translator, this translation was frequently copied into MSS of Chartier's works.

[5] I have italicized all MSS that also collect Chartier's French verse or Latin works.

BnF, Rothschild, 440	X		
BnF, Rothschild 2796	X		
Besançon, BM, 1791		X	
Douai, BM, 767			X
Moulins, BM, 26	X	X	
Poitiers, BM, 214	X		
Reims, BM, 918[6]			X
Rouen, BM, 930			X
Toulouse, BM, 826	X		
Valenciennes, BM, 304			X
Valenciennes, BM, 652	X	X	
Berlin, Kupferstichkabinett, 78 C 7 (Hamilton 144)	X	X	
Berlin, Kupferstichkabinett, 78 C 8 (Hamilton 146)	X	X	
Brussels, BR, II 1172	X	X	
Brussels, BR, 21521–31			X
Cambridge, Harvard Uni., Houghton Lib., 92	X	X	
Copenhagen, RL, Thott. 57 in f°		X	
Copenhagen, RL, 1768	X		X
Escorial, O. I. 14	X		
Geneva, Lib. of E. Droz		X	
Göttingen, BU, Philos. 98			X
Heidelberg, UB, Pal. Germ. 484		X	
The Hague, KB, 71 E 49			X

(*continued overleaf*)

[6] This is not included by Laidlaw in his table of MSS containing the *Curial*. Bourgain-Hemeryck includes it in her edition of the Latin works, Alain Chartier (1977), p. 141.

Appendix B

MSS	Quadrilogue	Esperance	Curial
The Hague, KB, 78 E 68		X	
London, BL, Cotton Julius E. V.	X	X	
London, BL, Harley 4402	X		
London, BL, Royal 19 A xii		X	
London, Clumber Sale, 941	X	X	X
Manchester, Chetham's Lib., Muniment A. 6.91	X		
Munich, Bibl. nat. gall., 10	X	X	X
New York, Pierpont Morgan Lib., 438		X	
Oxford, Bod., 421	X	X	X
Oxford, Bod., 864			X
Oxford, Bod., E. D. Clarke 34		X	X
Stockholm, RL, V. u. 22	X		
Turin, BN, L II 12	X		X
Vatican, Vat. lat. 1005		X	
Vatican, Reg. lat. 1338	X	X	
Vatican, Vat. lat., 4794	X		
Vienna, NB, 2619	X	X	
Vienna, NB, 3391			X
Pierre Le Caron, printed ed. (1489)	X	X	X

Key

Quadrilogue	*Quadrilogue invectif* (1422)
Esperance	*Le Livre de l'Esperance* (1428–30)
Curial	*Le Curial* (French translation of before 1447, Latin original dates from 1427)

MSS	Ep 1	Disc 1	Ep 2	AD	Disc 2	Disc 3	Har 1	DF	Curial	Inv 1	Inv 2	Disc 4	Ep 3
BnF, fr. 1267								X					
BnF, fr. 1123								X					
BnF, fr. 1124								X					
BnF, fr. 1128								X					
BnF, lat. 3127										X	X		
BnF, lat. 4329										X	X		
BnF, lat. 5961			X	X	X	X	X	X	X	X	X		
BnF, lat. 6254										X	X		
BnF, lat. 8757	X	X	X	X	X	X	X	X	X	X	X	X	X
BnF, lat. 10922								X	X	X			
BnF, lat. 14117								X					
BnF, lat. 15083										X	X		
BnF, lat. 18532								X					
Paris, Bibl. Mazarine, 940										X			
Paris, Bibl. Mazarine, 3893										X	X		

(continued overleaf)

7 I have italicized the manuscripts that also contain Chartier's French prose and emboldened those that contain verse works as well.

MSS	Ep 1	Disc 1	Ep 2	AD	Disc 2	Disc 3	Har 1	DF	Curial	Inv 1	Inv 2	Disc 4	Ep 3
Paris, Ste-Geneviève, 1992								X					
Paris, Bibl. de l'Université, 229									X				
Chantilly, Musée Condée, 438	X	X	X	X	X	X	X	X	X	X	X	X	X
Moulins, BM, 26								X					
Rouen, BM, 480								X					
Tours, BM, 978									X				
Berlin, *Kupferstichkabinett 78 C 7 (Hamilton 144)*								X					
Berlin, Staatsbibliothek, lat. fol. 366	X		X	X	X	X	X		X	X	X		X
Brussels, Bibl. Royale, 14370–71								X					
Cambridge, H.U., Houghton Lib., 92								X					

Manuscript	1	2	3	4	5	6	7	8	9	10	11
Einsiedeln, Monastery Lib., 3678									X	X	
Florence, Bibl. Riccardiana, 443	X		X			X			X	X	X
Giessen, Universitätsbibliothek, 1256									X	X	
Hildesheim, Dombibliothek, 737	X		X	X		X	X		X	X	
Liège, Bibl. Univ., Fonds Wittert 109							X		X	X	
London, BL, Cotton Julius E V							X				
London, BL, Harley 1883							X		X		
Oxford, Bod., E. Musaeo 213		X									
Toledo, Cabildo Toletano, VI 21	X		X	X		X	X		X	X	
Uppsala, UL, C 917			X	X							
Vatican, Ottoboni lat. 858	X	X	X								

(*continued overleaf*)

[8] Bourgain-Hemeryck notes that this manuscript contains a short paraphrased and imperfect extract from the *Curial*, Alain Chartier (1977), p. 133.

MSS	Ep 1	Disc 1	Ep 2	AD	Disc 2	Disc 3	Har 1	DF	Curial	Inv 1	Inv 2	Disc 4	Ep 3
Vatican, Ottoboni lat. 1651				X									
Vatican, Reg. lat. 1338								X					
Vatican, Reg. lat. 1676								X					
Vatican, cod. lat. 11548										X	X		
Vienna, NB, 3281				X									
Wolfenbüttel, Bibl. Herzog August, Helmstedt 376			X	X	X	X	X	X					

Key (in chronological order by category)

Ep 1   Epistula ad fratrem suum juvenem (1410–14)
Ep 2   Lettre à l'Université de Paris (August 1418–beginning of 1419)
Ep 3   Lettre sur Jeanne d'Arc (August–September 1429)
Disc 1 Discours à Charles VI sur les libertés de l'Église (March 1412?)
Disc 2 Premier discours à Sigismond (January–April 1425)
Disc 3 Second discours à Sigismond (January–April 1425)
Disc 4 Discours au roi d'Écosse (1428)
AD   Ad detestacionem belli gallici (January 1423)
Har 1 Harangue aux Hussies (January–April 1425)
DF   Dialogus familiaris (1426–February 1427)
Curial De vita curiali (Latin original—1427?)
Inv 1 Invectiva ad ingratum amicum (1427–8)
Inv 2 Invectiva ad invidum et detractorem (1427–8)

Bibliography

In the body of this study, after the first reference I refer to all editions and critical works by the author's name or the book title (if there is no named author) and the year of publication. In the case of two or more publications by the same author in the same year I also use letters to refer to each work as it is listed sequentially in the *Bibliography*, beginning with the second work. For example, Minnis (1991b) would refer to the second publication listed under Minnis for that year.

MANUSCRIPT SOURCES[1]

Chartier manuscripts

Paris, BnF, fr. 126 (BnF microfilms 10629: fols. 1–132, 10630: fols. 133-end, 721: miniatures)
Paris, BnF, fr. 832 (BnF microfilm 3403)
Paris, BnF, fr. 1123
Paris, BnF, fr. 1124
Paris, BnF, fr. 1125
Paris, BnF, fr. 1128
Paris, BnF, fr. 1130
Paris, BnF, fr. 1132
Paris, BnF, fr. 1133
Paris, BnF, fr. 1549
Paris, BnF, fr. 2249 (BnF microfilm 8125)
Paris, BnF, fr. 2263
Paris, BnF, fr. 2265
Paris, BnF, fr. 2861 (BnF microfilm 4682)
Paris, BnF, fr. 5339
Paris, BnF, fr. 12435
Paris, BnF, fr. 12436
Paris, BnF, fr. 12437
Paris, BnF, fr. 20026 (BnF microfilm 2122)
Paris, BnF, fr. 20055 (BnF microfilm 2437)
Paris, BnF, fr. 24441

---

[1] I have listed first all manuscripts found in the BnF in Paris, followed by those in other Paris libraries, in libraries in the rest of France, and then in libraries elsewhere (respecting alphabetical order).

Paris, BnF, fr. 25293
Paris, BnF, nouv. acq. fr. 4511–13
Paris, BnF, nouv. acq. fr. 6220–4 (6222: BnF microfilm 7944)
Paris, BnF, nouv. acq. fr. 6535
Paris, BnF, lat. 3127
Paris, BnF, lat. 4329
Paris, BnF, lat. 5961 (BnF microfilm 16422)
Paris, BnF, lat. 6254
Paris, BnF, lat. 8757
Paris, BnF, lat. 10922
Paris, BnF, lat. 14117
Paris, BnF, lat. 15083
Paris, BnF, lat. 18532
Paris, BnF, lat. 18583
Paris, BnF, fonds Rothschild 2796
Tours, Bibliothèque Municipale, 978
The Hague, Koninklijke Bibliotheek, 71 E 49
London, British Library, Cotton Julius E V
London, British Library, Harley 1883
London, British Library, Harley 4402
London, British Library, Lansdowne 380
Oxford, Bodleian Library, Bodley 421
Oxford, Bodleian Library, Bodley 864
Oxford, Bodleian Library, Canonici Misc. 213
Oxford, Bodleian Library, E. D. Clarke 34
Oxford, Bodleian Library, E Musaeo 213 (3703)
Sion, Bibliothèque Cantonale du Valais, Supersaxo 97bis (IRHT microfilm 10166)

Querelle de la Rose manuscripts

Paris, BnF, fr. 604 (1st *Rose* dossier)
Paris, BnF, fr. 835 (2nd *Rose* dossier)
Paris, BnF, fr. 12779 (1st *Rose* dossier)

Querelle de la Belle Dame sans mercy cycle and 'jeu des échecs' manuscripts

Paris, BnF, fr. 833 (BnF microfilm 3404)
Paris, BnF, fr. 924 (BnF microfilm 6275)
Paris, BnF, fr. 1127
Paris, BnF, fr. 1131
Paris, BnF, fr. 1169
Paris, BnF, fr. 1173 (Nicole de Saint-Nicolas)
Paris, BnF, fr. 1642 (BnF microfilm 6923)
Paris, BnF, fr. 1661

Paris, BnF, fr. 1727
Paris, BnF, fr. 2230
Paris, BnF, fr. 2253 (BnF microfilm 7627)
Paris, BnF, fr. 2264
Paris, BnF, fr. 14978 (5037, Guillaume de Saint-André)
Paris, BnF, fr. 15219
Paris, BnF, fr. 19139
Paris, BnF, fr. 19157 (poem on the game of chess)
Paris, BnF, fr. 20026 (BnF microfilm 2122)
Paris, BnF, fr. 24440
Paris, BnF, fr. 25435
Paris, BnF, fr. 25566 (Engreban d'Arras)
Paris, BnF, nouv. acq. fr. 4237
Paris, BnF, fonds Rothschild 440
Paris, Bibliothèque de l'Arsenal, 3521 (microfilm R 2330)
Paris, Arsenal, 3523 (microfilm R 2239)
Paris, Arsenal, 3650 (poem on the game of chess)
London, British Library, Royal 19 A iii

DICTIONARIES AND REFERENCE BOOKS

Bibliothèque Impériale: catalogue des manuscrits français, ancien fonds I (Paris: Firmin-Didot, 1868).

Brayer, Edith, *Catalogue of the French-language Medieval Manuscripts in the Koninklijke Bibliotheek (Royal Library), The Hague* (Paris: IRHT, 1954–6).

Briquet, C. M., *Les Filigranes. Dictionnaire historique des marques de papier*, 4 vols. (Leipzig: Hiersemann, 1923).

Cappelli, Adriano, *Dizionario di abbreviature latine e italiane*, 6th edn (Milan: Ulrico Hoepli, 1987).

Catalogue des livres de la bibliothèque de feu M. le duc de la Vallière, première partie, vol. 2 (Paris: de Bure, 1783).

Catalogue des livres de M. le baron James de Rothschild, vol. I (Paris: Morgand, 1884).

Catalogue général des manuscrits des Bibliothèques publiques des départements, vol. VII—Toulouse-Nîmes (Paris: Imprimerie Nationale, 1885).

Catalogue général des manuscrits des Bibliothèques publiques des départements, vol. VII—Grenoble (Paris: Plon, 1889).

Catalogue général des manuscrits des Bibliothèques publiques des départements, vol. XIV—divers (Paris: Plon, 1890).

Catalogue général des manuscrits des Bibliothèques publiques des départements, vol. XXV—Poitiers-Valenciennes (Paris: Imprimerie Nationale, 1894).

Catalogue général des manuscrits des Bibliothèques publiques des départements, vol. XXXIV—Carpentras 1 (Paris: Imprimerie Nationale, 1901).

218 *Bibliography*

Catalogue général des manuscrits des Bibliothèques publiques des départements, vol. XLI, supplément tome II: Caen-Luxeuil (Paris: Plon, 1903).

Catalogue général des manuscrits des Bibliothèques publiques des départements, vol. LI: manuscrits conservés dans les dépôts d'archives départementales (supplément) (Paris: Bibliothèque Nationale, 1956).

Catalogue général des manuscrits des Bibliothèques publiques de France: Paris, Bibliothèques de l'Institut, Musée Condé à Chantilly; Bibliothèque Thiers; Musée Jacquemart-André à Paris et à Chaalis (Paris: Plon, 1928).

Catalogue des manuscrits de la Bibliothèque de l'Arsenal, III, ed. H. Martin (Paris: Plon, 1900).

Delandine, A.-F., *Manuscrits de la Bibliothèque de Lyon, vol. I* (Paris/Lyon: Fr. Mistral, 1812).

Delisle, L., *Le Cabinet des manuscrits de la Bibliothèque impériale*, 3 vols. (Paris: Imprimerie Nationale, 1868–81).

Di Stefano, Giuseppe, *Dictionnaire des locutions en moyen français* (Montreal: CERES, 1991).

Falconer, Madan, *A Summary Catalogue of Western Manuscripts in the Bodleian Library at Oxford, vol. IV* (Oxford: Clarendon Press, 1897).

Godefroy, Frédéric, *Dictionnaire de l'ancienne langue française et de tous ses dialectes du IX*e *au XV*e *siècle*, 10 vols. (Paris: F. Vieweg, 1880–1902).

Hasenohr, Geneviève; Zink, Michel, *Dictionnaire des lettres françaises: le moyen âge*, rev. edn (Paris: Fayard, 1992).

Lewis, C. T.; Short, C., *A Latin Dictionary* (Oxford: Clarendon Press, 1996).

Morawski, Joseph, *Proverbes français antérieurs au XV*e *siècle* (Paris: Champion, 1925).

The New English Bible (Oxford: OUP, 1973).

Tobler, Adolf; Lommatzsch, Erhard; Christmann, H. H., *Altfranzösisches Wörterbuch: Adolf Toblers nachgelassene Materialien/bearb. und mit Unterstützung der preussischen Akademie der Wissenschaften hrsg. von Erhard Lommatzsch, weitergeführt von Hans Helmut Christmann*, 11 vols. (Berlin: Weidmann, 1915–2002).

Wartburg, Walther von, *Französisches etymologisches Wörterbuch: eine darstellung des galloromanischen sprachschatzes*, 2 vols. (Paris: Champion, 2003).

PRIMARY SOURCES

L'Abuzé en court, ed. Roger Dubuis (Geneva: Droz, 1973).

Alain Chartier, *Les Fais* (Paris: Pierre Le Caron, 1489). First edition of the complete works, including works wrongly attributed to Chartier. There were reprints of this edition by Pierre Le Caron for Anthoine Vérard in 1493–4; Michel Le Noir in 1514; Veuve Jean Trepperel and Jean Jeannot *c.*1515; Philippe Le Noir *c.*1520 and 1523; and Galliot du Pré in 1526.

—— *Les Oeuvres*, ed. André Duchesne (Paris: Samuel Thiboust, 1617).

—— *La Belle Dame sans mercy et les poésies lyriques*, ed. Arthur Piaget (Geneva: Droz, 1949).

—— *Le Quadrilogue invectif*, ed. E. Droz (Paris: Droz, 1950).

—— 'The Major Poems of Alain Chartier: A Critical Edition', ed. J. E. White (unpubd dissertation, University of North Carolina, 1962).

—— *The Poetical Works*, ed. James C. Laidlaw (Cambridge: CUP, 1974).

—— *Les Oeuvres latines*, ed. Pascale Bourgain-Hemeryck (Paris: CNRS, 1977).

—— *Poèmes*, ed. James C. Laidlaw (Paris: Union générale d'éditions, 1988).

—— *Le Livre de l'Esperance*, ed. François Rouy (Paris: Champion, 1989).

—— *Le Quadrilogue invectif*, trans. Florence Bouchet (Paris: Champion, 2002).

Alain de Lille, *Textes inédits*, ed. Marie-Thérèse d'Alverny (Paris: J. Vrin, 1965).

—— *Anticlaudianus or The Good and Perfect Man*, ed. James J. Sheridan (Toronto: Pontifical Institute of Medieval Studies, 1973).

—— *The Plaint of Nature*, ed. James J. Sheridan (Toronto: Pontifical Institute of Medieval Studies, 1980).

Alanus de Insulis, *Liber parabolarum*, ed. Jacques-Paul Migne, *Patrologia Latina Database* 210 (1993), 579–94.

L'Amant rendu cordelier a l'observance d'amours, ed. Anatole de Montaiglon (Paris: Firmin-Didot, 1881).

Andreas Capellanus, *On Love*, ed. P. G. Walsh (London: Duckworth, 1993).

Anne de Graville, *La Belle Dame sans mercy en Fransk Dikt*, ed. Carl Wahlund (Upsala: Almquist & Wiksells, 1897).

Antoine Loisel, *Institutes coustumieres* (Paris: Abel L'Angelier, 1611, 3rd edn, transcription and facsimile (Mayenne: Floch, 1935), no. 310).

Aristophanes, *The Frogs*, ed. Kenneth Dover (Oxford: Clarendon Press, 1997).

Aristotle, *The Poetics* and Longinus, *On the Sublime*, ed. W. Hamilton Fyfe (London: Heinemann, 1932).

—— *The Nicomachean Ethics*, ed. Harris Rackham (London: Penguin, 1966).

—— *De anima*, ed. Hugh Lawson-Tancred (London: Penguin, 1986).

—— *Posterior Analytics*; *Topica*, ed. G. P. Goold; trans. Hugh Tredennick and E. S. Forster (Cambridge, MA: Harvard University Press, 1997).

Les Arrets d'amours avec L'amant rendu cordelier, à l'observance d'amours, ed. N. Lenglet-Dufresnoy (Amsterdam: F. Changuion, 1731).

Arrêts d'amours, ed. Jean Rychner (Paris: Picard, 1951).

Les Aventures merveilleuses de Huon de Bordeaux, chanson de geste du XIII e siècle, ed. Jean Audiau (Paris: E. de Boccard, 1926).

Boccaccio, Giovanni, *Genealogie deorum gentilium libri*, ed. V. Romano, 2 vols. (Bari: G. Laterza, 1951).

—— *De casibus virorum illustrium* (*Des cas des nobles hommes et femmes*), ed. Patricia May Gathercole; trans. Laurent de Premierfait (Chapel Hill: University of North Carolina Press, 1968).

—— *Décaméron*, ed. Christian Bec (Paris: Librairie générale française, 1994).

Boethius, *The Theological Tractates and The Consolation of Philosophy*, ed. S. J. Tester (Cambridge, MA: Harvard University Press, 1997).

Brunetto Latini, *Li livres dou tresor*, ed. Spurgeon Baldwin and Paul Barrette (Tempe, AZ: Arizona Center for Medieval and Renaissance Studies, 2003).

Cassiodorus, *Institutiones divinarum et saecularium litterarum*, ed. Wolfgang Bürsgens, 2 vols. (Freiburg/New York: Herder, 2003).

Cent Nouvelles Nouvelles, ed. Franklin P. Sweetser (Geneva: Droz, 1966).

Chansons des trouvères, ed. Marie-Geneviève Grossel; S. N. Rosenberg; Hans Tischler (Paris: Librairie générale française, 1995).

Charles d'Orléans, *Ballades et rondeaux*, ed. Jean-Claude Mühlethaler (Paris: Librairie générale française, 1992).

Chaucer, Geoffrey, *The Complete Works*, ed. W. Skeat, 7 vols. (Oxford: Clarendon Press, 1894–7).

Chevalier aux dames, ed. Robert J. Fields (Paris: A. G. Nizet, 1980).

Chevalier des dames: le chevalier des dames du dolent fortuné, ed. Jean Miquet (Ottawa: University of Ottawa Press, 1990).

Chrétien de Troyes, *The Continuations of the Old French Perceval of Chrétien de Troyes*, ed. William Roach, Lucien Foulet, Robert Ivy, 4 vols. (Philadelphia: University of Pennsylvania Press, 1949–71).

Christine de Pizan, *Oeuvres poétiques*, ed. Maurice Roy, 3 vols. (Paris: Firmin-Didot, 1886–96).

—— *L'Avision Christine*, ed. Sister Mary Louise Towner (Washington: Catholic University of America Press, 1932).

—— *The Book of Fayttes of Armes and of Chyvalrye*, ed. A. T. P. Byles; trans. William Caxton, 1489 (London: EETS, 1932).

—— *Le Livre de la mutacion de Fortune*, ed. Suzanne Solente, 4 vols. (Paris: Picard, 1959).

—— *Ditié de Jehanne d'Arc*, ed. Angus J. Kennedy; Kenneth Varty (Oxford: Society for the Study of Medieval Languages and Literatures, 1977).

—— *Lamentacion sur les maux de la France*, in *Mélanges de langue et littérature française du Moyen Age et de la Renaissance offerts à Charles Foulon*, ed. Angus J. Kennedy (Rennes: Institut de français, Université de Haute Bretagne, 1980), vol. 1, 177–85.

—— *Cent Ballades d'amant et de dame*, ed. Jacqueline Cerquiglini (Paris: Union générale d'éditions, 1982).

—— *The Treasure of the City of Ladies*, ed. and trans. Sarah Lawson (London: Penguin, 1985).

—— *Le Livre de la cité des dames*, ed. Éric Hicks; and Thérèse Moreau (Paris: Stock, 1986).

—— *La Città delle dame*, ed. P. Caraffi; E. J. Richards (Milan: Luni, 1998).

—— *The Love Debate Poems*, ed. Barbara K. Altmann (Gainesville: University Press of Florida, 1998).

—— *Livre du chemin de lonc estude*, ed. Andrea Tarnowski (Paris: Librairie générale française, 2000).

—— *Le Livre de l'advision Cristine*, ed. Liliane Dulac; Christine Reno (Paris: Champion, 2001).

Christine de Pizan; Hoccleve, Thomas, *Poems of Cupid, God of Love: Christine de Pizan's Epistre au dieu d'Amours and Dit de la Rose; Thomas Hoccleve's The Letter of Cupid*, ed. Thelma S. Fenster; Mary Carpenter Erler (Leiden: Brill, 1990).

Cicero, *De inventione; De optimo genere oratorum; Topica*, ed. G. P. Goold; trans. H. M. Hubbell (Cambridge, MA: Harvard University Press, 1993).

—— *Select Letters*, ed. D. R. Shackleton Bailey (Cambridge: CUP, 1995).

Coluccio Salutati, *Epistolario*, ed. F. Novati (Rome: Instituto storico italiano, 1893).

Complainte de l'amant trespassé de deuil, et l'Inventaire des biens demourez du decés de l'amant trespassé de deuil, ed. Rose M. Bidler, *Le Moyen Français* 18 (1986), 11–105.

Le Cycle de La Belle Dame sans Mercy. Une anthologie poétique du XVe siècle (BNF MS FR. 1131), ed. David F. Hult; Joan E. McRae (Paris: Champion, 2003).

Danse Macabre of Women, ed. Anne Tukey Harrison (Kent/Ohio: Kent State University Press, 1994).

Dante Alighieri, *The Divine Comedy*, ed. G. L. Bickersteth (Oxford: Basil Blackwell, 1965).

—— *De vulgari eloquentia*, ed. Warman Welliver (Ravenna: Longo, 1981).

—— *The Divine Comedy*, trans. Peter Dale (London: Anvil Press Poetry, 1996).

Debat des herauts d'armes, ed. Léopold Pannier; Paul Meyer (Paris: Firmin-Didot, 1877).

Débat sur le 'Roman de la Rose', ed. Éric Hicks (Paris: Champion, 1977).

Débats du clerc et du chevalier dans la littérature poétique du moyen âge, ed. C. Oulmont (Paris: Champion, 1911).

Les Demandes d'amour, ed. Margaret Felberg-Levitt (Montreal: CERES, 1995).

Demetrius, *On Style*, ed. W. Rhys Roberts (London: Heinemann, 1932).

Deux moralités à la fin du moyen-âge et du temps des guerres de religion, ed. Jean-Claude Aubailly; Bruno Roy (Geneva: Droz, 1990).

Epistles on the 'Romance of the Rose' and other documents in the debate, ed. Charles F. Ward (Chicago: microfilm, 1911).

Eustache Deschamps, *Oeuvres complètes*, ed. Gaston Raynaud and le Marquis de Queux de Saint-Hilaire, 11 vols. (Paris: Firmin-Didot, 1878–1903).

—— *L'Art de dictier*, ed. Deborah Sinnreich-Levi (East Lansing, MI: Colleagues Press, 1994).

—— *Selected poems*, ed. Ian S. Laurie; Deborah M. Sinnreich-Levi; trans. David Curzon; Jeffrey Fiskin (New York/London: Routledge, 2003).

Évrart de Conty, *Livre des échecs amoureux*, ed. Anne-Marie Legaré; Françoise Guichard Tesson; Bruno Roy (Paris: Éditions du Chêne, 1991).

Familiar Dialogue of the Friend and Fellow, ed. Margaret S. Blayney (London/ New York/Toronto: OUP (EETS), 1989).

Fifteenth Century English Translations of Alain Chartier's 'Traité de l'Esperance' and 'Le Quadrilogue invectif', ed. Margaret S. Blayney, 2 vols. (London/New York/Toronto: OUP (EETS), 1974–80).

François de Monte-Belluna, *Le Tragicum argumentum de miserabili statu regni Francie*, ed. André Vernet, *Annuaire-Bulletin de la Société de l'Histoire de France 1962–3* (Paris: C. Klincksieck, 1964), 101–63.

François Villon, *Poésies complètes*, ed. J. Rychner and A. Henry, 3 vols. (Geneva: Droz, 1977).

—— *Poésies complètes*, ed. Claude Thiry (Paris: Librairie générale française, 1991).

—— *Lais, Testament, Poésies Diverses*, ed. Jean-Claude Mühlethaler (Paris: Champion, 2004).

Geoffrey of Vinsauf, *Documentum de modo et arte dictandi et versificandi (Instruction in the method and art of speaking and versifying)*, trans. Roger P. Parr (Milwaukee, WI: Marquette University Press, 1968).

—— *The Poetria nova and its Sources in Early Rhetorical Doctrine*, ed. Ernest Gallo (The Hague: Mouton, 1971).

George Chastelain, *Oeuvres*, ed. Kervyn de Lettenhove, 8 vols. (Brussels: F. Heussner, 1863–6).

Gérard Machet, 'Gérard Machet, confesseur de Charles VII et ses lettres', ed. Santoni (typewritten thesis, École des Chartes, 1968).

Guillaume Alexis, *Oeuvres poétiques*, ed. Arthur Piaget; Émile Picot, 3 vols. (Paris: Firmin-Didot, 1896–1908).

Guillaume de Deguileville, *Le Pèlerinage de l'âme*, ed. J. J. Stürzinger (London: Nichols & sons, 1895).

Guillaume de Lorris and Jean de Meun, *Le Roman de la Rose*, ed. Jean Dufournet (Paris: Gallimard, 1984).

—— *Le Roman de la Rose*, ed. Armand Strubel (Paris: Librairie générale française, 1992).

Guillaume de Machaut, *Le Jugement du roy de Behaigne and Remede de Fortune*, ed. William W. Kibler; James I. Wimsatt (Athens/London: University of Georgia Press, 1988).

—— *Le Jugement du roy de Navarre*, ed. R. Barton Palmer (New York/London: Garland, 1988).

—— *La Fontaine amoureuse*, ed. Jacqueline Cerquiglini-Toulet (Paris: Stock, 1993).

—— *Le Livre du voir dit*, ed. Paul Imbs; Jacqueline Cerquiglini-Toulet (Paris: Librairie générale française, 1999).

Horace, *Satires, Epistles and Ars poetica*, ed. H. R. Fairclough (Cambridge, MA: Harvard University Press, 1991).

Jacobus de Cessolis, *Le Jeu des eschaz moralisé*, ed. Alain Collet; trans. Jean Ferron (1347) (Paris: Champion, 1999).

Jardin de plaisance et fleur de rethorique, ed. in facsimile by E. Droz and A. Piaget, 2 vols. (Paris: Firmin-Didot, 1910–25), I: *facsimile*; II: *introduction and notes*.

Jean Courtecuisse, *L'Oeuvre oratoire française*, ed. Giuseppe di Stefano (Turin: G. Giappichelli, 1969).

Jean Froissart, *Oeuvres*, ed. Kervyn de Lettenhove, 28 vols. (Brussels: A. Scheler, 1867–77).

—— *'Dits' et 'débats'*, ed. Anthime Fourrier (Geneva: Droz, 1979).

Jean Gerson, *Oeuvres complètes*, ed. Palémon Glorieux, 10 vols. (Paris/New York: Desclée, 1960–73).

—— *Early Works*, ed. Brian P. McGuire (New York: Paulist Press, 1998).

Jean Juvénal des Ursins, *Écrits politiques*, ed. Peter S. Lewis, 3 vols. (Paris: C. Klincksieck, 1978–92).

Jean Lemaire de Belges, *Les Épîtres de l'amant vert*, ed. Jean Frappier (Lille: Giard/Geneva: Droz, 1948).

Jean de Meun, *Testament*, ed. Silvia Buzzetti Gallarati (Alessandria: Orso, 1989).

Jean Molinet, *Les Faictz et dictz*, ed. Noël Dupire, 3 vols. (Paris: SATF, 1936–9).

Jean de Montreuil, *Opera*, ed. Ezio Ornato, 4 vols. (Turin: G. Giappichelli, 1963–86), I: *Epistolario*; II: *L'Oeuvre historique et polémique*; III: *Textes divers, appendices et tables*; IV: *Monsteroliana*.

Jean Robertet, *Les Douze Dames de rhétorique, par maistre Jean Robertet*, ed. Louis Batissier (Moulins: Desrosiers, 1838).

—— *Oeuvres*, ed. Margaret Zsuppán (Geneva: Droz, 1970).

Jean Robertet; George Chastelain; Jean de Montferrant, *Les Douze Dames de rhétorique*, ed. David Cowling (Geneva: Droz, 2002).

Jean le Seneschal, *Les Cent Ballades*, ed. Gaston Raynaud (Paris: Firmin-Didot, 1905).

Jean de Werchin, *Le Songe de la barge*, ed. Joan Grenier-Winther (Montreal: CERES, 1996).

John of Salisbury, *Policraticus: Of the Frivolities of Courtiers and the Footprints of Philosophers*, ed. and trans. Cary J. Nederman (Cambridge: CUP, 1990).

Les Joies du gai savoir: recueil de poésies couronnées par le Consistoire de la gaie science, ed. Alfred Jeanroy (Toulouse: Édouard Privat, 1914).

Keats, John, *Selected Poems*, ed. John Barnard, rev. edn (London: Penguin, 1999).

Las Leys d'amors: manuscrit de l'Académie des Jeux Floraux, ed. Joseph Anglade, 4 vols. (Toulouse: Édouard Privat, 1919).

Livre des faits de Jean le Meingre, dit Boucicaut (1406/7–1409), ed. Denis Lalande (Geneva: Droz, 1985).

Macrobius, *Commentary on the Dream of Scipio*, ed. William Harris Stahl (New York: Columbia University Press, 1990).

Martial d'Auvergne, *Matines de la vierge*, ed. Yves Le Hir (Geneva: Droz, 1970).

Martin le Franc, 'Un poème inédit de Martin le Franc', ed. Gaston Paris, *Romania* 16 (1877), 383–437.

—— *Le Champion des dames*, ed. Robert Deschaux, 5 vols. (Paris/Geneva: Champion, 1999).

Matthew of Vendôme, *Ars versificatoria/The art of the versemaker*, trans. Roger P. Parr (Milwaukee, WI: Marquette University Press, 1981).

Michault Taillevent, *Un poète bourguignon du XV ^e^ siècle: Michault Taillevent: édition et étude*, ed. Robert Deschaux (Geneva: Droz, 1975).

Nicolas de Clamanges, *Opera omnia*, ed. J. Lydius (Leyden: Ludovicum Elzevirium & Henr. Laurentium, 1613).

—— *Opera omnia*, ed. J. Lydius (Farnborough: Gregg Press, 1967).

—— *Epistolario*, ed. D. Cecchetti (typewritten thesis, Turin, 1969).

Octovien de Saint-Gelais, *Le Sejour d'honneur*, ed. Frédéric Duval (Geneva: Droz, 2002).

Ovid, *The Love Poems*, ed. E. J. Kenney (Oxford: OUP, 1990).

Ovide moralisé en prose (texte du quinzième siècle), ed. Cornelis de Boer (Amsterdam: North-Holland Pub. Co., 1954).

Philippe de Mézières, *Le Songe du vieil pelerin*, ed. G. W. Coopland, 2 vols. (Cambridge: CUP, 1969).

Pierre d'Ailly, *Le Recueil épistolaire autographe*; Jean de Montreuil, *Les Notes d'Italie*, ed. G. Ouy (Amsterdam: North Holland Pub. Co., 1966).

Pierre Chastellain; Vaillant, *Les Oeuvres de Pierre Chastellain et de Vaillant: poètes du XV ^e^ siècle*, ed. Robert Deschaux (Geneva: Droz, 1982).

Pierre Fabri, *Le Grand et Vrai Art de pleine rhétorique*, ed. A. Héron, 3 vols. (Rouen: A. l'Estringant, 1889–90).

Pierre de Hauteville, *La Confession et testament de l'amant trespassé de deuil*, ed. Rose M. Bidler (Montreal: CERES, 1982).

Pierre Michault, *Le Procès d'Honneur féminin*, ed. Barbara Folkart, *Le Moyen Français* 2 (1978), special edition.

The Quarrel of the Belle Dame sans mercy, ed. and trans. Joan E. McRae (New York/London: Routledge, 2004).

Querelle de la Rose: Letters and Documents, ed. Joseph L. Baird; John R. Kane (Chapel Hill: University of North Carolina Press, 1978).

Quintilian, *The Institutio oratoria, vol. IV*, ed. H. E. Butler (London: Heinemann, 1922).

Quinze Joyes de mariage, ed. Joan Crow (Oxford: Basil Blackwell, 1969).

Recueil d'arts de seconde rhétorique, ed. Ernest Langlois (Paris: Imprimerie Nationale, 1902).

Recueil général des jeux-partis français, ed. Arthur Långfors; A. Jeanroy; L. Brandin (Paris: Champion, 1926).

Recueil de poésies françoises des XV ^e^ et XVI ^e^ siècles, ed. Anatole de Montaiglon (Paris: P. Jannet, 1855–78), 13 vols.

Renaissance Latin Verse: An Anthology, ed. Alessandro Perosa; John Sparrow (London: Duckworth, 1979).

Renaut de Beaujeu, *Le Bel Inconnu*, ed. Karen Fresco (New York/London: Garland, 1992).

Robert of Basevorn, *Forma praedicandi*, in *Three Medieval Rhetorical Arts*, ed. James J. Murphy (Tempe: Arizona Center for Medieval and Renaissance Studies, 2001).

Rondeaux et autres poésies du XV ᵉ siècle, ed. Gaston Raynaud (Paris: Firmin-Didot, 1889).

Roos, Richard, '*La Belle Dame sans mercy*', in *The Complete Works of Geoffrey Chaucer, vol. 7 (supplement): Chaucerian and other pieces*, ed. W. Skeat (Oxford: Clarendon Press, 1897), 299–326.

Sebillet, Thomas, *Art poëtique françois*, ed. Francis Goyet (Paris: Nizet, 1988).

Sedulius Scottus, *Sedulii Scotti carmina*, ed. Jean Meyers (Turnhout: Brepols, 1991).

Seneca, *Letters from a Stoic*, ed. and trans. Robin Campbell (London: Penguin, 1969).

——*Select Letters*, ed. Walter C. Summers (Bristol: Bristol Classical Press, 1990).

Le Songe de la Pucelle, ed. P. Aebischer, *Vallesia* 16 (1961), 225–41.

Le Songe du vergier, ed. Marion Schnerb-Lièvre, 2 vols. (Paris: CNRS, 1982).

Theocritus, *The Idylls*, ed. and trans. Robert Wells (London: Penguin, 1989).

Veterum scriptorum et monumentorum amplissima collectio, ed. E. Martène; U. Durand (Paris: Montalant, 1724).

Virgil, *The Eclogues; The Georgics; The Aeneid: Books 1–6*, ed. and trans. H. R. Fairclough, rev. edn (Cambridge, MA: Harvard University Press, 1986).

——*The Aeneid—A New Prose Translation*, ed. and trans. David West (London: Penguin, 1990).

——*The Aeneid: Books 1–6*, ed. R. D. Williams (Surrey: Nelson, 1992).

——*The Aeneid: Books 7–12*, ed. R. D. Williams (Surrey: Nelson, 1992).

——*The Eclogues and Georgics*, ed. R. D. Williams (Bristol: Bristol Classical Press, 1996).

SECONDARY SOURCES

Adams, Alison, 'The *Cent Nouvelles Nouvelles* in MS Hunter 252: The Impact of the Miniatures', *French Studies* 46 (1992), 385–93.

Aebischer, P., 'Le manuscrit Supersaxo 97ᵇⁱˢ de la Bibliothèque cantonale du Valais; le roman de "Ponthus et la belle Sidoine". Textes en vers', *Vallesia* 14 (1959), 245–69.

Angelo, Gretchen, 'A Most Uncourtly Lady: The Testimony of the *Belle Dame sans mercy*', *Exemplaria* 15/1 (Spring 2003), 133–57.

Angenot, Marc, *Les Champions des femmes: examen du discours sur la supériorité des femmes 1400–1800* (Montreal: University of Québec, 1977).

Ariès, Philippe; Margolin, Jean-Claude, *Les Jeux à la Renaissance: Actes du XXIIIᵉ Colloque International d'Études Humanistes, Tours—Juillet 1980* (Paris: J. Vrin, 1982).

Armstrong, Adrian, 'The Practice of Textual Transmission: Jean Molinet's *Ressource du Petit Peuple*', *Forum for Modern Language Studies* 33 (1997), 270–82.

—— 'The Deferred Verdict: A Topos in Late-Medieval Poetic Debates?', *French Studies Bulletin* 64 (Autumn 1997), 12–14.

—— *Technique and Technology: Script, Print, and Poetics in France, 1470–1550* (Oxford: Clarendon Press, 2000).

—— *The Virtuoso Circle: Competition, Collaboration and Complexity in Late Medieval French Poetry* (Arizona: Medieval and Renaissance Texts Studies, forthcoming in 2008/9).

—— ' "Leur temps est; le mien est passé": The *Querelle de la Belle Dame sans mercy*', in *The Virtuoso Circle: Competition, Collaboration and Complexity in Late Medieval French Poetry* (Arizona: Medieval and Renaissance Texts Studies, forthcoming in 2008/9).

Atwood, Catherine, *Dynamic Dichotomy: The Poetic 'I' in Fourteenth- and Fifteenth-Century French Lyric Poetry* (Amsterdam/Atlanta: Rodopi, 1998).

Autrand, Françoise, *Naissance d'un grand corps de l'Etat: les gens du Parlement de Paris 1345–1454* (Paris: Sorbonne, 1981).

Badel, Pierre-Yves, 'Pierre d'Ailly, auteur du *Jardin amoureux*', *Romania* 97 (1976), 369–81.

—— *Le 'Roman de la Rose' au XIVᵉ siècle: étude de la réception de l'oeuvre* (Geneva: Droz, 1980).

—— 'Le Débat', in *Grundriss der romanischen Literaturen des Mittelalters* VIII/1, ed. Daniel Poirion (Heidelberg: Carl Winter, 1988), 95–110.

Bahti, T., *Ends of the Lyric: Direction and Consequence in Western Poetry* (Baltimore/London: Johns Hopkins University Press, 1996).

Baird, Joseph L., 'Pierre Col and the *Querelle de la Rose*', *Philological Quarterly* 60 (1981), 273–86.

Baird, Joseph L.; Kane, John R., '*La Querelle de la Rose*: In Defense of the Opponents', *French Review* 48 (1974), 298–307.

Bakhtin M. M., *The Dialogic Imagination*, trans. Caryl Emerson; Michael Holquist (Austin: University of Texas Press, 1981).

—— *Rabelais and his World* (Bloomington: Indiana University Press, 1984).

Balard, Michel, *L'Histoire médiévale en France: bilan et perspectives* (Paris: Seuil, 1991).

Barthes, Roland, 'L'Effet de réel', *Communications* 11 (1968), 84–9.

Bautier, Robert-Henri, 'Chancellerie et culture au moyen âge', in *Cancelleria e cultura nel medio evo*, ed. Germano Gualdo (Vatican City: Archivio Segreto Vaticano, 1990), 1–75.

Bazàn, Bernardo C., *Les Questions disputées et les questions quodlibétiques dans les facultés de théologie, de droit et de médecine* (Turnhout, Belgium: Brepols, 1985).

Bec, Pierre, *La Joute poétique: de la tenson médiévale aux débats chantés traditionnels* (Paris: Les Belles Lettres, 2000).

Bédier, Joseph, 'La tradition manuscrite du *Lai de l'ombre*: réflexions sur l'art d'éditer les anciens textes', *Romania* 54 (1928), 161–96, 321–56.

Beltran, Evencio, 'Continuité de l'humanisme français au XVe siècle: L'exemple de Pierre de la Hazardière', in *L'Aube de la Renaissance*, ed. D. Cecchetti; L. Sozzi; L. Terreaux (Geneva: Slatkine, 1991), 123–36.

Bennett, Philip E.; Runnalls, G. A., *The Editor and the Text* (Edinburgh: Edinburgh University Press, 1990).

Bent, Margaret; Wathey, Andrew, *Fauvel Studies: Allegory, Chronicle, Music and Image in Paris, Bibliothèque Nationale de France, MS Français 146* (Oxford: Clarendon Press, 1998).

Bergeron, Réjean, 'Les Venditions françaises des XIVe et XVe siècles', *Le Moyen Français* 19 (1986), 34–57.

Berthelot, Anne, "Si moi ou autre vous regarde, les yeux sont faits pour regarder': la *Belle Dame sans mercy* ou la dame qui ne voulait pas jouer', in *La 'Fin'Amor' dans la culture féodale: Actes du colloque du Centre d'études médiévales de l'Université de Picardie Jules Verne, Amiens, mars 1991*, ed. Danielle Buschinger; Wolfgang Spiewok (Greifswald: Reineke-Verlag, 1994), 13–21.

Bijvanck, Willem Gertrud C., *Spécimen d'un essai critique sur les oeuvres de François Villon* (Leyde: De Brauk & Smits, 1882).

Billanovich, Giuseppe; Ouy, Gilbert, 'La Première Correspondance échangée entre Jean de Montreuil et Coluccio Salutati', *Italia medioevale e umanistica* VII (1964), 337–74.

Birnbaum, M. D., *Humanists in a Shattered World: Croatian and Hungarian Latinity in the Sixteenth Century* (Columbus, OH: Slavica Publishers, Inc., 1986).

Bischoff, Bernhard, *Latin Palaeography: Antiquity and the Middle Ages* (Cambridge: CUP, 1990).

Blakeslee, Merritt R., 'Lo Dous Jocx sotils: la partie d'échecs amoureuse dans la poésie des troubadours', *Cahiers de Civilisation Médiévale* 28 (1985), 213–22.

—— *Love's Masks: Identity, Intertextuality, and Meaning in the Old French Tristan Poems* (Cambridge: D. S. Brewer, 1989).

Blamires, Alcuin, *Woman Defamed and Woman Defended: An Anthology of Medieval Texts* (Oxford: Clarendon Press, 1992).

Blamires, Alcuin, *The Case for Women in Medieval Culture* (Oxford: Clarendon Press, 1997).

Blanch, R. J., *From Pearl to Gawain: Forme to Fynisment* (Gainesville: University Press of Florida, 1995).

Blanchard, Joël; Mühlethaler, Jean-Claude, *Écriture et pouvoir à l'aube des temps modernes* (Paris: PUF, 2002).

Blayney, M.S., 'Sir J. Fortescue and Alain Chartier's *Traité de l'Esperance*', *Modern Language Review* 48 (1953), 388–9.

Bloch, Marc, *Feudal Society I: The Growth of Ties of Dependence* (London: Routledge, 1965).

—— *Feudal Society II: Social Classes and Political Organization* (London: Routledge, 1965).

Bloch, R. Howard, *Medieval French Literature and Law* (Berkeley/London: University of California Press, 1977).

Bloom, Harold, *The Anxiety of Influence: A Theory of Poetry* (Oxford: OUP, 1973).

Blumenfeld-Kosinski, Renate, 'Two Responses to Agincourt: Alain Chartier's *Livre des Quatre Dames* and Christine de Pizan's *Epistre de la vie humaine*', in *Contexts and Continuities—Proceedings of the IVth International Colloquium on Christine de Pizan (Glasgow 21–27 July 2000) published in honour of Liliane Dulac*, ed. Angus J. Kennedy; Rosalind Brown-Grant; James C. Laidlaw; Catherine M. Müller, 3 vols. (Glasgow: Glasgow University Press: 2002), I: 75–85.

Bock, Gisela; Zimmermann, Margarete, 'Die *Querelle des femmes* in Europa: Eine begriffs- und forschungsgeschichtliche Einführung', in *Querelles. Jahrbuch für Frauenforschung 1997 Band 2: Die europäische 'Querelle des femmes': Geschlechterdebatten seit dem 15. Jahrhundert*, ed. G. Bock; M. Zimmermann (Stuttgart/Weimar: Verlag J. B. Metzler, 1997), 9–38.

Boitani, Piero; Torti, Anna, *Poetics: Theory and Practice in Medieval English Literature* (Cambridge: CUP, 1991).

Bolton, Maureen, 'The Lady Speaks: The Transformation of French Courtly Poetry in the XIVth and XVth Centuries', in *The Court and Cultural Diversity—International Courtly Literature Society 1995*, ed. Evelyn Mullally; John Thompson (Cambridge: D. S. Brewer, 1997), 207–17.

Bossy, Michel-André, *A Garland Anthology of Medieval Debate Poetry: Vernacular Works* (Paris: Garland, 1987).

Boudet, Jean Patrice; Millet, Hélène, *Eustache Deschamps en son temps* (Paris: Publications de la Sorbonne, 1997).

Bourdieu, Pierre, *Esquisse d'une théorie de la pratique* (Geneva: Droz, 1972).

—— *Outline of a Theory of Practice*, trans. Richard Nice (Cambridge: CUP, 1977).

—— *Ce que parler veut dire: l'économie des échanges linguistiques* (Paris: Fayard, 1982).

—— *Leçon sur la leçon* (Paris: Editions de Minuit, 1982).

—— *Homo academicus*, trans. Peter Collier (Cambridge: Polity Press, 1988).

—— *Le Sens pratique/The Logic of Practice*, trans. Richard Nice (Cambridge: Polity Press, 1990).

Bourdieu, Pierre; Wacquant, Loïc J. D., *An Invitation to Reflexive Sociology* (Cambridge/Oxford: Polity Press, 1996).

Bourgain, Pascale, 'Style professionel et style personnel: les différents niveaux stylistiques chez Alain Chartier, secrétaire de Charles VI', in *Cancelleria e cultura nel medio evo*, ed. Germano Gualdo (Vatican City: Archivio Segreto Vaticano, 1990), 169–85.

—— *Poésie lyrique latine du Moyen Age* (Paris: Librairie générale française, 2000).

Bowie, Malcolm, *Lacan* (London: Fontana, 1991).

Bozzolo, Carla, 'La Lecture des classiques par un humaniste français Laurent de Premierfait', in *L'Aube de la Renaissance*, ed. D. Cecchetti; L. Sozzi; L. Terreaux (Geneva: Slatkine, 1991), 67–81.

Bozzolo, Carla; Loyau, Hélène, *La Cour amoureuse dite de Charles VI*, 3 vols. (Paris: Le Léopard d'Or, 1982–92).

Brabant, Margaret, *Politics, Gender, and Genre: The Political Thought of Christine de Pizan* (Boulder/San Francisco/Oxford: Westview Press, 1992).

Brabant, Margaret; Brint, Michael, 'Identity and Difference in Christine de Pizan's *Cité des dames*', in *Politics, Gender, and Genre: The Political Thought of Christine de Pizan*, ed. Margaret Brabant (Boulder/San Francisco/Oxford: Westview Press, 1992), 207–22.

Brami, Joseph, 'Un lyrisme de veuvage: étude sur le je poétique dans la *Belle Dame sans mercy*', *Fifteenth-Century Studies* 15 (1989), 53–66.

Brown, Cynthia Jane, *The Shaping of History and Poetry in Late-Medieval France: Propaganda and Artistic Expression in the Works of the Rhétoriqueurs* (Birmingham, AL: Summa Publications, 1985).

—— *Poets, Patrons, and Printers: Crisis of Authority in Late-Medieval France* (Ithaca/London: Cornell University Press, 1995).

—— 'Allegorical Design and Image-Making in Fifteenth-Century France: Alain Chartier's Joan of Arc', *French Studies* 53/4 (1999), 385–404.

Brown-Grant, Rosalind, 'L'Avision Christine: Autobiographical Narrative or Mirror for the Prince?', in *Politics, Gender, and Genre: The Political Thought of Christine de Pizan*, ed. Margaret Brabant (Boulder/San Francisco/Oxford: Westview Press, 1992), 95–111.

—— *Christine de Pizan and the Moral Defence of Women: Reading beyond Gender* (Cambridge: CUP, 1999).

Brownlee, Kevin, *Poetic Identity in Guillaume de Machaut* (Madison: University of Wisconsin Press, 1984).

Brownlee, Kevin, 'The Practice of Cultural Authority: Italian Responses to French Cultural Dominance in *Il Tesoretto, Il Fiore*, and the *Commedia*', *Forum for Modern Language Studies* 33 (1997), 258–69.

—— 'Pygmalion, Mimesis, and the Multiple Endings of the *Roman de la Rose*', *Yale French Studies* 95 (1999), 193–211.

Brownlee, Kevin; Huot, Sylvia, *Rethinking the Romance of the Rose: Text, Image, Reception* (Philadelphia: University of Pennsylvania Press, 1992).

Busby, Keith, *Codex and Context: Reading Old French Verse Narrative in Manuscript*, 2 vols. (Amsterdam: Rodopi, 2002).

Busby, Keith; Kooper, Erik, *Courtly Literature: Culture and Context: Selected Papers from the 5th Triennial Congress of the International Courtly Literature Society, Dalfsen (The Netherlands)—August 1986* (Amsterdam/Philadelphia: John Benjamins Publishing Company, 1990).

Caillois, Roger, *Les Jeux et les hommes: le masque et le vertige* (Paris: Gallimard, 1967).

Calhoun, Craig; LiPuma, Edward; Postone, Moishe, *Bourdieu: Critical Perspectives* (Cambridge: Polity Press, 1993).

Calin, William, 'Intertextual Play and the Game of Love: The *Belle Dame sans mercy* Cycle', *Fifteenth-Century Studies* 31 (2006), 31–46.

Cannon, Christopher, 'Spelling Practice: The *Ormulum* and the Word', *Forum for Modern Language Studies* 33 (1997), 229–44.

Catach, Nina, 'La Ponctuation', *Langue française* 45 (1980), 16–27.

—— *La Ponctuation (histoire et système)* (Paris: PUF, 1994).

Cayley, Emma, 'Collaborative Communities: The Manuscript Context of Alain Chartier's *Belle Dame sans mercy*', *Medium Aevum* 71 2 (2002), 226–40.

—— 'Drawing Conclusions: The Poetics of Closure in Alain Chartier's Verse', *Fifteenth-Century Studies* 28 (2003), 51–64.

—— 'Debating Communities: Revealing Meaning in Late-Medieval French Manuscript Collections', *Neuphilologische Mitteilungen* 2 (2004), 191–201.

—— ' "Tu recites, je replique; et quant nous avons fait et fait, tout ne vault riens": Explorations of a Debating Climate in Early Humanist France', *Nottingham Medieval Studies* 48 (2004), 37–59.

—— 'Players and Spaces of Play in Late-Medieval French Manuscript Collections', in *Space: New Dimensions in French Studies*, eds. Emma Gilby; Katja Haustein (Bern: Peter Lang, 2005), 23–39.

—— 'MS Sion, Supersaxo 97[bis]: A pro-feminine reading of Alain Chartier's verse', in *Courtly Arts and the Art of Courtliness*, eds. Keith Busby; Chris Kleinhenz (Boydell & Brewer, forthcoming 2006).

Cecchetti, Dario, *Petrarca, Pietramala e Clamanges: storia di una "querelle" inventata* (Paris: CEMI, 1982).

Cecchetti, Dario; Sozzi, L.; Terreaux, L., *L'Aube de la Renaissance* (Geneva: Slatkine, 1991).

Cerquiglini, Jacqueline, *'Un engin si soutil': Guillaume de Machaut et l'écriture au XIVe siècle* (Geneva: Droz, 1985).

—— 'Le Dit', in *Grundriss der romanischen Literaturen des Mittelalters* VIII/1, ed. Daniel Poirion (Heidelberg: Carl Winter, 1988), 86–94.

—— 'Fullness and Emptiness: Shortages and Storehouses of Lyric Treasure in the Fourteenth and Fifteenth Centuries', *Yale French Studies* special issue (1991), 224–39.

—— *The Colour of Melancholy: The Uses of Books in the Fourteenth Century*, trans. Lydia G. Cochrane (Baltimore/London: Johns Hopkins University Press, 1997).

Champion, Pierre, *La Librairie de Charles d'Orléans* (Paris: Champion, 1910).

—— *Histoire poétique du quinzième siècle*, 2 vols. (Paris: Champion, 1923).

—— *Charles d'Orléans, joueur d'échecs*, rev. edn (Geneva: Slatkine Reprints, 1975).

Chesney, K., 'Some Notes on Lyrics of Alain Chartier', in *Mélanges offerts à M. Roques* 1 (Paris: Didier, 1950–2), 191.

Chinca, Mark, 'Knowledge and Practice in the Early German Love-Lyric', *Forum for Modern Language Studies* 33 (1997), 204–16.

Colby-Hall, Alice M., 'Frustration and Fulfillment: The Double Ending of the *Bel Inconnu*', *Yale French Studies* 67 (1984), 120–34.

Coleman, Joyce, *Public Reading and the Reading Public in Late-Medieval England and France* (Cambridge: CUP, 1996).

Combes, André, *Jean de Montreuil et le chancelier Gerson* (Paris: J. Vrin, 1942).

Connolly, J. L., *Jean Gerson: Reformer and Mystic* (Louvain: University Library, Uystpruyst, 1928).

Contamine, Philippe, *Des pouvoirs en France 1300–1500* (Paris: École Normale Supérieure, 1992).

—— *De Jeanne d'Arc aux guerres d'Italie* (Orléans: Paradigme, 1994).

Contamine, Philippe; Mattéoni, Olivier, *La France des principautés: les chambres des comptes aux XIVe et XVe siècles* (Paris: Comité pour l'histoire économique et financière de la France, 1996).

Cornilliat, François, *'Or ne mens': couleurs de l'éloge et du blâme chez les Grands Rhétoriqueurs* (Paris: Champion, 1994).

Coville, A., *Gontier et Pierre Col et l'Humanisme en France au temps de Charles VI* (Paris: Droz, 1934).

—— *Recherches sur quelques écrivains du XIVe et du XVe siècle* (Paris: Droz, 1935).

Cowling, David, *Building the Text: Architecture as Metaphor in Late Medieval and Early Modern France* (Oxford: Clarendon Press, 1998).

Curtius, Ernst Robert, *European Literature and the Latin Middle Ages* (London: Routledge & Kegan Paul, 1979).

Daly, Kathleen, 'Mixing Business with Leisure: Some French Royal Notaries and Secretaries and their Histories of France, c.1459–1509', in *Power,*

Culture, and Religion in France c.1350–c.1550, ed. C. T. Allmand (Bury St Edmunds, Suffolk: The Boydell Press, 1989), 99–115.

Delany, Sheila, 'History, Politics, and Christine Studies: A Polemical Reply', in *Politics, Gender, and Genre: The Political Thought of Christine de Pizan*, ed. Margaret Brabant (Boulder/San Francisco/Oxford: Westview Press, 1992), 193–206.

Delisle, Léopold, *Recherches sur la librairie de Charles V* (Paris: Champion, 1907).

Desmond, Marilynn; Sheingorn, Pamela, *Myth, Montage, & Visuality in Late Medieval Manuscript Culture: Christine de Pizan's 'Epistre Othea'* (Ann Arbor: University of Michigan Press, 2003).

Dickinson, Joycelyne Gledhill, *The Congress of Arras, 1435: A Study in Medieval Diplomacy* (Oxford: Clarendon Press, 1955).

Diekstra, F. N. M., 'The Poetic Exchange between Philippe de Vitry and Jean de le Mote: A New Edition', *Neophilologus* 70 (1986), 504–19.

Di Stefano, Giuseppe, 'Alain Chartier ambassadeur à Venise', in *Culture et politique en France à l'époque de l'humanisme et de la Renaissance*, ed. Franco Simone (Turin: Accademia delle Scienze, 1974), 155–68.

—— 'Le Lais Villon et le manuscrit de l'Arsenal', *Romania* 105 (1984), 526–51.

—— *De Villon à Villon: Le Lais François Villon, Ms. Arsenal, 3523* (Montreal: CERES, 1988).

Donato, Eugenio, 'Ending/Closure: On Derrida's Edging of Heidegger', *Yale French Studies* 67 (1984), 3–22.

Doutrepont, Georges, *La Littérature française à la cour des ducs de Bourgogne* (Paris: Champion, 1909).

Dragonetti, Roger, *Le Gai Savoir dans la rhéthorique courtoise* (Paris: Seuil, 1982).

—— 'Joufroi, Count of Poitiers and Lord of Cocaigne', *Yale French Studies* 67 (1984), 95–119.

Dronke, Peter, *The Medieval Lyric*, 3rd edn (Cambridge: D. S. Brewer, 1996).

Droz, Eugénie, 'Un recueil de manuscrits du XVe siècle de la bibliothèque de Claude-Enoch Virey', *Bulletin de l'IRHT* 15 (1967–8), 157–73.

Ducoudray, Gustave, *Les Origines du Parlement de Paris et la justice aux XIIIe et XIVe siècles* (Paris: Hachette, 1902).

Dulac, Liliane, 'Authority in the Prose Treatises of Christine de Pizan: The Writer's Discourse and the Prince's Word', in *Politics, Gender, and Genre: The Political Thought of Christine de Pizan*, ed. Margaret Brabant (Boulder/San Francisco/Oxford: Westview Press, 1992), 129–40.

Dulac, Liliane; Ribémont, Bernard, *Une femme de lettres au Moyen Age: études autour de Christine de Pizan* (Orléans: Paradigme, 1995).

Empson, William, *Seven Types of Ambiguity* (London: Penguin, 1995).

Evans, G. R., *Philosophy and Theology in the Middle Ages* (London: Routledge, 1993).

Farral, E., *Recherches sur les sources latines des contes et romans courtois du moyen âge* (Paris: Champion, 1913).

Felberg-Levitt, Margaret, 'Jouer aux *Demandes d'amour*', *Le Moyen Français* 39 (1995), 93–124.

Fenster, Thelma, ' "Perdre son latin": Christine de Pizan and Vernacular Humanism', in *Christine de Pizan and the Categories of Difference*, ed. Marilynn Desmond (Minneapolis/London: University of Minnesota Press, 1998), 91–107.

Fenster, Thelma S.; Lees, Clare A., *Gender in Debate from the Early Middle Ages to the Renaissance* (New York: Palgrave, 2002).

Ferguson, Margaret, *Dido's Daughters: Literacy, Gender, and Empire in Early Modern England and France* (Chicago/London: University of Chicago Press, 2003).

Ferrante, Joan M.; Economou, George D., *In Pursuit of Perfection: Courtly Love in Medieval Literature* (New York/London: Kennikat Press, 1975).

Ferrier, Janet M., 'The Theme of Fortune in the Writings of Alain Chartier', *Medieval Miscellany presented to Eugène Vinaver* (Manchester: Manchester University Press, 1965), 124–35.

Ferruolo, Stephen C., *The Origins of the University: The Schools of Paris and the Critics 1100–1215* (Stanford, CA: Stanford University Press, 1985).

Firth Green, Richard, '*Le Roi qui ne ment* and Aristocratic Courtship', in *Courtly Literature: Culture and Context*, ed. Keith Busby and Erik Kooper (Amsterdam/Philadelphia: John Benjamins Publishing Company, 1990), 211–25.

Fish, Stanley, *Is There a Text in this Class?: The Authority of Interpretive Communities* (Cambridge, MA: Harvard University Press, 1980).

—— 'Interpreting the *Variorum*', in *Modern Criticism and Theory: A Reader*, ed. David Lodge (London/New York: Longman, 1988), 310–29.

Fleming, John V., *The 'Roman de la Rose': A Study in Allegory and Iconography* (Princeton: Princeton University Press, 1969).

—— *Reason and the Lover* (Princeton: Princeton University Press, 1984).

Forhan, Kate Langdon, 'Polycracy, Obligation and Revolt: The Body Politic in John of Salisbury and Christine de Pizan', in *Politics, Gender, and Genre: The Political Thought of Christine de Pizan*, ed. Margaret Brabant (Boulder/San Francisco/Oxford: Westview Press, 1992), 33–52.

Foulet, Alfred; Speer, Mary B., *On Editing Old French Texts* (Lawrence: Regents Press of Kansas, 1979).

Furrow, Melissa, 'The Author and Damnation: Chaucer, Writing, and Penitence', *Forum for Modern Language Studies* 33 (1997), 245–57.

Gadamer, Hans-Georg, *Dialogue and Dialectic: Eight Hermeneutical Studies on Plato* (New Haven/London: Yale University Press, 1980).

—— *Truth and Method*, 2nd rev. edn (London: Sheed & Ward, 1988).

234   *Bibliography*

Gally, Michèle, 'Disputer d'amour: les Arrageois et le *jeu-parti*', *Romania* 107 (1986), 55–76.

—— 'Entre sens et non-sens: approches comparatives de la *tenso* d'oc et du *jeu-parti* arrageois', in *Il genere «tenzone» nelle letterature romanze delle origini (atti del convegno internazionale Losanna 13–15 novembre 1997)*, ed. Matteo Pedroni; Antonio Stäuble (Ravenna: A. Longo, 1999), 223–35.

Gathercole, Patricia, 'Illuminations on the Manuscripts of Alain Chartier', *Studi Francesi* 20 (1976), 504–10.

Gaunt, Simon, *Troubadours and Irony* (Cambridge: CUP, 1989).

—— *Gender and Genre in Medieval French Literature* (Cambridge: CUP, 1995).

Gaunt, Simon; Kay, Sarah, 'Introduction: Theory of Practice and Practice of Theory', *Forum for Modern Language Studies* 33 (1997), 193–203.

—— *The Troubadours: An Introduction* (Cambridge: CUP, 1999).

Gauvard, Claude, 'Les Humanistes et la justice sous la règne de Charles VI', in *Pratiques de la culture écrite en France au XVe siècle*, ed. Monique Ornato and Nicole Pons (Louvain-La-Neuve: Fédération internationale des instituts d'études médiévales, 1995), 217–44.

Gellrich, Jesse M., *The Idea of the Book in the Middle Ages: Language Theory, Mythology, and Fiction* (Ithaca/London: Cornell University Press, 1985).

—— *Discourse and Dominion in the Fourteenth Century: Oral Contexts of Writing in Philosophy, Politics and Poetry* (Princeton: Princeton University Press, 1995).

Giannasi, Robert, 'Chartier's Deceptive Narrator: *La Belle Dame sans mercy* as Delusion', *Romania* 114 (1996), 362–84.

Gilbert, Jane, 'The Practice of Gender in *Aucassin et Nicolette*', *Forum for Modern Language Studies* 33 (1997), 217–28.

Gilson, Etienne, 'Le message de l'Humanisme', in *Culture et politique en France à l'époque de l'humanisme et de la Renaissance*, ed. Franco Simone (Turin: Accademia delle Scienze, 1974), 3–9.

Glorieux, P., *La Littérature quodlibétique*, 2 vols. (Paris: Kain, 1925–35).

—— 'Les 572 Questions du ms de Douai 434', *Recherches de Théologie ancienne et médiévale* 10 (1938), 123–267.

Gorochov, Nathalie, *Le Collège de Navarre de sa fondation (1305) au début du XVe siècle (1418): histoire de l'institution, de sa vie intellectuelle et de son recrutement* (Paris: Champion, 1997).

Gossner, J. W., 'Two Medieval French *Congés d'Amour*', *Symposium* 9 (1955), 106–14.

Grafton, Anthony, *Rome Reborn: The Vatican Library and Renaissance Culture* (Washington/New Haven: Library of Congress/Yale University Press, 1993).

Gravdal, Kathryn, *Ravishing Maidens: Writing Rape in Medieval French Literature and Law* (Philadelphia: University of Pennsylvania Press, 1991).

Gros, Gérard, *Le Poète, la vierge et le prince: étude sur la poésie mariale en milieu de cour aux XIVe et XVe siècles* (Saint Étienne: University of Saint Étienne Press, 1994).

—— *Le Poème du puy marial: étude sur le servontois et le chant royal du XIVe siècle à la Renaissance* (Paris: Klincksieck, 1996).

Gros, Gérard; Fragonard, Marie-Madeleine, *Les Formes poétiques du moyen âge à la Renaissance* (Paris: Nathan, 1995).

Grössinger, Christa, *Picturing Women in Late Medieval and Renaissance Art* (Manchester/New York: Manchester University Press, 1997).

Gruber, Jörn, *Die Dialektik des Trobar: Untersuchungen zur Struktur und Entwicklung des occitanischen und französischen Minnesangs des 12. Jahrhunderts* (Tübingen: Niemeyer, 1983).

Guenée, Bernard, *Tribunaux et gens de justice dans le bailliage de Senlis à la fin du moyen âge* (Paris: Les Belles Lettres, 1963).

—— *Un roi et son historien: vingt etudes sur le règne de Charles VI* (Paris: Boccard, 1999).

Gunn, Alan M. F., *The Mirror of Love: A Reinterpretation of 'The Romance of the Rose'* (Lubbock: Texas Tech. Press, 1952).

Haidu, Peter, *The Subject Medieval/Modern: Text and Governance in the Middle Ages* (Stanford, CA: Stanford University Press, 2004).

Hanford, J., 'Classical Eclogue and Medieval Debate', *Romanic Review* 2 (1911), 16–43.

Hanley, Sarah, 'Identity Politics and Rulership in France: Female Political Place and the Fraudulent Salic Law in Christine de Pizan and Jean de Montreuil', in *Changing Identities in Early Modern France*, ed. Michael Wolfe (Durham, NC: Duke University Press, 1997), 78–94.

Hawcroft, Michael, *Rhetoric: Readings in French Literature* (Oxford: OUP, 1999).

Herrnstein Smith, Barbara, *Poetic Closure: A Study of How Poems End* (Chicago/London: University of Chicago Press, 1968).

Hicks, Eric, 'The Political Significance of Christine de Pizan', in *Politics, Gender, and Genre: The Political Thought of Christine de Pizan*, ed. Margaret Brabant (Boulder/San Francisco/Oxford: Westview Press, 1992), 7–15.

Hicks, Eric; Ornato, Ezio, 'Jean de Montreuil et le débat sur le *Roman de la Rose*', *Romania* 98 (1977), 34–64, 186–219.

Hill, Jillian, *The Medieval Debate on Jean de Meung's 'Roman de la Rose': Morality Versus Art* (Lewiston/Lampeter: Edwin Mellen Press, 1991).

Hoepffner, Ernest, '*Les Voeux du paon* et les *Demandes amoureuses*', *Archivum Romanicum* 4 (1920), 99–104.

Hoffman, E. J., *Alain Chartier, His Works and Reputation* (Geneva: Slatkine, 1975; 1st edn 1942).

Huber, Christoph; Lähnemann, Henrike, *Courtly Literature and Clerical Culture: Selected Papers from the Tenth Triennial Congress of the International*

Courtly Literature Society, Universität Tübingen, Deutschland 28. Juli–3. August 2001 (Tübingen: Attempto-Verlag, 2002).

Hüe, Denis, 'Dérives et grenouillages: l'eau et la politique à la fin du moyen âge', *L'Eau au Moyen Âge (Sénéfiance)* 15 (1985), 213–32.

Huizinga, Johan, *The Waning of the Middle Ages*, rev. edn (London: Penguin, 1990).

—— *Homo ludens: A Study of the Play-Element in Culture*, rev. edn (London: Routledge & Kegan Paul, 1998).

Hult, David F., 'Closed Quotations: The Speaking Voice in the *Roman de la Rose*', *Yale French Studies* 67 (1984), 248–69.

—— *Self-Fulfilling Prophecies: Readership and Authority in the First 'Roman de la Rose'* (Cambridge: CUP, 1986).

—— 'The Allegoresis of Everyday Life', *Yale French Studies*, 95 (1999), 212–33.

—— 'La Courtoisie en décadence: l'exemple de la *Belle Dame sans merci* d'Alain Chartier', in *Progrès, réaction, décadence dans l'Occident médiéval*, ed. Emmanuèle Baumgartner; Laurence Harf-Lancner (Geneva: Droz, 2003), 251–60.

Hunt, Tony, 'Aristotle, Dialectic and Courtly Literature', *Viator* 10 (1979), 95–129.

Huot, Sylvia, *From Song to Book: The Poetics of Writing in Old French Lyric and Lyrical Narrative Poetry* (Ithaca/London: Cornell University Press, 1987).

—— 'The Daisy and the Laurel: Myths of Desire and Creativity in the Poetry of Jean Froissart', *Yale French Studies* special issue (1991), 240–51.

—— *The 'Romance of the Rose' and its Medieval Readers: Interpretation, Reception, Manuscript Transmission* (Cambridge: CUP, 1993).

Ilvonen, Eero, 'Les *Demandes d'amour* dans la littérature française du moyen âge', *Neuphilologische Mitteilungen* 14 (1912), 128–44.

Jameson, Fredric, *The Political Unconscious: Narrative as a Socially Symbolic Act* (Ithaca, NY: Cornell University Press, 1981).

Jauss, Hans Robert, *Towards an Aesthetic of Reception* (Brighton: Harvester, 1982).

Jeanroy, Alfred, 'Un Duel poétique du XIIIe siècle', *Annales du Midi* 27/28 (1915–16), 269–305.

—— 'Boccace et Christine de Pisan. Le *De claris mulieribus* principale source du *Livre de la cité des dames*', *Romania* 48 (1922), 93–105.

Jeanroy, A.; Droz, E., 'Deux manuscrits de François Villon', in *Documents artistiques du XVe siècle* (Paris: Droz, 1932).

Jefferson, Lisa, *Oaths, Vows and Promises in the First Part of the French Prose Lancelot Romance* (Bern: Peter Lang, 1993).

Jodogne, Pierre, 'Recensioni: Jacques Lemaire, *Meschinot, Molinet, Villon: témoignages inédits*, étude du Bruxellensis IV 541, suivie de l'édition de quelques ballades, Bruxelles, 1979, 169 ("Archives et Bibliothèque de Belgique", special issue, 20)', *Studi Francesi* 72 (1980), 513–14.

Johnson, Leonard W., *Poets as Players: Theme and Variation in Medieval French Poetry* (Stanford, CA: Stanford University Press, 1990).

Joret-Desclosières, G., *Un Écrivain national au XVᵉ siècle: Alain Chartier* (Paris: Fontemoing, 1899, 4th edn).

Jung, Marc-René, 'Poetria: Zur Dichtungs-theorie des ausgehenden Mittelalters in Frankreich', *Vox Romanica* 30/1 (1971), 44–64.

Kay, Sarah, *Subjectivity in Troubadour Poetry* (Cambridge: CUP, 1990).

—— *The Chansons de geste in the Age of Romance* (Oxford: Clarendon Press, 1995).

—— *The 'Romance of the Rose'* (London: Grant & Cutler, 1995).

—— *Courtly Contradictions: The Emergence of a Literary Object in the Twelfth Century* (Stanford, CA: Stanford University Press, 2001).

Kay, Sarah; Rubin, Miri, *Framing Medieval Bodies* (Manchester: Manchester University Press, 1994).

Kay, W. B., '*La Belle Dame sans mercy* and the Success of Failure', *Romance Notes* 6 (1964), 69–73.

Keller, Adelbert von, *Romvart: Beiträge zur Kunde Mittelalterlicher Dichtung aus italienischen Bibliotheken* (Mannheim: F. Bassermann, 1844).

Kelly, Douglas, 'The Scope of the Treatment of Composition in the Twelfth and Thirteenth Century Arts of Poetry', *Speculum* 41 (1966), 261–78.

—— *Internal Difference and Meanings in the 'Roman de la Rose'* (Madison: University of Wisconsin Press, 1995).

Kelly, Joan, 'Early Feminist Theory and the *Querelle des femmes*, 1400–1789', *Signs* 8 (1982), 4–28.

Kennedy, Angus J.; Brown-Grant, Rosalind; Laidlaw, James C.; Müller, Catherine M., *Contexts and Continuities—Proceedings of the IVᵗʰ International Colloquium on Christine de Pizan (Glasgow 21–27 July 2000) published in honour of Liliane Dulac*, 3 vols. (Glasgow: Glasgow University Press: 2002).

Ker, N. R., *Medieval Manuscripts in British Libraries: Vol. 1* (Oxford: Clarendon Press, 1969).

Kermode, Frank, *The Sense of an Ending: Studies in the Theory of Fiction* (New York/London: OUP, 1967).

Kibler, William W., 'The Narrator as Key to Alain Chartier's *Belle Dame sans mercy*', *French Review* 52 (1979), 714–23.

Kinch, Ashby, 'Richard Roos' *La Belle Dame sans merci* and the Politics of Translation', forthcoming in *Journal of English and Germanic Philology*.

—— 'Playing at Death: the Suspended Subject of Middle English Lyric', unpublished article.

Kristeva, Julia, *Desire in Language: A Semiotic Approach to Literature and Art* (Oxford: Basil Blackwell, 1981).

Krynen, Jacques, *Idéal du prince et pouvoir royal en France à la fin du moyen âge (1380–1440)* (Paris: Picard, 1981).

—— *L'Empire du roi: idées et croyances politiques en France, XIIIe-XVe siècle* (Paris: Gallimard, 1993).

Laidlaw, James C., 'The Manuscripts of Alain Chartier', *Modern Language Review* 61 (1966), 188–98.

—— 'André du Chesne's Edition of Alain Chartier', *Modern Language Review* 63 (1968), 569–74.

—— 'Christine de Pizan—An Author's Progress', *Modern Language Review* 78 (1980), 532–50.

—— 'Alain Chartier and the Arts of Crisis Management, 1417–1429', in *War, Government and Society in Late Medieval France*, ed. Christopher Allmand (Liverpool: University of Liverpool Press, 2000), 37–53.

Langlois, E., *De artibus rhetoricae rhythmicae* (Paris: Émile Bouillon, 1890).

—— 'Le Jeu du roi qui ne ment et le jeu du roi et de la reine', *Romanische Forschungen* 23 (1902), 163–73.

—— 'Le Traité de Gerson contre le *Roman de la Rose*', *Romania* 45 (1919), 23–48.

Lausberg, Heinrich, *Handbook of Literary Rhetoric* (Leiden/Boston/Cologne: Brill, 1998).

Lavis, Georges, 'Le Jeu-parti français: jeu de réfutation, d'opposition et de concession', *Medioevo romanzo* XVI (1991), 21–128.

Lazard, Madeleine, 'Ventes et demandes d'Amour', in *Les Jeux à la Renaissance: Actes du XXIIIe Colloque international d'études humanistes, Tours—Juillet 1980*, ed. Philippe Ariès; Jean-Claude Margolin (Paris: J. Vrin, 1982), 133–49.

Lecoy, Félix, 'Guillaume de Saint-André et son jeu des échecs moralisés', *Romania* 67 (1942–3), 491–503.

—— 'Le *Jeu des échecs* d'Engreban d'Arras', *Le Moyen Français* 12 (1983), 37–42.

Le Duc, Alma, 'Gontier Col and the French Pre-Renaissance', *The Romanic Review* 7 (1916), 414–57.

Leff, Michael C., 'Boethius' *De differentiis topicis*, Book IV', in *Medieval Eloquence: Studies in the Theory and Practice of Medieval Rhetoric*, ed. James J. Murphy (Berkeley/Los Angeles/London: University of California Press, 1978).

Leger, Emile, *Le Seneschal d'Eu, poète du XIVe siècle: sa famille, ses exploits et ses ballades* (Neufchatel-en-Bray: Coeurderoy Frères, 1897).

Le Goff, Jacques, *Intellectuals in the Middle Ages*, trans. Teresa Lavender Fagan (Cambridge, MA/Oxford: Blackwell, 1993).

Léonard, Monique, *Le Dit et sa technique littéraire: des origines à 1340* (Paris: Champion, 1996).

Leppig, Linda, 'The Political Rhetoric of Christine de Pizan: *Lamentacion sur les maux de la guerre civile*', in *Politics, Gender, and Genre: The Political Thought of Christine de Pizan*, ed. Margaret Brabant (Boulder/San Francisco/Oxford: Westview Press, 1992), 141–57.

Lewis, Peter S., *Essays in Later Medieval French History* (London/Ronceverte: The Hambledon Press, 1985).

Lloyd, Michael, *The Agon in Euripides* (Oxford: Clarendon Press, 1992).

Lodge, David ed., *Modern Criticism and Theory: A Reader* (London/New York: Longman, 1988).

Luscombe, D. E., *The School of Peter Abelard: The Influence of Abelard's Thought in the Early Scholastic Period* (Cambridge: CUP, 1969).

Lusignan, Serge, *Parler vulgairement: les intellectuels et la langue française aux XIIIe et XIVe siècles* (Montreal: University of Montreal Press, 1987).

Maddox, Donald and Sturm-Maddox, Sarah, *Transtextualities: Of Cycles and Cyclicity in Medieval French Literature* (Binghamton, New York: Medieval and Renaissance Texts and Studies, 1996).

Marchello-Nizia, Christiane, 'Ponctuation et «unités de lecture» dans les manuscrits médiévaux, ou: je ponctue, tu lis, il théorise', *Langue Française* 40 (1978), 32–44.

—— 'Entre l'histoire et la poétique: le *Songe politique*', *Revue des Sciences humaines*, 55 (1981), 39–53.

—— *La Langue française aux XIVe e et XVe siècles* (Paris: Nathan, 1997).

McAuslan, Ian; Walcot, Peter, *Virgil* (Oxford: OUP, 1990).

McGerr, Rosemarie P., 'Medieval Concepts of Literary Closure: Theory and Practice', *Exemplaria* 1 (1989), 149–79.

—— *Chaucer's Open Books: Resistance to Closure in Medieval Discourse* (Gainesville: University Press of Florida, 1998).

McKeon, Richard, 'Rhetoric in the Middle Ages', *Speculum* 17 (1942), 1–32.

McKinley, Mary, 'The Subversive "Seulette"', in *Politics, Gender, and Genre: The Political Thought of Christine de Pizan*, ed. Margaret Brabant (Boulder/San Francisco/Oxford: Westview Press, 1992), 157–69.

McQuillan, Martin, *The Narrative Reader* (London/New York: Routledge, 2000).

McRae, Joan E., 'The Trials of Alain Chartier's "*Belle Dame sans mercy*": The Poems in Cyclical and Manuscript Context' (unpublished doctoral thesis, University of Virginia, 1997).

Mehl, Jean-Michel, *Les Jeux au royaume de France, du XIIIe au début du XVIe en France* (Paris: Fayard, 1990).

Mérindol, C. de, *Le Roi René et la seconde maison d'Anjou: emblématique, art, histoire* (Paris: Le Léopard d'Or, 1987).

Meyenberg, Regula, *Alain Chartier prosateur et l'art de la parole au XVe siècle* (Bern: Francke, 1992).

Meyer, Paul, 'Notice d'un recueil manuscrit de poésies françaises du XIIIe au XVe siècle, appartenant à Westminster Abbey', *Bulletin de la Société des Anciens Textes Français* 1 (1875), 25–36.

Meyers, Jean, 'Le Latin carolingien: mort ou renaissance d'une langue?', *Moyen Age* 5e série, 4 (1990), 395–410.

Minio-Paluello, L., 'Iacobus Veneticus Grecus, Canonist and Translator of Aristotle', *Traditio* 8 (1952), 265–304.

Minnis, Alastair J., *The Medieval Boethius: Studies in the Vernacular Translations of De consolatione philosophiae* (Cambridge: D. S. Brewer, 1987).

—— 'Theorizing the *Rose*: commentary tradition in the *Querelle de la Rose*', in *Poetics: Theory and Practice in Medieval English Literature*, ed. Piero Boitani; Anna Torti (Cambridge: D. S. Brewer, 1991), 13–36.

—— *Lifting the Veil: Sexual/Textual Nakedness in the 'Roman de la Rose'* (London: King's College, 1995).

Minnis, Alastair J.; Scott, A. B., *Medieval Literary Theory and Criticism c.1100–c.1375: The Commentary Tradition* (Oxford: Clarendon Press, 1991).

Moi, Toril, *Sexual/Textual Politics* (London/New York: Routledge, 1985).

Monfrin, J., *Humanisme et tradition au Moyen Age: l'humanisme médiéval dans les littératures romanes du XIIe au XIVe siècles* (Paris, 1964).

Monfrin, Jacques; Jullien de Pommerol, Marie-Henriette, *La Bibliothèque pontificale à Avignon et à Peñiscola pendant le grand schisme d'Occident et sa dispersion: inventaires et concordances*, 2 vols. (École Française de Rome: Palais Farnèse, 1991).

Mühlethaler, Jean-Claude, *Poétiques du quinzième siècle: situation de François Villon et Michault Taillevent* (Paris: Librairie A.-G. Nizet, 1983).

—— 'Les Masques du clerc pour parler aux puissants', *Moyen Age* 5e série, 4 (1990), 265–86.

—— '«Incipit Quadrilogium invectivum et comicum ad morum gallicorum correctionem». Dalla definizione della Satira all'uso degli animali nella letteratura impegnata ai tempi di Carlo VI: Alain Chartier e Eustache Deschamps', *L'Immagine riflessa*, N. S. Anno VII (1998), 303–29.

—— 'Disputer de mariage: débat et subjectivité: des jeux-partis d'Arras à l'échange de ballades et de rondeaux chez Eustache Deschamps et Charles d'Orléans', in *Il genere «tenzone» nelle letterature romanze delle origini (atti del convegno internazionale Losanna 13–15 novembre 1997)*, ed. Matteo Pedroni; Antonio Stäuble (Ravenna: A. Longo, 1999), 203–21.

Murphy, James J., *Rhetoric in the Middle Ages: A History of Rhetorical Theory from Saint Augustine to the Renaissance* (Berkeley/Los Angeles/London: University of California Press, 1974).

—— *Medieval Eloquence: Studies in the Theory and Practice of Medieval Rhetoric* (Berkeley/Los Angeles/London: University of California Press, 1978).

Murray, H. J. R., *A History of Chess* (Oxford: Clarendon Press, 1913).

O'Donovan, Oliver; O'Donovan, Joan Lockwood, *From Irenaeus to Grotius: A Sourcebook in Christian Political Thought* 100–1625 (Michigan/Cambridge, England: William B. Eerdmans Publishing Company, 1999).

Ong, Walter J., *Orality and Literacy: The Technologizing of the Word* (London/New York: Methuen, 1982).

Ornato, Ezio, 'Jean Muret: *De contemptu mortis*', in *Miscellenea di studi e richercha sul Quattrocento francese*, ed. Franco Simone (Turin: Giappichelli, 1967), 243–353.

—— *Jean Muret et ses amis: Nicolas de Clamanges et Jean de Montreuil* (Geneva: Droz, 1969).

Ornato, Monique; Pons, Nicole, *Pratiques de la culture écrite en France au XVᵉ siècle* (Louvain-La-Neuve: Fédération internationale des Instituts d'études médiévales, 1995).

Ouy, Gilbert, 'Humanisme et propagande politique en France au début du XVᵉ siècle: Ambrogio Migli et les ambitions impériales de Louis d'Orléans', in *Culture et politique en France à l'époque de l'humanisme et de la Renaissance*, ed. Franco Simone (Turin: Accademia delle Scienze, 1974), 13–42.

Ouy, Gilbert; Reno, C., 'Identification des autographes de Christine de Pizan', *Scriptorium* 34 (1980), 221–38.

Pächt, Otto; Alexander, J. J. G., *Catalogue of Illuminated Manuscripts in the Bodleian Library, Oxford: Vol. 1* (Oxford: Bodleian Library, 1966).

Paetow, Louis J., *Two Medieval Satires on the University of Paris: La Bataille des sept arts of Henri d'Andeli and the Morale scolarium of John of Garland* (Berkeley: University of California Press, 1914).

Pagès, A., 'La *Belle Dame sans mercy* d'Alain Chartier: texte français et traduction catalane', *Romania* 23 (1936), 481–531.

Paris, Gaston, *Medieval French Literature*, trans. Hannah Lynch (London: J. M. Dent, 1903).

Parker, Patricia A., *Inescapable Romance: Studies in the Poetics of a Mode* (Princeton: Princeton University Press, 1979).

Parkes, Malcolm B., *Scribes, Scripts and Readers: Studies in the Communication, Presentation and Dissemination of Medieval Texts* (London: Hambledon, 1991).

—— *Pause and Effect: An Introduction to the History of Punctuation in the West* (Aldershot: Scolar Press, 1992).

Paterson, Linda, *Troubadours and Eloquence* (Oxford: Clarendon Press, 1975).

Payen, Jean-Charles, *Littérature française 1: le moyen âge* (Paris: Arthaud, 1990).

Pedroni, Matteo; Stäuble, Antonio, *Il genere «tenzone» nelle letterature romanze delle origini (atti del convegno internazionale Losanna 13–15 novembre 1997)* (Ravenna: A. Longo, 1999).

Pellegrini, Angelo, 'Renaissance and Medieval Antecedents of Debate', *Quarterly Journal of Speech* 28 (1942), 14–18.

Perret, Michèle, 'Typologie des fins dans les oeuvres de fiction (XIe–XVe siècles)', *PRIS-MA* 14/2 (1998), 155–74.

Piaget, Arthur, 'Pierre Michault et Michault Taillevent', *Romania* 18 (1889), 439–52.

—— 'Oton de Granson et ses poésies', *Romania* 19 (1890), 237–59.

—— 'La Cour amoureuse dite de Charles VI', *Romania* 20 (1891), 417–54.

—— 'Jean de Garencières', *Romania* 22 (1893), 422–81.

—— 'L'Épitaphe d'Alain Chartier', *Romania* 23 (1894), 152–6.

—— 'Notice sur le manuscrit 1727 du fonds français de la Bibliothèque Nationale', *Romania* 23 (1894), 192–208.

—— 'Un prétendu manuscrit autographe d'Alain Chartier', *Romania* 25 (1896), 312–15.

—— ed., '*La Belle Dame sans merci* et ses imitations', *Romania* 30 (1901), 22–48, 317–51; 31 (1902), 315–49; 33 (1904), 179–208; 34 (1905), 375–428, 559–602.

Piaget, A.; Droz, E., 'Recherches sur la tradition manuscrite de Villon. I. Le manuscrit de Stockholm', *Romania* 58 (1932), 238–54.

Pickford, C. E.; Whitehead, F., 'The Introduction to the *Lai de l'Ombre*: Sixty Years Later', *Romania* 94 (1973), 145–56.

Planche, Alice, ' "Ainsi qu'en l'or le dyamant": autour d'une image d'Alain Chartier', *Medieval Miscellany presented to Eugène Vinaver* (Manchester: Manchester University Press, 1965), 345–54.

Poirion, Daniel, *Le Poète et le prince: l'évolution du lyrisme courtois de Guillaume de Machaut à Charles d'Orléans* (Paris: Slatkine Reprints, 1978).

—— 'Lectures de la *Belle Dame sans mercy*', in *Mélanges de langue et de littérature médiévales offerts à Pierre Le Gentil* (Paris: SEDES et CDU réunis, 1973), 691–705.

Pons, Nicole, 'Latin et français au XVe siècle: le témoignage des traités de propagande', in *Actes du Ve colloque international sur le moyen français, 6–8 mai, 1985, t. II, Le Moyen Français* (Milan: Vita e Pensiero, 1986), 67–81.

—— 'Les Chancelleries parisiennes sous les règnes de Charles VI et Charles VII', in *Cancelleria e cultura nel medio evo*, ed. Germano Gualdo (Vatican City: Archivio Segreto Vaticano, 1990), 137–68.

—— 'L'Historiographie chez les premiers humanistes français', in *L'Aube de la Renaissance*, ed. D. Cecchetti; L. Sozzi; L. Terreaux (Geneva: Slatkine, 1991), 103–22.

—— 'La Présence de Coluccio Salutati dans le recueil épistolaire de Jean de Montreuil', *Franco-Italica: Serie Storico-Letteraria* 1 (1992), 9–24.

Pöschl, Viktor, *The Art of Vergil: Image and Symbol in the Aeneid* (Michigan: University of Michigan Press, 1962).

Press, Alan R., 'Chrétien de Troyes's Laudine: A *Belle dame sans mercy*', *Forum for Modern Language Studies* 19/2 (1983), 158–71.

Putter, Ad, 'Animating Medieval Court Satire', in *The Court and Cultural Diversity—International Courtly Literature Society 1995*, ed. Evelyn Mullally; John Thompson (Cambridge: D. S. Brewer, 1997), 67–76.

Puttonen, Vilho, *Études sur Martial d'Auvergne suivies du texte critique de quelques arrêts d'amours* (Helsinki: Imprimerie de la Société de Littérature Finnoise, 1943).

Rashdall, Hastings, *The Universities of Europe in the Middle Ages*, 3 vols. (Oxford: Clarendon Press, 1987).

Reed, Thomas L., *Middle English Debate Poetry and the Aesthetics of Irresolution* (Columbia/London: University of Missouri Press, 1990).

Regalado, Nancy Freeman, 'Effet de réel, effet du réel: representation and reference in Villon's *Testament*', *Yale French Studies* 70 (1986), 63–77.

—— 'Gathering the Works: The 'Oeuvres de Villon' and the Intergeneric Passage of the Medieval French Lyric into Single-Author Collections', *L'Esprit Créateur* 33 (1993), 87–100.

Remy, Paul, 'De l'expression «partir un jeu» dans les textes épiques aux origines du jeu-parti', *Cahiers de Civilisation Médiévale* 17 (1974), 327–33.

Reno, Christine M., 'Christine de Pizan: "At Best a Contradictory Figure"?', in *Politics, Gender, and Genre: The Political Thought of Christine de Pizan*, ed. Margaret Brabant (Boulder/San Francisco/Oxford: Westview Press, 1992), 171–91.

Reynolds, L. D.; Wilson, N. G., *Scribes and Scholars: A Guide to the Transmission of Greek and Latin Literature* (Oxford: OUP, 1991).

Ribémont, Bernard, *Écrire pour dire: études sur le dit médiéval* (Paris: Klinck-sieck, 1990).

Rice, Winthrop H., 'Deux poèmes sur la chevalerie: le *Breviaire des nobles* d'Alain Chartier et le *Psaultier des villains* de Michault Taillevent', *Romania* 75 (1954), 55–65; editions, 66–97.

Richter, David H., *Fable's End: Completeness and Closure in Rhetorical Fiction* (Chicago: University of Chicago Press, 1974).

Rieger, Dietmar, 'Alain Chartier's *Belle Dame sans Mercy* oder der Tod des höfischen Liebhabers: Uberlegungen zu einer Dichtung des ausgehenden Mittelalters', in *Sprachen der Lyrik: Festschrift für Hugo Friedrich zum 70. Geburtstag* (Frankfurt am Main: Vittorio Klostermann, 1975), 683–706.

Roques, M., 'Etablissement de règles pratiques pour l'édition des anciens textes français et provençaux', *Romania* 52 (1926), 243–49.

Rouse, Richard H.; Rouse, Mary A., *Manuscripts and their Makers: Commercial Book Producers in Medieval Paris 1200–1500*, 2 vols. (Turnhout, Belgium: Harvey Miller Publishers, 2000).

Rouy, François, *L'Esthétique du traité moral d'après les oeuvres d'Alain Chartier*, (Geneva: Droz, 1980).

Rubin, David Lee, *The Knot of Artifice: A Poetic of the French Lyric in the Early 17th Century* (Columbus: Ohio State University Press, 1981).

Sansone, Giuseppe E., 'La *Belle Dame sans merci* et le langage courtois', *Le Moyen Français* 39–40–41 (1995–96), 513–26.

Sebeok, Thomas A., *Style in Language* (New York/London: The Technology Press of Massachusetts Institute of Technology, 1960).

Shapley, C. S., *Studies in French Poetry of the Fifteenth Century* (The Hague: Nijhoff, 1970).

Simone, Franco, *The French Renaissance: Medieval Tradition and Italian Influence in Shaping the Renaissance* (London: Macmillan, 1969).

—— *Culture et politique en France à l'époque de l'humanisme et de la Renaissance* (Turin: Accademia delle Scienze, 1974).

Small, Graeme, *George Chastelain and the Shaping of Valois Burgundy* (Bury St Edmunds, Suffolk: The Boydell Press, 1997).

Smith, Pauline M., *The Anti-Courtier Trend in Sixteenth-Century French Literature* (Geneva: Droz, 1966).

Söderhjelm, Jarl Werner, *Anteckningar om Martial d'Auvergne och hans Kärleksdommar* (Helsingfors: Öfversigt af Finska vet. soc. förhandl. 31, 1889).

Solente, Susan, 'Le *Jeu des échecs moralisés* source de la *Mutacion de Fortune*', in *Recueil de travaux offert à M. Clovis Brunel, tome II* (Paris: L'École des Chartes, 1955), 556–65.

Solterer, Helen, *The Master and Minerva: Disputing Women in French Medieval Culture* (Berkeley/London: University of California Press, 1995).

—— 'The Freedoms of Fiction for Gender in Premodern France', in *Gender in Debate from the Early Middle Ages to the Renaissance*, ed. Thelma S. Fenster; Clare A. Lees (New York: Palgrave, 2002), 135–63.

Speer, Mary B., 'Editing Old French Texts in the Eighties', *Romance Philology* 45 (1991), 7–43.

Stiennon, Jacques, *Paléographie du moyen âge*, 2nd edn (Paris: A. Colin, 1991).

Stock, Brian, *Listening for the Text: On the Uses of the Past* (Baltimore/London: Johns Hopkins University Press, 1990).

Swartz, David, *Culture & Power: The Sociology of Pierre Bourdieu* (Chicago/London: University of Chicago Press, 1997).

Swift, Helen, 'Alain Chartier and the Death of Lyric Language', *Acta Neophilologica* 35 (2002), 57–65.

Taylor, Craig, 'La *Querelle anglaise*: Diplomatic and Legal Debate during the Hundred Years War, with an Edition of the Polemical Debate "*Pour ce que Plusieurs*" (1464)' (unpubd doctoral thesis, University of Oxford, 1998).

—— 'Sir John Fortescue and the French Polemical Treatises of the Hundred Years War', *English Historical Review* 114 (1999), 112–29.

—— 'War, Propaganda and Diplomacy in Fifteenth Century France and England', in *War, Government and Society in Late Medieval France*, ed. Chistopher Allmand (Liverpool: University of Liverpool Press, 2000), 70–91.

—— 'The Salic Law and the Valois Succession to the French Crown', *French History* 15 (2001), 358–77.

Taylor, Jane H. M., *Dies illa: Death in the Middle Ages* (Liverpool: Cairns, 1984).

—— 'Order from Accident: Cyclic Consciousness at the End of the Middle Ages', in *Cyclification: The Development of Narrative Cycles in the Chansons de geste and the Arthurian Romances*, ed. Bart Besamusca *et al.*, Koninklijke Nederlandse Akademie van Wetenschappen Verhandelingen, Afd. Letterkunde, ns. 159 (Amsterdam etc.: Royal Netherlands Academy of Arts and Sciences, 1994), 59–73.

—— 'The Sense of a Beginning: Genealogy and Plenitude in Late Medieval Narrative Cycles', in *Transtextualities: Of Cycles and Cyclicity in Medieval French Literature*, ed. Sarah Sturm-Maddox; Donald Maddox (Binghamton, New York: Medieval and Renaissance Texts and Studies, 1996), 93–123.

—— 'Inescapable *Rose*: Jean Le Seneschal's *Cent Ballades* and the Art of Cheerful Paradox', *Medium Aevum* 67 (1998), 60–84.

—— *The Poetry of François Villon: Text and Context* (Cambridge: CUP, 2001).

—— 'Embodying the Rose: An Intertextual Reading of Alain Chartier's *La Belle Dame sans mercy*', in *The Court Reconvenes: Courtly Literature across the Disciplines*, ed. Barbara K. Altmann; Carleton W. Carroll (Cambridge: D. S. Brewer, 2003), 325–33.

Taylor, S. M., 'Les Vices de vilenie: la métamorphose des péchés capitaux et des vertus chez Alain Chartier', *Moyen Age* 5ᵉ série, 10 (1996), 73–9.

Terreaux, Louis, *Culture et pouvoir au temps de l'Humanisme et de la Renaissance: Actes du congrès Marguerite de Savoie: Annecy, Chambéry, Turin 29 avril–4 mai 1974* (Geneva: Slatkine/Paris: Champion, 1978).

Tessier, Georges, 'Le Formulaire d'Odart Morchesne (1427)', in *Mélanges dédiés à la mémoire de Félix Grat, II* (Paris: Pecqueur-Grat, 1949), 75–102.

Thiry, Claude, 'Débats et moralités dans la littérature française du XVᵉ siècle: intersection et interaction du narratif et du dramatique', *Le Moyen Français* 19 (1986), 203–44.

Thomas, A., *De Johannis de Monsterolio vita et operibus* (Paris: E. Thorin, 1883).

—— 'Alain Chartier, chanoine de Paris, d'après des documents inédits', *Romania* 33 (1904), 387–402.

Todorov, Tzvetan, *Mikhail Bakhtin: The Dialogical Principle* (Manchester: Manchester University Press, 1984).

Tompkins, Jane P. ed., *Reader-Response Criticism: From Formalism to Post-Structuralism* (Baltimore: Johns Hopkins University Press, 1980).

Toshiki, Ito, 'Les Débats dans la littérature française du moyen âge' (unpubd doctoral thesis, Paris, 1974).

Tournier, Claude, 'Histoire des idées sur la Ponctuation', *Langue Française* 45 (1980), 28–40.

Valois, Noël, *La France et le Grand Schisme d'Occident*, 4 vols. (Paris: Picard, 1896–1902).

Van Eemeren, Frans H.; Grootendorst, Rob, *Speech Acts in Argumentative Discussions: A Theoretical Model for the Analysis of Discussions Directed*

Towards Solving Conflicts of Opinion (Dordrecht, Holland/Cinnaminson, USA: Foris Publications, 1984).

Verger, Jacques, *Les Universités au moyen âge* (Paris: Quadrige/PUF, 1999).

—— *Gens de savoir dans l'Europe de la fin du moyen âge* (Paris: PUF, 2000).

Vernay, Philippe, 'Jehan, d'amour je vous demant: quelques considérations sur le jeu-parti français', in *Il genere «tenzone» nelle letterature romanze delle origini (atti del convegno internazionale Losanna 13–15 novembre 1997)*, ed. Matteo Pedroni; Antonio Stäuble (Ravenna: A. Longo, 1999), pp. 189–201.

Walravens, C. J. H., *Alain Chartier: études biographiques suivies de pièces justificatives, d'une description des éditions et d'une édition des ouvrages inédits* (Amsterdam: Meulenhoff-Didier, 1971).

Walther, Hans, *Das Streitgedicht in der lateinischen Literatur des Mittelalters* (Munich: Beck, 1920).

Weiss, Julian, ' "¿Qué demandamos de las mugeres?": Forming the Debate about Women in Late Medieval and Early Modern Spain (with a Baroque Response)', in *Gender in Debate from the Early Middle Ages to the Renaissance*, ed. Thelma S. Fenster; Clare A. Lees (New York: Palgrave, 2002), 237–81.

Weston, Jessie L., *From Ritual to Romance* (New York: Doubleday Anchor Books, 1957).

Willard, Charity Cannon, 'An Autograph Manuscript of Christine de Pizan?' *Studi Francesi* 27 (1965), 452–7.

—— 'Christine de Pizan: From Poet to Political Commentator', in *Politics, Gender, and Genre: The Political Thought of Christine de Pizan*, ed. Margaret Brabant (Boulder/San Francisco/Oxford: Westview Press, 1992), 17–32.

Williams, Sarah Jane, 'An Author's Role in Fourteenth Century Book Production: Guillaume de Machaut's "Livre ou je met toutes mes choses" ', *Romania* 90 (1969), 433–54.

Winn, Mary Beth, *Anthoine Vérard, Parisian publisher, 1485–1512: Prologues, Poems, and Presentations* (Geneva: Droz, 1997).

Witt, Ronald G., *Coluccio Salutati and his Public Letters* (Geneva: Droz, 1976).

—— *Hercules at the Crossroads: The Life, Works, and Thought of Coluccio Salutati* (Durham, NC: Duke University Press, 1983).

Wolfe, Michael, *Changing Identities in Early Modern France* (Durham/London: Duke University Press, 1997).

Zimmermann, Margarete, 'Vox femina, vox politica: The *Lamentacion sur les maux de la France*', in *Politics, Gender, and Genre: The Political Thought of Christine de Pizan*, ed. Margaret Brabant (Boulder/San Francisco/Oxford: Westview Press, 1992), 113–27.

Zumthor, Paul, *Essai de poétique médiévale* (Paris: Seuil, 1972).

—— 'The Impossible Closure of the Oral Text', *Yale French Studies* 67 (1984), 25–42.

Zutshi, Patrick N. R., 'The Office of Notary in the Papal Chancery in the Mid-Fourteenth Century', in *Forschungen zur Reichs-, Papst- und Landesgeschichte: Peter Herde zum 65, vol. 2.*, ed. Karl Borchardt; Enno Bünz (Stuttgart: Hiersemann, 1998), 665–83.

Index

I have not listed references to Alain Chartier as author and poet, since they are ubiquitous here. As in the *Bibliography*, I have usually listed medieval authors by given name, except in cases where they are more commonly known by their surname (e.g. Boccaccio). Italic numbers denote reference to illustrations.